Intellect, Affect, and God

THE TRINITY, HISTORY, AND THE LIFE OF GRACE

Intellect, Affect, and God

THE TRINITY, HISTORY, AND THE LIFE OF GRACE

Essays in Honor of Robert M. Doran, SJ

Edited by

Joseph Ogbonnaya
and Gerard Whelan, SJ

MARQUETTE UNIVERSITY PRESS

Marquette Studies in Theology
No. 91
Lonergan Studies, International Institute for Method in Theology
Joseph Ogbonnaya, General Editor

Library of Congress Cataloging-in-Publication Data

Names: Ogbonnaya, Joseph, 1968- editor. | Whelan, Gerard, 1959- editor.
Title: Intellect, affect, and God : the Trinity, history, and the life of grace / edited by Joseph Ogbonnaya and Gerard Kevin Whelan.
Description: First. | Milwaukee, Wisconsin : Marquette University Press, [2021] | Series: Marquette studies in theology ; no. 91 | Includes bibliographical references and index. | Summary: "The essays collected in this volume reflect on the various aspects of Robert M. Doran's (S.J.) interdisciplinary contribution to scholarship in the areas of integral ecology, philosophy, politics, culture, critical hermeneutics, systematic and pastoral theology, and economics for humane globalization"-- Provided by publisher.
Identifiers: LCCN 2020053593 | ISBN 9781626007208
Subjects: LCSH: Theology. | Doran, Robert M., 1939-
Classification: LCC BT80 .I58 2021 | DDC 230.2--dc23
LC record available at https://lccn.loc.gov/2020053593

Book Design by Carol Sawyer

∞The paper used in this publication meets the minimum requirements of the American National Standard for Information Sciences—Permanence of Paper for Printed Library Materials, ANSI Z39.48-1992.

Manufactured in the United States of America

CONTENTS

Section III

CRITICAL HERMENEUTICS / 109

Section IV

ECONOMICS OF HUMANE GLOBALIZATION / 169

Section V

SYSTEMATIC THEOLOGY / 211

Section VI

THE ONGOING APPROPRIATION OF DORAN'S WORK / 309

FOREWORD

It is an honor to write the Foreword for the second Festschrift for Robert M. Doran. It is fitting that there be a second celebration of his work. This is not only because he continues to influence a multitude of students and colleagues, but also because since the publication of the first Festschrift his thought has ventured into new areas of exploration and his publications have continued at a steady pace.[1]

Bernard Lonergan (1904–1984) once described Doran as "remarkably creative."[2] Prof. Doran has labored, perhaps more than anyone else, to facilitate a historical and intellectual legacy for Bernard Lonergan. When I think of an analogy for Doran's relationship with Lonergan, Jordan of Saxony (c. 1190–1237) comes to mind. Jordan became the first Master of the Order of Preachers following St. Dominic's death. He ensured Dominic's legacy by founding hundreds of priories during his tenure.

In terms of Lonergan's historical legacy, Doran established a digitization of many of Lonergan's unpublished writings on a website now accessible to anyone throughout the world. Furthermore, as a friend and trustee, he made good on a promise to Lonergan, on the latter's death bed in 1984, to ensure the publication of Lonergan's collected works. That promise recently came to final fruition in 2019 with the publication of the archival volume. This completed the planned twenty-five volumes of Collected Works, published by the University of Toronto Press. Third, after moving to Marquette University in 2006, Doran created the vibrant Lonergan Project, a community dedicated to promoting and developing Lonergan's thought. This also includes the establishment in 2017 of the International Institute for Method in Theology, of which many of the contributors to this Festschrift are involved. This list of accomplishments does not exhaust Prof. Doran's initiatives.

1. For the first Festschrift, see John Dadosky, Ed., *Meaning and History in Systematic Theology: Essays in Honor of Robert M. Doran, S. J.* Milwaukee, WI: Marquette University Press, 2009.

2. Bernard Lonergan, *Caring about Meaning: Patterns in the Life of Bernard Lonergan* Volume 82 of Thomas More Institute for Adult Education Montreal, (eds.) Pierrot Lambert, Charlotte Tansey, Cathleen Mary Going (Montreal: Thomas More Institute, 1982), 115.

In terms of Lonergan's intellectual legacy, Doran developed a further aspect to be added to Lonergan's three conversions, a fourth, psychological dimension, termed *psychic conversion*. Archival evidence corroborates Lonergan's endorsement of this development.[3] Second, in his tome *Theology and the Dialectics of History* (1990), Doran sought to implement an outline forged by Lonergan conceiving theology as inextricably connected with history.[4] Third, Doran has proposed a collaborative framework for developing a comprehensive, contemporarily relevant systematic theology. His establishment of the Lonergan Project at Marquette University has created a group of collaborators aiming to advance his goal. His own contribution to that endeavor includes a three-volume work on *The Trinity in History*, two of which are already complete. This three-volume work will no doubt form a capstone to a brilliant career.

I discovered Doran's work in 1991 when I was studying at the University of Dayton. I was intrigued by the recently published *Theology and the Dialectics of History*. Several years later I moved to Toronto and started my doctoral studies under his direction. After that, I was fortunate to work with him for several years at Regis College, before he moved to Milwaukee in order to take up the Emmett Doerr Chair in Catholic Systematic Theology at Marquette University. We have continued to collaborate over the years, and his friendship has been a true gift to my life. It was a highlight of my career to co-edit with him four volumes of Lonergan's Collected Works, especially *Method in Theology* (CWL 14).

Prof. Doran has a personal charism that is contagious when he is discussing Lonergan, and he brings a *gravitas* to the study of contemporary theology that is admirable and challenging. He is one of the clearest and most reliable interpreters of Lonergan's thought that I have encountered during my thirty years of studying Lonergan. Prof. Doran has not always received the honor and respect he deserves, but his personal sacrifices and hard work will provide a worthy example of research and scholarship for others to emulate in the years to come.

---

3. Lonergan states in a letter to a publisher: "Intellectual, Moral, and Religious conversion of the theologian are foundational in my book on method in theology. To these Doran has added a psychic conversion in his book on *Psychic Conversion and Theological Foundations*. He has thought the matter through very thoroughly and it fits very adroitly and snugly into my own efforts." A2280 (File 490.1/6), Archives, Lonergan Research Institute of Regis College, Toronto. Similarly, in a letter to Edward Braxton (February 12, 1975) Lonergan wrote: "I agree with Robert Doran on psychic conversion and his combining it with intellectual, moral, and religious conversion." File 132, p. 1, also from the Lonergan Archives.

4. Robert M. Doran, *Theology and the Dialectics of History* (Toronto: University of Toronto Press, 1990).

The testimony and legacy of Doran's lifework is well represented in this Festschrift. The editors are to be congratulated. I have known Prof. Gerry Whelan since my first days as a doctoral student. He was like an elder sibling who had managed to comprehend a range of ideas that were overwhelming to me at the time, and he was always patient and kind in our tutorial conversations. He has gone on to write two important books, one directly on Doran's work, and the other on Pope Francis with reference to Doran.[5]

Prof. Ogbonnaya has written creatively in endeavoring to apply Lonergan's work to a theory of sustainable development and, among other projects, has engaged Doran's work in terms of World Christianity. I had the joy of directing his dissertation, and since then, of watching his career flourish.[6]

I often tell my students struggling to understand Lonergan's thought: "On the one hand, Lonergan is not for everyone. On the other hand, Lonergan *is* for everyone." To the extent this is the case, Doran's writings on Lonergan and his own development of Lonergan's thought will be indispensable for the future of Lonergan studies. Lonergan scholars of the future will have to stand on the shoulders of Lonergan's work and Doran's work.

John D. Dadosky, PhD, STD
Professor of Philosophy and Theology
Director of the Msgr. John Mary Fraser Centre for Practical Theology
Regis College/University of Toronto

5. Gerard Whelan, S.J., *Redeeming History: Social Concern in Bernard Lonergan and Robert Doran* (Rome: Gregorian University Press, 2014) and *A Discerning Church: Pope Francis, Lonergan, and a Theological Method for the Future* (Mahwah, NJ: Paulist Press, 2019).

6. Joseph Ogbonnaya, *Lonergan, Social Transformation, and Sustainable Human Development* (Eugene, OR: Pickwick, 2013) and *African Perspectives on Culture and World Christianity* (Newcastle upon Tyne, UK: Cambridge Scholars Publishing, 2017).

INTRODUCTION

In 2009 John D. Dadosky organized the first series of essays in honor of Robert M. Doran, *Meaning and History in Systematic Theology* dwelt on Doran's work from 1967–2007. The work of Doran that gained most attention in these essays was *Theology and the Dialectics of History*, published in 1990, a work that operated primarily in Lonergan's fifth functional specialty, Foundations. The articles in Dadosky's publication were well received. The Australian Catholic Record stated that they, "witness to Doran's deep and creative development of Lonergan's work on the structure of the human mind, of decision-making and theological collaboration." In the last ten years, Doran has continued to be most productive, and the community of younger scholars interested in his work continues to expand. In this context, we consider it appropriate to make available a second series of essays honoring his work, especially, these more recent developments.

Already at the time of Dadosky's publication, Doran had begun to operate in the seventh functional specialty, Systematics. In 2005, he had produced *What is Systematic Theology?*, which promised a multi-volume work in systematic theology. Some essays in Dadosky's work already comment on this. Doran's central idea for this project had been conceived while he was editing Lonergan's treatise on the Trinity, which is now published as Volumes 11 and 12 of the *Collected Works of Bernard Lonergan*. Then, he had noticed that Lonergan makes brief reference to a "four-point hypothesis" that could integrate all systematic theology. In *What is Systematic Theology?*, Doran declares his intention to attempt just such an integration. Dadosky stated that readers could look forward to new strides in Doran's thought in successive years as Doran planned volumes in a book series that would be entitled: *The Trinity in History: A Theology of the Divine Missions*. Anthony J. Kelly shared this anticipation, stating, "Doran's new systematics, then, promises to show, on the common ground of flesh, blood, imagination and cultural experience, how a new historically-grounded systematics (appropriate to a "fourth stage of meaning" of living dialogue with the "other") might look in the hands of one who has notably assimilated and extended Lonergan's theological method."

Over the past decade, Doran has been true to his word. He produced two contributions to his book series: *Volume One: Missions and Processions*

(2012); and *Volume Two: Missions, Relations, and Persons* (2019.) In addition, he published various articles, expanding the e-book which gathers his work to include over fifty pieces. In addition to exploring Trinitarian themes, this e-book expounds upon the work of René Girard; traces the link between systematics and Ignatian spirituality; and relates Lonergan to von Balthasar. In addition to these developments, an important expression of how Doran's work is being received in academia is the annual Marquette University colloquium on doing systematic theology in a multi-religious world. Furthermore, a research network of academics has emerged from this annual event, the International Institute for Method in Theology. This institute is formed of groups of academics who collaborate with each other on diverse themes. To date, there are five such groups: systematic theology, philosophy, economics, ecology, and hermeneutics. It occurred to us to feature the work of these groups in this present collection of essays, marking as they do developments that have occurred subsequent to the publication of Dadosky's work. The first five parts of this present work correspond broadly to the themes being treated in the groups of the International Institute for Method in Theology. Indeed, most of the contributors to this present work are members of these groups. Part six of this work addresses a related theme. It comprises contributions from younger scholars and records how, in the last ten years, Doran's thought, not least as found in *Theology and the Dialectics of History*, continues to be applied to ever-more diverse contexts, both geographic and thematic.

Synopsis of the Chapters

Section One examines, analyzes and advances the concept of integral ecology central to Pope Francis's *Laudato si* with the various writings of Doran. Thus, in Chapter One, Lucas Briola, in "Dramatic Artistry in Our Common Home: Robert Doran and the Doxological Anthropology of Laudato Si'," shows how the work of Doran helps to answer Pope Francis's assertion in *Laudato si'*: "There can be no ecology without an adequate anthropology" (LS 118). Briola's contribution focuses on Doran's presentation of human authenticity, i.e. genuine personal values, as the "artistic" balance between limitation and transcendence, affect and intellect. He highlights the encyclical's doxological character and the priestly dominion that it accords to humans with respect to the environment. He relates this to Doran's notion of dramatic artistry. In Chapter Two, Eugene Schlesinger's "The Four-Point Hypothesis and the Possibility of Ecological Conversion" relates the ecological conversion to the four-point hypothesis of Doran. It puts to the test Doran's claims about the utility of the four-point hypothesis by (1) providing an account of the means whereby ecological conversion can be achieved, which (2) attends to the human causes of the crisis and need for a human solution, (3) without thereby underwriting an anthropocentrism which would only deepen the problem, and so appealing to God's grace. In Chapter Three, Christopher Krall's "Healing Vectors on the Mind: The Transformative Effects of Divine Grace at the Personal level of the Integral Scale of Values" seeks to provoke insight into the effects of divine grace in the created realm, especially the lives of human persons. From the physiological/ neurological changes that can occur through prayer and meditation all the way up to the cultural transformations that occur when healing grace inspires communities of people toward authenticity, grace can be demonstrated to be efficacious.

Section Two is devoted to the philosophical and psychological aspects of Doran's works with specific focus on psychic conversion and alterity. In Chapter Four, Jonathan Heaps, in "The Grandiosity of Experience," probes Lonergan's account of religious experience by coupling Doran's analysis of the psyche and Eugene Gendlin's account of embodied experiencing. He explores Gendlin's accounts of felt-experience as a kind of body-feeling and of the functions of symbolization in discerning the significance of our felt-meanings, particularly with regard to providing a phenomenological and hermeneutical tool for controlling the data of consciousness. He suggests that, by joining this to Doran's account of six levels of consciousness, one can build a frame on which the full breadth, weave, and texture of religious experiencing can be hung. Brian Bajzek's "Serving the Other: Robert Doran's Work at the Crux of Horizontal and Vertical Alterity," in Chapter Five, explores the role of otherness in Doran's philosophical-theological project. He traces a series of developments from Doran's earliest writings through his most recent reflections in *The Trinity in History Vol. II: Missions, Relations, and Persons*, and through this suggests that concern for the intersection of horizontal and vertical alterity is a subtle but central facet of Doran's thought. In Chapter Six, Gregory P. Floyd's "Lonergan's Turn to the Concrete and its Relevance for Doran's Notion of Psychic Conversion," argues that a key characteristic of Lonergan's critical realism and empirical notion of culture is an attentiveness to the concrete—a characteristic missing in classicism. However, he suggests that the concreteness of Lonergan's own account of consciousness needs to be expanded upon. He claims that Doran's notion of psychic conversion achieves this by grounding Lonergan's account of religious, moral, and intellectual conversion more deeply in the facticity of subject thus avoiding any slide into the static essentialism of thinking about substances. He also comments on the relevance of a notion of psychic conversion to broader themes in Lonergan's work.

Section Three on Critical Hermeneutics looks at Doran's work from scripture, poetry and religious pluralism. In Chapter Seven, Joseph Gordon's "Redrawing the Map: Scripture in the Dialectic of Culture after *The Trinity in History*" employs Bernard Lonergan's 1973 essay "Sacralization and Secularization" to explain that the authentic fruits of historical criticism represent a secularism to be promoted, while positivist and reductionist approaches to the text present in the guild of biblical scholarship exhibit secularism to be resisted. Conversely, he asserts that the premodern theological reading strategies which promoted the love of God and neighbor represent a sacralization to be promoted, while the utilization of the authority of Scripture in the promotion of clericalism, nationalism, racism, and sexism are sacralizations to be resisted. He concludes by discussing the role of scriptural interpretation in the promotion of cultural, personal, and religious values and discusses the relevance to reflection on scripture of Doran's recent work in volumes one and two of *The Trinity in History*. In Chapter Eight, Ryan Hemmer, in "Systems and Sequences: The Renewal of Theological Understanding and the Problem of Speculative Pluralism," builds on Doran's work on systematic theology as a genetic sequence of *theologies*. Hemmer's work shows how the sequence of systems is not only a genetic process over time, but also a complimentary, contrary, and contradictory dialectic at any given time. His chapter advances the notion of speculative pluralism as a basic heuristic structure for understanding the dynamics and relationships obtaining between distinct speculative projects, for coordinating collaboration between them, and for disengaging the regulative functions that discriminate between incompatible poles of contradictory theologies. In this way, he demonstrates that speculative pluralism expands upon Doran's account of genetic pluralism in a way analogous to Doran's own expansion of Lonergan's notion of systematics. Anne Carpenter's "Robert Doran, Hans Urs von Balthasar, and Poetry' in Chapter Nine, examines Doran's interpretation of Hans Urs von Balthasar's work, exploring both its beginnings and its continued development. She studies how Doran moves from rapprochement to appropriation, that is, from working toward a reconciliation between Lonergan and Balthasar to borrowing Balthasar in his theological studies of the Trinity and history. This borrowing results in a development of Balthasar, particularly with respect to a theology of history. One of the keys to Doran's explorations of Balthasar is the power of images in human thinking alongside their distinction from, their difference from, human understanding. Doran's "Lonerganian" rigor unveils a "Balthasarian" rigor that transcends a mere coming together over similarities of poetic vision.

Section Four reflects on the collaborative engagement of Doran's work with themes related to globalization including, world Christianity, ethics, economics and ecological debates. In Chapter Ten, Joseph Ogbonnaya's "World Christianity and Theology for World Cultural Humanity" argues that decades of cross-cultural encounter and actual practice of contextual theologies have dealt extensively with the issues of religion and culture to an extent that the debate between world Christianity and global Christianity is addressed. Thus, theologians should be preoccupied with the significance of world Christianity in our globalized world asking such questions as: "What role should contemporary Christianity play in the world stage characterized by the challenges of globalization?" A related question is: "What is the task of theology in evoking alternative communities towards peaceful and mutual coexistence of humankind? And how is theology to accomplish this?" He seeks answers to these questions in Doran's theology of world-cultural community. Cyril Orji's "Robert Doran—The Master Collaborator," in Chapter Eleven, argues that far from being a finished project, Lonergan intentionally designed his work like a symphony in which all the parts coalesce to make a beautiful whole only through the collaboration of a community of scholars. If there is a pair of words that captures Doran's role in the Lonergan project, it is "master-collaborator." Doran the master-collaborator has ensured that Lonergan's work does not remain an "unfinished symphony." This essay examines Doran's collaborative effort in the Lonergan project, particularly his role in bringing the Lonergan project into tune with the realities of World Christianity. In Chapter Twelve, Gerard Whelan in "Capitalism, Reform it or Reject it? The Encounter of Ethics and Economics in Current Ecological Debates," asserts that a key contribution of a critical realist approach to current ecological debates can be in providing foundations for negotiating their interdisciplinary character. He suggests that this can be particularly helpful in current ecological debates in helping economists and ethicists relate better with each other. He adverts to Lonergan's work on economics and ethics and to Lonergan's quip about one ethicist who he considered too utopian: "One might be inclined to ask whether our economic and social structure is not rather a sick man needing treatment than a dying man awaiting burial." Whelan suggests that such utopianism is found today among Christian ethicists who are so concerned to criticize capitalism that they do not place their moral weight behind arguments for carbon pricing. On the other hand, he recognizes that many such ethicists make an important contribution to envisioning what Doran would explain as a world-cultural-community that is constituted by a culture that values cosmological meaning as well as anthropological meaning.

Section Five concentrates on the developments in systematic theology accruing from Doran's writings. Responding to the COVID-19 pandemic, Cecille Medina-Maldonado, in "Bias, Conversion, and Grace in the Time of a Pandemic," in Chapter Thirteen, studies incoherent and confusing responses to the pandemic including, people's rejection of wearing masks, refusal of social distancing and other guidance from the Center for Disease Control, and the invoking of notions of rights and freedoms to justify this. She suggests that such positions are, ultimately, a result of dramatic bias. Hence, she concludes, there is the need for conversion aided by the grace of God. In Chapter Fourteen, Joseph Mudd's article "Transposing in Persona Christi: Toward a Theology of Priestly Ministry for the Third Millennium" reflects on current theologies of the priesthood and notes that it usually attends to the unique "ontological bond" between Christ and the priest. He then notes that, in *Pastores Dabo Vobis*, Saint John Paul II talks about a "psychological" bond as well. He explores the meaning of this psychological bond in relation to the contemporary crisis of authority in the church and by turning to Doran's analysis of integral human interiority and his notion of psychic conversion. What emerges is a theology of the priesthood on the level of the time that transposes classical categories into the categories of a methodical theology and offers a way forward for a church in crisis. In Chapter fifteen, Andrew T. Vink, in "Historical Soteriology and the Scale of Values: Ellacuría and Doran in Dialogue," engages Doran's project of the scale of values with liberation theology of Ignacio Ellacuría. He notes that Doran has engaged with Juan-Luis Segundo on issues such as connecting the scale of values with the principle of the preferential option for the poor. However, he suggests that yet greater parallels exist with Ellacuría's work, highlighting themes from Ellacuria such as: historical soteriology; the civilization of poverty and the civilization of wealth; and the notion of a crucified people.

In Chapter Sixteen, Gordon Rixon in "History Illumined by Discernment," links the notion of discernment of spirits in the *Spiritual Exercises of St. Ignatius* to Doran's attentiveness to the psyche, to affectivity, and to the struggle, at both conscious and unconscious levels, to be self-transcending. He draws on the four-point hypothesis to describe how spiritual consolation represents a participation in created grace. He explores how such grace produces fruits in self-transcending decision-making. Discussing the exercise of Ignatius, "Three Times of Making a Decision" he describes how the consoled individual engages in "the imitation and participation in charity infused actions that yield delightful and transparent fruits in history." Jeremy Blackwood's "Law of the Cross and the Mystical Body of Christ," in Chapter Seventeen, draws on Doran's work to examine on how René Girard can deepen our notion of the Law of the Cross. He appeals to the notion of psychic conversion as he connects the psyche with the fifth level consciousness of love and relates this to a theology of the Mystical Body. In Chapter Eighteen, Darren Dias, in "Trinity, Elemental Meaning and Psychic Conversion: A Pastoral Consideration," situates the issues of language, images and symbols within the theoretical frame of elemental meaning and psychic conversion.

Section Six entitled, "The Ongoing Appropriation of Doran's Work," representents how Doran's work, both recent and early, continues to be employed in various parts of the world: Europe, Africa, North America and Asia. It also relates Doran's works to diverse areas of politics, theology, psychology and missiology. In Chapter Nineteen, Josephat Rugaiganisa's "Psychic Conversion and the legacy of Julius K. Nyerere in Tanzania," relates the thought of Doran to that of Julius Nyerere, the first President of Tanzania. He comments on Nyerere's sincere Christian faith and finds parallels with Doran's thought on a number of issues, including cosmological culture, imperialism, victimization, the redemption of history. He concludes with reflections on employing Doran's thought in pastoral work in Tanzania. In Chapter Twenty, John P. Cush's "John Courtney Murray and the Situation as Source of Theology," recalls how Doran expands upon Lonergan's brief mention in *Method in Theology* of how the situation is a source of theology. He also pursues a hint offered by Doran that the work of John Courtney Murray represents an impressive example of a theology that is both methodical and respects the principle of the situation as source of theology. On the other hand, he suggests that there is an absence of psychic conversion in Murray, with the consequence lack of attention to symbol and cosmological values. Studying how Murray has remained an abiding influence on Catholic social ethics in North America, he speaks of the desirability of advancing the position in Murray's thought by adding considerations of psychic conversion. In Chapter Twenty-One, Jake Mudge, in "Psychic

Conversion, Psychotherapy, and Vocational Counselling," engages with the thought of Luigi Rulla, founder of the Institute of Psychology at the Gregorian University. He notes how the "vocational counselling" proposed by Rulla already employs the thought of Bernard Lonergan as a foundation for its interdisciplinary character. He suggests that the use of Lonergan could be more comprehensive in Rulla's thought, and also explores how Doran's notion of psychic conversion could enrich the approach of Rulla. However, he praises Rulla's basic approach and proposes that vocational counselling could be widely employed as an instrument for attaining psychic conversion. Finally, Jaime Vidal Zuñiga's "Foundations for Ecclesial Mission in Asia: The Relevance of General and Special Categories in Robert Doran" undertakes a task of relating Doran's thought to the pastoral priorities of the Federation of Asian Bishops Conferences (FABC). These priorities involve a "triple dialogue" with "Asian cultures, with Asian religions, and with the poor and oppressed of Asia." He finds that Doran's early work, in *Theology and the Dialectics of History*, is sufficient to ground the dialogues with cultures and with the poor, whereas he suggests that reference to Doran's account of the four-point hypothesis is necessary to provide foundations for interreligious dialogue.

Conclusion

The wealth of reflection of our contributing authors—often relatively young—confirms for the editors their intuition that the influence of Lonergan's thought continues to expand and that the innovations of Doran on issues such as psychic conversion and the four-point hypothesis are being widely received as an authentic expansion of this legacy.

Robert Doran passed away on January 21, 2021. There are no words for such a profound loss and, until we meet again, we shall miss him; his wisdom, his kindness, his intellect.

SECTION I

INTEGRAL ECOLOGY

CHAPTER ONE

DRAMATIC ARTISTRY IN OUR COMMON HOME

Robert Doran and the Doxological Anthropology of *Laudato Si'*

Lucas Briola

Saint Vincent College (Latrobe, PA)

"But the fundamental meaning important to us in art is that, just as the pure desire to know heads on to the beatific vision, so too the break from the ready-made world heads on to God. Man is nature's priest, and nature is God's silent communing with man."[1]

Robert Doran calls for a theology that responds to the contemporary situation.[2] In *Laudato si'*, Pope Francis describes that situation as one marked by the shrill cries of the earth and the poor. Doran has acted accordingly, most explicitly by establishing an "ecological culture" section within the recently formed International Institute for Method in Theology.[3] Guided by the thought of Bernard Lonergan, this initiative has already yielded fruitful theological work.[4] Several of those efforts employ

1. Bernard J. F. Lonergan, *Topics in Education*, ed. Robert M. Doran and Frederick E. Crowe, vol. 10 in *Collected Works of Bernard Lonergan* (Toronto: University of Toronto Press, 1993), 224–225.

2. Robert M. Doran, *Theology and the Dialectics of History* (Toronto: University of Toronto Press, 1990), 8, 12–16.

3. See Robert M. Doran, "The International Institute for Method in Theology: A Vision," available at https://www.lonerganresource.com/pdf/lectures/Doran_-_International_Institute_or_Method_in_Theology.pdf, accessed November 12, 2019.

4. See Joseph Ogbonnaya and Lucas Briola, eds., *Everything Is Interconnected: Towards a Globalization with a Human Face and an Integral Ecology* (Milwaukee, WI: Marquette University Press, 2019).

Doran and Lonergan's work to respond to Pope Francis's striking pronouncement that "there can be no ecology without an adequate anthropology" (*LS* 118). In my own work, I have used Doran's thought to reflect upon the doxological essence of *Laudato si'* and the doxological essence of the church's mission.[5] This essay brings that perspective to those previous anthropological studies.

My study proceeds in three parts. First, I rehearse Doran's conception of human authenticity as one of dramatic artistry and consider the theological significance of this claim. Second, I couple this emphasis with John Zizioulas's preference for "priesthood" as a more dramatic understanding of human responsibility within creation than the more conventional stewardship model. I also show how, given the doxological character of *Laudato si'*, this conversation elucidates the anthropology advanced in the encyclical. Third, I return to Doran's work and place it in conversation with this doxological, priestly anthropology. While Doran's categories solidify this anthropology, so too do the unique proposals of *Laudato si'* enrich Doran's work. I conclude by noting the enduring relevance of this discussion for the life of the church.

Doran and "Dramatic Artistry"

For Doran, human interiority and authenticity supply prime loci for the theological task. He follows his teacher, Lonergan, in this focus. According to Doran, Lonergan's expansion to an existential, fourth level of consciousness as well as acknowledgement of the important role of value and feelings on that level require a renewed attentiveness to the affective, aesthetic, and dramatic dimensions of human living. The deliberative function of this fourth level sublates both knowing and feeling and thus demands an integration of intellect and affect, the spirit and the body.[6]

Doran's notion of "psychic conversion" names this integrative task. For Lonergan and Doran alike, human authenticity is achieved through surrendering ourselves to the unrestrictedly self-transcending character of "the search for direction in the movement of life" and indeed the "passionateness of being" itself.[7] The experiential release of this undertow comes through psychic conversion, which Doran defines as "a transformation of

5. See, e.g., Lucas Briola, "Integral Ecology, Eucharist, and the Scale of Values: A Contribution of Bernard Lonergan" (PhD diss., The Catholic University of America, 2019).

6. See Bernard J. F. Lonergan, "*Insight* Revisited," in *A Second Collection*, ed. William F.J. Ryan and Bernard Tyrell (Philadelphia: The Westminster Press, 1974), 277.

7. Doran, *Theology and the Dialectics of History*, 45–49, 80, 218, 358.

the psychic component of what Freud calls 'the censor' from a repressive to a constructive agency in a person's development."[8] Psychic conversion most often takes the form of embracing the dialectical tension that is oneself, allowing one to straddle the transcendent insatiability of the human spirit and the biological-psychological limits of being embodied, the mix of *ruah* and clay that God has called "very good" (Gen 2:7).

Psychic conversion is no end unto itself, however. Just as Lonergan calls for a cognitive self-appropriation in *Insight*—"what am I doing when I am knowing?"—Doran suggests that the emergence of a fourth level of consciousness demands an analogous existential self-appropriation—"what am I doing when I am doing?" As Doran notes, Lonergan turns to drama and art when discussing authenticity in the everyday.[9] Indeed, in the light of psychic conversion, existential self-appropriation takes on a dramatic, artistic form. It is the psychic censor, after all, that sifts the requisite neural images both emerging out of our biological and psychological limitations and shaping how we imagine ourselves and our activities in the world. Contrary to Marxist, technocratic anthropologies that reduce human activity to managerial practicality and instrumental rationality, Doran seeks to retrieve an "artistic paradigm of praxis" so as to underscore the "dramatic artistry" of human living.[10] As he describes it:

> As the artist who works with oils and clay, music and words, must be capable of this release of empirical consciousness from instrumentalization, so too the dramatic artist who would make a work of art out of his or her own life must be able to abide in an empirical freedom of consciousness that allows there to emerge from the materials of one's life an inevitability of form analogous to that of a painting, a work of sculpture, or a symphony.[11]

Psychic conversion allows us to tell our story, to be attentive to the work of art that our lives are becoming or failing to become. Thus, creatively abiding between limitation and transcendence, matter and spirit, in accord with the movement of life becomes an inherently aesthetic enterprise.

---

8. Doran, *Theology and the Dialectics of History*, 59.

9. See Bernard J. F. Lonergan, *Insight: A Study of Human Understanding*, vol. 3 in *Collected Works of Bernard Lonergan*, ed. Frederick E. Crowe and Robert M. Doran (Toronto: University of Toronto Press, 2005), 210–231.

10. Doran, *Theology and the Dialectics of History*, 72, 399–401.

11. Doran, *Theology and the Dialectics of History*, 54.

These claims carry significant theological consequence, given the importance of dramatic artistry for constituting ourselves in deliberation and decision. Doran submits that "ethics is radically aesthetics."[12] Ethics is more than managing problems or, worse, utilitarian calculi. Instead, ethics is a creative task, a way of life that needs to be always learned and always more closely approximated. Moreover, as Doran has stressed especially in dialogue with Hans Urs von Balthasar, attention to the dramatic character of human authenticity "render[s] possible the critical use of poetic categories in systematic theology."[13] For theologians, poetic and symbolic descriptors provide more than a disposable husk. Instead, when grounded in systematic meaning, aesthetic meaning is constitutive of a theology that befits the third stage of meaning.[14] Otherwise, theology deforms into an arid and decadent relic detached from the richness of actual human living.

This art of self-appropriation is crucial for a theology that mediates redemption to the contemporary situation. Far from being a narcissistic endeavor, this spiritual exercise redounds beyond our selves to affect history and, indeed, our entire common home. In Doran's words, "we are left with the task of *healing an entire planet*. The healing can begin only when the subject returns to himself or herself through the explanatory mediation of cognitive and existential praxis."[15]

Laudato Si', Doxology, and a Priestly Anthropology

"There can be no ecology without an adequate anthropology," Pope Francis declares in *Laudato si'* (*LS* 118). While explicitly disavowing both "excessive anthropocentrism" and "biocentrism," the pope never specifies this more adequate anthropology. Even more startling, as Kevin Irwin notes, is the fading of the previously regnant model of "stewardship" in the encyclical as an adequate naming of the relationship between the human person and the

---

12. See Robert M. Doran, "Aesthetics and the Opposites," in *Theological Foundations, Volume One: Intentionality and Psyche* (Milwaukee, WI: Marquette University Press, 1995), 123 (hereafter, *Intentionality and Psyche*). See also, idem, "Aesthetic Subjectivity and Generalized Empirical Method," in *Intentionality and Psyche*, 328; and idem, *Psychic Conversion and Theological Foundations*, 2nd ed. (Milwaukee, WI: Marquette University Press, 2006), 104.

13. Robert M. Doran, *Subject and Psyche*, 2nd ed. (Milwaukee, WI: Marquette University Press, 1994), 104. See also, idem. "Lonergan and Balthasar: Methodological Considerations," *Theological Studies* 58 (1997): 61–84, esp. 82–83.

14. See John D. Dadosky, *The Eclipse and Recovery of Beauty: A Lonergan Approach* (Toronto: University of Toronto Press, 2014). For Lonergan's presentation of realms of meaning, see Lonergan, *Method in Theology* (New York: Herder and Herder, 1972), 81–85.

15. Doran, *Psychic Conversion and Theological Foundations*, 163. Emphasis added.

rest of creation.[16] *Laudato si'* intimates the need for a new anthropological paradigm beyond stewardship.

This shift recalls John Zizioulas and his critique of the stewardship model. For him, a stewardship ethic conveys a predominantly "managerial approach to nature" with a "utilitarian implication"; this model conjures images of nature as a "thing" to be overseen, organized, and distributed by humans.[17] Like Doran, Zizioulas believes that an excessive emphasis on productivity impoverishes the human vocation in our common home. Likewise, according to Zizioulas, the stewardship model expresses an overly conservationist and insufficiently creative approach to nature. It fails to disclose the *art* of living responsibly in our common home, and it fails to capture the irrepressibly creative character of the human person.[18]

Zizioulas finds the stewardship model lacking given the exigencies of the situation. If ethics is radically aesthetics, then stewardship cannot capture the dramatic character of caring for our common home. The stewardship model similarly fails to evoke the requisite neural images that convey the properly dramatic artistry of this care. Zizioulas insists that the ecological crisis cannot be resolved through purely ratio-ethical strategies as these replicate the very technocratic assumptions that have produced the crisis.[19] Zizioulas turns to doxology and liturgy as an aesthetic-dramatic alternative: in his words, "without a world-view that involves religious and what we may call liturgical attitudes to creation it will be impossible to reverse the alarming situation the world is facing today."[20] The words of *Laudato si'* echo this call: "rather than a problem to be solved, the world is a joyful mystery to be contemplated with gladness and praise" (*LS* 12). Praise, rather than technocratic management, best conveys the human creativity that our common home needs.

These sentiments help explain the uniquely doxological, liturgical tenor of *Laudato si'*. The encyclical borrows its title—"Praised be!"—from the famous doxology of Saint Francis. Words of praise bookend the

---

16. Kevin W. Irwin, *A Commentary on* Laudato si'*: Examining the Background, Contributions, Implementation, and Future of Pope Francis's Encyclical* (New York: Paulist Press, 2016), 119–120.

17. John D. Zizioulas, "Proprietors or Priests of Creation?," in *The Eucharistic Communion and the World* (New York: T&T Clark, 2011), 134.

18. Zizioulas, "Proprietors or Priests of Creation?," 135–136.

19. John D. Zizioulas, "Preserving God's Creation: Lecture One," *King's Theological Review* 12 (1989): 1–5, at 1–2.

20. John D. Zizioulas, "Preserving God's Creation: Lecture Two," *King's Theological Review* 12 (1989): 41–45, at 41.

document, explaining why, in his official presentation of *Laudato si'*, Cardinal Peter Turkson proposed that "the attitude upon which the entire Encyclical is based [is] that of prayerful contemplation."[21] Doxology shapes that prayerful contemplation and supplies a hermeneutical key for interpreting the encyclical and its proposals. This tone explains Denis Edwards's keen observation that affective language saturates the encyclical.[22] So too does it demonstrate why the encyclical provides a far more extensive meditation on the sacraments generally and the Eucharist specifically than any other social encyclical. By placing it within this doxological milieu, the encyclical intimates that its call to care for our common home involves dramatic artistry rather than rational management.

This doxological and liturgical frame should accordingly inform the adequate anthropology upon which ecology must stand. For his part, Zizioulas proposes a "priestly anthropology" as a complement to and perhaps even a replacement of stewardship. As he writes, "man has to become a liturgical being before he can hope to overcome his ecological crisis."[23] While Zizioulas admits the potential freight of clericalism that sacerdotal language carries, he hopes in particular to extract the offertory role of the priest, a duty incumbent on all.[24]

Zizioulas expounds the meaning of this responsibility through his relational ontology. As evolutionary science shows, human beings are "organically and inseparably linked with the natural world, particularly with the rest of creation."[25] At the same time, human creativity distinguishes them from the rest of creation. Specifically, Zizioulas understands rationality primarily as the unique human capacity to "collect what is diversified and even fragmented in this world and make a unified and harmonious world (*cosmos*) out of that."[26] Through this integrative action, and as ecstatic beings always stretching towards the transcendent, humans offer all creation to the God who is harmonious relation. Precisely as

---

21. Peter Turkson, "Conferenza Stampa per la presentazione della Lettera Enciclica «Laudato si'» del Santo Padre Francesco sulla cura della casa commune: Intervento del Card. Peter Kodwo Appiah Turkson," Bollettino: Sala Stampa della Santa Sede, June 18, 2015, https://press.vatican.va/content/salastampa/it/bollettino/pubblico/2015/06/18/0480/01050.html#eng, accessed October 14, 2019.

22. See Denis Edwards, "'Sublime Communion: The Theology of the Natural World in *Laudato Si'*," *Theological Studies* 77, no. 2 (2016): 377–391, at 386.

23. Zizioulas, "Preserving God's Creation: Lecture One," 2.

24. See Zizioulas, "Preserving God's Creation: Lecture One," 2.

25. Zizioulas, "Proprietors or Priests of Creation?," 136.

26. Zizioulas, "Proprietors or Priests of Creation?," 136.

members of creation, humans bring it towards the rest in God for which it yearns. As Zizioulas writes:

> The transcendence of the limits of creation, which is . . . the condition for its survival, requires on the part of creation a drive to absolute freedom. The fact that this drive was given to Man made the whole creation rejoice, in the words of St. Paul "awaiting with eager expectation the revelation of the glory of the children of God", i.e. of Man. Because Man, unlike the angels . . . forms an organic part of the material world, being the highest point in its evolution, he is able to carry with him the whole creation to its transcendence.[27]

To reject our organic connection to the world in this creative task, Zizioulas adds, is sin. To fall prey to the temptation to "be like God" (Gen 3:5) by attempting to create "out of nothing" is a rejection of this connectedness.[28] Likewise, in referring creation only to ourselves, we truncate creation's precarious orientation to God.[29] Embracing our creatureliness and referring creation to God, meanwhile, is the pinnacle of human personhood.

If sin inhibits this bridge-like vocation, then salvation through Christ somehow restores it. For Zizioulas, whereas Adam failed in this task, Christ the New Adam fulfills it. Christ, as the embodiment and recapitulation of creation, is the supreme Priest of Creation.[30] To participate in Christ's saving work accordingly entails conforming ourselves to his priestly vocation and learning the proper manner of relating to the natural world.

The church, precisely as the prolongation of this saving work, perpetuates this task "particularly through the sacraments."[31] In a unique way, the Eucharist enacts the culmination of this priestly offering in our lives. In Zizioulas's words:

> Through the Eucharist, the Church proclaims and realizes precisely this priestly function. The Eucharist consists in taking elements from the natural world, the bread and the wine which represent the created material world, and bringing them into

27. John Zizioulas, "Preserving God's Creation, Lecture Three," *King's Theological Review* 13 (1990): 1–5, at 3.

28. Zizioulas, "Proprietors or Priests of Creation?," 136.

29. Zizioulas, "Proprietors or Priests of Creation?," 138.

30. John Zizioulas, "Preserving God's Creation, Lecture Three," 5.

31. Zizioulas, "Proprietors or Priests of Creation?," 138.

> the hands of the human being, the hands of Christ who is the man *par excellence* and the priest of creation, in order to refer them to God.[32]

Rather than referring creation to ourselves—this is sin—the church through the Eucharist offers creation back to its Creator. Creation becomes a gift to be celebrated rather than an object to be manipulated. Through the work of human hands, the natural world finds its final fulfillment: "this is my Body, . . . this is my Blood."

Humans liberate creation by giving voice to it such that the groanings of creation become its rejoicings. Thus, humankind's relationship to creation is far more profound than a functional one; it is a "cultural" one. That is, for Zizioulas, "the priest is in this sense an *artist*: he takes the material world in his hands (the bread and the wine, for example, in the case of the Eucharist, which are perishable by nature) and lifts it up to acquire eternal divine meaning."[33] While the stewardship model betrays overly managerial implications, this priestly anthropology better conveys the dramatic artistry of human responsibility in our common home. And the Eucharist illustrates this "art" in a unique, unsurpassable way. The Eucharist must become a way of life for all, a way to imagine ourselves in the world: "we are all born priests, and unless we remain so throughout our lives we are bound to suffer the ecological consequences we are now experiencing."[34]

Zizioulas's proposal of a priestly anthropology helps flesh out the otherwise inchoate anthropology tendered in *Laudato si'*. In fact, Zizioulas presided at the official presentation of *Laudato si'* as an ecumenical observer and extolled how the encyclical makes "human beings instead of proprietors of creation act as its priests" such that "the human being leads this cosmic chorus of glorification to the Creator as the priest of creation."[35] In *Laudato si'*, Pope Francis roots the intrinsic value of all creatures in their

---

32. Zizioulas, "Proprietors or Priests of Creation?," 138–139. See also Paul McPartlan, "Praying with Creation: Cosmic Aspects of Eucharist," *Liturgy News* 40, no. 3 (Sept. 2010): 6–10.

33. Zizioulas, "Proprietors or Priests of Creation?," 139–140. [Emphasis added.]

34. Zizioulas, "Proprietors or Priests of Creation?," 141. See also David Cloutier, *Walking God's Earth: The Environment and Catholic Faith* (Collegeville, MN: Liturgical Press, 2014), 117–125.

35. John D. Zizioulas, "A Comment on Pope Francis' Encyclical *Laudato Si'* by Elder Metropolitan John (Zizioulas) of Pergamon" (June 18, 2015), https://www.patriarchate.org/-/a-comment-on-pope-francis-encyclical-laudato-si-, accessed December 5, 2019.

ability to "give [God] glory" (*LS* 69); he decries biodiversity loss, as "thousands of species will no longer give glory to God by their very existence" (*LS* 33). This claim is a biblical one; the pope discusses how the Psalms frequently have us join with sun and moon, stars and water, in a single chorus of glorifying God (*LS* 72). He concurs with the Japanese bishops that "to sense each creature singing the hymn of its existence is to live joyfully in God's love and hope" (*LS* 85). Likewise, "when we can see God reflected in all that exists, our hearts are moved to praise the Lord for all his creatures and to worship him in union within them" (*LS* 87). Equipped with Zizioulas's extended reflections on this theme, readers can detect the encyclical's emphasis that all creation, including human beings, strains to reach its Creator through praise.

Nevertheless, again in view of Zizioulas's thought, while always themselves a part of this chorus, human beings play a special role in mediating this praise. Pope Francis names Saint Francis of Assisi as an "example *par excellence*" for "drawing all creatures into his praise" as opposed to viewing them through mere "intellectual appreciation or economic calculus" (*LS* 11). After all, it was Saint Francis who famously preached to the birds so that through their glorification of God, creation might be restored to its original harmony. It was Saint Francis who composed the "Canticle of the Creatures" in which God is praised *by* creation precisely through humans praising God *for* creation: *Laudato si'*![36] Saint Francis thus models the meaning of caring for our common home. As opposed to the twin errors of "biocentrism" and "excessive anthropocentrism," we too "are called to lead all creatures back to their creator" by joining with yet also bringing forth creation's sacrifice of praise (*LS* 83). The doxological tenor of the encyclical and Zizioulas's proposals both suggest that this call is a priestly one, to offer creation back to God. To neglect this mediatory role is "how we end up worshipping earthly powers, or ourselves usurping the place of God, even to the point of claiming an unlimited right to trample his creation underfoot" (*LS* 75). As an alternative, the call to mediate creation's praise affords an opportunity to conform ourselves to Christ's own cosmic priesthood, to see with "the gaze of Jesus" (*LS* 96). Seen through this Christological light, "the creatures of this world no longer appear to us under merely natural

36. See Roger D. Sorrell, *St. Francis of Assisi and Nature: Tradition and Innovation in Western Christian Attitudes toward the Environment* (New York: Oxford University Press, 1988), esp. 110–111, 140. The "by" and "for" refer to the controversial ambivalence of the Italian "*per*" in the Canticle (e.g., "*Laudato si, mi signore, per sora Luna e le Stelle*"; on this debate, see *St. Francis of Assisi and Nature*, 115).

guise because the risen One is mysteriously holding them to himself and directing them towards fullness as their end" (*LS* 100). Ecological conversion, the dramatic art of caring for our common home, climaxes in joining with and bringing forth this tidal movement towards God.

Finally, this call helps explain why *Laudato si'* devotes such considerable space to the Eucharist. For Pope Francis, "it is in the Eucharist that all that has been created finds its greatest exaltation" (*LS* 236). The Eucharist offers human beings the means to participate in this sacerdotal offering back of the world, the Christic art of caring for our common home:

> Joined to the incarnate Son, present in the Eucharist, the whole cosmos gives thanks to God. . . . The world which came forth from God's hands returns to him in blessed and undivided adoration: in the bread of the Eucharist, "creation is projected towards divinization, towards the holy wedding feast, towards unification with the Creator himself" (*LS* 236).[37]

In the cosmic celebration of the Eucharist, all creation, through the human person, resounds its praises to God.[38] The Eucharistic celebration liberates the groanings of creation, sacramentalizing its stretching forth towards God. Making the Eucharist a way of life and a way of imagining our role in our common home dramatically narrates our calling within it.

Laudato si', when read in tandem with Zizioulas's proposals, presents a compelling and engaging vision of our role within creation. At the same time, however, more reflection is needed. Zizioulas sagely desires to capture the properly dramatic character of human responsibility over excessively rational-ethical, technocratic conceptions. Precisely through this emphasis, though, Zizioulas occasionally rejects what Lonergan refers to as the "systematic exigence."[39] In this vein, Doran stressed the need to ground poetic, aesthetic categories in explanatory theory, which can provide a systematic

---

37. Pope Francis cites here Pope Benedict XVI's *Homily for the Mass of Corpus Domini* on June 15, 2016. For Joseph Ratzinger's own articulation of a priestly anthropology, see, e.g., Joseph Ratzinger, *God and the World: A Conversation with Peter Seewald*, trans. Henry Taylor (San Francisco: Ignatius Press, 2002), 89; and idem., "The Spirit of the Liturgy," in *Theology of the Liturgy*, Joseph Ratzinger Collected Works (vol. 11), ed. Michael J. Miller (San Francisco: Ignatius Press, 2014), 13, 42, 84, 107.

38. Pope Francis notes how generally the sacraments offer "a privileged way in which nature is taken up by God to become a means of mediating supernatural life. . . . Water, oil, fire and colors are taken up in all their symbolic power and incorporated in our act of praise" (*LS* 235).

39. See, e.g., Zizioulas, "Preserving God's Creation, Lecture Three," 1. For Lonergan on the "systematic exigence," see his *Method in Theology*, 82.

understanding of a descriptive phrase like "priest of creation." Moreover, *Laudato si'*, as a social encyclical operating on the level of practical common-sense, cannot answer these exigencies on its own. To this end and following Lonergan, Doran can provide some systematic categories for substantiating the aims of Catholic social teaching.[40]

Doran's Work in a Doxological, Cosmic Key

While Doran's thought can substantiate this dramatic account, so too can the priestly anthropology of *Laudato si'* enrich Doran's work as a response to the contemporary situation. Although others have brought Doran's work to bear on the question of the "adequate anthropology" that *Laudato si'* urges, none have done so in light of the encyclical's indisputably doxological tenor.[41] What follows supplements those studies. So too does it reply to Doran's invitation in the first volume of *The Trinity in History* to detail the relationship between religious and personal values within the scale of values.[42]

Doran's insistence that the dramatic artistry of human living involves a tensive balance between poles of limitation and transcendence, matter and spirit, deserves deeper analysis. On a personal level, the pole of limitation represents unconscious neural movements, but, in an even deeper way, so too does it represent our dependency on the earth and biological processes, whether for insights or for vital goods. Indeed, on a cultural level, limitation takes the form of "cosmological meanings and values," which are "rooted in the affective and thus biologically based sympathy of the human organism with the rhythms and processes of nonhuman nature."[43] Transcendence, meanwhile, manifests itself on the personal level in the drive towards intelligence, truth, goodness, and being itself. Culturally, "anthropological

40. See, e.g., Patrick Brown, "'Aiming Excessively High and Far': The Early Lonergan and the Challenge of Theory in Catholic Social Thought," *Theological Studies* 72 (September 2011): 620–644; Rohan Michael Curnow, *The Preferential Option for the Poor: A Short History and a Reading Based on the Thought of Bernard Lonergan* (Milwaukee, WI: Marquette University Press, 2012); and Joseph Ogbonnaya, *Lonergan, Social Transformation, and Sustainable Human Development* (Eugene, OR: Pickwick Publications, 2013).

41. See Thomas Hughson, "Interpreting *Laudato Si'*: What Does It Mean to Be Human?," in *Everything Is Interconnected*, 159–177; Gerard Whelan, "The Human Person: Cause or Solution of the Ecological Crisis?," *St. Augustine Papers* 17, no. 1/2 (2016): 5–22; and Neil Ormerod and Cristina Vanin, "Ecological Conversion: What Does it Mean?," *Theological Studies* 77, no. 2 (2016): 328–352.

42. See, e.g., Robert M. Doran, *The Trinity in History: A Theology of the Divine Missions, Volume 1: Missions and Processions* (Toronto: University of Toronto Press, 2012), 349.

43. Doran, *Theology and the Dialectics of History*, 510; see also 507, 511.

meanings and values" stress the distinctly human in the world, conceiving "history as a process involving the contribution of human insight, reflection, deliberation, and decision."[44] Authenticity in history demands the balancing of these two poles first and foremost in the human person.

I propose that the priestly anthropology of Zizioulas and *Laudato si'* aesthetically names this taut balancing. Conceiving humans as joining with and alongside all creation's praise of God maintains humankind's belonging with creation (limitation). At the same time, conceiving humans as mediating and offering forth this praise to God maintains humankind's unique role within the cosmos through their pursuit of meaning (transcendence). So too do Doran's categories guard against excessively anthropocentric distortions of this priestly anthropology that worry someone like Michael Northcott.[45] Any correct understanding of a priestly anthropology must ensure that it maintains the limitation pole of the dialectic, that humans join with and participate in creation's praise of God. To emphasize the transcendence pole of the dialectic too much produces what Doran labels "the mechanomorphic imperialism of perverted anthropological truth" in which "the source of order becomes the human will for domination rather than participation."[46] Conversely, to stress limitation too much and neglect the unique mediating role of humans within this praise produces the biocentrism rejected by Pope Francis in *Laudato si'*. The categories of limitation and transcendence preserve the mediatory value of a priestly anthropology.

Dramatic artistry in our common home requires more than maintaining dialectical balances, however; instead, dramatic artistry is a dynamic reality, the creative unfolding of these linked but opposed principles of change. Transcendence and limitation cooperate within the human person as the ever-transcending yearnings for intelligibility and meaning create not *ex nihilo* but by patiently attending to the lower-order rhythms of nature that limit them. By so doing, we participate in the "upward but indeterminately directed dynamism" of the universe[47] and unleash the passionateness of being

44. Doran, *Theology and the Dialectics of History*, 510.

45. See Michael Northcott, *The Environment and Christian Ethics* (New York: Cambridge University Press, 1996), 131–132.

46. Doran, *Theology and the Dialectics of History*, 513, 543. See also 511: "The ecological crisis generated by the . . . displacement [in the direction of transcendence] is due to our allowing the apparent linearity of humanly constituted history to play fast and loose with the apparent cycles of nature, interfering with them in such a cavalier fashion as to introduce into a disoriented culture another, mechanomorphic, process of experience and symbolization."

47. Lonergan, *Insight*, 477.

itself, now rightly understood as creation's groundswell of praise that groans to be released. As Doran writes in an especially provocative early passage:

> What is good, is good for the whole person, and not simply for the upper reaches of consciousness. The lower manifolds are themselves energically, indeterminately, heading for the same good that higher conjugates understand, affirm, and choose. An intentionality open to things as they are is receptively instrumental in the flourishing of psyche and organism. The whole of creation groans in expectation of the liberation of the children of God.[48]

Through being attentive, being intelligent, being rational, and being responsible, humans bring these lower manifolds of creation closer to their "higher good," their transcendent end in the God who is love. Otherwise, in Doran's words, "we forget what the universe uttered when the body spoke through the psyche to intentionality."[49] When the human person is authentic, the sub-atomic movements, chemical processes, and biological phenomena that undergird human intentionality all transcend themselves, just as the subject does in surrendering to the unrestricted character of being. To seek the "direction in the movement of life" is to participate in and mediate this hymn of the universe.

Nevertheless, as Doran makes apparent, personal authenticity remains impossible to sustain, dramatic artistry impossible to fashion, on our own. Given the cul-de-sac of sin and biases, we need what Lonergan calls an "antecedent willingness," fulfilled only through the gift of God's grace.[50] Zizioulas speaks of our participation in Christ's cosmic priesthood. This Christological reference describes what Doran labels a "soteriological differentiation of consciousness"—taking on the mind of Christ (Phil 2:5), to see with the eyes of Jesus (*LS* 96)—that allows for this creative balancing of transcendence and limitation in our own lives. The work of art that we make of our lives is no longer our own: "dramatic artistry is God's work before it is our own, and God's work of art is ultimately the Risen Body of

---

48. Doran, *Psychic Conversion and Theological Foundations*, 230. See also "Dramatic Artistry in the Third Stage of Meaning," in *Intentionality and Psyche*, 253, where after a similar passage, Doran states: "And so we have perhaps the starting point of a contemporary mediation through transcendental method of the biblical insight that the whole of creation groans in expectation, waiting for the liberation of the children of God."

49. Doran, "Insight and Archetype: The Complementarity of Lonergan and Jung," in *Intentionality and Psyche*, 296.

50. Lonergan, *Insight*, 660, 690.

God's faithful servant who remained obedient even unto death."[51] Authentic dramatic artistry takes the shape of the Law of the Cross, behind which is, in Lonergan's words, "the chief act of religious worship, the act of sacrifice. . . . It is the spirit of adoration . . . more simply and more solidly recognizing [God's] supreme dominion and surrendering to Him all that one is with all one's heart and all one's soul and all one's mind and all one's strength."[52] By patterning the drama of Christ's own doxological obedience, we offer ourselves and all the lower manifolds of creation to God as a "sacrifice of praise" (Heb 13:15).

As Doran demonstrates in his most recent work, the life of grace is profoundly Trinitarian, and so this praise ultimately participates in the reciprocal doxology that is the Triune God. The *ekstasis* of worship participates in the *ekstasis* of the Trinity. Christ the High Priest brings creation into this relationship, and through conformity to the mission of the Son that fulfills the mission of the Spirit, humans bring all creation to join in the joyful dance of the divine *perichoresis*. In Doran's words:

> The state of grace is an interpersonal situation, where the founding persons are the divine Three, and where we are all invited to allow ourselves to be caught up, in prayer and in life, individually and communally, in the circumcession of divine life. Our participation in the divine relations through grace is an elevation also of our relatedness to our fellow men and women, *and in fact to all creation*.[53]

Through the self-transcending character of the human spirit, the passionateness of creation reaches its fulfillment in the passionateness of Triune relation. "Trinitarian theology is inherently doxological," Catherine Mowry

---

51. Doran, *Theology and the Dialectics of History*, 206; see also 358.

52. Bernard J. F. Lonergan, "The Mass and Man," in *Shorter Papers*, vol. 20 in *Collected Works of Bernard Lonergan*, ed. Robert Croken, Robert Doran, H. Daniel Monsour (Toronto: University of Toronto Press, 2007), 95–96. See also Bernard J. F. Lonergan, "The Notion of Sacrifice," Latin text with translation by Michael Shields *in Early Latin Theology*, vol. 19 in *Collected Works of Bernard Lonergan*, ed. Robert M. Doran and H. Daniel Monsour (Toronto: University of Toronto Press, 2011), 29–31, 37. For an extended reflection on the doxological pattern that determined Christ's own life, see Edward Schillebeeckx, *Christ, the Sacrament of the Encounter with God* (New York: Sheed and Ward, 1963), esp. 17–19, 30, 37–39.

53. Robert M. Doran, *The Trinity in History: A Theology of the Divine Missions, Volume 2: Missions, Relations, and Persons* (Toronto: University of Toronto Press, 2019), 34. Emphasis added. For an extended treatment of the ecological significance of Doran's Trinitarian theology, see Eugene R. Schlesinger, "A Trinitarian Basis for a 'Theological Ecology' in Light of *Laudato Si'*," *Theological Studies* 79, no. 2 (2018): 339–355.

LaCugna reminds us.[54] From below, participation in the drama of the Trinity takes the shape of praise; in Lonergan's words, "religious conversion is transferring oneself into the world of worship."[55] Doxology shapes unmistakably the relationship between personal and religious values.

For Zizioulas and *Laudato si'* alike, the Eucharist makes this cosmic doxology tangible. Doran has admitted the need to articulate more clearly the place of sacraments within his theological system, believing that such a project might enhance sacramental theology as well.[56] Each Eucharistic celebration, along with inviting us into the Triune God, enacts this dramatic artistry of our priestly duty within our common home. If the integral scale of values rests upon religious values, then the Eucharist, as a way of life, helps secure the integrity of personal, cultural, social, and vital values as well as the processes that undergird vital values. The Eucharist, "sacrament of salvation," transforms the cries of the earth and the poor into a symphony of praise to our Triune God.[57]

Conclusion

Pope Francis's 2019 Lenten Message was stunning in its cosmic scope. Meditating on Romans 8:19—"For creation waits with eager longing for the revealing of the children of God"—the pope discussed how our cooperation with God's redemptive purposes helps redeem all creation. While sin ruptures creation, "when the love of Christ transfigures the lives of the saints in spirit, body and soul, they give praise to God. Through prayer, contemplation and art, they also include other creatures in that praise, as we see admirably expressed in the 'Canticle of the Creatures' by Saint Francis of Assisi." To praise God is creation's salvation, as "all creation is called, with us, to go forth 'from its bondage to decay and obtain the glorious liberty of the children of God' (Rom 8:21)."[58] Conversion in our common

54. Catherine Mowry LaCugna, *God for Us: The Trinity and Christian Life* (San Francisco: Harper Collins Publishers, 1991), 368.

55. Bernard J. F. Lonergan, "An Interview with Fr. Bernard Lonergan, S.J.," ed. Philip McShane, in *A Second Collection*, 217.

56. Robert M. Doran, *What Is Systematic Theology?* (Toronto: University of Toronto Press, 2005), 70, 74.

57. See Lucas Briola, "Hearing and Answering the One Cry of Earth and Poor: An Integral Ecology, Eucharistic Healing, and the Scale of Values," in *Everything Is Interconnected*, 119–135.

58. Francis, "Message of His Holiness Pope Francis for Lent 2019," October 4, 2018, https://press.vatican.va/content/salastampa/en/bollettino/pubblico/2019/02/26/190226d.html, accessed October 5, 2019.

home, during Lent and elsewhere, requires configuring our own personhood, imagining our own dramatic artistry, in this manner. This message illustrates that the doxological backdrop of *Laudato si'* and its priestly anthropology are not anomalies. The far-ranging work of Robert Doran, this essay has shown, helps us grasp what claims like these mean.

Meanwhile, the work of John Zizioulas, the proposals of *Laudato si'*, and the cosmic mysticism of both place Doran's work more firmly in an ecological key. Reading Doran's work in a doxological key likewise draws out the dynamism of his proposals. It is to Doran's great credit that, following Lonergan, he leaves his project open-ended and always receptive to further development. It is up to his students to serve the work of this great theologian by always placing it in conversation with the ever-evolving contemporary situation in our common home.

CHAPTER TWO

ECOLOGICAL CONVERSION, SOCIAL GRACE, AND THE FOUR-POINT HYPOTHESIS

Eugene R. Schlesinger

SANTA CLARA UNIVERSITY (SANTA CLARA, CA)

Introduction:

Buried away in a tome of scholastic-in-form Latin prose originally intended for seminarians, we find the following speculative proposal:

> There are four real divine relations, really identical with the divine substance, and therefore there are four very special modes that ground the external imitation of the divine substance. Next, there are four absolutely supernatural realities, which are never found uninformed, namely, the secondary act of existence of the incarnation, sanctifying grace, the habit of charity, and the light of glory. It would not be inappropriate, therefore, to say that the secondary act of existence of the incarnation is a created participation of paternity, and so has a special relation to the Son; that sanctifying grace is a participation of active spiration, and so has a special relation to the Holy Spirit; that the habit of charity is a participation of passive spiration, and so has a special relation to the Father and the Son; and that the light of glory is a participation of sonship, and so in a most perfect way brings the children of adoption back to the Father.[1]

With this "four-point hypothesis," Bernard Lonergan gestures towards an integration of trinitarian theology, Christology, and soteriology. His

1. Bernard Lonergan, *The Triune God: Systematics* (orig. *De Deo Trino: Pars Systematica* [1964], ed. Robert M. Doran and H. Daniel Monsour, trans. Michael G. Shields, vol. 12 in *Collected Works of Bernard Lonergan* (Toronto: University of Toronto Press, 2007), 471, 473.

proposal attempts a coherent account of how human beings are recruited into and come to participate in the relations that constitute the eternal, infinite life of God. The four-point hypothesis is a creative enough synthesis to be debated and discussed in its own right, but the work of Fr. Robert Doran has taken it further than this somewhat modest provenance, seeing in it the potential for a "unified field structure" for systematic theology.[2]

Meanwhile, Pope Francis has devoted much of his energy to calling our attention to the pressing urgency of environmental degradation. In his landmark Encyclical, *Laudato si'*, Pope Francis has called the church to an ecological conversion,[3] paralleling his call for a pastoral and missionary conversion in his earlier Apostolic Exhortation, *Evangelii gaudium*.[4] This call for ecological conversion comes in recognition of the particularly pressing nature of the ecological crisis, which continues to cast a rather ominous shadow and which experts warn us is approaching the point of irreversibility. Radical conversion is needed because radical change must occur, and it must occur without delay.

Any theology responsive to the signs of the times must squarely face the environmental crisis and respond to Francis's call to an integral ecology. This is the case not only because of the particular teaching office exercised by the bishop of Rome, but because this crisis is of a sort as to threaten the very future of the planet. This essay marshals Doran's articulation of the four-point hypothesis in service of Pope Francis's call to ecological conversion. Beginning with some ecological touchstones from *Laudato si'*, it notes a dialectic between the need for a human solution to the ecological crisis and the need for a solution beyond ourselves. It then turns to the four-point hypothesis to meet this dialectical requirement by producing an account of human action that is empowered by and participates in the divine life, making it possible to affirm both a human solution and a solution beyond ourselves. In addition, this account of divine and human activity provides the basis for an understanding of ecological conversion. By sharing in the divine life through the divine missions, human beings come to share in a judgment of value and an act of

---

2. See, e.g., Robert M. Doran, "The Starting Point of Systematic Theology," *Theological Studies* 67 (2006): 750–76; idem., *The Trinity in History: Volume 1: Missions and Processions* (Toronto: University of Toronto Press, 2013).

3. Pope Francis, *Laudato Si': On Care for Our Common Home*, nos. 226–231 The Holy See (Vatican website), May 24, 2015, http://w2.vatican.va/content/francesco/en/encyclicals/documents/papa-francesco_20150524_enciclica-laudato-si.html.

4. Pope Francis, *Evangelii Gaudium*, nos. 25–33, The Hole See (Vatican website), November 24, 2013, http://w2.vatican.va/content/francesco/en/apost_exhortations/documents/papa-francesco_esortazione-ap_20131124_evangelii-gaudium.html.

unrestricted love that extend not only to humans but to the whole creation, and are recruited into a collaboration with one another and with God himself to work for the protection of the most vulnerable, including the earth itself.

Laudato si': The Proper Contours of a Response to Ecological Crisis

Laudato si' is a sprawling spiritual work, which provides a rich theological account of the environment and the urgency of ecological conversion. In attending to Pope Francis's ecological teaching, three emphases of the Encyclical's perspective are particularly salient for our purposes.

First, true to his Latin American roots, Francis notes that "ecojustice" is tied to human justice. The environmental crisis disproportionately affects the poor and vulnerable of the world. Insofar as the church is tasked with working for an integral human development, the natural environment must also be cared for. Indeed, the earth is the common home of humanity, meaning that for human persons to flourish, so too must the eco-system(s) of which we are an integral part. Francis goes so far, though, as to note that the earth itself is the victim of injustice. Among the poor and vulnerable on whose behalf the church exercises a preferential option, the earth, our common mother and sister, must be included.[5]

Second, a complex dialectic between humanity and the rest of creation must be observed and maintained. On the one hand, an improper anthropocentrism has caused untold harm, as human beings misunderstand their unique status within the created order, and appeal to that status as justification for exploitative relationships with the earth's resources. In contrast, humanity is not other than the creation. The Genesis creation story roots us in the dust of the earth: the same as other creatures (Gen 2:7, 19). A fundamental equality pervades our relationship to the plants and animals of the earth, on whom we depend and to whom we are responsible.[6] On the

5. Pope Francis, *Laudato si'*, nos. 2, 43–52, 156–62.

6. Pope Francis, *Laudato si'*, nos. 66–69. Denis Edwards notes a similar dynamic, but roots it in a recognition of the intrinsic worth of all creatures ("'Everything Is Interconnected': The Trinity and the Natural World in Laudato Si'," *Australasian Catholic Record* 94, no. 1 [2017]: 84; "Earth as God's Creation The Theology of the Natural World in Pope Francis' Laudato Si'," *Phronema* 31, no. 2 [2016]: 4–8; "'Sublime Communion': The Theology of the Natural World in *Laudato Si'*," *Theological Studies* 77, no. 2 [2016]: 380–83). This recognition is valid, important, and clearly held by Francis. I shall return to the intrinsic value of the created order below, when considering the healing and creative vectors, and Doran's transposition of the category of sanctifying grace into the terms and relations of intentionality analysis.

other hand, though, there is an ineffaceable and unique human dignity that must not be dispensed with. Humanity, rather than any other creature, is created in the image of God.[7]

Finally, and related to this dialectic of humanity: the solution to the ecological crisis must be a human one. This is the case at two levels. First, all the evidence indicates that climate change and other aspects of the ecological crisis are the result of human activity.[8] Because this is the case, it can only be through a change in human activity that this crisis can be addressed and, by the grace of God, corrected. Second, because the environmental and human crises are intertwined, it follows that in order to properly address the needs of the environment we must address the needs of fellow human beings, and vice-versa.[9] From this, it follows that a transformation of humanity is a *sine qua non* of the church's environmental mission. We do not aim to merely change our behavior, though of course we do that. Rather, the values, dispositions, and orientations of human beings from which our behavior flows, must be transformed.

The Scale of Values and the Need for a Solution Beyond Ourselves

When Francis calls for "ecological conversion," it is precisely to this transformation that he gestures.[10] By indicating the need for human transformation, Francis alerts us to the fact that, while the ecological crisis does require a human solution, it also requires a solution beyond ourselves. The transformation required exceeds our capacities. This can be borne out by one of Doran's chief contributions, namely his development of Lonergan's integral scale of values in his theory and theology of history.[11]

7. Pope Francis, *Laudato si'*, no. 90. See further Reinhard Marx, "'Everything Is Connected': One the Relevance of an Integral Understanding of Reality in *Laudato Si'*," *Theological Studies* 77, no. 2 (2016): 295–307.

8. Pope Francis, *Laudato si'*, nos. 101–36.

9. Pope Francis, *Laudato si'*, nos. 137–62

10. Pope Francis, *Laudato si'*, nos. 226–31.

11. The scale of values is introduced in Bernard J. F. Lonergan, *Method in Theology* (Toronto: University of Toronto Press, 1971), 31–33; Doran's work has significantly expanded upon the concept, noting its global dimensions, and especially the way in which the whole is conditioned by divine grace, especially the proposed category of "social grace." *Theology and the Dialectics of History* (Toronto: University of Toronto Press, 2001), 83–114; idem, *Trinity in History*, 1:83–107; idem, *The Trinity in History: A Theology of the Divine Missions. Volume 2: Missions and Relations* (Toronto: University of Toronto Press, 2019), 36. 63–64.

The normative scale of values ascends from vital values such as food, water, shelter; to social values, which ensure the adequate and just distribution of those vital values; thence to cultural values, which inform social values so that there is a commitment to such just distribution; and thence to personal values, as authentic subjects inform the culture so that some meaning and purpose beyond sheer ongoing existence can be discerned and articulated; and, capping the scale of values, to religious values. The love of God (here both a subjective and an objective genitive) flows through women and men, leading them to commit themselves to the flourishing and right order of the integral scale of values.[12]

Each successive level of the scale of values depends upon the lower levels: a culture cannot be sustained if people are starving; scrambling to get by leaves little time for discernment of spirits and choosing the good. At the same time, though, when problems arise at the lower levels, they cannot be addressed at those levels: insufficient recurrence of or access to food and water can only be resolved by attending to social values, asking where the disorder is that impedes just distribution and recurrence. A dysfunctional society requires renewal at the level of culture, and so on. As Doran puts it:

> Briefly, the gift of God's love, that is, the gift of the Holy Spirit (religious values) is the condition of the possibility of sustained personal integrity (personal value); persons of integrity represent the condition of possibility of genuine meanings and values informing ways of living (cultural values); the pursuit of genuine cultural values is a constitutive dimension in the establishment of social structures and intersubjective habits (social values) that would render more probable something approaching an equitable distribution of vital values to the human community (vital values).[13]

The impossibility of resolving problems at the lower levels at their own level or from below is illustrated by such responses to the ecological crisis as the purchase of carbon credits by the wealthy. Through mathematical prestidigitation, they are able to attain a net neutral impact on the environment without actually making any changes to their patterns of consumption. In such cases, the ledgers may balance, but the actual problems facing our environment remain unaddressed. In a similar matter, simplistic calls for population control avoid the deeper issues of human injustice and the

12. Doran, *Theology and the Dialectics of History*, 99–114; idem *Trinity in History*, 1:83–107.

13. Doran, *Trinity in History*, 1:86.

refusal to make concrete changes.[14] Indeed, such calls for population control are often directed towards poorer communities, which amounts to the suggestion that we alleviate poverty by eliminating the poor. Even if such solutions are not intrinsically eugenicist, they need only slight modification to become such.

The urgency of the environmental crisis lies at the level of vital values: the depletion of resources, and, more pressingly, the excessive emission of carbon dioxide into the atmosphere leading to abnormally higher temperatures, and so melting polar ice, rising sea levels, etc. Any possible solution to the crisis, though, will depend upon transformed ideals at the higher levels. This higher-level transformation is, ultimately, the work of God and his grace, transforming human horizons and commitments, and elevating human capacities and collaboration. It is precisely here that the "unified field structure" for systematic theology is able to demonstrate its relevance for the question of ecological conversion, for it attends to the nature of that divine action upon humanity; an action which liberates and accompanies human action.

The Four-Point Hypothesis and the Transformation of Humanity

In order to properly assess the four-point hypothesis we must first locate it within its native context of trinitarian theology, and especially the theology of the divine missions. The basic position on the divine missions which undergirds the four-point hypothesis is articulated by Bernard Lonergan in the systematic portion of his *The Triune God*, in which he updates and refines the Thomistic teaching that the missions of the Son and the Holy Spirit are identical to their processions, only with a created term (Lonergan 2007, 455–67).[15]

Lonergan's refinement is twofold. First, he clarifies that "the mission of a divine person is constituted by a divine relation of origin in such a way that it still demands an appropriate external term as a consequent condition."[16] With this statement Lonergan makes clear that the constitution

14. Pope Francis, *Laudato si'*, no. 50. *See further*, Marx, "Everything Is Connected," 305–6.

15. Lonergan, *Triune God: Systematics*, 455. Thomas Aquinas develops his account of the divine missions in *Summa Theologiae* 1.43.1–7. See Jeremy D. Wilkins, "Why Two Divine Missions? Development in Augustine, Aquinas, and Lonergan," *Irish Theological Quarterly* 77, no. 1 (2012): 55–64, for an account of Lonergan's thought as a development of Aquinas's.

16. Lonergan, *Triune God: Systematics*, 455.

of the missions is in God. Recognizing this vigorously upholds the infinity and aseity of God, while also allowing us to recognize the contingency of the missions, and, hence, the gratuity of grace.[17] Lonergan's second refinement is to provide a more differentiated account of the missions' terms. Aquinas understood the invisible missions of the Son and the Holy Spirit having their term in sanctifying grace,[18] and the visible mission of the Son's term in the assumed humanity of the incarnation.[19] Lonergan, though, specifies four created terms for the missions: the *esse secondarium* of the incarnation, sanctifying grace, habitual charity, and the light of glory. He further suggests that they are created participations of the four divine relations, which constitute the life of God: paternity, active spiration, passive spiration, and filiation, respectively.[20]

The four-point hypothesis clarifies the nature and the purpose of the divine missions. They consist in the divine life directed outwards toward humanity for the purpose of bringing human beings to share in that same divine life. The divine missions must be understood in terms of their formal effects upon humanity, for otherwise it is unintelligible to speak about a divine person being "sent."[21] Our introduction into God's life occurs through our intellectual, moral, and religious transformation. By grace, human beings are brought into friendship with God and have our relationship with earthly realities reconfigured. Ecological conversion is a special instance of this reconfiguration, directed towards the value of the created order, and which involves human beings at the psychic, intellectual, moral, and religious levels.[22]

---

17. Lonergan, *Triune God: Systematics*, 439–47. See further, Doran, *Trinity in History*, 1:41–57. This account of contingent predication, then, does represent a genuine refinement of and advance upon Aquinas's articulation. For instance, in his masterful treatment of Thomas's trinitarian theology, Giles Emery argues that the divine missions are constituted by both the relation of origin and the created term. *The Trinitarian Theology of Saint Thomas Aquinas*, trans. Francesca Aran Murphy (Oxford: Oxford University Press, 2007), 364–69. Such a viewpoint brings problematic metaphysical consequences, as noted above. And yet, Emery is a careful and responsible reader. The fact is that Aquinas's position is liable to be interpreted in this way because it is less developed. Lonergan's refinement forecloses this possibility.

18. *Summa Theologiae* 1.43.3.

19. *Summa Theologiae* 1.43.7

20. Lonergan, *Triune God: Systematics*, 471, 473. See above for the full quotation.

21. E.g., *Summa Theologiae* 1.43.1; Lonergan, *Triune God: Systematics*, 483–91.

22. See Neil Ormerod and Cristina Vanin, "Ecological Conversion: What Does It Mean?," *Theological Studies* 77, no. 2 (June 2016): 328–52.

As ground-breaking as the four-point hypothesis is, Doran recognizes that it also needs further refinement in order to serve as a part of a unified field structure for systematic theology. He provides this refinement in two key areas. First, he transposes the scholastic categories used in Lonergan's earlier formulation into categories drawn from the intentionality analysis that came to characterize Lonergan's later work, which allows for greater precision. The supernatural reality that the scholastics and the early Lonergan called sanctifying grace is a synthetic category, incorporating a wide range of biblical teaching, which may be summarized thus:

> To those whom God the Father loves [1] as he loves Jesus, his only begotten Son, (2) he gives the uncreated gift of the Holy Spirit, so that (3) into a new life they may be (4) born again and (5) become living members of Christ; therefore as (6) justified, (7) friends of God, (8) adopted children of God, and (9) heirs in hope of eternal life, (10) they enter into a sharing in the divine nature.[23]

Doran expresses this complex of biblical affirmations as "the recalled reception (memoria) of the gift of God's love . . . grounding a subsequent set of judgments of value (faith)," while the reality previously identified as habitual charity is expressed as "a return of love (charity) participating in the Proceeding Love that is the Holy Spirit, which establishes a special relationship with the indwelling Father and Son."[24] The former (memoria and faith) participate in active spiration, while the latter (charity) participates in passive spiration. Put another way, we recognize and affirm that we have been loved unconditionally, just as the Father loves the Son, and are motivated by that recognition to make our own return of love. There is a twofold movement: we are loved unrestrictedly, and we come to love in return. In this way, we share in the trinitarian relations, and "are divinized not by a quasi-formal cause but by elevation to conscious *relations* to each of the divine persons . . . [which] participate in the divine relations."[25]

Our entry into the divine relations has the concrete effect of transforming our human relationality as well, fostering collaboration in service

23. Bernard J. F. Lonergan, "Supplementary Notes on Sanctifying Grace [Translated from *De Gratia Sanctificante: Supplementum* (1951–1952)]," in *Early Latin Theology*, ed. Robert M. Doran and H. Daniel Monsour, trans. Michael G. Shields, Collected Works of Bernard Lonergan 19 (Toronto: University of Toronto Press, 2011), 581. See also Doran, *Trinity in History*, 1:20.

24. Doran, *Trinity in History*, 1:17. See his further elaboration on pp. 166–67.

25. Doran, *Trinity in History*, 2:12.

of the reign of God, which is, formally, the integral functioning of the scale of values.[26] The incarnation expresses "God's meaning, Logos, Word" within the realm of human meaning, thereby informing cultural values, which in turn, "inform the integral dialectics of community at the level of social values," thereby ensuring the "equitable distribution of vital goods to the whole human family."[27] This allows us to ground our understanding of the triune God both in terms of an analogy drawn from the natural order (the operations of intentional consciousness) and from the supernatural order (our participation in the life of God).[28] Crucially, it enables us to affirm that we come to participate in the processions from act to act—a judgment of value (the procession of the Word), and an act of love (the procession of the Holy Spirit)—that we analogically understand to constitute the life of God. In other words, our values and loves are transformed through the act of God and come to imitate the values and loves of God.

The second refinement offered by Doran is to integrate the four-point hypothesis with a theology of history, which attends to the dynamics of progress and decline, the vectors of creating and healing, and the proper functioning of the integral scale of values, and so prevents the four-point hypothesis from remaining overly abstract and disconnected from either the concrete reality of women and men and their activity in the world or from the historical dynamism enacted and inaugurated by Jesus of Nazareth and continued by him through the community of the church and other persons of good will.[29] This is a crucial dimension of ecological conversion, then, for it foregrounds for us the centrality of human agency and the effects that this has in the world.

Pope Francis's call for ecological conversion pushes us to recognize that our agency in the world has a critical impact on the environment. Our historical activity has pushed us to the brink of disaster, but by God's grace, we can make the needed about-face, and direct our historical energies to reversing not just cultural and social decline, but ecological decline. I shall return to this point below.

---

26. Doran, *Trinity in History*, 2:36, 63–65.

27. Doran, *Trinity in History*, 2:5.

28. Doran, *Trinity in History*, 1:142–62.

29. Doran, *Trinity in History*, 1:139–41; 2:33–36, 149–66. Doran's earlier work in the functional specialization of foundations provides the theoretical underpinning for this later development within systematic theology (*Theology and the Dialectics of History*).

The Problem of Anthropocentrism

This emphasis on the transformation of humanity, though, might seem to reduce our concerns once more to anthropocentrism. On the one hand, *some* degree of anthropocentrism is probably unavoidable. As *Laudato si'* reminds us, the biblical witness does recognize a unique status and vocation for humanity among God's creatures.[30] This is all the more pronounced by the incarnation of the eternal Logos as human. Indeed, given the human causes of the ecological crisis, any viable solution will have to involve human activity. On the other hand, there are indeed problematic forms of anthropocentrism which must be avoided. The four-point hypothesis, and especially Doran's refinement of it, helps us to avoid these problematic anthropocentrisms even as it points toward the possibility of and means for a properly human solution.

The soteriological transformation of humanity is a higher integration of our "lower" functions and operations, especially those of intentional consciousness. It takes the underlying manifold of human nature and sublates it, rendering it capable of producing new operations, beyond what it is capable of by nature.[31] This is the meaning of the supernatural order, which, as we have seen for Lonergan and Doran, is itself a concretion of the divine missions, the life of God.[32] The supernatural order sublates humanity's

30. Pope Francis, *Laudato si'*, no. 90.

31. Lonergan, *Insight: A Study of Human Understanding*, ed. Frederick E. Crowe and Robert M. Doran, Collected Works of Bernard Lonergan 3 (Toronto: University of Toronto Press, 1992), 718–25; idem, *Method in Theology*, 105–7.

32. Lonergan only refers to the supernatural order as such in his explicitly theological writings (e.g., *Grace and Freedom: Operative Grace in the Thought of St. Thomas Aquinas*, ed. Frederick E. Crowe and Robert M. Doran, Collected Works of Bernard Lonergan 1 [Toronto: University of Toronto Press, 1988]; *The Triune God: Systematics, Translated from* De Deo Trino: Pars Systematica *(1964) by Michael G. Shields*, ed. Robert M. Doran and H. Daniel Monsour, Collected Works of Bernard Lonergan 12 [Toronto: University of Toronto Press, 2007]; "The Supernatural Order [Translated from *De Ente Supernaturali: Supplementum Schematicum* (1946–1947)]," in *Early Latin Theology*, ed. Robert M. Doran and H. Daniel Monsour, trans. Shields, Collected Works of Bernard Lonergan 19 [Toronto: University of Toronto Press, 2011], 52–255; "Supplementary Notes on Sanctifying Grace"; "God's Knowledge and Will [Translated from '*De scientia atque voluntate Dei*' (1949–1950)," in *Early Latin Theology*, ed. Robert M. Doran and H. Daniel Monsour, trans. Michael G. Shields, Collected Works of Bernard Lonergan 19 [Toronto: University of Toronto Press, 2011], 257–411). In *Method in Theology*, Lonergan transposed the notion of sanctifying grace into the idiom of a dynamic state of being in love with God (106–7). These developments are traced in H. Daniel Monsour, "Bernard Lonergan's Early Formulation of the Foundational *Nexus Mysteriorum* in God's Self Communication in Creation," in *Meaning and History in Systematic Theology: Essays in Honor of Robert M. Doran*, ed. John D. Dadosky (Milwaukee: Marquette University

intentional consciousness, which itself integrates the lower manifold of the psyche, which in turn is the sublation of a manifold of neurological events.[33]

This sublation characterizes not just humanity and our place in the supernatural order, but also the entire universe of proportionate being. The otherwise coincidental events ignored by physicists are the data of chemistry; the coincidental events ignored by the chemist are the data of biology, and so forth.[34] Humanity finds its place within the universe as the sublation of the non-rational creation, directed beyond itself towards God. This understanding of humanity coheres with both the scientific perspective that understands us as the outcome of a process of evolution, and the theological perspective which sees us as not only the result of evolutionary process, but as directed by this process's outcome (our intellectual consciousness) towards God.[35] Crucially, the upward vector of energy does not do away with the integrities of the lower levels (physics remains valid, even though there exists chemistry, the psyche retains its importance even though we engage in intentional operations, reason retains its dignity, even with the advent of supernatural faith and divine revelation). Rather, the process preserves and elevates them.

Hence, just as humanity preserves and integrates the "lower" manifolds of the non-rational creation, the salvation of humanity requires the preservation of the created order in its totality. The salvation and transformation of human beings is necessarily the salvation, transformation, and preservation of the entire cosmos, of which we are an integral part (cf. Rom. 8:19–23). Through the divine missions, we are recruited into collaboration with God and decisively re-oriented in our relationship to God, ourselves,

---

Press, 2009), 375–404; J. Michael Stebbins, *The Divine Initiative: Grace, World-Order, and Human Freedom in the Early Writings of Bernard Lonergan* (Toronto: University of Toronto Press, 1995). In the philosophical work *Insight*, Lonergan limits himself to the data of human consciousness, rather than anything known through supernatural revelation, and so he simply notes that the divine solution to the problem of evil must be some sort of higher integration, which involves the transformation and elevation of human intelligence, but leaves unspecified its precise material content because this would require more than the heuristic structure available to natural human self-reflection (719–25, 740–50).

33. See Lonergan, *Insight*, 230, 281, 289–91, 492–94, 718–25, 740–50; idem *Method in Theology*, 101–7, 120–24; and especially Doran, *Theology and the Dialectics of History*, 19–63.

34. Lonergan, *Insight*, 230, 281, 289–91, 492–94

35. Cf. Lonergan, *Insight*, 284–93; Pope Francis, *Laudato si'*, nos. 65–66. See also the excellent exposition of Lonergan's account of emergence in Benjamin J. Hohman, "The Glory to Be Revealed: Grace and Emergence in an Ecological Eschatology," in *Everything Is Interconnected: Towards Globalization with a Human Face and an Integral Ecology*, ed. Joseph Ogbonnaya and Lucas Briola (Milwaukee: Marquette University Press, 2019), 179–98.

and the rest of creation. Our historical activity is directed away from short-sighted folly, and its resultant destructive behaviors, and towards attentiveness, intelligence, reasonableness, and responsibility.[36]

The enactment of these transcendental precepts—"Be attentive, Be intelligent, Be reasonable, Be responsible"[37]—takes the concrete form of commitment to an integral scale of values,[38] which forms a major component of Doran's theory of history and heuristically anticipates the reign of God.[39] Human activity and historical developments unfold with reference to and according to the dynamics of "vital, social, cultural, personal, and religious values in an ascending order."[40] As with the emergence of humanity from the non-rational creation, the scale of values is characterized by a set of mutually conditioning relationships. The lower levels are presupposed by the higher ones, but the higher values are required for the proper functioning of the lower. Without sufficient food and water (vital values), human beings cannot constitute themselves in an orderly society (social values), and apart from the stability provided by a social order, cultural values cannot be cultivated. Nevertheless, inadequate access to food and water cannot be addressed at the level of vital values. Instead, as noted above, vital values depend upon social values for their recurrence, while social values depend upon cultural values for their formation and enactment, and cultural values derive from the personal values of women and men of integrity. At the top of the scale, and conditioning the whole, are religious values. The dynamic state of being in love with God leads authentic subjects to work for the integral functioning of the entire structure, which, in terms derived from special theological categories, is understood "as a fidelity to the just and mysterious law of the cross."[41]

The scale of values, then, displays not only a sublation of lower manifolds into higher integrations (an upward movement), but also a downward movement insofar as the lower levels' proper functioning depends upon the higher levels, which turn out to "condition the possibility of the recurrent

---

36. Lonergan, *Method in Theology*, 20.

37. Lonergan, *Method in Theology*, 20.

38. Lonergan, *Method in Theology*, 31–33. See further Ormerod and Vanin, "Ecological Conversion," 336–44, for an account of the scale of values and ecological conversion within the framework of moral conversion.

39. Doran, *Theology and the Dialectics of History*, 93–114; idem, *Trinity in History*, 1:85–107; 2:63–64, 134.

40. Lonergan, *Method in Theology*, 31.

41. Doran, *Theology and the Dialectics of History*, 107–14 [113].

realization of the more basic levels."[42] Hence, there is a complementarity between these movements from below and from above, the vectors of creating and healing, respectively.

Lonergan develops this theme in his essay "Healing and Creating in History," where he writes, "just as the creative process, when unaccompanied by healing, is distorted and corrupted by bias, so too the healing process, when unaccompanied by creating is a soul without a body . . . for a single development has two vectors, one from below upwards, creating, the other from above downwards, healing."[43] This twofold movement allows us to affirm both the centrality of human agency, because the creating vector is a genuine movement from below, and of divine grace, because this upward finality is comprehended and depends upon God and his action in and for the world.

The healing of creation is not simply the result of the upward striving of and from the lower levels, but is rather the result of divine grace, a grace that does not abolish, but rather supposes and perfects nature. The perspective we have developed here allows us to see that this Thomistic maxim refers not only to the human nature, but also to "nature" in its more commonsense understanding, for humanity is the rational sublation of the upward striving creative vector, and the focal point of the downwardly transforming healing vector. In saving humanity God saves not just humanity, but the whole creation. The movement of the healing vector does not terminate upon impact, but rather proceeds downward through the lower levels, which are presupposed and sublated by the human creature.

With the four-point hypothesis transposed into the framework of religiously differentiated consciousness, we find both another safeguard against anthropocentrism and a goad towards ecological responsibility. Through the created participation in Paternity that is the incarnate Word, human beings hear the divine summons to friendship and collaboration. Participating in the unrestricted love that is Active Spiration through the love of God poured into our hearts by the Holy Spirit (Rom 5:5), we recognize that all is gift: the creation, our own existence, and especially our coming to share in the divine life, and that the love of God, which we gratefully receive, extends not only to us, but to the environment as a whole, of which we are integral components. As we participate in that return of love that is

42. Doran, *Theology and the Dialectics of History*, 100.

43. Bernard J. F. Lonergan, "Healing and Creating in History," in *A Third Collection: Papers*, ed. Frederick E. Crowe (Mahwah: Paulist, 1985), 107–8. See also the significant development of this theme in Doran, *Theology and the Dialectics of History*, 31–33, 174–76, 221–28, 242–53.

Passive Spiration by our own acts of love, we extend that love also to the beloved creation.

Finally, through participation in the judgment of value that is Filiation through the light of glory, anticipated now by eschatological hope,[44] we learn to value the creation which God has judged to be "very good" (Gen 1:31). Further, we recognize that our own return as children of the Father is bound up with the restoration of all things, including the non-human creation. As *Lumen Gentium* puts it, "The human race as well as the entire world, which is intimately related to man and attains to its end through him, will be perfectly reestablished in Christ."[45] It is not just that the world is preserved for our own sake, but that the world is an object of divine love. It is not just a good of order promoting the recurrence of the particular goods we need, but is itself a particular good, valued by God for its own sake.[46]

Divine love decenters us, even as it radically affirms us. We are decentered, not in the sense of a demotion, or of being lost as mere specks in the cosmos, but in the sense of recognizing that the center of all things is the God of love. This God wills our being and our wellbeing, along with the being and wellbeing of the rest of creation. As that portion of the creation capable of rational thought and, by grace, capable of God, we have a special responsibility toward the rest. When humanity is understood in this sense, as the intellectual sublation of the upward striving creative vector, and the focal point of the downwardly transforming healing vector, we are led to affirm that humanity is saved for the environment's sake, for the Scriptures promise that our complete restoration will also be the restoration of the cosmos (Rom 8:19–23; 2 Pet 3:13; Rev 21–22).

---

44. Doran, *Trinity in History*, 1:57.

45. *Dogmatic Constitution on the Church, Lumen Gentium* (November 21, 1964), no. 48, http://www.vatican.va/archive/hist_councils/ii_vatican_council/documents/vat-ii_const_19641121_lumen-gentium_en.html.

46. Lonergan's notion of the good of order is developed in *Insight*, 238–39, 619–20, 628–29; *Method in Theology*, 48–52. Crucially, in his trinitarian theology, he notes that, with reference to God, the good of order and the good of act are only conceptually, and not really distinct (*Triune God: Systematics*, 421–34, cf. 257–61). Hence it is possible for a good of order to itself be a particular good. Hughson suggests the scale of values be supplemented by the addition of natural values, which support vital values, at the base. "Interpreting *Laudato Si'*: What Does It Mean to Be Human?," in *Everything Is Interconnected: Towards Globalization with a Human Face and an Integral Ecology*, ed. Joseph Ogbonnaya and Lucas Briola (Milwaukee: Marquette University Press, 2019), 159–78.. I believe that this would complement my proposal of seeing the environment as both a good of order and a particular good.

Conclusion

In the face of such a pressing and urgent crisis, it would seem that an appeal to abstruse reflection upon trinitarian theology and precise scholastic distinctions is a step in the wrong direction. Yet that is exactly what this essay has offered. Nevertheless, it is precisely because of the urgency of the environmental situation that this theoretical attention to the divine missions and their transformation of humanity is needed. It has become increasingly clear that, though this is a problem of our own making, its solution lies beyond our capacities.

The four-point hypothesis provides us with an account of how God the Trinity has effected and continues to effect the transformation of humanity. It is just this sort of transformation that is needed if we are to take the decisive action required to address the crisis of environmental degradation. Indeed, our transformation by the salvific act of the Trinity obliges us to take up responsibility for the rest of the earth. The interaction of the creative and healing vectors provides an account of how environmental restoration can be the result of both divine and human activity. In this way, we affirm the need for decisive action on the part of humanity without thereby re-enshrining an anthropocentric perspective. These resources decenter humanity in two crucial ways: by acknowledging the priority of divine grace (in such a way as to also uphold human responsibility and freedom), and by affirming that the created order is both a good of order and a particular good worthy of preservation in its own right.

It is through the graced action of the Son's humanity (*esse secondarium*/paternity) and the unrestricted love given to us in him by the Holy Spirit (sanctifying grace/active spiration) that we learn to make our own return to God in love (charity/passive spiration), returning home as children of the Father (light of glory/filiation), with the rest of the creation rejoicing at the revelation of the freedom of the children of God (Rom 8:21). Through the divine missions, God has reached out to embrace and redeem the entire created order, beginning with humanity.[47]

47. Portions of this essay first appeared in Eugene R. Schlesinger, "A Trinitarian Basis for a 'Theological Ecology' in Light of Laudato Si'," *Theological Studies* 79, no. 2 (June 1, 2018): 339–55.

CHAPTER THREE

HEALING VECTORS ON THE MIND

The Transformative Effects of Divine Grace Within the Integral Scale of Values

Christopher Krall

Marquette University (Milwaukee, WI)

Humanity needs divine grace. God's blessings ground the rational and provide the motivation for the practice of a faith tradition. The human instinct for survival may impel humans to seek out and find those activities and resources that seem to offer security, healing, and strength to face impending challenges. People have in the past and continue to use prayer as a means to seek for such security and comfort, especially related to health and well-being.[1] Results from the 2008 Pew Research survey sampling over 36,000 adults in the United States indicated that 92% of those surveyed believe in God, 60% believe in a personal god, and "most Americans agree with the statement that many religions–not just their own–can lead to eternal life." The actual practice of the religious traditions causes the numbers to drop as 54% attend religious services at least once or twice per month, 39% on a weekly basis. Of those people surveyed, 58% say that they pray daily.[2] A collaborative study from the National Center for Health Statistics, National Center for Complementary and Alternative Medicine, and the Center for Disease

1. See Joseph Bulbulia, "Nature's Medicine: Religiosity as an Adaptation for Health and Cooperation," in *Where God and Science Meet: How Brain and Evolutionary Studies Alter Our Understanding of Religion, Vol. 1: Evolution, Genes, and the Religious Brain*, ed. Patrick McNamara (Westport CT: Praeger Publishers, 2006), 87–122.

2. Luis Lugo, Sandra Stencel, John Green, Gregory Smith et. al., eds., *U.S. Religious Landscape Survey: Religious Beliefs and Practices: Diverse and Politically Relevant* (Washington, DC: Pew Forum on Religion and Public Life, 2008), 4–5.

Control found that 62% of Americans used some form of complementary and alternative therapy in the last twelve months that included prayer, 43% prayed specifically for their own health, 24.4% had asked others to pray for them.[3] Despite how a majority of Americans in these surveys believe in a God and over half of all those surveyed pray on a somewhat regular basis, the Pew Research survey indicates that "a significant minority of Americans say that their prayers result in definite and specific answers from God at least once a month (31%) and nearly one-in-five adults (19%) saying they receive direct answers to specific prayer requests at least once a week . . . [while] members of most other religious traditions tend to be less likely to report familiarity with this kind of direct interaction with the divine."[4] The discrepancy in the data conveys the sad reality that people, in general, are in need of and hopeful for divine assistance but tend not to recognize or acknowledge that they receive grace when or if it comes.

Specialists within the field of neuroscience are looking for the effects of prayer by examining the synaptic growth and the activation of distinct brain regions occurring when a person meditates or prays.[5] Much research has been published and is currently being conducted using MRI brain-imaging technology to establish the physiological effects of (especially Buddhist) meditation and focused mindfulness practices. A recent meta-analysis concluded "that meditation does indeed have positive effects on cognitive and emotional processes, . . . [and] meditation appears to be reliably associated with altered anatomical structure in several brain regions."[6] There are strong correlations of cerebral changes, strengthened synaptic connections, and the enhanced ability for self-regulation with the amount of meditation practiced.[7]

---

3. Patricia M. Barnes, Eve Powell-Griner, Kim McFann, and Richard L. Nahin, "Complementary and Alternative Medicine Use Among Adults: United States, 2002," Advance Data from Vital and Health Statistics 343 (2004), https://www.cdc.gov/nchs/data/ad/ad343.pdf.

4. Lugo et al., *U.S. Religious Landscape Survey*, 13–14.

5. As an example of this see Patrick McNamara, *The Neuroscience of Religious Experience* (New York: Cambridge University Press, 2009).

6. Kieran C. R. Fox, Savannah Nijeboer, Matthew L. Dixon, James L. Floman, Melissa Ellamil, Samuel P. Rumak, Peter Sedlmeier, and Kalina Christoff, "Is Meditation Associated with Altered Brain Structure? A Systematic Review and Meta-Analysis of Morphometric Neuroimaging in Meditation Practitioners," *Neuroscience and Biobehavioral Reviews* 43 (2014), 48–73, 69.

7. For examples see Frédéric Rosenfield, "The Benefits of Meditation, A Scientific Reality" in *The Healing Power of Meditation: Leading Experts on Buddhism, Psychology, and Medicine*

Neuroscience research is also showing correlations between the intentional fostering of love, compassion, and gratitude by means of contemplative methods and mindfulness-based practices, and changes in the brain. People's ability to adapt to adverse conditions also improves dramatically through such practices. Neuroplasticity is the term given to the change in neural structures, connections, and functions of the brain due to the use and abuse of the brain.[8] Health benefits are shown to result when people are intentionally mindful, grateful, and hopeful in their behavioral patterns. Despite all of this research on the changes of the physical structures of the brain when meditative practices are performed, people are not always convinced or comforted that a supernatural force of love is indeed active and working in the world through each person's life.

Robert Doran, in his theological and psychological works, crafts a robust theory of the powerful effects of divine grace in the created world. Doran's perspective helps to manifest the radical transformations that divine grace can cause in the broken world of suffering and sadness and points to the Kingdom of God in the hoped-for world to come.[9] Basing his thought on the writings of Bernard Lonergan, Doran does not limit the power and scope of divine grace to the healing of one person's illness, clarity in one's discernment process, or the activation of a group of neurons in the brain of a person practicing meditation. Rather, Doran has worked for the last thirty years on "the hypothesis about how it can be that the very life of the triune God is communicated to human beings."[10] When the triune God does communicate with humanity, Doran insists that the whole human cosmos is dramatically transformed. He writes, "the world to be changed is one constituted by that nihilism of meaning and value that for Lonergan would be the final upshot of a 'longer

Explore the Health Benefits of Contemplative Practice, ed. Andy Fraser (Boston: Shambhala Publications, 2013), 35–44; Amit Sood and David T. Jones, "On Mind Wandering, Attention, Brain Networks, and Meditation," *Explore: The Journal of Science and Healing* 9 no.3 (2013), 136–41; Evan Thompson, *Waking, Dreaming, Being: Self and Consciousness in Neuroscience, Meditation, and Philosophy* (New York: Columbia University Press, 2014).

8. See Daniel Goleman and Richard J Davidson, *Altered Traits: Science Reveals How Meditation Changes Your Mind, Brain, and Body* (New York: Avery Press, 2017); Norman Doidge, *The Brain's Way of Healing: Remarkable Discoveries and Recoveries from the Frontiers of Neuroplasticity* (New York: Viking, 2015).

9. Progress, decline, and redemption are categorized within the fifth set of theological categories in Lonergan's schemes. See Robert M. Doran, *Theology and the Dialectics of History* (Toronto, Ontario: University of Toronto Press, 1990), 712.

10. Robert M. Doran, *The Trinity in History: A Theology of the Divine Missions*, vol. 1: *Missions and Processions*, (Toronto: University of Toronto Press, 2013), x.

cycle of decline.' But through a substantive change in constitutive meaning, that world can become one constituted by the meanings and values informative of integrity in the dialectical realms of the subject, culture, and social order of the community."[11] This paper explores Robert Doran's development of his vision of divine grace, which is inspired by Lonergan's extensive work and writings. Doran seeks to understand "the meanings constitutive of that praxis of the reign of God through which the human world itself is changed."[12] The praxis of the reign of God in the created world is the perspective of divine grace which not only inspires humanity toward lives of hope in the creative work toward peace on earth, but also impels people toward the salvation of their souls.

This paper has one main section with two following implications. First, in the first volume of Doran's *The Trinity in History*, he recounts the theological debate that developed since Lonergan's death regarding the presence of a fifth level of consciousness.[13] Doran asserts, based on findings in some of Lonergan's archived work and the analysis of recent scholars, especially Jeremy Blackwood, that Lonergan did indeed advocate for a fifth level of consciousness which is "the consummation of unconscious desire, which is to be understood as a self-possessed handing over of one's central form to the determination of another in which is effected the co-presence of the operator and the person who is the object of the operation."[14] The elevation of the fifth level of consciousness is what Lonergan considers vertical finality, the blossoming forth of that which is finest in man,[15] and is the totality of self-transcendence. As

---

11. Doran *Theology and the Dialectics of History*, 5.

12. Doran *Theology and the Dialectics of History*, 5.

13. To see the full historical progression of this discussion, start first with Robert M. Doran, "Consciousness and Grace," *Method: Journal of Lonergan Studies* 11, no. 1 (1993), 51–76; then see Michael Vertin, "Lonergan on Consciousness: Is There a Fifth Level?" *Method: Journal of Lonergan Studies* 12, no. 1 (1994), 1–36; then see Robert M. Doran, "Revisiting "Consciousness and Grace," *Method: Journal of Lonergan Studies* 13, no. 2 (1995), 151–60; then see Patrick H. Byrne, "Consciousness: Levels, Sublations, and the Subject as Subject," *Method: Journal of Lonergan Studies* 13, no. 2 (1995), 131–50; then see Tad Dunne, "Being in Love," *Method: Journal of Lonergan Studies* 13, no. 2 (1995), 161–76; then see Christiaan Jacobs-Vandegeer, "Sanctifying Grace in a 'Methodical Theology'," *Theological Studies* 68 (2007), 52–76; then see Jeremy Blackwood, "Sanctifying Grace, Elevation, and the Fifth Level of Consciousness," *Method: Journal of Lonergan Studies N.S.* 2, no. 2 (2011), 143–62; Doran summarizes this discussion in Doran, *The Trinity in History: vol 1*, 125–131.

14. Blackwood, "Sanctifying Grace, Elevation," 162.

15. See Bernard J.F. Lonergan, *A Third Collection; Papers by Bernard J.F. Lonergan, S.J.*, ed. Frederick E. Crowe, S.J. (New York: Paulist Press, 1985), 27.

Blackwood encapsulates from a number of Lonergan's writings, the fifth level is constituted by "the self-forgetting of love . . . answering the question, 'What would you have me do?'"[16]

Doran associates the fifth level with the elevated act of human loving as a sublation of experiencing, understanding, judgment, and decision. This sublation of previous levels of cognition allows for the reception of sanctifying grace, the gift from God eliciting interpersonal relationships and awakening what Lonergan poetically describes as "a new principle [that] takes over and, as long as it lasts, we are lifted above ourselves and carried along as parts within an ever more intimate yet ever more liberating dynamic whole."[17] Falling in love is a profoundly personal excitation. It is a metaphysical elevation that expands a person's horizons of conscious knowing through the three Scholastic epistemological principles of the light of the intellect (philosophy), to the light of faith (theology), to the light of glory (the beatific vision). Divine grace is necessary to inspire a person to be moved to love and then to accept aspects of faith. Accepting faith involves an expansion of the person's horizon from simply knowing natural/proportionate objects to knowing supernatural/disproportionate objects, such as divine love in the beatific vision. The divine grace of elevation (*gratia elevans)* sets up a distinction between unelevated or natural knowledge and elevated or supernatural knowledge. Lonergan teaches that the affirmation of faith, which can only happen with elevating grace in the light of faith, has to do with the level of judgment because it "enable[s] one to see the reasonableness of faith as acquired; for this reasonableness by which a person adheres to and relies upon God's knowledge is above nature."[18] As each of the levels of consciousness, namely, the empirical, intelligent, rational, and reasonable, work to acquire natural knowledge, they also can be elevated by divine grace to enter the supernatural light of glory. Blackwood suggests that "there appears to be no reason why this definition [of elevation] could not be extended to all the levels of consciousness, such that at each of the levels of both knowing and deliberating, an elevated subject has two formal objects–the natural/proportionate and the supernatural/disproportionate."[19]

16. Blackwood, "Sanctifying Grace, Elevation," 158.

17. Lonergan, *A Third Collection*, 175.

18. Bernard J. F. Lonergan, "Analysis of Faith" in *Method: Journal of Lonergan Studies* 20, no. 2, (2002): 125–154. 146.

19. Blackwood, "Sanctifying Grace, Elevation," 148.

Doran responds to Blackwood's suggestion by saying that "the details remain to be worked out for the levels of experience and understanding."[20] The first section of this paper will attempt to work out the details of the elevation, through divine grace (*gracia elevans*) of the levels of experience and understanding by examining the personal transformations of one who is engaged in the knowing process. Starting at the synaptic level of the physical brain, then expanding to the five sensations, and then broadening the scope of examination to the process of understanding, precisely because there is a sublation of each of the levels into the fifth level of consciousness, each preliminary level of consciousness acquires a two-fold importance. Blackwood and Doran have each developed the aspects of the elevation in the levels of judgement and decision, but research is still needed in the first two levels that accounts for the elevation of the total person knowing and falling in love.

A first corresponding implication of the elevation of the levels of consciousness is what Lonergan referred to as a unified field of consciousness, which will be compared to what neuroscience considers a unified field potential within the brain structure.[21] A second outcome of elevated levels of consciousness is an outward movement of self-appropriated individuals into the community of humanity as they assume a collective responsibility for the care and advancement of humanity as a whole. Doran's vision of the creative upward vector of humanity advancing toward the Kingdom of God matched with the healing vector of grace from God pouring down into the created world of suffering, reveals the reality, power, efficaciousness, and expansiveness of the divine action. As Doran says poignantly, "the real human subject emerges into genuine autonomy only through the grace of the rule of God, which is not so much an interdividual or intersubjective reality as an interpersonal one."[22]

The explanatory account of the elevation of the first two levels of consciousness.

Can supernatural grace be *experienced*? Prima facia, it would seem that since grace is supernatural and the only way human persons can have any kind of experience is through the empirical sensations of material objects in the

20. Doran, *The Trinity in History: vol 1*, 129.

21. See Bernard J.F. Lonergan, *Insight: A Study of Human Understanding*, Collected Works of Bernard Lonergan 5, (Toronto: University of Toronto Press, 1992), 349.

22. Doran, *The Trinity in History: vol 1*, 311.

created world, then an experience of supernatural objects would be impossible. Lonergan asks, "Can man know more than the intelligibility immanent in the world of possible experience? If he can, how can he conceive it? If he can conceive it, how can he affirm it? If he can affirm it, how can he reconcile that affirmation with the evil that tortures too many human bodies, darkens too many human minds, hardens too many human hearts?"[23] And yet, the human rationality can know that which is beyond the immanent realm of possible experience. Because Doran and Blackwood, especially, have helped to reveal in Lonergan's works the presence of a fifth level of consciousness, that of falling in love, the possibilities arise for interpersonal and transcendental experiences, that have empirical elements. In his essay "Openness and Religious Experience," Lonergan explains that the first three levels of consciousness, namely, the empirical, intellectual, and rational "are isomorphic with the relations of potency, form, and act in the Aristotelian-Thomist tradition."[24] The fourth and fifth levels of consciousness involving responsibly judging and falling in love, direct and guide each intentional action rationally decided upon in the third level of consciousness.

Lonergan describes the human person as naturally in a state of potency as open to ever-more experiences. In his first book *Insight*, he explains, "deep within us all, emergent when the noise of other appetites is stilled, there is a drive to know, to understand, to see why, to discover the reason, to find the cause, to explain."[25] In "Openness and Religious Experience," a later paper, Lonergan explains that this pure desire to know is one of three potencies of the human person which he calls the openness as fact; "it is referred to by Aristotle when he speaks of the wonder that is in the beginning of all science and philosophy. It is referred to by Aquinas when he speaks of the natural desire to know God by his essence."[26] The source of transcendence in human persons is the unrestricted desire to know, but the limited capacity to attain knowledge in the physical human brain is the paradox in which humanity finds itself.[27] Thus, a second sense of potency or openness that Lonergan names in "Openness and Religious Experience," is openness as achievement. Because of the limitations of human knowing despite the unlimited desire to know, "there are needed not only precepts,

23. Lonergan, *Insight*, 23.

24. Bernard J.F. Lonergan, *Collection,* Collected Works of Bernard Lonergan 4 (Toronto: University of Toronto Press, 2005), 185.

25. Lonergan, *Insight*, 28.

26. Lonergan, *Collection*, 186.

27. See Lonergan, *Insight*, 661.

methods, and criticism, but also a formulated view of our knowledge and of the reality our knowledge can attain. . . . All of [our] thinking and acting have to be worked out and successfully applied to actual thinking and actual acting."[28] The human potency of study, of the labor of applying the pure desire to know to the actual process of knowing, while fighting off fatigue, forgetfulness, unclarity, distractions, and wavering motivation is the potential of the achievement of knowledge. Lonergan explains, "There is a contrast, almost an antimony, between the primordial fact and achievement, for the primordial fact is no more than a principle of possible achievement, a definition of the ultimate horizon that is to be reached only through successive enlargements of the actual horizon. But such successive enlargements only too clearly lie under some law of decreasing returns."[29] The pure desire to know all things about all things is not satisfied until the human person knows God face to face. However, because of the reality of human sinfulness, biased perspectives of the truth, and limitations in human achievement, the vision of God cannot be *achieved*.

What keeps the effort for knowledge in check and unbiased? Lonergan acknowledges a third type of potency that he names openness as gift. Only divine grace, a healing grace (*gratia sanans*) can purify human intentions that are blinded by biases and disordered by wayward affections. Only healing grace can wrestle from humans all of the patterns and habits of inauthenticity so as to expose once again the pure, detached, disinterested desire to know the truth. Divine grace can also enlarge or elevate the horizons of human consciousness (*gracia elevans*). Lonergan explains that there are "enlargements that are naturally possible in man. But there is also an ultimate enlargement, beyond the resources of every finite consciousness, where there enters into clear view God as unknown, when the subject knows God face to face, knows as he is known. This ultimate enlargement alone approximates to the possibility of openness defined by the pure desire."[30] These three potencies of fact, achievement, and gift, give rise to the central form of the human person, what Lonergan considers the essence of the soul, the unified wholeness of the human person.[31] From this central form, the concrete, intelligent person acts with dynamic and performative conscious subjectivity, manifesting the unity of potency, form, and

28. Lonergan, *Collection*, 186.

29. Lonergan, *Collection*, 186–187.

30. Lonergan, *Collection*, 187.

31. For more on the central form, see Lonergan, *Insight*, 460–463 and Jacobs-Vandegeer, "Sanctifying Grace in a 'Methodical Theology'," 71.

act through attentively experiencing, intelligently understanding, rationally judging, reasonably deciding, and sublating each of these previous actions by falling in love.

Doran and Blackwood both emphasize that the grace that elevates (*gracia elevans*) can be extended to each level of consciousness "such that at each of the levels of intentional consciousness, an elevated subject has two formal objects, the natural/proportionate and the supernatural/disproportionate."[32] Blackwood explains that for the level of cognition, "the elevation of central form and the consequent horizon known as the light of faith elevate judgement by allowing the subject to know with God's own knowledge."[33] Before a person is able to make an elevated judgement, an elevated act of experience must first happen. Lonergan defines the absolutely supernatural as "that which exceeds the proportion of any and every finite intellect."[34] Since human persons are limited to a finite intellect, when a human person considers a supernatural object, Lonergan explains how the intellect has two operations. The first operation seeks to understand the essence or quiddity of material objects or "other supernatural goods by way of negation, analogy, and extrapolation, [and] do nothing that exceeds the natural proportion of a finite intellect."[35] The second intellectual operation of a human person allows for the attainment of the transcendental objects of truth and being. Lonergan explains how he uses the analogy of the natural light of the human mind to refer to the power human persons possess to make reasonable judgements after asking reflective questions. To know any truth beyond what the natural light of human reasoning can obtain requires divine grace or "a proportionate light," possessed by God alone whose divine light is natural to God's essence. The blessed in heaven have an immediate vision of God and enjoy the light of glory. Those who believe in the proper way and do not cling to or rely upon their own limited understandings or knowledge but upon God's light and God's knowledge are able to glimpse the light of glory.[36]

Nevertheless, is it possible for a human person to *experience* a supernatural object? To answer this question, it is helpful to get a sense of the cognitive understanding of the process of human experiencing. George

32. Blackwood, "Sanctifying Grace, Elevation," 148.

33. Blackwood, "Sanctifying Grace, Elevation," 148.

34. Lonergan, "Analysis of Faith," 136.

35. Lonergan, "Analysis of Faith," 136.

36. Lonergan, "Analysis of Faith," 137.

Lakoff and Mark Johnson, in *Philosophy in the Flesh: The Embodied Mind and Its Challenge to Western Thought*, explain that, "conscious thought is the tip of an enormous iceberg. It is the rule of thumb among cognitive scientists that unconscious thought is 95 percent of all thought—and that may be a serious understatement. Moreover, the 95 percent below the surface of conscious awareness shapes and structures all conscious thought. If the cognitive unconscious were not there doing this shaping, there could be no conscious thought."[37] Just one example of the enormous amount of experienced yet unconscious mental thought is visual processing. Rods and cones within the retina of the eye gather light as visual stimuli and transfer the information to the optic nerve which transports this information through the optic chiasm to the lateral geniculate nucleus (LGN) and from the LGN to the visual cortex, as well as many other regions within the cortex.[38] The phenomenon of blindsight illustrates how much unconscious perception is happening. When a person's visual cortex is damaged, rendering the person clinically blind, they cannot consciously "see" anything even though the eyes and optic nerves are intact. This person's unconscious visual processing capacities are tested by the person being subjected to the clinical trial of walking through a hallway riddled with obstacles. Without consciously able to see any aspects of the hallway or the obstacles within the hallway, the person who has this "blindsight" capacity is successfully able to maneuver around each obstacle. When the person is asked why she moved around the box or over the broken glass, this person cannot give any explanation.[39] The point that blindsight illustrates is that the first level of consciousness, that of experience, happens as the five sensations gather data from the external environment, the brain processes the information, and signals are sent to the corresponding muscle-groups for movement. However, the higher levels of conscious understanding, judgement, and decision are not yet activated. This example of blindsight and the many ways the cognitive processes unconsciously process the experienced data of the senses is the natural/proportionate formal object of the level of experience.

---

37. George Lakoff and Mark Johnson, *Philosophy in the Flesh: The Embodied Mind and its Challenges to Western Thought* (New York: Basic Books, 1999), 13.

38. For a more detailed explanation of visual processing, see Eric R. Kandel, James H. Schwartz, and Thomas M. Jessell, eds., *Principles of Neuroscience*, 5th Edition (New York: McGraw-Hill Medical Book Co., 2013), 556–601.

39. For a more detailed explanation on the phenomenon of blindsight, see Kandel et al., *Principles of Neuroscience*, 1375.

The supernatural/disproportionate formal object at the level of experience is also possible. Lakoff and Johnson explain that the unconscious processing "creates the entities that inhabit the cognitive unconscious—abstract entities like friendships, bargains, failures, and lies—that we use in ordinary unconscious reasoning. It thus shapes how we automatically and unconsciously comprehend what we experience."[40] Unconscious processing of experienced stimuli determines much about how conscious perceptions are understood and actions are decided upon. A concrete example of the experienced but unconscious perception of elevating grace is Ignatius' first way of discernment.[41] Ignatius describes the experience, "when God our Lord so moves and attracts the will that a devout soul without hesitation, or the possibility of hesitation, follows what has been manifested to it. St. Paul and St. Matthew acted thus in following Christ our Lord."[42] The person receiving this divine grace that elevates the will certainly experiences profound sensations, but the conscious levels of understanding, judgement, and decision cannot and do not engage, at least not at the moment. If the person who receives such elevating grace does attempt to understand, judge, or decide about the supernatural movement of the will, hesitation and doubt may arise. Without attentiveness to the experiences of divine grace due to lack of attention, physical blindness, deafness, numbness, mental biases, and close-mindedness, divine grace can go by unnoticed. Jesuit poet Gerard Manley Hopkins recognizes the pervasiveness of God's grandeur in the created world:

> "The world is charged with the grandeur of God.
> It will flame out, like shining from shook foil;
> It gathers to greatness, like the ooze of oil . . ."[43]

The book of Numbers also captures the concept of unconscious supernatural experience poetically:

---

40. Lakoff and Johnson, *Philosophy in the Flesh*, 13.

41. On several occasions, Doran refers to St. Ignatius of Loyola's third time of making an election in connection to making a responsible decision. See Doran, *The Trinity in History: vol 1*, 129; Robert M. Doran, "Ignatian Themes in the Thought of Bernard Lonergan: Revisiting a Topic That Deserves Further Reflection," *Lonergan Workshop 19*, Fred Lawrence, ed. (Newton, MA: Boston College: 2006), 83–106.

42. Saint Ignatius of Loyola, *The Spiritual Exercises*, Louis J. Puhl, trans. (Chicago: Loyola Press.

1951), 74.

43. Gerard Manley Hopkins, *Poems and Prose*, W.H. Gardner, ed. (New York: Penguin Books, 1985), 27.

"The oracle of one who hears what God says,
and knows what the Most High knows,
Of one who sees what the Almighty sees,
in rapture and with eyes unveiled.
I see him, though not now;
I observe him, though not near . . ." (Num 24: 16–17).

God's wisdom, as the supernatural formal object to human experience is beyond what human consciousness can understand, judge, or decide. Nevertheless, the sensed experience of divine grace can impel a person into love, which elevates the person's central form and allows for an enhanced perception of all of existence.[44] The person is in love.

The second level of consciousness in a subject elevated by grace can also have two formal objects, the natural/proportionate and the supernatural/disproportionate. Empirically, a person receives data from one or more of the five senses, consciously and unconsciously processes the sensory stimuli, but then does not yet make judgments about whether or not the conscious processing is accurate and true. This is the state that Lonergan would consider the world of immediacy.[45] Lonergan describes this world as that of the infant, living in the present moment and taking in the environment's data through the five senses and having insights of discovery. As the infant grows and the brain develops so as to gain capacities in questioning the perceived data and checking the accuracy of the gained insights, the world mediated by meaning opens. This world includes the past, present, and future and is rich and varied with possibilities, facts, hopes, and dreams. Even when a person is in this world of rational meanings and purposes, there are moments when insights into understanding are directed to formal

44. There is a long theological tradition of the enhancement of the senses through divine grace. For example see Saint Augustine on eyes of faith, "Sermon 38 on the New Testament," in *Nicene and Post-Nicene Fathers, First Series*, vol. 6, Philip Schaff, ed. (Buffalo, NY: Christian Literature Publishing Co., 1888); Augustine, "Sermon 239: Preached During the Easter Octave," in *The Works of Saint Augustine (4th Release), Sermons, (230–272B) on the Liturgical Seasons*, vol III/7, Edmund Hill, trans. (New Rochelle, NY: New City Press, 1993), 64. Thomas Aquinas, *Summa Theologiae*, Blackfiars, eds (New York: McGraw-Hill Company, 1964), Ia,78,a4; Aquinas also discusses the *vis cogitativa*, see Anthony J. Lisska, *Aquinas's Theory of Perception: An Analytic Reconstruction* (Oxford, UK: Oxford University Press, 2016), 237–273.

45. For more on the world of immediacy in contrast with the world mediated by meaning, see Bernard J.F. Lonergan, *Method in Theology* (New York: Herder and Herder, 1972), new edition is in the Collected Works of Bernard Lonergan 14 (Toronto: University of Toronto Press, 2017), 76–77.

objects that do not undergo the scrutiny of rational judgement. A neurological example of the mental processing of a natural formal object of understanding without proper judgement is known as Capgras syndrome. These patients are convinced that one in close relation, usually a husband or wife, has been replaced by an impostor. They claim that the person who is similar if not identical in appearance, is in fact a different person.[46] This phenomenon is caused by the accurate grasp of the empirical data from the senses, but the lack of emotional energy that usually accompanies the managing, formulating, and understanding of the sensory stimuli of the beloved companion so as to make an accurate assessment on the identity of the companion. As a result, the patient recognizes his wife with accurate attentive sensory data collection, but inaccurately understands that the person in front of him is an impostor who dresses and acts like his wife. The disconnect between the rational processing of the sensory data and the emotional affective movements aroused by the data indicates that there can be formal objects of understanding that are not yet or cannot yet be objects of the higher levels of consciousness of judgement and decision.

Precisely because there is a fifth level, that of falling in love, the level of understanding can also have supernatural formal objects. In a lecture given in Quebec in 1975 entitled "Christology Today," Lonergan discusses the emergence of religious consciousness and identifies the transformational moment when a person is struck profoundly by supernatural grace and consciously understands the experienced effects of this grace, but cannot articulate why the experiences are important or how they have come about. Such an experience is just the opposite of that of the Capgras patient. Here, a person glimpses the supernatural reality of God and experiences powerful emotions connected to the indwelling presence of unconditional love and a confrontation with absolute truth such that any rational judgments of the experience and understanding fail to comprehend the full essence of God. Lonergan writes, "the measure that this transformation is effective, development becomes not merely from below upwards but more fundamentally from above downwards. There has begun a life in which the heart has reasons which reason does not know. There has been opened up a new world in which the old adage, *nihil amatum nisi prius cognitum*, yields to a new truth, *nihil vere cognitum nisi prius amatum*."[47] The person understands that

46. See Kandel et al, *Principles of Neuroscience*, 1378.

47. Bernard J.F. Lonergan, "Christology Today: Methodological Reflections," in *A Third Collection*, 77. [Nothing is loved unless it is first known; Nothing is truly known unless it is first loved.]

he or she is deeply loved. The formal object of understanding is supernatural as the indwelling love of God floods the person's conscious from above downward with the theological virtues. When supernatural indwelling happens, the level of understanding is elevated through *gracia elevans*, and the person's horizons are expanded far beyond individualistic or selfish pursuits even though the person may not be able to make a judgment or decision based on the supernatural experiences and understandings.

One of the consequential aspects that results from God's grace flooding a person's consciousness which elevates each of the levels of consciousness is what Lonergan called a unified field of consciousness. Each level of consciousness contributes a unique and specified function in the knowing process. Jacobs-Vandegeer summarizes Lonergan's writings, "The essence of the soul *manifests* itself interiorly as the unified field of consciousness, the principle of unity in the dynamic performative diversity of existential subjectivity. Since this interior awareness reveals the soul, it pertains to the infusion of grace."[48] Theoretical understanding of the unified field of consciousness can be related to the neurological models of a unified field potential in the synaptic interconnections within the human brain. Thanks to the advancement of brain-imaging technology, Lonergan's postulations of the unification of the diverse acts of consciousness can be correlated to harmonious physical actions happening within the structures of the human brain as it processes the sensations of the exterior environment, seeks to understand the meaning of the sensations, judges the accuracy of the perceptions, and decides upon the best course of action to take because of the acquired knowledge.

Neuroscientists use the term interoceptive awareness to explain how the components of the brain activated for higher-order cognitional thinking (such as the insula cortex and the anterior cingulate cortex [ACC]), integrates with and regulates the components of the brain utilized for emotion production, regulation, survival control, and limbic system processing (such as the limbic system, brain stem, and cerebellum). Analyzing how the two contrasting processes interact in the physical structures of the brain and the behavioral outcomes, Elizabeth Stanley explains that "since the insula and the ACC together provide top-down control of survival brain processes regulating stress and emotions, we can improve the functioning of this regulatory loop by cultivating interoceptive awareness. We do this building our capacity to pay attention to physical sensations and sensory

48. Jacobs-Vandegeer, "Sanctifying Grace in a 'Methodical Theology'," 71.

stimuli, such as sights, sounds, and smells."[49] Lonergan and Doran both use the terminology of "from below upward" to refer to the creative labor and growth of human persons as well as "from above downward" to refer to the healing and elevating grace of the divinity entering into the human world. In the same way, neuroscience is recognizing the higher ordered cognitional thinking that allows for regulation "from above downwards" of the survival and emotional aspects of the person. Is it the case that when divine grace elevates the consciousness of a person, as described by Lonergan and Doran, there is a strengthening of the ACC and insula, among other brain components, so as to enhance the unified field of consciousness and allow for greater attentive interoceptive awareness and a healthy regulation of rational thinking and acting? More research is needed to explore this interdisciplinary area.

A second implication of the infusion of divine grace into a person's unified consciousness, beginning at the level of experience and sublating up to the fifth level of falling in love, involves the integral scale of values first conceived by Lonergan in *Method in Theology* and then developed by Doran especially in *Theology and the Dialectics of History* and further articulated in *What is Systematic Theology*. Doran's work is an expansive vision of the efficaciousness of grace throughout creation. When individuals are elevated to supernatural levels of consciousness through the reception of divine grace and when they are willing to cooperate with this grace, healing and transformation become possible in communities and throughout the human population. Persons in love expand their conscious awareness so as to be moved outward into communities and assume a collective responsibility for the care and advancement of humanity. Doran's vision of the creative upward advancements of humanity toward the Kingdom of God matched with the healing grace from God pouring down into the created world of suffering, reveals the reality, power, efficaciousness, and expansiveness of divine action. The human creative vector "from below upward" is the human potential for building a flourishing civilization structured by the integral scale of values. The vector "from above downward" is God's healing grace permeating through and directing the labors of humanity.[50] Doran's

49. Elizabeth A. Stanley, *Widen the Window: Training Your Brain and Body to Thrive During Stress and Recover from Trauma* (New York: Penguin Random House, 2019), 246.

50. Lonergan's concept of the integral scale of values provides a systematic structure for understanding the transformational effects in authentic persons who have transcended themselves so as to transform the society and culture. See Lonergan, *Method in Theology*, 47–52; Doran, *Theology and the Dialectics of History*, 527–560.

The Trinity in History II, explores the intricacies of the radical transformations that become possible when grace from the Trinitarian God is infused into the cosmos. He develops what Lonergan referred to as the law of the cross by explaining how "the supreme good may be regarded (as it is by Lonergan) as the "form" of the economy of salvation introduced into the "matter" of a human race infected with original sin, burdened with actual sins, entangled in the penalties of sin, alienated from God, and divided both within individuals and between them socially."[51] When grace comes into the broken world, "It is in effect an elevation of human relations to participation in the divine relations. But, like every form, its emergence is in accord with probabilities, and in this case the probabilities 'regard the occurrence of [our] intelligent and rational apprehension of the solution and [our] free and responsible consent to it.'"[52]

In conclusion, humanity is in need of and hopeful for divine assistance, but we tend not to recognize or acknowledge when we receive grace. Doran's hope-filled perspective helps to illuminate the elevating transformation that divine grace can bring to the broken world and points to the communication of the triune God which heals the world and establishes the reign of the Kingdom of God in this world and forever.

---

51. Robert M. Doran, *The Trinity in History: A Theology of the Divine Missions*, vol. 2: *A Theology of the Divine Missions*, (Toronto: University of Toronto Press, 2019, 41.

52. Doran, *The Trinity in History*, vol. 2., 41.

SECTION II

PHILOSOPHY

CHAPTER FOUR

THE GRANDIOSITY OF EXPERIENCE

Jonathan Heaps
St. Edward's University (Austin, TX)

Prologue

My contribution is, in a certain respect, the repayment of a debt. Students owe their teachers myriad debts, likewise advisees their advisors and dissertators their directors. Fr. Robert Doran has been all three and more for me. But none of these general debts could I hope to reasonably repay. What follows repays a very specific debt and my repayment is funded by the dividends of Fr. Doran's shrewd investment. The initial capital consisted in a book recommendation: Eugene Gendlin's 1978 self-help book, *Focusing*.[1] Ever preoccupied with the technical details (as my reader will soon discover), I found my way from *Focusing* to its academic predecessor, 1962's *Experiencing and the Creation of Meaning*.[2] Gendlin's account of "experiencing" and its role in meaning has transformed my appreciation of what Bernard Lonergan called, "interiority." You will find in what follows the fruits of Fr. Doran's investment. I hope that my reader may draw on this mutual fund of insight and seed his or her own campaign of intellectual development.

Introduction

The following is occasioned by a pair of nested problems. They are questions I cannot hope to answer here. Indeed, they are questions that Lonergan, Gendlin, and Doran have gone a long way to answering for us. I will only manage to zoom in closely on one element implied by these questions.

1. Eugene Gendlin, *Focusing* (New York: Bantam Dell, 2007).

2. Eugene Gendlin, *Experiencing and the Creation of Meaning: A Philosophical and Psychological Approach to the Subjective* (Evanston, IL: Northwestern University Press, 1997).

There is a general, philosophical question. "Meaning is experienced," Gendlin insists in *Experiencing and the Creation of Meaning*.[3] This experience of meaning is not merely residual. For Lonergan, that conscious operations are *conscious* is essential to the mediating function of meaning.[4] For Gendlin, the subjective experience of meaning has an integral function in human meaning itself.[5] In light of this integral function, how do academic disciplines that investigate objects constituted by meaning integrate the subjective experience of meaning into their scientific—i.e., theoretical and explanatory—controls of meaning and belief? How, in other words, can subjective experience find its integral place beside explanation in the humanities?

Nested within, but irreducible to this general, philosophical question, there is a specific, theological question. Theology in what Fr. Lonergan called the "third stage of meaning"—that stage which explicitly thematizes and founds itself upon interiority—proposes to investigate human experiences of meanings both human *and divine*.[6] Of course, the above philosophical problem likewise afflicts theology. However, theology's twofold object imposes a unique challenge. How will the theoretical concepts, heuristics, types, etc., of theology integrate the subjective human experiences of these meanings without *a priori* bracketing, excluding, or otherwise occluding divine meanings qua *divine*?

By invoking the challenge of founding method in *Geisteswissenschaft* and appending to it the problem of transcendent knowledge, I set down two questions that cannot possibly be addressed in the space of a short essay. But their conjunction suggests an initial challenge and calls out for the means to meet it. These two preliminary topics will occupy us below.

An Initial Challenge

Methodically taking the subjective experience of meaning in hand poses an initial challenge, whether in the general case of the humanities or the specific case of theology. In the general case, Gendlin identifies this initial challenge with the "symbolic character" of meaningful experience:

---

3. Gendlin, *Experiencing*, 44.

4. For a brief, clear exposition of the mediating and constitutive functions of meaning in human consciousness, see Bernard J. F. Lonergan, "*Existenz* and *Aggiornamento*," in *Collection*, ed. Frederick E. Crowe and Robert M. Doran, vol. 4 in *Collected Works of Bernard Lonergan* (Toronto: University of Toronto Press, 1988), 224–7.

5. Gendlin, *Experiencing*, 60–89.

6. Bernard Lonergan, *Method in Theology*, ed. Robert M. Doran and John D. Dadosky, vol. 14 in *Collected Works of Bernard Lonergan* (Toronto: University of Toronto Press, 2017), 90–93.

> However, an inquiry into felt [e.g., experienced] meaning must be able to refer to and examine felt meaning as such—not only in its symbolizations. . . . If symbolization is involved in every case of meaning, and if inquiry itself can proceed only in terms of symbols, how can we hope to inquire into the experienced dimension of meaning as such?[7]

Gendlin is by no means pessimistic about this general and initial challenge, for he takes a stand on the integral function that the subjective experience of meaning plays in human meaning itself. But to insist on the exigence that brings the challenge to light is not yet the same as resolving it. Nor is this challenge idiosyncratic to Gendlin's construal of the issue. Lonergan repeatedly returns to this initial challenge under both its general and specifically theological forms. He notes the general challenge for the humanities when considering the various *Geisteswissenschaften* in his 1968 lecture, "The Absence of God in Modern Culture." Lonergan (following Wilhelm Dilthey) distinguishes them from the natural sciences:

> In the human sciences . . . there are of course data, but the data are data for human science not simply inasmuch as they are given but only inasmuch as there attaches to them some commonsense meaning. Thus, one could send into a law court as many physicists, chemists, and biologists as one pleased with as much equipment as they desired. They could count, measure, weigh, describe, record, analyze, dissect to their hearts' content. But it would be only by going beyond what is just given and by attending to the *meaning* of the proceedings that they could discover they were dealing with a court of law; and it is only insofar as the court of law is recognized as such and the appropriate meanings are attached to the sounds and actions that the data for a human science emerge.[8]

This specific difference between the natural and human sciences comes with a danger:

> Precisely because everyday, commonsense meaning is constitutive of the data for a human science, phenomenology and hermeneutics

---

7. Gendlin, *Experiencing*, 46.

8. Lonergan, "The Absence of God in Modern Culture," in *A Second Collection*, ed. Robert M. Doran and John D. Dadosky, vol. 13 in *Collected Works of Bernard Lonergan* (Toronto: University of Toronto Press, 2016), 89.

> and history assume basic importance. . . . Clearly such an emphasis on meaning and such elaborate techniques for the study of meanings greatly reduce the relevance of counting, measuring, correlating, and so move the *Geistewissenschaften* away from the ambit of natural science and towards a close connection with—or a strong reaction against—idealist, historicist, phenomenological, personalist, or existentialist thought. . . . [But] is modern science to be conceived and worked out in total independence of philosophy or is it not? . . . At least until philosophers reach, if not agreement, then comprehensiveness in their disagreements, it would be suicidal for scientists not to insist on their autonomy. . . . In the measure that [*Geisteswissenschaften*] insist on their specific difference from the natural sciences, they risk losing their autonomy and becoming the captive of some fashion or fad in philosophy.[9]

If I may be forgiven for such voluminous block-quoting, perhaps it will be for the sake of this central point Lonergan is setting up. In the humanities, commonsense meanings make up the objects of study, but the instruments of study are themselves formalized meanings: scholarly, scientific, and/or philosophical meanings. Consequently, there remains both the problem of accurately linking the givenness (that is, the subjective experience) of the meanings under study with their symbolization, but also of discerning which tools reliably and accurately establish this link. But here the problem becomes recursive, for the tools too are made of meanings, and so their evaluation involves the same troublesome challenge: how do I tease out from the formal systems of symbolic relations (logical, genealogical, phenomenological, what-have-you) the experience that makes them meaningful, that makes them data in the human sciences at all? From here it is not a long walk to the labyrinthine halls of post-structuralism (which seem, of late, to have opened unto the stark—if level—mustering grounds of materialist theory).

The difficulty does not vanish if one turns to face directly this general challenge at its root in critical realist philosophy. Even if one works out how to knock down this sticky wicket, there remains to communicate one's solution. But communication is a matter of meaning. Lonergan flags this problem in the introduction to *Insight*:

9. Lonergan, "Absence," 89–91.

> It is not the answer itself that counts so much as the manner in which it is read. For the answer cannot but be written in words; the words cannot but proceed from definitions and correlations, analyses and inferences; yet the whole point of the present answer would be missed if a reader insisted on concluding that I must be engaged in setting forth lists of abstract properties of human knowing. The present work is not to be read as though it described some distant region of the globe which the reader never visited, or some strange and mystical experience which the reader never shared. It is an account of knowledge. Though I cannot recall to each reader his personal experiences, he can do so for himself and thereby pluck my general phrases from the dim world of thought to set them in the pulsing flow of life.[10]

Thus we see Lonergan gesture at both the challenge of integrating meaning's subjective experience into the communication of modern philosophical conclusions, but also at the very beginning of a solution to the challenge.[11] The instruments of philosophical analysis, argumentation, and reportage will only have significance if the reader can correlate them with the data they propose to explain. But the data are a subjective experience of the meaningfulness of the symbols by which the analysis, argumentation, and reportage are effected. Lonergan reassures the reader that, yes, you have had these experiences. Lonergan also exhorts the reader to "pluck" the subjective experience of meaning evoked by his "general phrases" from their own "pulsing flow of life." This is the right track, as far as it goes. The challenge heuristically implies this avenue of address. Still, the challenge

10. Bernard J. F. Lonergan, *Insight: A Study of Human Understanding*, ed. Frederick E. Crowe and Robert M. Doran, vol. 3 in *Collected Works of Bernard Lonergan* (Toronto: University of Toronto, 1992), 13.

11. I should be careful not to give the impression that this challenge is entirely a product of the modern "Copernican" turn to the subject in philosophy. Lonergan took some early note of this problem by recognizing that it had afflicted the mind of St. Thomas Aquinas and, in some measure, been addressed by the same. Lonergan writes, "the Aristotelian term [*to ti ên einai*] was a logical effort to isolate understanding and form, and one has only to consider the difficulties of such isolation to grasp why Aquinas dropped this Aristotelian effort as abortive and proceeded on lines of his own. Because the act of understanding—the *intelligere proprie*—is prior to, and cause of, conceptualization, because expression is only through conceptualization, any attempt to fix the act of understanding, except by way of introspective description, involves its own partial failure; for any such attempt is an expression, and expression is no longer understanding and already concept" (Bernard F. J. Lonergan, *Verbum: Word and Idea in Aquinas*, ed. Frederick E. Crowe and Robert M. Doran, vol. 2 in *Collected Works of Bernard Lonergan* [Toronto: University of Toronto Press, 1997], 38).

persists: how to travel it? By going to the trouble to read with intelligent interest "some such book as *Insight*."[12] Still, the challenge persists. It appears again in *Method in Theology*. Lonergan warns from the outset that, if one cannot find a way to pivot from the book's formal account of the transcendental method to a subjective experience of the accumulation and progression of conscious and intentional operations in which it concretely consists, "[the reader] will find not merely this chapter but the whole book about as illuminating as a blind man finds a lecture on color."[13]

This initial challenge posed by the integral function that subjective experience plays in human meaning is not only refracted through the lens of philosophy into the various human sciences. It also casts its pallid light on the field of theology. Both John the Baptist and Christ himself (if I may take an ambitious example) cast their knowledge of the Kingdom of God to their disciples in images and parables, in signs and symbols, acknowledging that laying hold of their significance required "ears to hear."[14] It is pedantic to note, of course, that their listeners were possessed of ears, but it does underline the inward aspect in which this "hearing" was intended. There was some subjective experience of meaning required to receive what they had to say and lacking it meant missing the point.

This inward aspect, this integral subjective experience of meaning is not merely an accident of figurative language or commonsense contexts of communication. After all, differences in scriptural interpretation gave rise to the various controversies of Christianity's first centuries, which were in turn met by the adaptation of Hellenistic philosophical categories to set down doctrinal definitions and a clarifying grammar of interpretation. But such "classical controls" on Christian belief hardly put an end to theological controversy in the intervening centuries.[15] Instead they gave rise to the aggregation of doctrines and a voluminous "sentence commentary" tradition. Commentary is no less symbolically constituted than direct discourse, and so emerged the recursive iteration of commentary upon commentary upon commentary. Even the heroic effort of no less a genius than St. Thomas Aquinas to fit the accretion of doctrines into a synthetic scheme or two could not prevent the scholastic fragmentation that followed, for the high rigors of logical inference are subject to the integral function of

12. Lonergan, *Method in Theology*, 11n4.

13. Lonergan, *Method in Theology*, 11.

14. Matt 11:15; Mark 4:9, 23; Luke 8:8, 14:35.

15. Regarding classical controls of meaning, see Bernard J. F. Lonergan, "Dimensions of Meaning," in *Collection*, especially 235–40.

meaning's subjective experience as well. Nor should we be surprised at the plurality of Thomisms that blew in with the spirit of Vatican I and *Aeterni Patris*.

But besides the realm of meaning established by the deployment of theoretical controls on meaning and belief, there is the realm opened up by positively recognizing the integral role played in human meaning by the subjective experience of meaning. This realm stands not only adjacent to the realms of common sense and theory (as they seem to stand merely adjacent to one another), but, precisely because of subjective experience's integral function in meaning, interiority stands to commonsense and theory as ground and principle of their differentiation. Lonergan situates his discussion of religious experience at the fulcrum of this transition:

> This gift we have been describing really is sanctifying grace but notionally differs from it. The notional difference arises from different stages of meaning. To speak of sanctifying grace pertains to the stage of meaning when the world of theory and the world of common sense are distinct but, as yet, have not been explicitly distinguished from and grounded in the world of interiority. To speak of the dynamic state of being in love with God pertains to the stage of meaning when the world of interiority has been made the explicit ground of the worlds of theory and of common sense. It follows that in this stage of meaning the gift of God's love first is described as an experience and only consequently is objectified in theoretical categories.[16]

Sublating the communicative contexts of religious common sense and theoretically controlled theology into the realm of interiority (and so explicitly the conscious and existential horizon set out by being in love with God) ushers in significant advances. It allows one to transpose the significance of meanings from one realm to another: from common sense to theory and back again, and also from both common sense and theory into the realm of interiority. This latter transposition allows for a critical evaluation of common sense and theoretical meanings in theology, insofar as it adverts to a body of evidence given in the subjective experience of those meanings. This is of inestimable value for modern persons endeavoring to discern dialectically which among Christianity's accretions of symbol, doctrine, and theory present achievements meriting appropriation and promotion

16. Lonergan, *Method*, 103.

and which amount to aberrations and nonsense in need of repudiation.[17] Beyond verifying or establishing realm equivalence between meanings, theology that takes its place in the realm of interiority may also set out on the methodical task of cumulatively and progressively investigating the experiences, the expressions/"words", and the dialectical development of religion, making new discoveries on the basis of available evidence, both material and "interior."

It may appear, then, that our initial challenge has been swept away. *Au contraire.* Rather, the challenge has been rendered acute:

> So [we are] confronted with the three basic questions: What am I doing when I am knowing? Why is doing that knowing? What do I know when I do it? With these questions one turns from the outer realms of common sense and theory to the appropriation of one's own interiority, one's subjectivity, one's operations, their structure, their norms, their potentialities. Such appropriation, in its technical expression, resembles theory. But in itself it is a heightening of intentional consciousness, an attending not merely to objects but also to the intending subject and his acts. And as this heightened consciousness constitutes the evidence for one's account of knowledge, such an account by the proximity of the evidence differs from all other expression.[18]

Here we encounter a specter in the general case that also haunts theology in the realm of interiority.

In the case of theology, for example, Lonergan offers a sequential procedure for the methodical treatment of what Thomistic theology knows as sanctifying grace: first we would describe God's love as subjectively experienced, then enrich that experience and its attendant phenomena via objectification in theoretical categories. But there are two transitions in this procedure that, as to their interiority, remain opaque. First, there is the transition from the experience-as-experienced to the experience-as-described.

---

17. The grounding stability and mobilizing force such transposition provide to a systematic theology can be witnessed in Doran's still-unfolding trilogy, *The Trinity in History*, two volumes of which have been published as of my writing. (Robert M. Doran, *The Trinity in History: A Theology of the Divine Missions, Volume 1: Missions and Processions* [Toronto: University of Toronto Press, 2012]; Robert M. Doran, *The Trinity in History: A Theology of the Divine Missions, Volume 2: Missions, Relations, and Persons* [Toronto: University of Toronto Press, 2019]).

18. Lonergan, *Method*, 80.

True, Lonergan treats of the expression of religious experience, but largely in terms of its spontaneous and commonsense modes. But the specialized avenues of observation and description that in *Insight* he calls "prescientific" are not distinguished and fit, *mutatis mutandis,* into the horizon of the humanities.[19] From out of this lacuna there arises a first question: how does one move from being in love with God *as experienced* to being in love with God *as described*, and not merely spontaneously, but *methodically*?

Second, there is the transition from the experience-as-described in a methodical and scholarly fashion to its "objectification in theoretical categories." In the case of religious experience, Lonergan brings theoretical categories of grace up from the history of Catholic theology to meet his modern description of the subjective experience of transcendent meaning, of divine love. In this way and to the extent that one is able to pluck from the flow of life experiences that could be so described and objectified, the realm equivalence and on-going value of sanctifying grace as a theological concept is verified. It is true as well that transposition and verification are important methodical controls on theological meaning. Still, the cumulative and progressive process by which descriptions of subjective experience in theology are objectified in (and so enriched by) special theological categories remains opaque precisely because of the initial challenge that is our present topic.

Although Lonergan offers a technical expression of the dynamics and elements involved in the derivation of theological categories in the 11th chapter of *Method,* "Foundations," by his own reckoning it "resembles theory" and he acknowledges that "just as one can be a very successful scientist and yet have very vague notions regarding (one's) own intentional and conscious operations, so too a person can be religiously mature . . . (and yet) unable to associate any precise meaning with the words I have used."[20] Lonergan's sketch of the derivation of theological categories bears the same challenge as describing the religious experience from which they are, in the first instance, derived: the integral function in human meanings of the subjective experience of meaning needs to be taken in hand, to be "appropriated" so that the whole enterprise will not collapse back into a flat complex of symbolic relations. Without it, we risk merely pushing the *phantasmata* around. This initial, but pervasive challenge, therefore, calls out for the exposition of a *technique* by which to a) lay hold of the subjective experience of meaning and b) begin to consciously, deliberately, and methodically

19. Lonergan, *Insight*, 86–7.

20. Lonergan, *Method*, 271.

integrate that experience with phenomenological and theoretical elements in the humanities generally and theology specifically.

A Technique for Attention

Attention is selective. Some things impose themselves upon our attention: the sudden noise, the rapid movement, the scald of heat, the prick of pain, the dragging anchor of malaise, the jangle of anxiety, etc. Still, one may take hold of this selective function and direct one's attention, whether to the text, to the melody, to the smell of the tea, the growing warmth of gratitude, etc. Whether imposed from without or directed from within, the selective function of attention is focal. In other words, the direction of one's attention does not excise what has not been selected, but rather relegates it to a background field. This field, to the extent it falls into the background, consists in that of which one is conscious, but to which one is paying no particular attention. This same field, however, remains proximate to the focal center of attention, so that if attention wanders, is pulled, or is directed somewhere else, the new object of attention will be drawn from its penumbra. Occasionally we may become so engrossed by a narrow, intense focus that it takes rather a lot to draw our attention anywhere else, so that it seems like the penumbra of the background field has dropped away entirely—though it certainly has not. Conversely, sometimes a wash of focal indifference can fall spontaneously over our attention. We "space out." We seem to lose our sense of the distinctness of thought and sensation of the senses themselves, even of the boundary between ourselves and the field of experience, of the positionality of our experiencing, etc. We are conscious, but we are not paying attention.

On a first level of analysis, we may imagine that this background field consists in several intersecting planes of conscious experience: an auditory plane of sounds, a visual plane of shapes and colors, a tactile plane of textures, pressures, etc., and an olfactory plane of flavors and aromas. To this complex of experiential planes, we might—if we are inducted into the differentiations of consciousness that pertain to the realm of interiority—add the planes of intellectual and rational intentionality, the planes of value-intending feeling and deliberation, of intersubjective and interpersonal attachment, and of psychical image construction, promotion, and censorship. We would thereby complexify the field in, from, and among which attention makes its focal selections. Thus, one may direct one's attention not only among the data of sensitive consciousness or among the data of intentional consciousness as in parallel, but non-intersecting fields. Rather, attention may be directed among any of the data given across any of these intersecting planes. In principle, attention may shift from exterior focal objects to interior ones and, indeed, insofar as the interior objects are themselves subjective acts intending exterior ones, it may prove a winning strategy (because interiority can prove elusive) to begin with the more familiar data of sense and, as it were, follow the winding thread back to the various data of consciousness.

All of this multiplication and complexification of attention amounts to only a differentiation of its basic selective function. There remains the fact of a focal center and the penumbra of a background field. But what is a mere matter of fact is not explained. Why can attention navigate between a variety of central foci and this variegated background field? What undergirds these transitions and by what means are they effected? For this, we will have recourse to Gendlin's notion of "experiencing." Gendlin uses the word "experiencing" to refer directly to the concreteness of "*raw*, present, ongoing . . . experience."[21] He describes it as follows:

> But regardless of the many changes in *what* we feel—that is to say, really, *how* we feel—there always is the concrete present flow of feeling. At any moment we can individually and privately direct our attention inward, and when we do that, there it is. Of course, we have this or that specific idea, wish, emotion, perception, word, or thought, but we *always* have concrete feeling, an inward sensing whose nature is broader. It is a concrete mass in the sense that it is "there" for us.[22]

This "experiencing" that is "there" for us is concrete in that it is given globally and so, in itself, given indistinctly. It is that in and among which focal selection is made. It is not, however, merely the background, for the background is necessarily that which is not what is selected for attention. Experiencing is no less what is selected for attention than it is the background that falls into attention's penumbra. Gendlin continues,

> Experiencing is a constant, ever present, underlying phenomenon of inwardly sentient living, and therefore there is an experiential side of anything, no matter how specifically detailed and finely specified, no matter whether it is a concept, an observed act, an

21. Gendlin, *Experiencing*, 11 (emphasis in the original).

22. Ibid. (emphasis in the original).

> inwardly felt behavior, or a sense of a situation. We can be very modest, or very grandiose, about experiencing. In a modest way we can say: experiencing is simply feeling, as it concretely exists for us inwardly, and as it accompanies every lived aspect of what we are and mean and perceive. Or we can be very grandiose about it and say that for the sake of (this or that aspect of) experiencing mankind do all they do in a lifespan. Within experiencing lie the mysteries of all that we do.[23]

At a technical level, we are proximately concerned with this modest identification of experiencing with the fundamental concreteness of "inwardly sentient living." But the grandiosity of experiencing is of more general interest, insofar as it links this description of meaning's situation within subjective experience with those data pertinent to the humanities, to the *Geisteswissenschaften*. To be obtuse to the unitary horizon of attention and its penumbral background is to be obtuse to a body of evidentiary data that pervade the humanities, both as to their objects and their methods.

If we want to philosophically explore the diverse functions of meaning, its elements, and its realms for ourselves, then some integral body of data thereupon will be selected for our attention from out of our experiencing. At this point, however, we find a photo negative of our initial challenge above: to draw experiencing into the focal length of our attention is, on the one hand, to render it meaningful by allowing it to function in the creation or recognition of meaning. On the other, rendering experiencing or some element of experiencing meaningful is to draw the experience of its meaningfulness into the focal length of our attention and so to set other facets of our experiencing into the penumbral background of consciousness. Moreover, insofar as selecting meanings for attention involves symbolization, we have also found the wellspring of the above initial challenge.[24] It becomes inviting, thanks to the all-too-human prejudice in favor of biological extroversion, to "pretend that we are only what we seem externally, and that our meanings are only the objective references and the logical meanings of our words."[25] We risk, in other words, forgetting the grandiosity of experiencing.

To insist that experiencing not enter the frame of meaning is to privilege immediacy in a fashion that diminishes the grandiosity of experiencing.

---

23. Ibid., 15.

24. "Meaning occurs for us when something experienced assumes a symbolic character" (ibid., 45).

25. Ibid., 16.

It is the function that experiencing plays in the creation and recognition of meaning that allows us to enter the fully human world mediated by meaning, and so that lends to experiencing the grandiosity of human poetry, politics, and piety. It would be a mistake parallel to the eclipse of meaning's subjective experience, one made in the name of objective reference and logical control. Instead, we ought to develop a technique in attention that deliberately, even methodically directs attention to meaning-as-felt. This technique, however, should not be mistaken for some kind of automated process. Insofar as it is sentient, it must emerge within the pulsing flow of life. Insofar as it generates and recognizes meaning, it must proceed according to the dynamism of intellectual consciousness and be governed first of all by the autonomy of inquiry. Insofar as it is *techné*, it must be appropriated, developed, and refined through the habits that constitute practical mastery. Consequently, the technique by which the subjective experience of meaning would be appropriated by and integrated into the humanities must also be a habit, a practice, a discipline.

When it comes to the humanities, in their retrieving and reflecting upon the meanings of persons and cultures distributed across time and geography, this technique will consist in a refinement, a sub-differentiation of empathic imagination. In some fields, where for example ethnography is of the essence, this can be a habit of intersubjective attunement, a body-to-body listening. In others, where textual and other forms of artificial expression mediate between the researcher and their sources, the accent will fall upon the imaginative aspect of this empathic imagination. One will have to develop a subtlety of feeling in representation, an interior repertoire of considerable range. No less will one need to attune this quality and tone of felt meaning to, not the expressive embodiment of another living person, but the impressions they have left in the materiality of our built environment. One will need, in the limit, a willingness to admit to the focal length of attention the full range of human sensibility. Such, I think, is the fundamental significance of psychic conversion for method in the humanities.[26]

This technique cannot be restricted to the role that felt meaning plays in the mediation of meaning from source to scholar. For, as I noted above, not only are the objects of the humanities, but also their methodical tools and controls made out of meanings. At a first level of analysis, this means developing a real apprehension of a field's methodical outlook in addition

26. Robert M. Doran, *Subject and Psyche*, 2nd ed. (Milwaukee, WI: Marquette University Press, 1994); Robert M. Doran, "Psychic Conversion," *The Thomist* 41, no. 2 (1977): 200–236.

to familiarity with its extant body of understanding. This requires an attention to and so an inward feel for the types, models, and heuristics in use, as well as the abstractive viewpoint taken by its driving questions. The genuineness with which one appropriates these operational elements of one's field mark the minor authenticity of a scholar therein. To the extent it is lacking, one is a hack.

At a deeper level, if one would methodically contribute to a field in the humanities, one needs an attunement to what is not yet accomplished and those means of accomplishment not yet developed and distributed. For this, one must appreciate, must feel viscerally, must be kept awake at night not by unanswered questions already asked, but the tension and tug of questions not yet asked. Now, one might get lucky and have such unasked questions occasioned by some new discovery, some new datum. In the normal course, however, discoveries are answers to the question already asked and data are found relevant in light of the same. The major authenticity that moves a field forward not from incremental insight to incremental insight, but from paradigm to paradigm, from epoch to epoch begins in attention to the persistent, but indeterminate notion that the field itself is unevenly intelligible and imperfectly rational and that the responsibility to remedy the situation begins, at least in part, with *me*.

Where we have focused until now on a technique for attention to meaning as recognized in human cultures or as an implement of methodical control, now we find an exigence for a technique in attention to the meaning that originates in scholars themselves. It is the meaning of our spontaneous desire for perfect intelligibility and for absolute rationality. It is the meaning we would make of ourselves if we would but give these deeper intellectual misgivings voice and follow with painstaking care the scholarly path to which they would call us. Consequently, this scholarly technique in attention, at this deeper level, directs our attention back onto ourselves as potential wellsprings of authentic meaning and, in any case, fulcra of liberty. To direct my attention to myself (or, more precisely, to the experience of my own felt meaning) in this deliberate, methodical way is to make a decision. It is to decide that I merit attention, not merely as an object of observation, but also as a subject experiencing. It is to value myself simultaneously as originating and terminal value.[27] This attention to myself in my experiencing *qua* mine cannot, despite superficial misgivings, really consist in idiocy or solipsism. For my experiencing has any content at all

27. On the distinction between originating and terminal value, see Lonergan, *Method*, 50.

always only because it originates in self-transcendence, however distorted or mitigated. Rather, this deliberate attention to myself in my experiencing and its present entirety is also a laying-hold of the knot in which all the threads of my meaningful experiencing are tied together. It is, as suggested above, the root of all methodical investigation, verification, explication, etc. It is the ground floor of the control of meaning in the realm of interiority.

At the same time (and to the extent that I prove able), this deliberate and methodical attention to myself consists in an act of submission. It consists in submission insofar as the focal center of attention dilates to encompass the circumference of present experiencing itself. It is a submission to the present state of experiencing, such as it is. It is a submission to the habits of attention that draw me away from the contemplative task. It is a submission to the meanings that make up my horizon of experiencing, including the absurdities I have allowed to masquerade as facts or—worse—profundities. It is submission to an experience of the meaning I have made of myself, such as I presently am. It is a deliberate and methodical (and habitual and disciplined) effort to attune myself to the reality of my experiencing on that reality's terms.

All of this, of course, is very general. It contemplates the place a technique and habit of what has come to be called "mindfulness" might have in the methodical control of meaning for the humanities. What, however, of our special concern with theology among the *Geisteswissenschaften*? We come upon a conclusion by inference that Sarah Coakley derived experimentally: that contemplative practice will be central to theology at the level of Christianity's present circumstances.[28] On the surface, this is only an application of our general conclusions to the special case of theology, and not insofar as it is special, but as an instance of the humanities in general. However, Coakley, in a manner not unlike Lonergan, "acknowledges the primacy of such contemplation for [theology] *not* as a quest for some sort of authenticating 'religious experience,'"—that is, some data on God—"but as an attentive openness of the whole self (intellect, will, memory, imagination, feeling, bodiliness) to the reality of God and of the creation."[29] Contemplative prayer dilates the focal center of attention beyond even the entirety of one's own experiencing, taking the circumference of God's love

---

28. See Sarah Coakley, *God, Sexuality, and the Self: An Essay 'On The Trinity'* (Cambridge: Cambridge University Press, 2013); for a recounting of the "experimental" character of this derivation, see Sarah Coakley, "Prayer as Crucible: How My Mind Has Changed," *The Christian Century*, March 9, 2011.

29. Coakley, *God, Sexuality, and the Self*, 88.

in the Spirit, God's willingness in Christ, God's desire for everything that is. Of course, the self-transcendence of being in love with God's own love is not the sort of thing one can acquire through even the most rigorous ascetic discipline of attention. It must be received as a gift. For the whole self, experiencing this gift occasions an existential question: "Will I love [God] in return, or will I refuse? Will I live out the gift of [God's] love, or will I hold back, turn away, withdraw?"[30] But for theology as a scholarly discipline, the question takes a methodical cast: will I endeavor rigorously, though always-imperfectly to understand (and to understand by the light of) what God has made of me, what God has in and through me made my experiencing to mean? To borrow Kierkegaard's idiom, are we willing to—and here we turn the glass around to look through theology at all the *Geisteswissenschaften*—render scholarship that "rests transparently on the power that established it?"[31]

30. Lonergan, *Method*, 112.

31. Søren Kierkegaard, *The Sickness Unto Death: A Christian Psychological Exposition for Upbuilding and Awakening*, ed. and trans. Howard V. Hong and Edna H. Hong (Princeton, NJ: Princeton University Press, 1980), 14.

CHAPTER FIVE

SERVING THE OTHER

Engaging Doran's Work at the Crux of Horizontal and Vertical Alterity

Brian Bajzek

Marquette University (Milwaukee, WI)

1. Introduction

This paper offers an initial examination of the connections between otherness and Robert Doran's philosophical-theological project. Tracing a series of developments from Doran's early career through his recent reflections in *The Trinity in History: Vol. II*, I suggest that concern for the intersection of horizontal and vertical alterity is a subtle but central facet of Doran's thought. As I will illustrate, Doran consistently prioritizes and provides resources for the authentic navigation of the subject's relation(s) with God's otherness, the otherness of her fellow human beings, and the inherent intersection and reciprocal ethical importance of such "vertical" and "horizontal" alterity. While Doran has only recently begun to highlight the connections between his work and postmodern philosophy's prioritization of alterity, this increased emphasis is neither an unnecessary addition to his thinking, nor a merely descriptive cul-de-sac within the explanatory project of Trinitarian Systematics. Instead, Doran's recent writings and ongoing research are the culmination of a lifetime both intellectually and performatively ordered toward serving those rendered least and othered most.

This paper is intended as a preliminary engagement with these issues, offering a springboard for a larger project analyzing Doran's ministry as concrete witness and service to the image of God in the face of the Other.[1]

1. As I will note below, much of my application of Doran's work involves dialogue with Emmanuel Levinas. Like many postmodern philosophers, Levinas often capitalizes "Other" to stress alterity's irreducibility and importance. For the sake of consistency, I capitalize all occurrences of 'Other' that refer either to a particular personhood (Levinas' '*autrui*') rupturing the horizon of the subject, or to the principle of alterity itself (Levinas' '*autre*').

This initial piece will lay the groundwork for reading Doran through the lens of the postmodern turn to alterity, and for beginning the nuanced and rewarding work of exploring the connections between his writings and his HIV/AIDS ministry. My own engagement with Doran's homilies from healing masses and his written reflections on serving HIV/AIDS patients have convinced me that this ministry must be understood as an (perhaps even *the*) hermeneutical key for unpacking Doran's deference to the Other. I am also convinced that his time assisting those afflicted with this agonizing and ostracizing disease has had a profound impact upon his nuanced—and increasingly frequent—calls for conversion concerning the theological status quo and its treatment of race, sex, sexuality, gender, interreligious dialogue, and secularity. The present essay will serve as prolegomenon to the more complex project of defending these claims and their implications. For now, I will situate Doran's work within the context of recent shifts to prioritize otherness in philosophy and theology, then highlight and expand upon key moments in Doran's development regarding the turn to horizontal and vertical alterity.

2. The Fourth Stage of Meaning

I shall begin by introducing John Dadosky's investigations of a fourth stage of meaning, which a number of Doran's recent writings have referenced as an important development of Lonergan's thought.[2] Dadosky asserts that Lonergan's work with the stages of common sense, theory, and interiority is incomplete without the identification of a fourth stage: a turn to transcendent otherness.[3] Resourcing Lonergan's later writings and a wide range of archival material, he cites multiple places where Lonergan references a fourth stage, resonant with developments in postmodern philosophy,

2. See, for example, Robert M. Doran, *The Trinity in History: A Theology of the Divine Missions, Volume One: Missions and Processions* (Toronto: University of Toronto Press, 2012), 101, 130–31.; Robert M. Doran, "Invisible Missions: The Grace That Heals Disjunctions," in *Seekers and Dwellers: Plurality and Wholeness in a Time of Secularity*, ed. Philip J. Rossi (Washington, D.C.: The Council for Research in Values and Philosophy, 2016), 247–67, at 262–63. Robert M. Doran, *The Trinity in History: A Theology of the Divine Missions: Volume Two: Missions, Relations, and Persons* (Toronto: University of Toronto Press, 2019), 128, 133.

3. See John D. Dadosky, "Is There a Fourth Stage of Meaning?," *Heythrop Journal* 51, no. 5 (2010): 768–80; John D. Dadosky, "Midwiving the Fourth Stage of Meaning: Lonergan and Doran," in *Meaning and History in Systematic Theology: Essays in Honor of Robert M. Doran, SJ*, ed. John D. Dadosky (Milwaukee: Marquette University Press, 2009), 71–92; John D. Dadosky, "Further Along the Fourth Stage of Meaning: Lonergan, Alterity and 'Genuine' Religion," *Irish Theological Quarterly* 85, no. 1 (February 2020): 64–79.

pointing to a collective "movement from presence to oneself as knower to presence to the Other through mutual self-mediation."[4] The transcendental exigence prompts this movement, and its unique consequences in contemporary history are indicative of an epochal shift, bringing "the subject beyond interiorly differentiated consciousness to the world of the Other, both vertically and horizontally, as being-in-relation and in love."[5]

Humanity's acknowledgment of a "vertically" transcendent Other is not a new phenomenon. The experience of vertical alterity is exemplified by our ancestors' sacred stories, texts, rituals, etc. Dadosky suggests, however, that Lonergan's later writings point to an even further concretization of the relationship with the surplus of vertical alterity. If allowed to flourish, such development will blossom into mutual self-mediation among world religions, the seeds of which were sown in the ecumenical, interreligious, and intercultural developments of the twentieth century. Dadosky also frames such radical reorientation in terms of "horizontal" alterity, writing, "We can derive from this, therefore, that the fruits of unrestricted loving include not just a recognition and response to a transcendent Other in a vertical sense but also horizontally to the Other—family, friends, neighbors, society and, perhaps most importantly, one's enemies."[6]

Within a contemporary context, this love of one's enemies carries an unprecedented urgency. Although human beings have always been ethically obligated to care for the needs of others, humanity as a whole must now respond to (1) unprecedented global connectivity and communicative capacity, and (2) the possibility of nuclear annihilation, biological or chemical warfare, widespread ecological devastation, etc. The Other can now be eradicated instantly, indiscriminately, and sweepingly. The fourth stage of meaning results from both the intensified expression of a primordial obligation, and the emergence of new opportunities and dangers, all of which must be met with relational attentiveness, intelligence, reasonableness, responsibility, and lovingness. Just as the operations of consciousness have always structured human knowing, but only become fully thematizable with the emergence of the third stage, the always-already-present importance of alterity is brought into full focus in the fourth stage.

My own work builds upon Dadosky's arguments for a fourth stage of meaning by examining intersubjectivity's importance to the intersection of

---

4. "Is There a Fourth Stage of Meaning?," 772.

5. "Midwiving the Fourth Stage of Meaning," 81.

6. Ibid., 76.

horizontal and vertical alterity.[7] This work is primarily rooted in a Lonergan/Levinas dialogue. While Levinas argues that the faces of *all* human beings exhort me toward a radical self-forgetfulness, he emphasizes the importance of response to the marginalized, utilizing the biblical exemplars of the poor, the widow, and the orphan as those Others to whom we ought to be most attentive.[8] Drawing from both Lonergan and Levinas, I have explored how our commonality is an ever-present reality that is concretely expressed in each encounter, where we are met by an ethical obligation to self-forgetful deference. All human persons are linked to one another, obligated by this intersubjective exigence, which is rooted in divine justice and love. This simultaneity of distinct subjectivity and inherent connection, divine injunction and human expression, radical otherness and intrinsic similarity creates a tension, one that provides a stumbling block both for proponents of postmodern deference to the Other and for those hesitant to elevate it to a methodological principle. The arguments I offer for overcoming this tension are directly indebted to Doran's work with dialectic.[9] I am convinced that many of Doran's insights offer tremendous resources for moving forward into the fourth stage of meaning. I am also convinced that this is not a coincidence. Doran's recent statements in support of the fourth stage are themselves an outer expression of meanings that have always been implicitly, elementally present in his work. His writings have ever more explicitly manifested this meaning over the course of his career, and it is to his writings that we must now turn.

3. Relevant Developments in Doran's Writings

In this section, I will examine several subtle but essential moments in Doran's development regarding otherness and its place in philosophical and theological reflection. Unpacking these selections in conversation with one another (and occasionally illustrating their importance in my work and Dadosky's), I will suggest that the resources offered in these writings are intentionally at the service of a philosophical-theological project for the Other.

7. Brian Bajzek, "Alterity, Similarity, and Dialectic: Methodological Reflections on the Turn to the Other," *International Philosophical Quarterly* 57, no. 3 (September 2017): 249–66.; Brian Bajzek, "Cruciform Encounter in a Time of Crisis: Enfleshing an Ethics of Alterity," *Theological Studies* 80, no. 1 (March 2019): 79–101.; Brian Bajzek, "Intersubjectivity, Illeity, and Being-in-Love: Lonergan and Levinas on Self-Transcendence," *The Heythrop Journal*, At Press, http://dx.doi.org/10.1111/heyj.12353.

8. Bajzek, "Cruciform Encounter in a Time of Crisis," 86–88.

9. See, for example, Bajzek, "Alterity, Similarity, and Dialectic," 257–66.

3.1 *Authenticity, Transcendence, and Symbol:* Subject and Psyche (*1977*)

Many of Doran's most pastorally powerful insights are directly derived from his groundbreaking assertion that psychic conversion plays a necessary role in the full flourishing of attentive, intelligent, reasonable, responsible, loving subjectivity. Although it may initially seem strange to suggest that psychic conversion is always already ordered toward the "movement from presence to oneself as knower to presence to the Other through mutual self-mediation" (Dadosky's description of the fourth stage of meaning, cited above), Doran's own observations in *Subject and Psyche* corroborate this claim, especially when these observations are read in light of his later insights.[10] By providing precise tools for integrating the inherent tension of limitation and transcendence present in the multi-faceted movement of subjectivity, especially as this movement is ordered toward both authentic, deferential treatment of one's fellow human beings *and* the dynamic statement of being-in-love with God, Doran offers tremendous tools for reflecting upon the horizontal alterity, vertical alterity, and even the complex tension of otherness and similarity present in the dialectic of the subject.

Central to Doran's arguments in *Subject and Psyche* is his recognition that Jung's work is problematically indebted to Kant. This truncates Jung's ability to adequately account for both self-transcendence's relationship to reality *qua* reality, and its openness to the ultimate reality of the divine. In *Subject and Psyche*, Doran treats this Kantian baggage in terms of the connections between the intending intention of being, the psyche, and the fourth level of consciousness, relating existential self-constitution in community and in ultimate relation to God as fourth-level operations:

> Jung needlessly short-circuits the teleology of the psyche, by reason of his epistemological confusion, and so ultimately traps psychic unfolding in an intrapsychic erotic *cul de sac*, in an eternal return, in a perpetually recurring psychic stillbirth. The absence of a clear notion of cognitional self-transcendence prevents Jung from vigorously accenting the dynamism to self-transcendence immanent in the psyche itself. There is a kind of love that is beyond the wholeness of the mandala. The psychology of Jung

10. Robert M. Doran, *Subject and Psyche*, Second Edition (Milwaukee: Marquette University Press, 1994).

> breaks down when the process of individuation invites one to surrender to such love. But so, perhaps, does all psychology unless psychic process is sublated into the movement of existential subjectivity to the authenticity of self-transcendence.[11]

Doran would soon follow Lonergan's lead and begin to frame existential self-constitution in direct connection to a sublating relational fifth level of consciousness: a level of love.[12] When read through the lens of a fifth level, the clarification by contrast offered in this paragraph illustrates psychic conversion's direct connection to both horizontal and vertical alterity. If we understand "psychic process [as] sublated into the movement of existential subjectivity to the authenticity of self-transcendence," and this movement is always ordered toward fulfillment in love (the topmost level of intentional consciousness), then the process of psychic conversion (and, for that matter, subjectivity itself) is always inherently oriented toward both the 'horizontal' Other and the divine Other. The full teleology of self-transcendence must go further than the immanentism of the idealist, opening itself to the love of God that transfigures previous horizons by flooding our hearts, overflowing into the expectation defying love of neighbor and prioritization of those most marginalized or othered. Psychic conversion is a necessary part of this process, especially when the symbolic baggage blocking self-transcendence is rooted in inauthentic concepts of God (e.g., God as hateful accuser or vengeful punisher), or of oneself and/or others (e.g., as inherently aberrant, inadequate, or inferior).[13]

---

11. Ibid., 19. As I note in "Alterity, Similarity, and Dialectic," this psychic immanentism parallels a problem among those that posit alterity as absolutely unknowable in order to avoid either reducing 'knowing' to a mere synthesis of phenomena and concepts or allowing such concepts to over-determine 'knowing' as a violent, reductive enterprise. I am convinced that Lonergan's positions on judgment and Doran's positions on dialectic hold the key for overcoming the Kantian baggage at the root of this problem.

12. For a thorough overview and defense of this development in Lonergan's and Doran's work, see Jeremy W. Blackwood, *And Hope Does Not Disappoint: Love, Grace, and Subjectivity in the Work of Bernard J. F. Lonergan, S.J.* (Milwaukee: Marquette University Press, 2017).

13. Doran's work with HIV/AIDS patients struggling to overcome their socially, culturally, religiously, and even personally inflicted baggage regarding God, sexuality, love, and sin is especially resonant with *Subject and Psyche* on this point. Those othered on the basis of a sexual orientation deemed 'inherently disordered' suffer through no fault of their own. As Doran laments, this psychic injury often comes at the hands of religious institutions, including the Catholic Church. For a moving, nuanced reflection upon real life examples of such psychic wounds and their healing, see Robert M. Doran, "AIDS Ministry as a Praxis of Hope," in *Jesus Crucified and Risen: Essays in Spirituality and Theology*, ed. William P. Loewe and Vernon J. Gregson (Collegeville, MN: Liturgical Press, 1998), 177–93.

Doran also suggests that Kantian baggage is responsible for a Jungian problem in relating concepts, archetypes, and universalization. This problem is exemplified by Jung's assertion that the archetypes he discusses are themselves *a priori* concepts universally present in—and formative for—all cultures. While Doran is not opposed to the idea of universally relevant symbols, he follows Lonergan in stressing that the only *a priori* facet of human knowing is cognition's operational structure, not its contents.[14] By advocating a shift from Jung's language of "symbolic *a priori*" to "symbolic function" and "collective unconscious" to "archetypal function," Doran avoids making concepts *a priori*, violently transcultural (i.e., epistemologically imperialist), and reductively determinative. This insight holds tremendous potential for affirming postmodernity's prioritization of surplus and irreducibility, while also standing by the conviction that meaning can be truly communicated, understood, and affirmed, whether intra- or interculturally.

In his 2005 text, *What is Systematic Theology?*, Doran laments the difficulty some have with maintaining both of these principles, as many only reach a liminal space regarding alterity: "the postmodern emphasis on otherness that also does not acknowledge the ongoing process of self-transcendence to the other as a normative source of meaning."[15] Here, openness to alterity is not the problem (and, when Doran's other writings are read in conversation with this remark, the openness to alterity is *the* positional element described in this quote about "ambiguities of completeness" in human development). The issue is the inability of much postmodern thought to reconcile the simultaneity of otherness and similarity, sacrificing the latter to save the former. As I will outline below, Doran's later writings offer resources for overcoming this methodological stumbling block.

The inherent links between psychic states, the dynamic state of being-in-love, and the treatment of the Other coalesce into an important feature of Doran's thought. In *What Is Systematic Theology?*, he confirms this continuity between his early work with psychic conversion and his eventual treatment of horizontal alterity:

> My earlier writings emphasized that symbolic or psychic operator as what is released into potential appropriation through what I am

14. *Subject and Psyche*, 190–95.

15. Robert M. Doran, *What Is Systematic Theology?* (Toronto: University of Toronto Press, 2005), 163.

> calling psychic conversion. But what I am after in speaking of psychic conversion includes as well the other two dimensions of what now I am calling an aesthetic and dramatic operator, and *they were never totally excluded from my intentions or neglected in what I tried to say regarding this foundational dimension.* [. . .] And because this 'symbolic operator' is the root from below of all that happens in this 'dimension of its own' on the part of the passionateness of being, *these earlier emphases cannot be passed by as we extend our consideration to the other two elements of this operator: its role as accompanying the operations of intentional consciousness in feeling, and its role as overarching the entire structure of intentional consciousness in moving us beyond intersubjectivity and solidarity into personal and existential relation with the other.*[16]

When read in light of these later statements, the presentation of psychic conversion in *Subject and Psyche* clearly anticipates Doran's later discussions of both the vertically transcendent Other and all those toward whom unrestricted being-in-love self-forgetfully overflows in deferential actions. In the process of psychic conversion, "one learns to distinguish symbols which further one's orientation to truth and value from those which mire one in myth and ego-centered satisfactions."[17] The dangers presented by those symbols that "mire one in myth" include the aforementioned tendency to project anthropomorphic inadequacies (e.g., vengefulness, hatred, or bigotry) onto God, who is decidedly "other" than these symbolic reductions. As Doran's dialogue with Girardian mimetic theory in *The Trinity in History* establishes, those symbols that solely strive for egoic satisfactions deviate intersubjectivity, reducing the horizontal Other to a use object or rival.[18] In both cases, psychic conversion (which is itself rooted in cooperation with grace, whether thematized as such or not) is necessary to overcome the inauthenticity fostered by symbolic disorder. To more fully explore how this reintegration of the dialectic of the subject connects to deference to the Other, we must now pivot to key methodological advances offered by Doran's *Theology and the Dialectics of History*.

16. *Ibid.*, 167.

17. *Subject and Psyche*, 220.

18. *The Trinity in History, Vol. 1*, 196–226.

3.2 Dialectic and Suffering Servanthood: Theology and the Dialectics of History (1990)

As noted above, I understand Doran's expansion and application of Lonergan's work with dialectic to be a tremendous contribution to philosophy and theology, especially in its import to postmodern conversations concerning alterity, similarity, and the mistaken presumption that the two must be incompatible. I am convinced that there are still significant insights to be mined from the application of these categories, especially as they can help those interested in the convergence of alterity and similarity overcome current tendencies toward false dichotomies, divisiveness, and polarization.

In *Theology and the Dialectics of History* (*TDH*), Doran expands upon Lonergan's discussion of "different types of differences," identifying two overarching categories of dialectics: First, dialectics of contradictories, which present an either/or, and—on the other hand—dialectics of contraries, which inhere in a both/and, wherein a principle of limitation and a principle of transcendence exist in productive tension.[19] My own work argues that the relationship between alterity and similarity is usually construed as contradictory.[20] I am also convinced that this mistake causes many problems, including postmodernity's occasional inability to reconcile the need to maintain surplus and irreducible alterity with the very real judgments of fact and value that constitute objective knowledge. Instead of understanding the Other and the similar as irreconcilable, bringing the combination of Lonergan's cognitional theory and Doran's analysis of dialectic to bear on the problem allows for the possibility of identifying alterity and similarity for what they really are: the interdependent poles of a dialectic of contraries. This insight has been instrumental in the development of my own work with Lonergan and Levinas, but its implications extend far beyond any one project.

Understood as a dialectic of contraries, the dual poles of alterity and similarity can work in a creative push-and-pull without implying false consistency among all differing positions, or suggesting that the alterity each person or group embodies is so radical as to preclude any real knowledge or mutuality. Instead, thematizing the dialectical relationship between alterity and similarity in this way opens up the possibility of meaningful exchange,

19. Robert M. Doran, *Theology and the Dialectics of History* (Toronto: University of Toronto Press, 1990), 10.

20. Bajzek, "Alterity, Similarity, and Dialectic," 257–66.

as people, groups, or ideas perceived as different are not automatically understood as oppositional. Doran's work offers the tools for maintaining alterity's irreducibility and mystery while *also* affirming the possibility of meaningfully knowing the Other. Although Doran does not directly identify this dialectic in his work, he has been supportive of my suggestion that it offers further insight into the advancement of the fourth stage of meaning. I will return to this dialectic reframing below. For now, my remaining reflections on *TDH* will focus on another of the book's significant themes, one relevant to contemporary discussions of inauthenticity toward the Other, as well as the transformative role the church might play in the drama of present polarization.

Doran begins *TDH* by reflecting upon the differences between the situation facing the church in his own time and that of Lonergan several decades prior: "What for [Lonergan] was the specter of nihilism looming on the horizon and calling for a foundation of thought at once empirical, critical, dialectical, and normative, is for us an increasingly dominant characteristic of our situation."[21] Doran concludes that, in recent years, this threat has evolved into a pervasive reality, against which he proposes the construction of a systematic theology, "elaborat[ing] in this new context the meanings constitutive of that praxis of the reign of God through which the human world itself is changed."[22] Central to this praxis is "the paradigm of the church as the Community of the Suffering Servant."[23] This model provides the church with a self-understanding rooted in "[cooperation] with God in working out [the] solution to the problem of evil."[24] Such cooperation entails participation in the Paschal Mystery, the defining characteristic

---

21. *Theology and the Dialectics of History*, 4. Given the recent rise of nationalist and/or populist movements, typified perhaps most perilously by Trumpism and QAnon in the United States, this closedminded nihilism is now more influential than at any point in recent memory. When the label of "Fake News" is so frequently used to handwave away any facts deemed inconvenient to one's own ideology, self-appropriation and conformity to the integral scale of values are in shockingly short supply. A parallel upsurge in dramatic, individual, and group biases among certain vocal sectors of church leadership also indicate that shorter and longer cycles of decline are currently unfolding in both the secular and religious spheres of public life. Unfortunately, the most painful consequences of decline are especially detrimental to those people already marginalized on the basis of their otherness. As Doran argues, the church is missionally obligated to oppose these trends.

22. Ibid.

23. Robert M. Doran, "Suffering Servanthood and the Scale of Values," ed. Fred Lawrence, *Lonergan Workshop* 4 (1983): 44. "Suffering Servanthood and the Scale of Values," was eventually expanded into the fifth chapter of *TDH*, so I will quote from them interchangeably.

24. Ibid.

of which is the just and mysterious Law of the Cross, responding to evil and hate with unflinching love.[25]

Such love runs counter to the systems that constitute the current dynamics of dominant power at play in the world. Insofar as the church acts as this Suffering Servant, it will combat the oppression, maldistribution of goods, and widespread social sin that perpetuate evil in contemporary societies. Within a Christian context, Doran concludes that conformity to the Law of the Cross and the vision of the Deutero-Isaian Suffering Servant must be the catalyst for transformation.[26] The community that is truly Christian must, therefore, act as the community of the Suffering Servant. This community must oppose the systems that perpetuate the prosperity of the powerful while increasing the strife and struggles of those marginalized and othered on the basis of social status, race, gender, sex, sexuality, religion, etc.[27] If the church intends to cooperate with God in the solution to the problem of evil, a task which entails the reversal of inauthenticity and oppression, it must take seriously the preferential option for the poor and the call of liberation theology to address and oppose the sources of "the hell of the night of private suffering" inflicted upon the marginalized members of the human community.[28]

Doran's primary target in these reflections is dangerously unfettered capitalism. Given the attention movements like Black Lives Matter have recently called to the connections between economic inequality and systemic racism (as well as misogyny, homophobia, and transphobia), Doran's comments are just as resonant as they were in 1990, perhaps even more pressingly so. The intersectional applicability of Doran's work has only become more obvious as his career has unfolded, reaching new heights in a place many might not expect such intersectionality and openness to alterity: systematic theological reflections on the Triune God.

3.3 Imitating and Participating in Perfect Relationality: The Trinity in History *(2012–Present)*

The two completed volumes of Doran's *The Trinity in History: A Theology of the Divine Missions* present his most developed account of the starting

25. *Theology and the Dialectics of History*, 111–14.

26. Ibid., 113.

27. "Suffering Servanthood and the Scale of Values," 64.

28. Ibid.

point" for "a Catholic systematic theology on the level of our time."[29] This starting point is the "unified field structure" offered by Lonergan's insights into the Trinity in history and the theory of history constituted by a positional cognitional theory, epistemology, and metaphysics.[30] A detailed analysis of the trinitarian hypothesis at the core of this theology is beyond the scope of the present paper, but in the briefest possible summary, the Four-Point Hypothesis provides the key for articulating how human relationality can (and must) be drawn into the perfect relationality that *is* the immanent Trinity.[31] The missions of the Son and Spirit break through the contingent vicissitudes of history, healing humanity's rivalry, bias, bigotry, and other divisions, drawing us into grateful remembrance of our being loved by the Father, who "makes his sun rise on the evil and on the good, and sends rain on the righteous and on the unrighteous" (Matthew 5:45, NRSV, used throughout).

Resourcing the ecclesiological heuristic presented in *TDH*, Doran explicitly identifies the Christian community's calling to participate in these missions by uniquely embodying the Law of the Cross and serving as the community of the suffering servant.[32] Far from falling into religious exclusivism, however, Doran's trinitarian systematics provide some of the clearest examples of his multi-faceted deference to grace's universal, mysterious presence and activity.. In Chapter 10 of *The Trinity in History, Vol. 1*, Doran stresses that although this law of love is most fully incarnate in the person and actions of Jesus of Nazareth, it is exemplified by more than just Christians.[33] This law is operative when anyone responds to inauthenticity and injustice with actions that performatively speak the words, 'I love you, hate does not get the final say.' Whether thematized as Christian or not, this love participates in Jesus' love, the only thing capable of overcoming and soteriologically subverting decline.

In *Vol. 2*, Doran pushes these suggestions even further into the fourth stage of meaning, taking direct aim at those religious authorities that would deny the presence of dignity and grace among those marginalized on the

---

29. *The Trinity in History, Vol. 1*, 6.

30. Ibid., 17–18.

31. Bernard J.F. Lonergan, *The Triune God: Systematics*, ed. Robert M. Doran and Daniel Monsour, trans. Michael G. Shields, Collected Works of Bernard Lonergan, Volume 12 (Toronto: University of Toronto Press, 2009), 471. For a basic overview of the terms and relations involved in the Four-Point Hypothesis, see Chs. 2, 3, and 7 of *The Trinity in History, Vol. 1*.

32. *The Trinity in History, Vol. 1*, 361, n. 45.

33. Ibid., 227–57.

basis of social status, race, gender, sex, sexuality, religion, etc.: "There is neither Jew nor Greek, male nor female, rich nor poor, straight nor gay, white nor person of color; if there is, and if the existence of such exclusions is based in some religious word, that word itself is inauthentic, and the sacralization of activities and groups based on such a word must be dropped."[34] In contrast to such exclusion, Doran highlights the universal mediation of grace through the invisible and visible missions of the Son and Spirit. Doran places special emphasis on the opposition between exclusionary practice masquerading under the moniker of 'religion' and the actions of Jesus, the self-emptying servant that prioritizes the hungry, the thirsty, the sick, the imprisoned, stating in no uncertain terms, "Truly I tell you, just as you [do] to one of the least of these who are members of my family, you [do] to me" (Matt 25:40).

In his interactions with those ostracized by his social, cultural, and religious milieu (e.g., tax collectors, lepers, adulterers, a Samaritan woman, a man born blind, a centurion with a sick servant), Jesus provides the paradigm for ministering to the marginalized. He also openly challenges falsely sacralized presumptions about who is or is not 'sinful,' 'unclean,' 'holy,' or 'unholy.' As I have argued elsewhere, these actions obliterate reductive expectations for the Image of God, and for the relationship between otherness and similarity. In Christ and through Christ, alterity and similarity converge perfectly.[35] As the Word become flesh, Jesus is both fully human and fully divine, and he is perfectly loving of both humanity and divinity. He humbles himself relative to both his fellow human beings and his Father in Heaven. Jesus embodies complete openness to the will of the Father and the promptings of the Spirit, even when this openness almost certainly ensures overwhelming suffering (cf., Matt 26:36–46). In doing so, Christ draws vertical alterity into an unprecedented, redeeming relationship with the similarity he shares with all of us: his humanity. By doing so, Christ directly opposes mythic presumptions that frame God in opposition to all but a chosen few. Doran's Christological reflections support and strengthen this claim, emphatically arguing for the simultaneous importance of Christ's divinity, his missional understanding of his own divinity, his concrete opposition to injustice within a real socio-cultural milieu, and—most importantly—his unprecedented mediation of divine meaning

34. Robert M. Doran, *The Trinity in History: A Theology of the Divine Missions, Volume Two: Missions, Relations, and Persons* (Toronto: University of Toronto Press, 2019), 40.

35. "Cruciform Encounter in a Time of Crisis," 91–94.

in history, inaugurating the reign of God through the universal offering of the Paschal Mystery.[36]

This is key to the brilliance of Doran's project: his work is rooted in a deep Christian faith, but it is precisely in his reflections upon the central mysteries of Christianity that he is most inclined to highlight both the universality of the missions of the Son and Spirit, and how grace is mediated in and through the ones "other" than (and even ostracized by) those that serve as the face for the majority of Catholic theology. It is not a coincidence that his recent writings place so much emphasis on the presence of actual grace in the whole of human living.[37] Implicit in Doran's assertions advancing Lonergan's complex work with the positive and negative forms of both sacralization *and* secularization is the recognition that it is precisely in encounter with the horizontal Other that the nominally religious so frequently fails, and where secular society often exemplifies authentic religiosity. Here, Doran echoes the spirit of Matthew 25, reminding us that the face of Christ is not merely present in the pews of parishes; it is made visible in the silent suffering of the one thrown out of his home for his homosexuality, the refugee fleeing religious persecution, or the immigrant separated from her children at the border for breaking the law while brown. It is here that we are *all* called to serve as community of the Suffering Servant, helping to alleviate the agony of those with whom Christ most explicitly identified. As Doran points out, "Matthew 25 makes it very clear that such responses are what qualify as 'pleasing' to the Son of Man, that is, as formal effects of *gratia gratum faciens*, the grace that makes us pleasing, sanctifying grace, or actual grace that, once accepted or acquiesced to, elevates to the supernatural order."[38] If we wish to be like Christ, therefore, we must dedicate ourselves to the service of the those rendered least and othered most.

4. Conclusion

As far back as *Subject and Psyche*, Doran's work anticipated that, implicit in the intersection of horizontal and vertical alterity is the demand to disentangle how our mythic, idolatrous, perhaps even accusatory or adversarial ideas of divinity undermine our ethical relationality and self-transcendence, *and* how our complacent, closeminded, totalizing, even violent approaches

36. *The Trinity in History, Vol. 2*, 163–66.

37. Ibid., 37–64.

38. Ibid., 41.

to the horizontal demands of alterity undermines our understanding(s) of God. This illuminates a fundamental but often-overlooked truth: our treatment of those others with whom we interact "horizontally" speaks a word expressing our understanding of vertical alterity (and vice versa). In the decades since he first proposed the possibility of psychic conversion, the words spoken by Doran's work at the intersection of horizontal and vertical alterity have offered tremendous resources for those seeking to grow in faith, hope, and love.

Although my overview of Doran's career has been far too brief to cover all he can contribute to the turn to alterity, I hope I have at least demonstrated that his writings exemplify the best of Christian philosophy and theology on the level of our time. For Doran, systematic rigor need not come at the expense of interpersonal openness, and faith is expressed not through conquest or exclusion, but through solidarity with those with whom Jesus of Nazareth most identified. I am excited to see how Doran's future writings—both including and following the final volume of *The Trinity in History*—develop the insights I have outlined. Although this paper is only the beginning to a much larger, project, I found it quite edifying to research and write. It is a privilege to examine and present the insights of one that so truly strives to act *in persona Christi*, offering his work and life as a service to the God always-already reaching out in and through the face of the Other.

CHAPTER SIX

CRITICAL REALISM, FACTICITY, AND PSYCHIC CONVERSION

Gregory P. Floyd
Seton Hall University (South Orange, NJ)

"We are subjects, as it were, by degrees."[1]
—Bernard Lonergan

The goal of this chapter is to revisit Robert Doran's account of psychic conversion and to situate it within two contexts. The first context is that of Lonergan's account of critical realism. The second context is that of the hermeneutics of facticity given a specific shape by the thought of Martin Heidegger, but also widely appropriated to various degrees, both directly and indirectly, by many twentieth century philosophers and theologians. I hope to show that the grounds for a positive assessment of Doran's account of psychic conversion are not only the authoritative grounds of Lonergan's own positive appraisal, nor only the heuristic completeness it brings to his account of consciousness. In addition to these, I will argue that a third warrant can be found in Lonergan's own critical realism, which, in adducing an empirical principle of knowledge and the primordial ambiguity of human consciousness, requires that the empirical and ambiguous dimensions of the knower herself also be adequately understood and sublated, in Lonergan's particular sense of that term, which is to say, drawn up into and made constitutive in an integrated life that desires to understand what it can of truth and to do what it can in the service of goodness. This "positional" grounding of psychic conversion throws into relief

1. Bernard Lonergan, "The Subject" in *A Second Collection*, CWL vol. 13, eds. Robert Doran and John Dadosky (Toronto: University of Toronto Press, 2016), 69.

certain embodied and situated dimensions of Lonergan's thought that help us appreciate his own distinct way into the hermeneutics of facticity. The principal claim defended is that the self-transcending subject envisioned by Lonergan achieves her most authentic performance when she undergoes not only intellectual, moral, and religious conversion, but psychic conversion as well. Critical realism demonstrates the need for psychic conversion by clarifying the way knowledge is dependent on self-transcendence. Such self-transcendence is dependent on an ongoing and differentiated process of conversion. Psychic conversion assures that at the highest level of integration, that process is not only intellectual, moral, and religious, but also affective and embodied.

I. Critical Realism

Across his extensive and varied authorship, Lonergan defended an epistemological position he called critical realism. Critical realism is a response to a philosophical predicament; it does not emerge full-grown and clothed from the mind of any single philosopher. The context of specific questions to which critical realism supplies an answer is developed over the course of philosophical history. Therefore, while Lonergan claims it is implicitly at work at any number of moments across that history, it is only formulated in an explicit way as the result of problematic questions concerning being, knowing, and objectivity in the modern period.

The critical realist account of knowing seeks to respond to various erroneous and mutually incompatible views such as empiricism, idealism, and subjectivism. According to Lonergan, each of these views was founded on an insight worth developing, but which required significant revision and redirection. For example, critical realism enabled him to offer a strong affirmation of the modern emphasis on the empirical component in human knowing without capitulating to the scientific reductionism expressed in materialism.[2] Variants of empiricism such as materialism and naturalism fail to understand that the empirical encompasses both the "data of sense" and the "data of consciousness." These two forms of experience together supply the empirical foundations indispensable to fully human knowing and living.

2. Materialism is the position that reality is exhausted by nature, and therefore empirical science is adequate to the discovery of reality. More specifically, naturalism holds that there is nothing supernatural. This rejection is generally extended to all non-material realities.

Opposed to a naïve empiricism is the rationalism that topples over quickly into idealism. In Lonergan's compact philosophical history, the modern dialectic of the question of knowing is constituted by the emergence of rationalism in Descartes, which reaches a form of philosophical maturity in the idealism of Kant, and ultimately Hegel. From the perspective of transcendental idealism, prior forms of commonsense and philosophical realism alike are thought to be "naïve." This is to say, commonsense realism and its philosophical elaboration lack an adequately nuanced account of how we come to understand and know reality. The common person simply asserts that objects are there to be "seen" for what they are. The naïve realist proposes a theory whereby such objects are known through concepts that, at least on some accounts, simply "pop" into one's mind. Naïve realism, therefore, is a "confrontationalism" in which the mind is confronted by reality which somehow imposes its conceptualities onto it. Its greatest limitation was that it held concepts "to be primitive and beyond analysis or explanation."[3] Such an account seemed arbitrary and unable to deal with the reality of error. More problematically, it led to a misleading dichotomy between concepts and intuitions, things in the mind and things in the world.

According to Lonergan, moving through the idealist critique of naïve realism is a necessary step to a more adequate and encompassing critical realism because it shows the inadequacy or, more precisely, the immaturity of a realism that suffers less from being incorrect than it does from being underdeveloped. Yet, if idealism makes clear the constitutive role reason plays in our discernment of reality, it pays too high a price for its insight. Lonergan consistently refers to idealism as the "halfway house"[4] on the way to full understanding because it mistakes the rational constituent in reality, for all of reality, or its only criterion. Idealism, while correctly discerning and emphasizing the role reason plays in the constitution of reality, does not attend adequately to the empirical realities that underpin our rational knowledge without wholly determining it. In different ways, therefore, both realism and idealism are guilty of the fallacy of composition, namely, of inferring that what is true of a component in knowing is true of the whole of knowing. Yet in empathizing two distinct components in knowing—the

---

3. For this quote, and a more extended treatment of confrontationalism, see Richard Liddy, *Transforming Light*, (Collegeville: Liturgical Press, 1993), 176ff.

4. See for example, Bernard Lonergan, *Insight*, CWL Vol. 3, eds. Crowe and Doran (Toronto: University of Toronto Press, 1992), 22. Also: *Understanding and Being*, CWL Vol. 5, eds. E. Morrelli and M. Morrelli, (Toronto: University of Toronto Press, 1990), 277.

given reality which all our questions, propositions, and judgments presuppose and the inquiring mind that questions, proposes, and judges—each system contributes a part of the solution. Human knowing is not a single act, but a set of interlocking operations that, when functioning correctly, results in the true clarification of our given experience that we call objective knowledge. Thus, what the two strands of epistemology clarify for us in the history of philosophical difference is the compound nature of human knowing, rooted in what Lonergan calls the polymorphic nature of human consciousness. In contrast to idealism, he writes,

> ". . . we affirm the realism of the *res cogitans* for human knowing and the realism of the *res extensa* for elementary knowing; while the two realities may be coincident, the two knowings must be distinguished and kept apart; and it is failure to keep them apart that originates the component of aberration in our dialectic of philosophy."[5]

Corresponding to these two forms of human knowing are the two worlds an inquirer comes to know through them: the world of the infant and the larger encompassing world of the adult. The world of the infant is the world that we can see and touch and taste and feel and smell, and that world is immediate—quite literally at our fingertips and before our eyes. It is a world we share with other sentient animals; a world navigated largely by the instinct to avoid pain and pursue pleasure. It is also the world articulated with increasing sophistication and in increasing detail by the empirical sciences. From such a world as infants we draw our first sense of what is real. No one who has held a hungry baby, experienced bodily illness, or accompanied a loved one to the end of life can doubt the inveterate and indisputable truth of physical reality. Yet, we do not live most of our lives in this world, at least not only there. Upon further inspection, we discover that the immediate world of our sensible perception is too small for us. It cannot accommodate the richness of human desire, the complexity of human consciousness, or the reach of human destinies. Thus, the small world of our animal spontaneity gives rise to, and is gradually encompassed by, a world of meaning that is distinct, but no less real.

The world of human meaning, in contrast to the world of immediacy, is not a world we are born with, but a world we are born into. It is a world that precedes us, this world of values and ideals, of institutions and societies,

5. Bernard Lonergan, *Insight*, 421–23.

of family, nation, and global community. It is, in other words, a fully human world that, at its best, is a world proportionate to the greatest of our capacities for wonder, discovery, and creation, as well as feeling, compassion, and healing. Our gradual entrance into this world of human meaning inaugurates a broader understanding of what is real. For the critical realist, this fully human reality is truer because it is more comprehensive: it can tell us more about who we are and what there is by including what we know of our native animal spontaneities and yet moving beyond them to broader horizons of knowledge and value that transcend and direct them. "Only the critical realist can acknowledge the facts of human knowing and pronounce the world mediated by meaning to be the real world; and he can do so only inasmuch as he shows that the process of experiencing, understanding, and judging is a process of self-transcendence."[6]

In response to the naïve realist, therefore, the critical realist claims that, "the reality known is not just looked at; it is given in experience, organized and extrapolated by understanding, posited by judgment and belief."[7] One implication of this account of knowing and being is that truth is conceived as an achievement, something which a human inquirer works her way up to. It is a process to which she must devote herself, and not simply a matter of having or not having a sudden correct intuition. Grasping the underlying cognitional structure of knowing that produces concepts and judgments also allows critical realism to elaborate a detailed account of error. As a process of structured components that are themselves cognitive operations, human knowing is something that can go wrong at a number of different points. Much of human error is inadvertent, but its effects are no less real. For critical realism, therefore, it is not enough to have a correct account of cognitional structure, but in appropriating its exigencies one must decide for a willingness to engage in ongoing self-transcendence, which includes an openness to acknowledging when one's attending, understanding, judging, or deciding has been misguided, partial, deliberately selective, or one of any number of other ways we are likely to go wrong in our knowing.

The revelation that authentic human existence is self-transcending clarifies two further aspects of the world mediated by meaning. The first is that the parameters of the world mediated by meaning are defined by possibility. As the world of speculative, moral, and ultimate concern, it is

6. Bernard Lonergan, *Method in Theology*, eds. Doran and (Toronto: University of Toronto Press), 239.

7. Lonergan, *Method*, 238.

the world in which we ask not only what is, but also what might be, what should be, and why it matters. It is in this sense that Lonergan claims that,

> "the world mediated by meaning is not just given. Over and above what is given there is the universe that is intended by questions, that is organized by intelligence, that is described by language, that is enriched by tradition."[8]

According to Lonergan, the world's great religions are one source for the kinds of ultimate questions that reveal the human world to be more than the world of sense, instinct, and simple satisfaction. The world's great religions reveal the human world as a world defined by what we can ask about and not merely by what is actual at any given point in time.

Humanity's possible world, as the final line above makes clear, is also always a shared world. This shared world is mediated to us by a variety of traditions and is one which we navigate with the help of these traditions. Such traditions, however, can also be a source of limitation. The possibility of error is not only individual, but also communal. Therefore, a further aspect of the world mediated by meaning is its vulnerability to decline: "besides fact there is fiction, besides truth there is error, besides science there is myth, besides honesty there is deceit."[9] Full human understanding is always a precarious exercise. Our realism, therefore, must be critical; that is, it must be reflective on its own performance, hopeful, but at the same time suspicious of its attainments.

Disambiguating these dual realisms and their distinct criteria does not remove the insecurity of the world mediated by meaning; however, it does allow us to take its full measure. This is also to take the measure of ourselves as inquirers who seek after truth, but do so according to our nature and the vulnerabilities that beset it. These can lead to error, but also to truth and to an awareness of the interdependent and collaborative nature of human knowing. We need one another to ask all the relevant questions and to answer them.

The stakes are high. Critical realism is an epistemological position, but it bears directly upon the existential and ethical dimensions of life. For Lonergan, these latter questions about what to make of ourselves are primary, yet, to reach adequate answers presupposes "that we have escaped the

8. Lonergan, "Origins of Christian Realism," 241.

9. Lonergan, "Origins of Christian Realism," 241.

clutches of naïve realism, empiricism, critical and absolute idealism, that we have succeeded in formulating a critical realism."[10]

II. Completing the Turn to the Subject: Gilson's Instructive Counter-Argument

It is interesting that Lonergan chose to call his position critical realism despite its point of departure in the idealist critique of naïve realism. The term itself is not Lonergan's invention but has a long prehistory. The most immediate context for his own use appears to be that of Britain in the early decades of the 20th century.[11] Much hinges on how we interpret the modifier "critical" in the term. For Lonergan, it has at least two related senses. Certainly, it carries the sense of a reflective exercise on the fact and complex performance of human knowing. But it also bears a dialectical relation to the critical project of Kant in asking, "what are the conditions of knowledge of objects?"[12]

In the latter respect, critical reason can be interpreted as "a further unfolding of a tendency in idealist speculation itself to recognize that 'the basis of all logical necessity is the necessity of fact,' and to proceed on the basis of that recognition to concretize the abstract self-conscious ego of Kant as a developing conscious self."[13] Yet, at the same time, if critical realism must pass through the idealist critique of naïve realism, it does so on the way to a new and deeper realism: "[It] claim[s] to have found a ground for realism beyond idealism—not, so to speak, before or beneath idealism . . ."[14] Critical realism, therefore, transcends and sublates both naïve realism and idealism (or rationalism, more broadly) because it recognizes both an empirical principle of knowledge, doggedly asserted by the pre-critical realist, as well as the constituent role of consciousness in being, like the idealist. Rather than two opposed principles that we must choose

10. Lonergan, "Origins of Christian Realism," 242–43.

11. See Mark Morelli, "The Realist Response to Idealism in England and Lonergan's Critical Realism" in *Method,* 21 (2003), pp.1–23. Morelli claims: "Critical Realism, as a name for a philosophical position, gained currency in British and American philosophy in the late nineteenth and early twentieth centuries. It appeared initially as a translation from German" (9). After detailing five distinct approaches each called critical realism that the model proposed by Dawes Hicks is the one closest to Lonergan's account, even though it remains deficient in essential respects from Lonergan's perspective.

12. Morelli, *Critical Realism,* 15.

13. Quoted in Morelli, *Critical Realism,* 18.

14. Morelli, *Critical Realism,* 11.

between, Lonergan contended that these are two components in a complex and compound structure of knowing.

A particularly forceful advocate of naïve realism and trenchant critic of approaches like Lonergan's was the great philosopher and historian of medieval thought, Etienne Gilson. His critique and Lonergan's response helps us see the greater explanatory power of critical realism, which enables a more developed phenomenology of rational consciousness, and also provides grounds for responding to idealist claims, where Gilson thought one must simply take a dogmatic stand on first principles. Gilson asserted that there was no higher viewpoint capable of integrating realism and idealism: "You can start with thought or with being, but you cannot do both at the same time."[15] One must begin either with epistemology (thought) or metaphysics (being), but only one could be first philosophy. Furthermore, such a stand was a matter of arbitrary choice because logically, both realism and idealism were internally consistent, once an individual accepted one or the other set of first principles. Since those first principles could not, by definition, be demonstrated one must simply choose.

Against this position, however, Lonergan argued that, "what is methodologically primary is neither metaphysics nor epistemology, but rather cognitional theory, that is, the articulation of cognitive performance, of what we are doing when we are knowing."[16] In other words, a "phenomenology of coming to know"[17] supplies the deeper ground upon which the dialectic between realism and idealism can be adjudicated. It was the original and most trenchant critic of idealism, Søren Kierkegaard, who remarked that no flight of conceptual speculation was so rarified that it could dispense with the human speculator. Following Kierkegaard, Lonergan cautions us not to treat philosophy or theology as "so objective that it is independent of the mind that thinks it."[18] The task, therefore, was not to adjudicate between the claims of being and thinking, but rather to grasp the normative structure of intentional consciousness that was operative in every act of knowing being. Lonergan's method which, tellingly, is referred to as both

15. Etienne Gilson, *Thomist Realism and the Critique of Knowledge*, trans. M.A. Wauck (San Francisco: Ignatius Press, 1986), 84.

16. Paul St. Amour, "Lonergan and Gilson on the Problem of Critical Realism" in *The Thomist* 69 (2005), 576.

17. Bernard Lonergan, *Philosophical and Theological Papers: 1965–1980*, CWL 17. Edited by Croken and Doran, (Toronto: UTP, 2004), 429.

18. Lonergan, "Philosophy of God and Theology" in *Philosophical and Theological Papers: 1964–1980*, CWL, Vol 17, (Toronto: UTP, 2004), 113.

the transcendental method or the generalized empirical method, "moves beyond the horizon of idealist immanentism by clarifying precisely how intentionality is intrinsically related to being."[19]

That relatedness of mind to matter was the product of a twofold intrinsicism: "Human experience is patterned by both biological and intellectual exigencies, and each maintains its own distinct criterion of the real."[20] This is the fundamental ambiguity at the heart of human consciousness, as we have seen. These dual criteria of the real are not a reason for skepticism or voluntarism, but rather facts that make possible a more precise and comprehensive theory of human understanding, objectivity, and being. When adverted to, they produce a new differentiation of consciousness: "Lonergan negotiated the apparent incompatibility of these two realisms, not by attempting to eliminate one or the other, nor by attempting to consolidate the two into a single unified realism, but by differentiating and validating distinct biological and intellectual patterns of experience."[21] When seen together, these distinct components can be understood as constituting equiprimordial operations of human consciousness, experiencing and understanding, which are irreducible to one another and incomplete without each other. The givenness of the world of sensible experience and the givenness of conscious intentionality are equally indisputable and equally incapable of bearing the full freight of human knowing on their own.

Ultimately, for Lonergan, the cognitional structure of consciousness is deeper than the systematic formulations of realism and idealism, and underlying their respective logical consistencies. Therefore, bearing in mind that the ancient Greek word for principle, *arche*, incudes the sense of "source," we can see the meaning of Lonergan's claim that what is properly basic is *not* logical first principles, as Gilson assumed, but rather the normatively structured operations of human understanding and the method according to which they proceed. Thus, as St. Amour notes, for Lonergan,

> "Logic promotes clarity, coherence, and rigor within an established horizon. But method is what originates horizons, and effects transitions from already established horizons to new horizons that more adequately satisfy the human desire to know."[22]

---

19. St. Amour, *Lonergan and Gilson*, 582.
20. St. Amour, *Lonergan and Gilson*, 584.
21. St. Amour, *Lonergan and Gilson*, 585.
22. St. Amour, *Lonergan and Gilson*, 572.

Method (*methodos*, the way) here denotes not an inflexible and presupposed set of procedural norms, but rather the always already operative functions of human understanding in the discovery of reality. It is the way or path of thought. A methodical approach in distinction from a dogmatic approach recognizes the interlacing of logical operations (deduction, induction, inference) and cognitional operations (experiencing, understanding, imagining, weighing, judging, observing, hypothesizing, experimenting, verifying) in the discovery of reality. Such a method is properly basic because it is rooted in cognitional operations that are always operative in any form of human understanding. Therefore, it provides a normative ground from which various philosophical horizons can be "clarified, assessed, and rationally adopted or rejected."[23]

Critical realism, therefore, moves beyond idealism in order to complete the turn to the subject, which reveals itself to be not, as Gilson thought, a turn away from the givenness of things, but instead to what is first for us—namely, ourselves—rather than what is first in itself. We are now in a position to take the full measure of this subject who discloses herself as what Robert Sokolowski has called, the "dative of manifestation."[24] This is the being "to whom" an understanding of being is given. Lonergan helps us see the precise way in which that understanding unfolds itself in a structured set of interdependent operations.[25] Precisely because it stands at the end of a process, the apprehension of truth is an achievement, a task to which the human inquirer must apply herself. For that reason, achieving truth and resolving to become an "agent of truth"[26] is not only a matter of intelligence, but also of willingness and something requiring conversion.

III. The Origins of Christian Realism: A Second Way into Critical Realism

The forgoing has been a philosophical account of the various motivations one might have for accepting critical realism as a position on the nature of

23. St. Amour, *Lonergan and Gilson*, 572.

24. Robert Sokolowski, *Introduction to Phenomenology*, (Cambridge: Cambridge University Press, 2000), 32.

25. Summing up his own position later in life, Lonergan wrote: "Critical Realism is the philosophical position that states that the real is that which is known by the three-fold process of attentive experience, intelligent inquiry, and responsible judgment. Reality is that which is known by totality of correct judgment." Bernard Lonergan, "An Interview with Fr. Bernard Lonergan, S.J.," in *A Second Collection*, eds. Ryan and Tyrrell, (Toronto: University of Toronto Press, 1996), 209–230.

26. Robert Sokolowski, *The Phenomenology of the Human Person*, (Cambridge: Cambridge University Press, 2008), 1–4 and *passim*.

knowing, objectivity and being. However, as a philosopher who was also a theologian, Lonergan countenances a distinct set of motivations for critical realism rooted in the history of Christian theology. These motivations amount to a case for realism as the implicit epistemological position of the Christian scriptures and also, as evidenced by the early church councils, and the emerging epistemological position of Christian theology.

The ambiguity of realism is something we encounter frequently when we know how to attend to the interwoven worlds of sense and meaning that constitute our natural, daily environment. However, the distinction of the two worlds and their different criteria of understanding can also be forced upon us under certain circumstances. According to Lonergan, the early theological debates of the Christian church were one such set of circumstances. The need to define and adjudicate between definitions of "the real" revealed, at one and the same time, the operative philosophies of different early church fathers as well as distinct criteria for judging claims belonging to the world mediated by meaning.

According to Lonergan, the early Christological debates forced the theological tradition to confront certain philosophical questions head on.[27] Tertullian, Origen, and Athanasius each proposed a solution to the controversies of their day according to distinct conceptions of the real. In ways that parallel more modern debates between empiricists and idealists, Tertullian argued for the real divinity of the Son according to a Stoic materialism that held whatever was real was corporeal, while Origen argued for the immateriality of both Father and Son according to a middle Platonist idealism, for which the non-corporeal was most real. Each account of the real, one rooted in the world of immediacy and the other in the world mediated by meaning, led to inadequacies in formulating what it meant for the Son to be real and also really distinct from the Father. It is only with Athanasius that there begins to emerge a method leading to judgment beyond the presumption of mere sense or meaning. Athanasius provides not an answer but a rule: "Whatever is said of the Father is said of the Son, except that the Son is the Son and not Father."[28] This rule is a heuristic device, a form of judgment, "a proposition about propositions." It specifies the conditions that must be fulfilled for a true statement about Father and Son to obtain,

27. He writes that, "The proximate involvement of Christianity in the problems of realism arose in the developments effected in Christological thought in the third, fourth, and fifth centuries." Lonergan, "Origins of Christian Realism," 245.

28. Lonergan, "Origins of Christian Realism," in *A Second Collection*, eds. Ryan and Tyrrell, (Toronto: University of Toronto Press, 1996), 250.

without yet determining if those conditions are in fact fulfilled. Augustine follows suit for the same reasons when he offers a heuristic definition of "person" in his discussion of the Trinity. Such a heuristic method discerns the shape that a possible answer must take before attempting to supply the determinate answer. This, Lonergan notes, is the method of Socrates asking for definitions of immaterial realities such as justice, virtue, and piety. He clarified the form that such a definition would take—*omni et soli*—prior to judging if such a reality was the case. What is real, for Athanasius and Augustine, is what is able to be judged as fulfilling the conditions for truth.

Lonergan sees implicit in the scriptural witness, and emerging gradually in the theological dialectics of the early church, that "there was developing a new mode of understanding."[29] This new mode of understanding originates as a biblical realism that "is present only implicitly, and not acknowledged explicitly."[30] In other words, there is a commonsense realism, latent in the biblical narratives for which the criterion of the real is not what is visible alone. Moreover, while this position is latent in the vast majority of scriptural exegeses and theologies, it is nonetheless functionally active to various degrees:

> ". . . from the beginning the word of God contained within it an implicit epistemology and ontology, but what was there implicitly become known explicitly only through a dialectic process that was spread over time; and this dialectic process was all the more complex as the real roots of the problem were touched only indirectly."[31]

Thus, just as the critical exigence of Socrates moved philosophy from the opinions of the agora to the systematic approach of Aristotle, so too in early Christianity there was, "a puzzling undertow, a concern for clarity and coherence, that was destined eventually to add to the ordinary language of the bazaars and to the religious language of the gospels the incipient theological language of the Greek councils."[32] We see, in the latter case, the way in which grappling with religious questions can lead to philosophical insights.

29. Bernard Lonergan, *The Way to Nicea*, 16.

30. Bernard Lonergan, *The Way to Nicea*, 129.

31. Bernard Lonergan, *The Way to Nicea*, 133.

32. Bernard Lonergan, *The Way to Nicea*, viii.

Apart from the historical precedence of realism in the Christian tradition, there are at least two further distinctly Christian motivations for appropriating a critical realism. First, as we have seen, key theological questions cannot be answered adequately if we have not made the conscious move into the world mediated by meaning and disambiguated distinct criteria of the real. Tertullian and Origen propose different accounts of Christology not because they read different sacred texts, but because they interpreted those scriptures according to "differing notions of reality," the former according to a Stoic materialism for which the real is corporeal and the latter according to a Platonic idealism in which the real is an idea. It is Athanasius with his "implicit thrust to realism"[33] who is able to transpose the correct insights of both into a new fuller context.

As with our earlier philosophical discussion of critical realism, here too, the value is that it is an epistemological position nuanced enough to encompass the insights of both accounts. And, according to Lonergan, Christianity has a stake in each:

> ". . . both the world of immediacy and the world mediated by meaning [are] vital to [Christianity]: the world of immediacy because of religious experience, because of God flooding our hearts through the Holy Spirit given to us (Rom. 5:5); the world mediated by meaning because divine Revelation is God's own entry into man's world mediated by meaning."[34]

Here Lonergan articulates a further religious motivation for appropriating critical realism that is twofold. First, in its retention of experience, critical realism preserves the world of immediacy as a place of possible encounter with the divine. Second, in its acknowledgement of the constitutive role of understanding, judgment, and decision in the subject's self-constitution, critical realism can supply a robust account of the constitutive role of meaning, including the meaning of Revelation, in transforming individuals and communities. It can accommodate the divine word and deed with equal agility.

Thus, in Lonergan's account, what originates as a "dogmatic realism" founded on the authority of scripture undergoes a dialectical development resulting in a differentiation of consciousness from the commonsense categories of biblical narrative to the theoretic-philosophical categories of the early councils. Grappling with the meaning of God's revelation led to a

33. Lonergan, "Origins of Christian Realism," 245.

34. Lonergan, "Origins of Christian Realism," 260.

revelation of the meaning of knowing and being. "If it was the word of God, considered as true, that led from the gospels to the dogmas, it was the same word from the same point of view, that brought about what we have described as differentiation of consciousness."[35]

Grappling with the meaning of Revelation also led, indirectly, to a new meaning of the human being. In struggling to understand the religious truths of her tradition, the Christian discovers further truths about herself, that are not themselves scriptural truths: "[The] ambiguity of realism was not among revealed truths. Christians had to find out for themselves . . ."[36] What followed was a slow process of philosophically discerning the conditions of meaning, language, truth, and falsity and therewith the entire economy of intelligibility that obtains in the world mediated by meaning. A world, "not known by experience alone, nor by ideas alone, or in conjunction with experience, but by true judgment and beliefs."[37]

IV. A Differentiated Empirical Principle

These two realisms and their corresponding worlds are both rooted in "the given as given" and therefore, for Lonergan, they can be related genetically rather than merely dialectically.. There is an empirical principle that is the source of both forms of knowledge. The key to disambiguating and then relating them, as we have seen, is grasping that the given extends not only to the data of sense but also to the data of consciousness. For the human inquirer, there is not only the immediacy of her sense experience, but also of her cognitional life. The world mediated by meaning is mediated to us through operations that are themselves immediate, given in and as conscious performance. Knowledge of ourselves, therefore, no less than knowledge of the world, begins with empirical consciousness, a basic being-with being that motivates our concern to understand it. Critical realism is the epistemological theory that results from Lonergan's cognitional theory, his transcendental method or, more to our point here, his generalized empirical method.

This expanded empirical principle that applies equally to entities, artifacts, and ideas enables critical realism to ground an account of historical consciousness, which determined much of the "new context" in which philosophy

35. Bernard Lonergan, *The Way to Nicea*, 9.

36. Lonergan, "Origins of Christian Realism," 260.

37. Lonergan, "Origins of Christian Realism," 261.

and theology set out to answer questions.[38] The "slow" and "bloody" entrance of history into Catholic thought involved turning from a classicist to an empirical notion of culture, turning from a deductive to an empirical notion of theology, and turning from abstract "substances" to concrete "subjects" who grasp theological truth from out of the resources of their concrete and contingent lives. The historical is, as it were, the empirical stretched over time, and this has significant implications for our understanding of truth, which naïve realism cannot meet well, but which critical realism is better equipped to handle by appealing to not the purported universality of terms that originated in radically different times and places,[39] but rather to the immanent structure of consciousness operative across such times and places.

That differentiated empirical principle applies not only to what is to be known (the noema) but also to the process of knowing (the noetic) because knowing is not simple intuition or picture thinking, but instead a process of interrelated acts culminating in judgment and decision. What guarantees the truthfulness of one's judgments is not a predetermined theoretical framework, but a cognitional method. The success of that method, however, depends on the authenticity of the inquirer, which is not the product of a single act of assent, but an on-going self-appropriation that requires a set of fundamental shifts in horizon, which Lonergan named conversions. The need for conversion indicates at one and the same time the precarious contingency of the human pursuit of truth and value, and the important role of hope in this process. We are capable of discovering some measure of truth and discerning some degree of goodness, yet at the same time without contradiction, Lonergan could observe,

> "We do not know ourselves very well; we cannot chart the future, we cannot control our environment completely or the influences that work on us; we cannot explore our unconscious and preconscious mechanisms. Our course is in the night; our control is only rough and approximate; we have to believe and trust, to risk and dare."[40]

---

38. Bernard Lonergan, "Theology in its New Context" in *A Second Collection*, CWL vol. 13, eds. Doran and Dadosky, (Toronto: University of Toronto Press, 2016), 48–59

39. See for example Lonergan's strong remarks on the meaning of "person" in theology: "When classicist assumptions are pushed to the point of denying matters of fact, I feel I must disagree. The meaning of the term 'person' at Chalcedon is not what commonly is understood by the term today, and theologians at least have to take that fact into account" (*Origins of Christian Realism*, 260).

40. Bernard Lonergan, "Existenz and Aggiornamento" in *Collection*, CWL vol. 4 (Toronto: University of Toronto Press, 2005), 224.

Lonergan's three-fold notion of conversion is rich and phenomenologically grounded. Yet, these conversions each occur at the level of a fully conscious subject. They are conversions experienced most intensely at the levels of judging, deciding and loving. Yet, as is clear to anyone who has undergone a measure of such radical change, it is not merely one's approach that undergoes an about-face, nor merely the operational dimensions of judging, deciding, and loving, but also one's aesthetic life as well. In a more complicated way, and often according to a different and slower timeline, one's sensitive spontaneity is also reoriented as a result of conversion and, in return, makes fidelity to the ongoing nature of conversion more consistent. These embodied and affective dimensions of existence remain unthematized in Lonergan's compact account of subjectivity. Absent a fuller understanding of this aesthetic and existential dimension, we run the risk of a disembodied account of the subject, which, precisely on account of the empirical principle of knowledge, would be an incomplete account.

Robert Doran's elaboration of a fourth "psychic" conversion seeks to address this dimension of Lonergan's work and bring the aesthetic and intellectual dimensions of human subjectivity into an existential completeness that provides a fuller account of the ongoing process of self-transcendence. It does so by extending Lonergan's account "downward" into the empirical consciousness and sensitive experience of the knower. Ultimately, it grounds these conversions more deeply in the facticity of human subjectivity. Let us turn to that account now.

V. Doran on Psychic Conversion

An analysis of psychic conversion requires that we first specify what is meant here by the psyche, to which dimension of consciousness the psyche belongs, and what is meant by conversion. According to Doran, the term psyche denotes, "the sequence of sensations, memories, images, conations, emotions, bodily movements and spontaneous intersubjective responses,"[41] that attend and are sublated by "higher" cognitional operations. The psyche is the "transcendental aesthetic dimension of our subjectivity."[42] As such, it is part of what is missing from the "neglected subject" of much traditional philosophy, and metaphysics, in particular.[43]

41. Robert Doran, *Psychic Conversion* (Milwaukee: Marquette University Press, 2006), 139.

42. Robert Doran, *Psychic Conversion*, 139.

43. See section one of Lonergan's "The Subject" in *A Second Collection*, CWL vol. 13, eds. Doran and Dadosky, (Toronto: University of Toronto Press, 2016), 60–63.

Lonergan begins to remedy this neglect by using his critical realism to undertake a phenomenology of cognitional interiority which grants equal priority to the data of sense and consciousness.

Doran's account of the psyche supplements that effort by showing us in greater degree and depth the empirical consciousness upon which the operations of cognitional structure are founded. That empirical dimension of consciousness includes the sensitive stream of external sensation, in addition to the internal operations of registering, imagining, associating, and remembering.[44] It is where the wonder native to our nature originates, which is the source of the distinctive exigence that unfolds in the normative pattern of inquiry, judgment, and decision. It also enables us to recover the embodied and affective dimensions of human subjectivity. This fundamental incarnated facticity of consciousness is essential to a complete account of the subject because, "all operations and feeling that constitute experience as such have a bodily basis."[45] Any account that lacks a robust analysis of the psyche, therefore, runs the risk of providing a disembodied account of interiority, which would misrepresent authenticity as an intellectual exercise and truncate the reach of self-transcendence.

The recovery of the psyche also enables a more adequate account of the nature and role of feelings in the life of the subject. Feelings which, though they originate at the empirical level of consciousness, are taken up and made constitutive in the supervening operations of consciousness, adding to them color, texture and the drama that make of the philosopher a *lover* of wisdom, and not merely an idle speculator. It is often feeling that first disposes us to attend to ourselves, to our inner lives that so often surprise us by their capacity to be moved by beauty, suffering, and goodness in the world around us. "It is primarily because of feelings," Doran argues, "that we can speak of the experience of the data of consciousness."[46]

Yet, to speak of the merely empirical dimension of human consciousness is already an abstraction, because for the human subject empirical consciousness is always already existential consciousness: "the empirical . . . always receives the direction of its intentionality from the same existential determinants that set intelligent and rational consciousness upon their course . . ."[47] Thus, existential consciousness, "integrates

---

44. Robert Doran, *Psychic Conversion*, 176.

45. Robert Doran, *Psychic Conversion*, 176.

46. Robert Doran, *Psychic Conversion*, 176.

47. Robert Doran *Psychic Conversion*, 177.

the affective and cognitional dimensions of consciousness."[48] That integration is not without mutual effect. Empirical consciousness founds, through its own sublation, the other levels of consciousness, yet it is also changed by that sublation. It is transformed by the exigencies of consciousness that demand that affectivity participate in the subject's self-transcendence. Not only our minds and wills, but also the embodied and emotional dimensions of our existence are to be recreated. They, in turn, become more fertile ground for the antecedent willingness that disposes us to comply with the exigencies for knowledge and goodness that transformed them.

What we have been describing is worth noting, as it is related to a key development in Lonergan's thought from the publication of *Insight* to the publication of *Method in Theology*. The latter lacked an account of existential consciousness and so it did not recognize that distinct category of feelings which are intentional responses to values.[49] Thus, it is only with *Method* that the desire to know is set within the fuller context of the subject's existential drama, which helps us to see its dignity and gravity, but also its precariousness and vulnerability, to the vicissitudes of bias. In uniting the sensitive and the intelligent dimensions of conciousness, existential consciousness "extends further the reach of self-transcending subjectivity in decision and responsible action."[50] This invites the artistic structuring of one's decisions in dialogue with judgments of fact and value and makes of one's life a dramatic and artistic act of creating. Additionally, because sensitive consciousness is the home of the aesthetic dimensions of human existence, it is therefore "the link between intelligent and nonintelligent emergent probability."[51] It is the meeting place of space and time and that which transcends them. Therefore, this union, at the same time, sublates emergent probability and draws it up into the world mediated by meaning.

What then does it mean for the psyche and, with it, empirical consciousness to be converted? Functionally, for Lonergan, conversion is what enables ongoing self-transcendence that in turn produces authenticity. Substantively, conversion is the expansion of one's horizon, or the broadening of one's field of knowledge and interest. It leads to wider concern and greater interest. In each of its forms, it entails a turning around that is in some sense always

48. Robert Doran *Psychic Conversion*, 71.

49. Robert Doran *Psychic Conversion*, 74.

50. Robert Doran *Psychic Conversion*, 93.

51. Robert Doran *Psychic Conversion*, 184; Doran also refers to it as "the meeting ground of matter and spirit" (184).

a turning from the self to another. Therefore, conversion, notwithstanding its distinct forms, is always at root, "an about-face from self-absorption or self-enclosure to self-transcendence," a movement, sudden or gradual, "beyond the isolation of the subject, beyond a constantly self-referential horizon, to self-transcendence."[52] The notion of psychic conversion enables us to grasp the way in which this self-transcendence is not only intellectual, but also affective. Yet, there is an important dissimilarity between psychic conversion and intellectual, moral, and religious conversion and it is rooted in the distinct forms of human consciousness distinguished by critical realism.

> "We are conscious in two ways: in one way, through our sensibility, we undergo rather passively what we sense and imagine, our desires and fears, our delights and sorrows, our joys and sadness; in another way, through our intellectuality, we are more active when we consciously inquire in order to understand, understand in order to utter a word, weigh evidence in order to judge, deliberate in order to choose, and exercise our will in order to act."[53]

Intellectual, moral, and religious conversion pertain to the "more active" form of human consciousness. Psychic conversion, on the other hand, is the transformation of its "more passive" dimension rooted in sensibility. In fact, it is "establishing the connection between the two ways of being conscious."[54] It is rooted in the insight, itself rooted in the experience of the self-transcending subject, that our sensitive and affective lives are not unaffected by the fundamental shifts in horizon that occur through intellectual, moral, and religious conversion. If attended to carefully, we see that over time and often indirectly, "the sensitive stream of consciousness is being changed by the very performance of these intentional operations."[55] The embodied dimensions of our subjectivity not only co-constitute our self-transcendence as a necessary condition, but also gradually come to participate in the full flourishing of the authentic human person. Psychic conversion, then,

> "consists in the development of the capacity for internal communication in the subject among spirit (intellectual, rational, deliberative,

---

52. Robert Doran, "What Does Bernard Lonergan Mean by 'Conversion'?" *Lecture presented at the University of St. Michael's College, University of Toronto* (2011), 4.

53. Bernard Lonergan, *The Triune God: Systematics*, CWL 12, trans. Michael G. Shields, ed. Robert M. Doran and H. Daniel Monsour (Toronto: University of Toronto, 2007), 139.

54. Robert Doran, "What Does Bernard Lonergan Mean by 'Conversion'?", 20.

55. Robert Doran, "What Does Bernard Lonergan Mean by 'Conversion'?", 20.

> and religious consciousness), psyche (sensitive consciousness) and the organism (the unconscious), by means of the attentive, intelligent, rational, and existentially responsible and decisive negotiations of one's imaginal, affective, and intersubjective spontaneity."[56]

It is the antecedent higher integration of the manner of existence of the human person that is required for her to accept and promote the higher viewpoints entailed in intellectual, moral, and religious self-transcendence.

Thus, psychic conversion, as the therapeutics of empirical consciousness, is central to the dynamics of existential consciousness because, first, it establishes the connection between cognitional theory in the empirical, embodied, and factical existence of the subject, and second, because in identifying the further, passive, transformation of spontaneous sensitivity, it brings the transformation of the subject to a heuristic completion. By virtue of a virtuous and deepening circularity, psychic conversion supports the ongoing self-transcendence of intellectual, moral, and religious conversion, but is also brought about through them.[57] A number of consequences follow from this.

First, as we have seen, psychic conversion originates the ongoing integration sought by existential consciousness: "For, the advancing authenticity, the fulfilled affectivity, and the responsible direction of one's work that make the flourishing human personality are functions of a decision to implement the capacities of conscious intentionality for detachment, disinterestedness, and objectivity at each level,"[58] including that of our sensitive spontaneity. The fuller integration brought about through psychic conversion is one reason Lonergan comes to accord a priority to existential consciousness.[59] It is only with the existential subject that we see more clearly the "dramatic finality" that sublates the normative order of inquiry and understanding, by enlisting it in the constitution of one's life.[60] This "existential concern for the

---

56. Robert Doran, *Psychic Conversion*, 52.

57. ". . . in addition to aiding the other three conversions psychic conversion is a function of these conversions" (Robert Doran, *Psychic Conversion*, 225).

58. Robert Doran, *Psychic Conversion*, 72.

59. Bernard Lonergan, "The Subject" in *A Second Collection,* CWL vol.13, eds. Robert Doran SJ and John Dadosky, (Toronto: University of Toronto Press, 2016). Here he speaks of "affirming the primacy of the existential" (73).

60. It also sublates empirical consciousness: "The dramatic pattern of experience is sensitive consciousness sublated by the fourth level of intentionality. It is that organization of the sequence of sensations, memories, images, emotions, conations, associations, bodily movements and spontaneous intersubjective response whose cohesive principle is the intentionality of dramatic artistry . . ." (Robert Doran, *Psychic Conversion*, 52).

drama" of one's "existential autobiography" situates intelligent and rational development and makes them not general exercises in knowing, but specific exercises of personal self-transcendence and participation in the human good.

Second, for this reason, psychic conversion is essential to the success of the transcendental method: "Psychic conversion is key to the completion of the finality of the task of transcendental method."[61] That finality is the ongoing self-transcendence of the knower, which is made possible through ongoing conversion. Psychic conversion, in particular, assists in transforming the empirical and sensitive dimensions of our existence where bias often originates. It not only promotes development, but also helps to overcome bias.

Third, the promotion of transcendental method, however, is itself at best a penultimate goal. The more encompassing finality is that of the human good. Psychic conversion, in bringing to heuristic completion the method by which we pursue self-transcendence in the development of authenticity, contributes to the "existential appropriation of the responsibility to reverse the longer cycle of decline."[62] It makes us more willing participants in creating and healing.

Fourth, when seen through the eyes of religious love, we grasp the further redemptive dimension of this higher integration, and its increased capacity to cooperate, because of an antecedent willingness borne of grace through which "even human sensitivity [is enabled] to participate in the divine solution to the problem of evil."[63] Psychic conversion enables us to be more receptive to religious love and to more faithfully reflect it. It makes possible our participation not only in a narrative of progress, but also one of redemption.

VI. Conclusion: Authenticity and Facticity

Psychic conversion and the integration it intends is not only a real possibility for human subjectivity, but also an essential component in human flourishing. It is essential in a twofold sense. Negatively, it helps eliminate the underlying conditions that lead to biased forms of understanding and choosing. Our oversights spring from inauthenticity[64] and "we are

61. Robert Doran, *Psychic Conversion*, 175.

62. Robert Doran, *Psychic Conversion*, 191.

63. Robert Doran, *Psychic Conversion*, 43.

64. Doran writes, "obstacles to performing the intentional operations can arise . . . from a psychic resistance to raising relevant questions . . ." (*Psychic Conversion*, 20).

cognitively disoriented because, more radically, we are existentially disoriented, terrified, resourceless, impoverished, estranged from our genuine being."[65] Positively, it is necessary for the full flourishing of the authentic individual who, as a result of it, not only inquires, chooses, and loves with a capacious authenticity, and in doing so restructures his or her own manner of being in the world. We will conclude by examining each of these in turn.

Both the negative and positive functions of psychic conversion are manners of attending to the subject's facticity. While, as traditional metaphysics insisted, it is not an essential property of the human essence to be at this time or from that place, it is in fact a universal feature of any human being to be at some time and in some place. The contemporary notion of facticity, given particular shape by the thought of Martin Heidegger,[66] designates these conditions of historical contingency that, while contingent, are nonetheless necessary. We live and move and have our manner of being amidst, in Doran's repeated phrase, "the movement of life."[67] That movement can be designated as facticity, "that world of meanings and relations that is undetachable from life itself."[68] This largely pre-reflective dimension of life is rooted in empirical consciousness. It is prior to and more encompassing than our intellectual dispositions toward the world, than our shapes and patterns of consciousness. It encompasses our total concourse with the world that is at one and the same time embodied, affective, intelligent, and intersubjective. It is through that concourse, moreover, that we both constitute our world and are constituted by it.

The negative or critical function of psychic conversion includes the curtailment of feelings that would inhibit the unrestricted desire to know from setting in motion the normative structure of cognitional interiority. It provides a "defensive circle for the integrity of the search."[69] Our thrownness, one dimension of which is the givenness of our being from above downward, is a matrix of authentic and inauthentic influences. It is simultaneously the condition of our openness to the intelligibility of being, and also for becoming, "closed off" to it. Existential consciousness as rooted in empirical consciousness is thus the site of the equiprimordiality according to which we are at once, in Heidegger's terminology, "in the truth

65. Robert Doran, *Psychic Conversion*, 115.

66. See for example First course, PRL, BT.

67. Robert Doran, *Psychic Conversion*, e.g., 19, 33, 169, 175, 179, 181, 182, 198.

68. Daniel O. Dahlstrom, "Facticity" in *A Heidegger Dictionary* (London: Bloomsbury, 2013), 72.

69. Robert Doran, *Psychic Conversion*, 143.

and untruth."[70] Doran's notion helps us appreciate the degree to which Lonergan stands in a long tradition stretching from Augustine through Kierkegaard to us for which error is always a result of turning in on oneself, described by Augustine as *curvatus in se* and by Kierkegaard as *inclosing reserve*. All basic sin is selfishness.

What is required in response to this is openness, and that is achieved through psychic conversion in its positive contribution to the full flourishing of the existential subject. Through the mediation of psychic conversion, the empirical strata of facticity become intelligible and malleable and thus potentially complicit in the human good. This, "therapy of self-possession,"[71] however, does more than enable the personal authenticity of the existential subject.

That subject, like all human subjects, is also the meeting place of matter and spirit, the link between intelligent and nonintelligent emergent probability. If the human being is world process becomes self-conscious, then the authentic self-transcending person is the capacity for emergent probability to deliberately bring about moral and healing schemes of recurrence: ". . . when emergent probability becomes intelligent and free . . . recognition for the distinct quality of existential foundations leads to a distinction between the real human world as it is and the good human world as it is to be realized."[72]

Through the human being, the world becomes a place hospitable to moral goodness, and its history becomes autobiography. This "real human world" is also the place where immanent intelligibility opens itself to the possibility of transcendent intelligibility. Through psychic conversion, sensitive spontaneity is mediated to cognitional activity and becomes "the opening onto existential and religious awareness."[73] Here sensitivity and intentionality, "are reconciled with each other when they become the place of conscious encounter between radically finite historically conscious proportionate being and absolute transcendence intelligibility, reality, truth, and value."[74] If this is the story of the human world reaching out towards transcendence, it can also be told in reverse order. Through psychic conversion the divinely originated solution to the problem of evil, so to speak, reaches through consciousness into the entirety of the human: "In this way,

70. Martin Heidegger, *Being and Time*, H55ff.

71. Robert Doran, *Psychic Conversion*, 91.

72. Robert Doran, *Psychic Conversion*, 111.

73. Robert Doran, *Psychic Conversion*, 231.

74. Robert Doran, *Psychic Conversion*, 154.

the divinely originated solution to the problem of evil penetrates to the sensitive level of human life."[75] And through a psychically converted humanity, the divine solution is mediated to the non-human material world.

In her openness to transcendence, the human subject becomes open to the possibility that just as psychic conversion enables the heuristic completeness of the foundational quest for human authenticity, so too the gift of a universal willingness in the order of grace brings to heuristic completion the redemptive arc of history, a still higher integration borne of "the discovery of the bending of God in history toward the soul in grace."[76] Thus, the empirical and existential dimension of the human becomes not only the meeting place of matter and mind, but also between the human and the transcendent. This makes possible a still higher integration and a more radical and universal willingness that provides a more capacious existential foundation of the concrete historical process of the human good.

It is critical realism that enables us to see the distinct dimensions of the self, and their distinct and equally constitutive contributions to human knowing. It reveals the constitutive role of authentic subjectivity in knowing, doing, and loving. Therefore, it is critical realism that necessitates not only a triply-converted consciousness, but the higher and deeper integration of the material and spiritual, bodily and intellectual dimensions of human being brought about through psychic conversion. Authenticity is borne out most completely in an integrated way of life, not only in particular judgments and decisions, but in a manner of being in the world.

75. Robert Doran, *Psychic Conversion*, 240.

76. Robert Doran, *Psychic Conversion*, 152.

SECTION III

CRITICAL HERMENEUTICS

CHAPTER SEVEN

'REDRAWING THE MAP'

Insights from the Work of Robert M. Doran on the Place of Christian Scripture in the Dialectic of Culture

Joseph K. Gordon

Johnson University (Knoxville, TN)

In 1990, Robert M. Doran, S.J. published *Theology and the Dialectics of History* (1990), a foundational account of change in history which builds upon both the work of Bernard Lonergan, S.J. and Doran's own extensive reading in the fields of sociology, psychology, and philosophy of history.[1] Despite its explanatory usefulness, Doran's work has not received near the attention or acclaim it deserves, especially outside of the community of scholars devoted to advancing the achievements of Bernard Lonergan.[2] That foundational text, complemented and extended by Doran's subsequent monographs *What is Systematic Theology?* (2005), and *The Trinity in History* (volume 1, 2012, volume 2, 2019), is profoundly helpful in the ways it identifies, organizes, and addresses the challenges of contemporary theological reflection.[3] The present essay explores the usefulness of Doran's work for one

1. Robert M. Doran, *Theology and the Dialectics of History* (Toronto: University of Toronto Press, 1990).

2. My hope is that this festschrift, and the work of the International Institute for Method in Theology (IIMIT), will help to remedy this neglect. See Robert M. Doran, "The International Institute for Method in Theology: A Vision," https://www.lonerganresource.com/pdf/lectures/Doran_-_International_Institute_for_Method_in_Theology.pdf. The first volume produced by the participants in the IIMIT is Joseph Ogbonnaya and Lucas Briola, eds. *Everything is Interconnected: Towards a Globalization with a Humane Face and an Integral Ecology* (Milwaukee: Marquette University Press, 2019). Many of its contributions refer to and build upon Doran's achievements.

3. See Robert M. Doran, *What is Systematic Theology?* (Toronto: University of Toronto Press, 2005); Robert M. Doran, *The Trinity in History: A Theology of the Divine Missions,*

set of significant contemporary conversations in the theological and religious studies academies—reflection on the place of Christian Scripture in the work of Christian theology in our contemporary historically-conscious situation.[4] "History," of course, is a contested, variably understood term in the guilds of biblical scholarship, theology, and religious studies. Doran's work can shed a great deal of light on the historical particularity manifest in Christian Scripture, and on the challenges and opportunities of historical, theological, and contextual approaches for engaging, understanding, appreciating, and utilizing Christian Scripture at the level of our own times.

In order to elaborate on the usefulness of Doran's work for the topic I have identified, I will need to begin by rehearsing the empirical notion of culture operative in Doran's work, first articulated by Bernard Lonergan. I will then explain the relevance of Doran's work in *Theology and the Dialectics of History* for understanding both the cultural variability of Christian Scripture and for understanding its theological usefulness and purposes today. Finally, I will explain the relevance of Doran's work for evaluating the products of contemporary engagement with Scripture.

The Plurality and Plasticity of Culture(s) and Christian Scripture

However Christians might conceive of the divine origins and authority of Christian Scripture, it is nevertheless constituted by artifacts that reflect the meanings and values of its ancient authors, tradents, and communities of reception. While Christians affirm the sacredness and divine provenance of Christian Scripture, it is and still remains "a human activity."[5] The

---

Volume 1: Missions and Processions (Toronto: University of Toronto Press, 2012); Robert M. Doran, *The Trinity in History: A Theology of the Divine Missions, Volume 2: Missions, Relations, and Persons* (Toronto: University of Toronto Press, 2019).

4. When I refer to Christian Scripture or Scripture throughout this essay I have in mind the texts of the Christian Bible, Old and New Testaments. Differing Christian communities possess differing canonical collections, of course. On the challenge of identifying and understanding the precise scope of Christian Scripture today, see Joseph K. Gordon, *Divine Scripture in Human Understanding: A Systematic Theology of the Christian Bible* (Notre Dame, IN: University of Notre Dame Press, 2019).

5. The phrase is Wilfred Cantwell Smith's. See *What is Scripture?: A Comparative Approach* (Minneapolis, MN: Fortress, 1993), 18, 183, 203. Smith has in mind all texts held sacred by specific religious traditions. I affirm that Christian scripture is additionally a divine activity. A fuller account of the simultaneity of these judgments—that scripture is the result of and serves as an instrument of both human and divine acts—would require a much fuller account of the character and relationship of divine and human freedom. I have offered one such account in Gordon, *Divine Scripture in Human Understanding*, 85–97.

scriptures are, and reflect, human culture. It is impossible to understand them well, therefore, without giving adequate attention to the nature, or intelligibility, of human culture. A general examination of culture will provide a basis for locating, and so understanding, the scriptures as reflecting and instantiating the human cultures of their authors, redactors, tradents, and readers.[6]

"Culture refers," Kathryn Tanner writes, "to the whole social practice of meaningful action, and more specifically to the 'meaning dimension' of such action—the beliefs, values, and orienting symbols that suffuse a whole way of life. This meaning dimension of social action cannot be localized in some separate sphere specifically devoted to intellectual or spiritual concerns."[7] Recent cultural theory, as Tanner has summarized, emphasizes the hybridity and permeability of cultures.[8] The plurality, plasticity, and historicity of human cultures have come into focus since the Enlightenment. "Culture" is not primarily a static achievement with rigid boundaries, but is instead a plastic process of groups and individuals seeking to understand their antecedent organizations and to express and create those understandings. Culture is therefore differentiated from the social.

The social, Lonergan writes, designates a "way of life, a way in which people live together in some orderly and therefore predictable fashion."[9] The social is constituted by the ordered structures of family, state, law, economy, technology, and religious organizations. Human beings have developed such organizations in both organic and distinctly intentional manners, and such organizations, upon their development, recurrently operate and function without regular critical reflection or intervention. Such structures and organizations, as history has taught us, however, are subject to development and breakdown as much as they are subject to such cyclical recurrence. Human beings, especially contemporary ones, are not content to simply let

6. I utilize the metaphorical language of "locating Scripture" in Gordon, *Divine Scripture in Human Understanding*, 7–8, 24–25. Chapters three and four of that work "locate" Christian Scripture within the economic work of the Triune God and within human cultural history, respectively. The present essay extends the work of that fourth chapter by utilizing Doran's work on the dialectics of history to better specify the location of Scripture within human cultural history.

7. Tanner, "Cultural Theory," 527.

8. Tanner, "Cultural Theory," 530–531. Tanner contrasts these features of culture with a modern, "common-sense" view of culture, which insisted on the stability and rigidity of culture as an accomplishment.

9. Bernard Lonergan, "The Absence of God in Modern Culture," in *A Second Collection*, Collected Works of Bernard Lonergan 13, eds. Robert M. Doran and John D. Dadosky (Toronto: University of Toronto Press, 2016), 87.

things as they are, either. Humans, Lonergan writes, "wish to understand their own doing. They wish to discover and to express the appropriateness, the meaning, the significance, the value, and the use of their way of life as a whole and in its parts. Such discovery and expression constitute the cultural."[10] Culture "is the meaning of a way of life."[11] Lonergan, like Tanner, argues that culture does not exclusively designate the peak achievements of human expression. All human acts of meaning are cultural. "Culture," writes Dale Martin, "is everywhere human beings are."[12]

Since Lonergan's understanding of culture explicitly deals with meaning, it is instructive to consider his elaborate account of meaning. Lonergan argues that meaning plays a constitutive role in human living:

> It is the fact that acts of meaning inform human living, that such acts proceed from a free and responsible subject incarnate, that meanings differ from nation to nation, from culture to culture, and that, over time, they develop and go astray. Besides the meanings by which man apprehends nature and the meanings by which man transforms it, there are the meanings by which man thinks out the possibilities of his own living and makes his choice among them. In this realm of freedom and creativity, of solidarity and responsibility, of dazzling achievement and pitiable madness, there ever occurs man's making of man.[13]

Lonergan gives a helpful taxonomy of human meaning in *Method in Theology*. "Meaning," he writes, "is embodied or carried in human intersubjectivity, in art, in symbols, in language, and in the lives and deeds of persons."[14] While the meanings communicated through intersubjectivity and symbols are largely pre-reflective and spontaneous, and artistic meaning is non-instrumental,

---

10. Lonergan, "The Absence of God in Modern Culture," 87.

11. Lonergan, "The Absence of God in Modern Culture," 87.

12. Dale B. Martin, *Biblical Truths: The Meaning of Scripture in the Twenty-first Century* (New Haven: Yale University Press, 2017), 216.

13. Lonergan, "Theology in its New Context," in *A Second Collection*, Collected Works of Bernard Lonergan 13, eds. Robert M. Doran and John D. Dadosky (Toronto: University of Toronto Press, 2016), 54.

14. Bernard Lonergan, *Method in Theology*, Collected Works of Bernard Lonergan 14, eds. Robert M. Doran and John D. Dadosky (Toronto: University of Toronto Press, 2017), 55. In chapter three of *Method*, Lonergan gives extensive accounts of each of these types of meaning. They all have in common their intentionality as human acts and their intelligible ordering as the products of that intentionality. See Lonergan, *Method in Theology*, 71–74 on the sources, acts, and terms of human meaning.

linguistic meaning serves a primarily instrumental purpose.[15] Language is useful for communicating meaning; it is an extremely versatile instrument. Language enables the infant to emerge from the world of the immediacy of her nursery—mediated only through the immediacy of tasting, smelling, touching, seeing, and hearing into the much wider world mediated by meaning unbounded by space and time and open to as-yet-undefined possibilities. Language, Lonergan writes, "structures the world about the subject. Spatial adverbs and adjectives relate places to the place of the speaker. The tenses of verbs relate times to his present. Moods correspond to her intention to wish, or exhort, or command, or declare. Voices make verbs now active and now passive and, at the same time, shift subjects to objects and objects to subjects."[16] When we transition into the world mediated by human meaning, we have access to not only that which is immediate to us through our senses, but to a "far larger world revealed through the memories of other persons, through the common sense of community, through the pages of literature, through the labors of scholars, through the investigations of scientists, through the experience of saints, through the meditations of philosophers and theologians."[17]

15. Lonergan's account of the carriers of meaning is much more elaborate than this, but a more adequate treatment is beyond the scope of this essay. Also, Lonergan affirms, of course, that language can be artistic and symbolic. See Lonergan, *Method in Theology*, 55–95 for his more extensive discussion of meaning.

16. Lonergan, *Method in Theology*, 68–69. Just prior to this, Lonergan writes that language strongly conditions, and even restricts our understanding of the world. Even so, however, our conscious intentionality—that is, our self-transcendent capacity in experience, insight, judgment, and freedom—allows us to move beyond previous boundaries imposed by our language. The human ability to learn different languages, and the insufficiency of certain languages for communicating specialized understandings and judgments, demonstrates this self-transcendent capacity and the boundedness of certain linguistic systems. Language is an extremely useful tool for navigating our world, but our wonder, questioning, new insights, and new grasp of the truth in judgment are the means of creating new linguistic tools to meet needs and desires that the current language cannot. So we can supplement the common sense language of a specific group with technical languages across cultures, and subsequent developments (see, for instance, the technical languages of mathematics, physics, chemistry, biology, psychology, sociology, philosophy, and theology) provide new word resources and new grammars which differentiate our consciousness and provide us greater freedom. Language is so important to this development, but language itself is on the move. It "makes questions possible," writes Lonergan, but "intelligence makes them fascinating." Bernard Lonergan, "Faith and Belief," in *Philosophical and Theological Papers 1965–1980*, Collected Works of Lonergan, ed. Robert C. Croken and Robert M. Doran (Toronto: University of Toronto, 2004), 30–48, here 33, see also idem, "Self-Transcendence: Intellectual, Moral, Religious," in *Philosophical and Theological Papers 1965–1980*, 313–331, at 317.

17. Bernard Lonergan, *Method in Theology*, 29.

While navigating the world of immediacy only requires one to attend to one's senses, navigating the world mediated by meaning requires much more. One must supplement attentiveness with wonder, with questions, with intelligent insights and hypotheses. One must supplement those further with reflection on the adequacy of our understandings—and the expressions, understandings, and judgments of others—to reality, and finally, one must supplement those with responsible deliberation about the good. The operations associated with attentiveness, intelligence, reasonableness, and responsibility become the means through which we can navigate both the world of our senses and the world(s) mediated by meaning of human cultures.

It is also illuminating to relate culture to what is distinctive about the human persons who produce it. Human persons are the ones who reflect on the social order, and human persons are the ones who imagine new possibilities that could change it. Both of these capacities, the capacity for truthful understanding and judgment concerning social orders, and the capacity for exercising freedom, reflect elements of the self-transcendence characteristic of human persons across cultures, throughout time and irrespective of geographical location. Because of their natures as experiencers, understanders, judgers, and deciders, human persons are the producers of new cultures. They are also the understanders and changers of existing social arrangements and antecedent cultures. Human persons are able to both explain what is the case in social orders and to transform them through their own exercise of freedom. While culture reflects the capacity for human reflection upon social and vital realities, it is a concrete product of human persons operating through their aforementioned capacities for self-transcendence in experience, understanding, judgment, and decision.[18] Attentiveness, intelligence, reasonableness, and responsibility, then, are the criteria for passing judgment on cultures.

The plurality and plasticity of human cultures are evident throughout Christian Scripture. The historically, generically, and linguistically diverse texts included in Christian Scripture reflect the manifold meanings and values of ancient people. The texts were created and disseminated in the ancient social arrangements of their communities of origin and reception,

18. Anyone familiar with Lonergan's work will recognize these four as the "levels of consciousness." This metaphor of "levels" provides Lonergan a means of differentiating different degrees of human self-transcendence in the unfolding of "a single transcendental intending of plural, interchangeable objectives." Bernard Lonergan, "The Subject," in *A Second Collection*, 69–86, at 81. For introduction to the levels and their relationships see Bernard Lonergan, "Cognitional Structure," in *Collection*, CWL 4, ed. Frederick E. Crowe and Robert M. Doran (Toronto: University of Toronto, 1988), 205–221; Lonergan, *Method in Theology*, 10–17; and Lonergan "The Subject," in *A Second Collection*, 60–74.

with all of their particular religious, political, familial, and economic realities. Those diverse texts both assume and critically evaluate those existing social orders. The authors of those texts, whether communal or individual, write through their own understandings, judgments, and decisions.

It is customary in Bible-centric Christian denominations and sects to differentiate between ideas and values in the language of Scripture which are "merely cultural," and those which are "timeless truths."[19] But the fact of the matter is that everything in Scripture is culturally located. Scripture includes as many cultured perspectives as it has authors, redactors, and tradents.[20] Awareness that all human culture is empirical, including the diverse cultures reflected in the texts of Christian Scripture, precludes Christian believers from assuming a classicist approach to Scripture. The goal of returning to, or promoting, the ideal of singular normative biblical culture—whether we would locate it in the past—"behind" or "in" the text—itself, in the present—"in front of the text"—in our actualization of it, or in some future as-yet-unrealized synthesis, is untenable. To put things starkly, there is no singular, ideal, biblical culture, theology, or worldview.[21] To the extent that past approaches to scripture, whether premodern, modern, or postmodern, were tied to such a notion, they are no longer tenable. We can no longer posit either the discovery or the dissemination of a single normative biblical culture as the goal of biblical exegesis or as the goal of the contemporary

19. For just one example of a standard, widely used evangelical textbook that makes reference to the timelessness of certain texts of Scripture (or even of principles derived by interpreters as timeless), see J. Scott Duvall and J. Daniel Hays, *Grasping God's Word: A Hand's On Approach to Reading, Interpreting, and Applying the Bible*, 3rd ed. (Grand Rapids: Zondervan, 2012), 45, 200, 238, 262, 313, 316, 351, 356, 365, 390.

20. Lonergan affirms the theological diversity of Scripture, referring to the work of Albert Deschamps, in *Method in Theology*, 161.

21. Though I think Tanner is largely correct in her articulation of the problematics of the cultural historicity of Christian life and thought, she could be read as presenting the dissemination of a single Christian culture as the goal of Christian thought and praxis. She writes, for instance, "What brings Christians together . . . across the wide array of times and places covered by Christian cultural forms, is their common concern to figure this all out. Christian culture amounts to a joint project of making something out of the rather underdeveloped and quite disparate cultural materials that all their lives revolve around. The unity of Christian culture is sustained by a continuity of fellowship, by a willingness, displayed across differences of time and place, to admonish, learn from, and be corrected by all persons similarly concerned about the true character of Christian living." Kathryn Tanner, "Cultural Theory," in *The Oxford Handbook of Systematic Theology*, ed. John Webster, Kathryn Tanner, and Iain Torrance (New York: Oxford University, 2007), 527–542, here 540. An approach informed by Lonergan's work, and Doran's, would allow that the "common concern to figure this all out," and the "joint project of making something out of the rather underdeveloped and quite disparate cultural materials," would result in a plurality of relatively authentic cultural, personal, and religious achievements of Christian communities.

application of Scripture. Despite the cultural plurality of Scripture, however, it is still possible to receive it as authoritative and unified in its purposes. Doing so, however, requires construing its authority in a non-classicist way.

Scripture as Culture: Or Scripture in the Dialectics of History

In the previous section I gestured towards a differentiated way of considering the relationships between 1) social arrangements, 2) specific cultural meanings and values, and 3) human persons in their concrete self-transcendence. The social, cultural, and personal, however, are also situated in relationship to vitality and the religious. The vital needs of human persons and communities must be met for social orders to function in the first place. Moreover, Christians have affirmed that God has entered into our situation, transforming persons, cultures, and societies from above downwards. Lonergan accounts for such differentiations and relations in his scale of values:

> We may distinguish vital, social, cultural, personal, and religious values in an ascending order. Vital values, such as health and strength, grace and vigor, normally are preferred to avoiding the work, privations, pains involved in acquiring, maintaining, restoring them. Social values, such as the good of order which conditions the vital values of the whole community, have to be preferred to the vital values of individual members of the community. Cultural values do not exist without the underpinning of vital and social values, but nonetheless they rank higher. Not on bread alone doth man live. Over and above mere living and operating, men have to find a meaning and value in their living and operating. It is the function of culture to discover, express, validate, criticize, correct, develop, improve such meaning and value. Personal value is the person in his self-transcendence, as loving and being loved, as originator of values in himself and in his milieu, as an inspiration and invitation to others to do likewise. Religious values, finally, are at the heart of the meaning and value of man's living and man's world.[22]

The differing levels of values are hierarchically arranged, with the recurrence of values at lower levels conditioning the probable emergence of values at higher levels. For instance, communities must have food, shelter, and

22. Lonergan, *Method in Theology*, 32–33.

security (vital values) for stable social arrangements. In turn, stable social arrangements condition the probability of cultural achievements in the production and promotion of meaning and values (cultural values). The inculturation or education of persons through actual cultural achievements is a means of self-discovery and authentic human living (personal values). Moreover, persons are created to "search for God and perhaps grope for him and find him" (Acts 17.27). That natural desire for God, though, is seldom followed well by actual persons. Christians have traditionally held that its fulfillment can only come about through the work of God.[23] From above downwards, higher values transform realities at the lower levels of values. The love of God that is Godself (religious values) floods the hearts of persons (Rom 5.5) transforming them to live, decide, judge, understand, and attend to reality (personal values). In turn, they become producers of meaning and value (cultural values), and those authentic meanings and values transform social situations for the better (social values), with the *telos* of a more just and equitable distribution of the vital goods necessary for the survival, and thriving, of humanity (vital values).[24]

In *Theology and the Dialectics of History*, Robert M. Doran has provided a rich elaboration of the historical dynamism of Lonergan's scale of values. Doran identifies the specific dynamics at the levels of personal, social, and cultural levels, and argues that specific dialectics, or tensions, constitute those dynamics.[25] The dynamics and dialectics provide a heuristic for understanding the actual changes of progress, decline, and redemption in history. Doran reiterates two dialectics already identified by Lonergan. The first is a dialectic in communities between practical intelligence and spontaneous intersubjectivity. The second is a personal dialectic between the way our consciousness exercises censorship because of its dramatic formation and "the neural demands that would reach a conscious integration in image and affect."[26]

---

23. For a recent explanation of the natural desire to see God and the concrete human experiences of createdness and redemption, see Randall S. Rosenberg, *The Givenness of Desire: Concrete Subjectivity and the Natural Desire to See God* (Toronto: University of Toronto Press, 2017) and the literature cited therein.

24. See the left side of figure 1: "The Scale of Values." I am grateful to Jeremy Blackwood and Jonathan Bernier for providing helpful feedback on this diagram.

25. See Doran, *Theology and the Dialectics of History*, 93–107 and passim.

26. Doran, *What is Systematic Theology?* 170. I will not spend extensive time reflecting on either of these dialectics, but work remains to be done on both 1.) the instrumental value of Scripture for facilitating psychic conversion and 2.) on the ways that engagement with Scripture serves as a transformative impetus influencing both spontaneous intersubjectivity and practical intelligence. My focus for now is on the place of Scripture in culture, and so the rest of this essay will focus on the place of Scripture in the dialectic of culture.

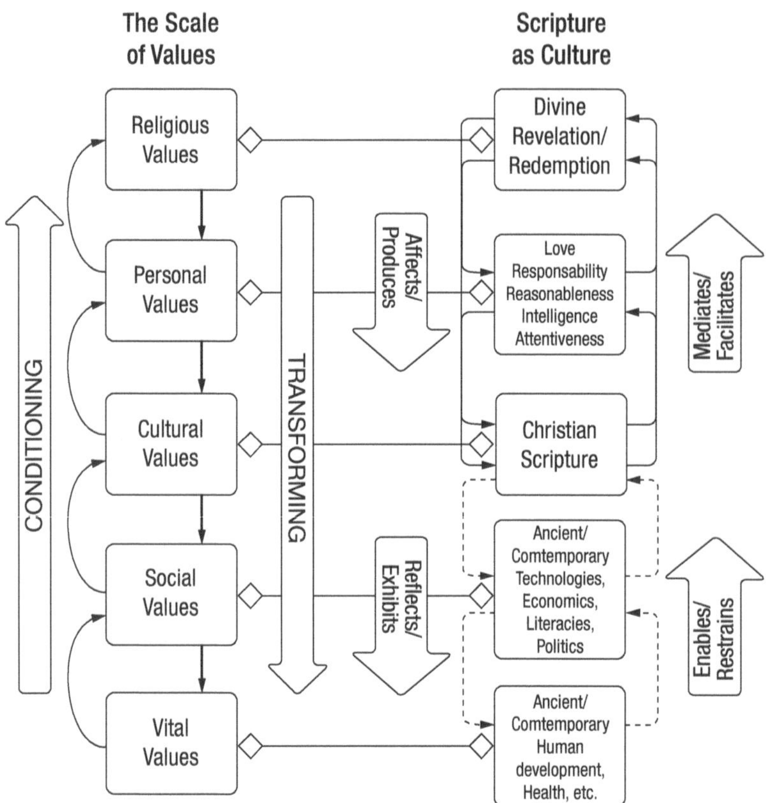

Figure 1: The Scale of Values and Scripture as Culture

Doran adds a third dialectic to those identified by Lonergan. Drawing on the work of Eric Voegelin, he articulates a dialectic at the level of culture, or human meanings and values, between cosmologically constitutive meanings and anthropologically constitutive meanings.[27] Cosmologically constitutive meanings take notice of, and defer to, the constraint and harmony of the rhythms and orders of the cosmos: of seasons, days, and lives as the measure of human living. Many human cultures have measured human persons and human communities primarily against these given rhythms, and have promoted the pursuit of harmony with such orders to be the apex of human living.[28]

27. Doran, *Theology and the Dialectics of History*, 474–558.

28. While such emphases are perhaps more common in premodern and non-western cultures, they are not absent from the modern world. For one example, see the rich literary oeuvre of Wendell Berry. The work of the Ecology wing of the IIMIT is emphasizing the need for persons, communities, and cultures to recognize the limitations of human reach and so has a stake.

Anthropologically constitutive meanings instead take notice of the virtually infinite reach of the human soul. Human persons and human communities, in the reach of their self-transcendence, actually measure the non-human world, human societies, and human cultures through our practices of understanding, judgment, and decision. These two approaches to meaning reflect a human tension between limitation (cosmological) and transcendence (anthropological) at the level of culture.

The tension between these approaches must be maintained if persons and communities are to be authentic. In order to be what we are created to be, we must both recognize and commit ourselves to the full reach of our self-transcendence, intellectual, moral, and religious. The cultural products of anthropological and cosmological constitutive meaning display the truth that human persons are experiencers, understanders, judgers, and deciders (personal values). We must nevertheless remember that we are dust, and to dust we will return. Concrete communities and cultures have seldom held these realities of the human condition in their appropriate tension, and so we have lived and decided inauthentically. We have often not respected our limitations, and we have often refused the reach of our built-in orientation to God. "Both cosmological and anthropological constitutive meaning," Doran writes,

> Stand in need of the soteriological higher synthesis that would integrate one with the other; and this is so because the psyche without direction from the spirit and the spirit without a base in the psyche are the two features of the constant and permanent structure of the human that stand in need of redemption.[29]

In the concrete, human persons and communities have refused the limitations and exigencies of our humanity; such a refusal manifests our moral impotence. We need divine help to heal the damage such sinful refusals have wrought. Christian faith holds that God has offered, and continues to offer, such help. The God who has created us has sent his Son into our situation, and has poured out his Spirit on all flesh, revealing and facilitating our redemption, and in that process, revealing Godself. It remains to detail the place of Christian Scripture in such dialectics and dynamics.

Certain developments in vital and social values set the conditions, or create the possibilities, for the writing, redaction, canonization, and transmission of Scripture, but it is primarily to be located at the level of cultural values (see the right side of figure 1: "Scripture as Culture").[30] As cultural,

29. Doran, *Theology and the Dialectics of History*, 510.

30. I will not discuss the ways in which ancient and contemporary social arrangements constrain and enable the creation and maintenance of Scripture any further in this essay, but

Christian Scripture reflects the transience, permeability, development, and decline characteristic of human meaning-making. It bears witness to the historicity of human meaning. As a human artifact, Christian Scripture unsurprisingly reflects the aforementioned tensions between limitation and transcendence. Scripture bears witness to the two poles of cosmologically and anthropologically constitutive meaning. The teachings of Qoheleth in Ecclesiastes represent a paradigmatic scriptural example of cosmologically constitutive meaning. As Qoheleth states, "for everything there is a season, and a time for every matter under heaven. A time to be born, and a time to die; . . ." (See Eccl 3.1–8; see also Gen 2.19). Paradigmatic examples of anthropologically constitutive meaning in Scripture occur in the creation narratives of Genesis 1–3, where humanity is created in the image and likeness of God and is given the task of stewarding the created world (Gen 1.26) and naming the animals (Gen 2.19). In bearing witness to human self-transcendence and limitation, Christian Scripture has stood the test of time as a preeminent cultural achievement, or "classic," that is "assumed to disclose permanent possibilities of meaning and truth."[31] Christians have historically received Christian Scripture as mediating more than merely human meanings. In the included figure, I have located it in human culture and have diagrammed its relationships to vital, social, personal, and religious values. Christians have received it as having been produced by, and mediating, not only human authenticity, but also divine revelation. In the next section of this essay, I will explain the place of engagement with Scripture in cultural values, but before I do so it is necessary to say more about its relationships to personal and religious values.

As a human activity, Christian Scripture reflects the decisions, judgments, understandings, and sensations of its authors, redactors, and communities of reception (personal values). Those judgments are all historically-located and historically-conditioned, and so none can be understood as "timeless" in any unqualified way. While Christian Scripture does reflect the historicity of human culture, Christians have held that it *is able* to *usefully* (τὰ

it is important to acknowledge, and not take for granted, the historical contingencies of Scripture on such social circumstances. For more on the material history of Christian Scripture, with some reflections on the social and vital conditions of its production and transmission, see Gordon, *Divine Scripture in Human Understanding*, 167–209.

31. David Tracy, *The Analogical Imagination: Christian Theology and the Culture of Pluralism* (New York: Crossroad Publishing, 1981), 68. For helpful discussion of Tracy's notion of the classic, and his later references instead to "fragments," see Stephen Okey, *A Theology of Conversation: An Introduction to David Tracy* (Collegeville: Liturgical Press, 2018), 76–97.

δυνάμενά and ὠφέλιμος, see 2 Tim 3.15–16) testify—prophetically and apostolically—to Jesus Christ, the fullness of God's self-revelation in history.[32] Among its meanings are the judgment that "with all wisdom and insight [God] has made known to us the mystery of his will, according to his good pleasure that he set forth in Christ, as a plan for the fullness of time, to gather up all things in him, things in haven and things on earth" (Eph 1.10). Scripture is the privileged linguistic instrument which mediates the testimony of the prophets and apostles to the divine and human meaning of Jesus Christ, the Son of God incarnate, born of a virgin, who preached and enacted the reign of God, who was crucified under Pontius Pilate, died, appeared to his disciples, and ascended to the right hand of the Father.[33] Among the values of Scripture are the beatitudes (Matt 5.1–12), the fruit of the Spirit (Gal 5.22–23), and the commands ultimately to love God, self, neighbor, and even enemy (see Deut 6.5; Lev. 19.18; Matt 5.43–48, 22.37–40; Rom 12.9–21; 1 Pet 3.9–12). As inspired by the Holy Spirit, Scripture is eminently and divinely useful for inculcating such values in its readers and hearers. These meanings and values have their place alongside many others in Scripture, but it is possible to set them as the terminal goals of Christian Scriptural interpretation.

The approach I have outlined above I have elaborated elsewhere, and so I will not dwell on it longer in this essay except to express it briefly in five theses:

1. All of Christian Scripture is instrumental to the message of God's work of reconciling all things in Christ (Eph 1.8–10).[34]
2. Christian Scripture *is* the history of Christian Scripture.[35]
3. The message of God's reconciling work in history is instrumental to the reality, or actuality, of that work itself.[36]
4. The message *is* the history of actual developments in understanding and expression of the reality of God's reconciling work.[37]

32. On the usefulness of Scripture for such purposes, see Gordon, *Divine Scripture in Human Understanding*, 248–260.

33. For a much fuller articulation of this position, see Gordon, *Divine Scripture in Human Understanding*, 228–247.

34. See Gordon, *Divine Scripture in Human Understanding*, 69–112.

35. See Gordon, *Divine Scripture in Human Understanding*, 167–209.

36. See Gordon, *Divine Scripture in Human Understanding*, 69–112.

37. See Gordon, *Divine Scripture in Human Understanding*, 33–67, 69–112.

5. Human beings produced and subsequently engage the texts of Scripture, in distinct historic cultures, under the conditions of finitude, fallibility, fallenness, self-transcendence, and redemption.[38]

Within this perspective, we could conceive of the normativity of Scriptural engagement not in its producing a specific static product—such as the one true biblical culture/"what the Bible says"/etc.—but instead in its production of fruit which demonstrate that its subjects are abiding in the true vine (John 15).[39] Such fruit represents what Lonergan calls personal values, and in the limit, religious values. If revelation is understood, with Lonergan, as the entry of divine meaning into history/culture most fully in the interpersonal, dramatic, symbolic, linguistic, and incarnate meaning of Jesus Christ, then the *telos* of fully theological engagement with Scripture is not the discovery or dissemination of a normative static biblical culture but instead the transformation of its individual and communal readers so that they understand and participate in that revelatory, saving work through the Holy Spirit. The goal of engagement with scripture is to have the mind of Christ and so to grow in the love of God, neighbors, and even enemies in greater and greater degrees. Such an approach fruitfully marries the premodern Christian judgment that Scripture is divine pedagogy with the modern/postmodern recognition of the historicity of culture.[40] Having explored the dynamic nature of Scripture as culture, dependent upon and reflecting vital and social realities, but also being produced through and mediating divine revelation and human self-transcendence, it remains for us to explore briefly the place of Scripture in the dialectic of culture itself.

Scripture and Culture: On the Exigencies and Norms of Interpretation and Application

Despite its fascinating and messy material history, contemporary religious readers and hearers, professional exegetes, and theologians receive Christian Scripture as a relatively fixed whole.[41] Nevertheless, and notwithstanding the protests of biblicists, unmediated access to "what the Bible

38. See Gordon, *Divine Scripture in Human Understanding*, 113–166.

39. For the problems with referring to "what the Bible says" see *Divine Scripture in Human Understanding*, 27–31.

40. See Gordon, *Divine Scripture in Human Understanding*, 115–122, 248–251.

41. See Gordon, *Divine Scripture in Human Understanding*, 223.

says," is neither possible nor desirable.[42] No one merely repeats the text as it is "already-out-there-now." All readings, interpretations, and applications are historical, selective, and constructive. Christian Scripture, once determined and produced, seems inevitably to produce scriptural culture.[43] Despite unfavorable social circumstances prior to the legalization of Christianity, it did not take long in Christian history for biblical commentary to emerge and flourish as a new literary genre.[44] The exegetical choices of ancient Christians evident in the development of lectionaries, in preaching, in catechesis, in artistic creation, and even in more "spontaneous" private and communal reading and use in recent times are no less creative than the composition of commentaries. Every Christian throughout Christian history picks and chooses what to emphasize, elaborate, dismiss, elevate, explain, and ignore in Scripture. The question is not whether interpretation and application and their products should continue. We should instead seek to determine the norms for the production of authentic scriptural culture in exegetical work, commentaries, preaching, lectionaries, catechesis, education, preaching, and art. Scripture (as culture) begets culture, but not all culture is equally beneficial or good.

In *Divine Scripture in Human Understanding*, I have argued that the norms of Scriptural interpretation and use are the same subjective norms of human nature—attentiveness, intelligence, reasonableness, responsibility, and love. Interpretations are authentic when they reflect and promote those human, and in the case of love, divine, values. I conclude this essay with some more specific suggestions for evaluating the various cultural products of engagement with Scripture. Instead of producing a single, static, normative biblical culture, engagement with Scripture has produced a plurality of cultural achievements. Future engagement with Scripture, whether scholarly, religious, or otherwise, should produce a plurality of relatively authentic cultural products. Such cultural products should reflect both the

42. On biblicism, see Christian Smith, *The Bible Made Impossible: Why Biblicism is not a Truly Evangelical Reading of Scripture* (Grand Rapids: Brazos Press, 2012). See also Gordon, *Divine Scripture in Human Understanding*, 27–31.

43. By this I mean that Christian communities that possess Scripture inevitably produce varied interpretive scriptural products, including commentaries, sermons, liturgies, litanies, and works of art. For accounts of such cultural productivity, see for example, Guy G. Stroumsa, *The Scriptural Universe of Ancient Christianity* (Cambridge: Harvard, 2016), Frances M. Young, *Biblical Exegesis and the Formation of Christian Culture* (Peabody: Hendrickson, 1997), David Lyle Jeffrey, *In the Beauty of Holiness: Art and the Bible in Western Culture* (Grand Rapids: Eerdmans, 2017), David Lyle Jeffrey, *People of the Book: Christian Identity and Literary Culture* (Grand Rapids, Eerdmans, 1996).

44. See Young, *Biblical Exegesis* and Stroumsa, *The Scriptural Universe.*

intrinsic cosmological limitations of human experience and human being in the world, and the lofty reach of human self-transcendence. Such products should hold the dialectic between cosmological and anthropological meaning(s) in tension, taking care not to overemphasize either side.

In volume one of *The Trinity in History: Missions and Processions*, Robert Doran identifies a heuristic in Lonergan's later work that I also find useful for evaluating historic productions of scriptural culture. Doran points readers to a posthumously published paper of Lonergan's, "Sacralization and Secularization," to ask "*which historical arrangements in human affairs* should be sacralized, and which desacralized; which should be secularized, and which desecularized?"[45] While the language of his question indicates that Doran has social arrangements in view, the same question can be asked with respect to the production of cultural artifacts which are interpretations of Christian Scripture. Which interpretive products of engagement with Scripture are sacralizations to be approved, and which ought to be rejected? Which secularizations ought to be approved, and which rejected?

Readers will have recognized that I have identified specific biblical meanings and values to promote as the divine intentions of Christian Scripture. It is easy to argue that the meanings and values I have chosen are sufficiently "biblical." They are judgments which the language of Scripture mediates. However, there are plenty of other biblical meanings and values in the variegated cultural historicity of Scripture that I have not emphasized. I hold as a matter of commitment and conviction that the meaning or message of Christian Scripture is as follows: God is reconciling all things in Christ through the outpouring of his Spirit on all people. Scripture is intended by God to mediate that meaning. I have identified the biblical values of the beatitudes, the fruit of the Spirit, and the commands to love God, self, neighbor, and enemies as the values of Scripture that Christian Scripture is intended to mediate. All theological and religious approaches which take analogous approaches to the meanings, values, and intentions of Scripture are sacralizations to be fostered. Such sacralizations promote the

45. Doran, *The Trinity in History, Volume 1: Missions and Processions*, 228. The promotion of authentic sacralizations and secularizations resonates with Ben F. Meyer's call for the development of a hermeneutical approach to Scripture which instantiates the ideals of both ancient Alexandria and ancient Antioch. "The most pressing exigence in biblical hermeneutics today is for a critical synthesis of Antioch and Alexandria, i.e.," he writes, "for the projecting of horizons at once fully differentiated by a historical consciousness and fully open to the transcendent mystery of salvation." Ben F. Meyer, *Critical Realism and the New Testament* (Eugene: Pickwick, 1989), 33.

just and mysterious law of the cross, the redemptive way of Jesus Christ, the Son of God incarnate, which returns good for evil.[46]

The history of Christian use of Scripture, however, is marked by the theological and religious employment of Scripture in the service of both the meanings and values I have identified above *and* in the service of moral atrocities.[47] The latter are sacralizations to be denounced and dropped. "Setting the standard of sacralizations to be dropped . . . ," Doran writes, "are any and all attempts to employ the name or word of God or any other sacral trappings to justify not only natural evils but also persecution, exclusion, and scapegoating both of carriers of the genuine religious word and, given the character of that word itself, of anyone else."[48] The violence recorded in Scripture itself, and literalistic readings of the "disturbing divine behavior" of the God of Scripture, have proven eminently useful to those seeking to justify moral atrocities with divine authority.[49] Christian readers must repent of such readings and must instead find intelligible, reasonable, responsible, and loving ways to read such texts. The movement afoot to recover a distinctly theological hermeneutic for reading Christian Scripture must discern, and authentically judge, between sacralizations to be promoted and sacralizations to be rejected.[50]

Finally, I conclude with proposals regarding secularizations to be promoted and secularizations to be rejected with respect to the production of scriptural culture. Historical-critical work, or, "the attempt to understand by the use of all available critical tools what the biblical author wished to convey to the original audience for which he wrote," manifests the incredible

46. On "the law of the cross," see Bernard Lonergan, *The Redemption*, Collected Works of Bernard Lonergan 9, eds. Robert M. Doran, H. Daniel Monsour, and Jeremy D. Wilkins, trans. Michael Shields (Toronto: University of Toronto Press, 2018), 197–264; Doran, *Theology and the Dialectics of History*, 113–114, 203–206; Doran, *The Trinity in History, Volume 1: Missions and Processions*, 228–240; Doran, *The Trinity in History, Volume 2: Missions, Relations, and Persons*, 38–42.

47. See Eric Seibert, *The Violence of Scripture: Overcoming the Old Testament's Troubling Legacy* (Minneapolis: Fortress Press, 2012). Seibert's work draws heavily from the wells of many recent contextual and liberationist studies. Seibert details the ways Scripture has been used to justify chattel slavery, the dehumanization of women, anti-Judaism and anti-Semitism, racisms and nationalism, and violence against LGBTQI peoples.

48. Doran, *The Trinity in History, Volume 1: Missions and Processions*, 228.

49. See Eric Seibert, *Disturbing Divine Behavior: Troubling Old Testament Images of God* (Minneapolis: Fortress Press, 2009).

50. On theological interpretation, see Joseph K. Gordon, "On the (Relative) Authenticity of Theological Interpretation of Scripture," *Lonergan Review* 9, no. 1 (2018): 78–102, and the literature cited therein.

reach of human attentiveness, intelligence, reasonableness, and responsibility with respect to the historicity of Scripture.[51] As I have noted above, the plurivocity and particularity of Scripture are now largely taken for granted thanks to the gargantuan efforts of historical critics. To the extent that historical-critical scholars promote such attentiveness, intelligence, reasonableness, and responsibility, their work is a secularization to be fostered.[52] The work of measuring up to the diverse particularity of Christian Scripture demands an unapologetic, ongoing commitment to raising and answering historical, sociological, anthropological, and ethical questions of the texts of Scripture boldly.

Such historical-critical work, though, has not been practiced in ideologically or theologically neutral ways. While premodern Christians practiced a religious, or scriptural Bible, developments since the Enlightenment have resulted in the cultural creation of an academic Bible.[53] The community devoted to the academic Bible, through the work of its scholarship, has erected "an impenetrable wall between systematic theology and its historical religious sources."[54] Historical critics have often rightly criticized superficial and ideologically violent employments of Scripture by less-educated but religiously committed interpreters. Such criticism is sometimes exercised from positions of incomplete personal development.[55] Secularism, naturalism, positivism, and liberalism have served as the philosophical and (anti)-theological grounds for such critiques. But such positions, despite their relative authenticity, refuse what would be necessary to meet the self-transcendent exigencies of human nature, and so are a truncation of personal values. As Doran writes, "welcoming genuine secularization will entail resisting secularism; for genuine secularization is the fruit of attentiveness, intelligence, reasonableness, and responsibility, while secularism

---

51. The definition comes from Karl Paul Donfried, *Who Owns the Bible? Toward the Recovery of a Christian Hermeneutic* (New York: Crossroad, 2006), 14.

52. For three recent defenses of historical-critical work that repay careful study, see John C. Collins, *The Bible after Babel: Historical Criticism in a Post-Modern Age* (Grand Rapids: Eerdmans, 2005); Joseph A. Fitzmyer, *The Interpretation of Scripture: In Defense of the Historical-Critical Method* (Mauwah: Paulist Press, 2008); and Roy A. Harrisville, *Pandora's Box Opened: An Examination and Defense of Historical-Critical Method and Its Master Practicioners* (Grand Rapids: Eerdmans, 2014).

53. On the academic Bible and the scriptural Bible, see Michael Legaspi, *The Death of Scripture and the Rise of Biblical Studies* (New York: Oxford University Press, 2010).

54. Lonergan, *Method in Theology*, 258.

55. Some readers may think this claim is not easily defensible. I only mean that historical-critics, like all persons, are not invincibly attentive, intelligent, reasonable, and responsible.

depends on neglecting or denying the finality, the upwardly determinately directly dynamism, of authentic intentionality."[56]

Attentive, intelligent, reasonable, and responsible engagement with Scripture recognizes that the texts are not merely culturally diverse, but that it is possible to understand and relate the various cultural (and religious) perspectives of the authors of Scripture genetically and dialectically. Such engagement can result in the judgment that revelation is progressive in Scripture and that it culminates in the meaning of Jesus Christ, and in the value of adhering to the kingdom of God that he preached, practiced, and enacted in his life, death, resurrection, and ascension.[57] That engagement with scripture has produced such fruit in the lives of the saints is undisputable.[58] Even so, it has proven equally useful as an instrument of selfishness and evil.[59] Christian engagement with Scripture will only reach the truth, then, if its subjects are authentic. This applies Lonergan's general axiom that "genuine objectivity is the fruit of authentic subjectivity" to all of the specific acts—including reading, hearing, meditating upon, teaching, preaching, liturgically using, theologizing, investigating, questioning, wondering about, imagining, and any others—encompassing Christian engagement with Scripture.[60] This authenticity requires us to recognize the cultural historicity of Scripture; in the providence of the Triune God, at this time in history we must recognize the folly of a classicist notion of culture. Scripture neither reflects, nor is intended to produce, a singular normative culture, theology, or worldview. Authenticity requires more than this, however, because the ultimate goal of engagement with Scripture, as Augustine rightly states, is to increase our love of God and neighbor (see *De doc. Chr.* I.36.40). The *telos* of this authenticity is in supernatural faith, hope, and love, but it has as its personal conditions of possibility the attentiveness in experience, intelligence in understanding, reasonableness in judgment, responsibility in decision, and love in being and action of its hearers, readers, interpreters, exegetes, stewards, and ministers. Against such things there is no law.

---

56. Doran, *The Trinity in History, Volume 2: Missions, Persons, and Relations*, 38.

57. On revelation as progressive in Scripture, see Gordon, *Divine Scripture in Human Understanding*, 230–231, 235; Doran, *The Trinity in History, Volume 2: Missions, Persons, Relations*, 39.

58. For examples, see C. Clifton Black, ed., *Reading Scripture with the Saints* (Eugene, OR: Pickwick, 2014).

59. For some significant examples, see Jim Hill and Randy Cheadle, *The Bible Tells Me So: Uses and Abuses of Holy Scripture* (New York: Anchor Books/Doubleday, 1996); Seibert, *The Violence of Scripture.*

60. See Lonergan, *Method in Theology*, 292.

The approach to Scripture in the dialectic of culture articulated in this essay is certainly open to further specifications. From these initial reflections, though, it is clear that Robert Doran's work on anthropological and cosmological meaning and their soteriological integration through obedience to the law of the cross, and his astute interpretation and employment of Lonergan's work on the scale of values and secularizations and sacralizations to be dropped and advanced, provide fecund resources for "redraw[ing] the map" of theological reflection, locating Scripture and scriptural interpretation clearly in the redemptive work of God in history and in the dynamics of human culture.[61]

61. See Robert M. Doran, "The International Institute for Method in Theology: A Vision," 25.

CHAPTER EIGHT

SYSTEMS AND SEQUENCES

The Renewal of Theological Understanding and the Problem of Speculative Pluralism

Ryan Hemmer

Academic Marketing Specialist, Fortress Press

Introduction

Theologians working in the tradition of Bernard Lonergan have grown accustomed to waiting. We have been doing so for a long time and for many things: waiting for Lonergan's Latin textbooks on trinitarian theology, Christology, and grace to be made available in a critical and accessible form; waiting for departments of theology to recognize the importance of Lonergan to the ongoing labor of theological education; waiting for the climate of theological opinion to shift away from its fifty-year aversion to systematic theology; and waiting for a Lonerganian theologian to move beyond the mediating phase of recovering Lonergan's thought and into the mediated phase of doing systematic theology in the first person. Apart from rumors, whispers, and a few notable and noble efforts, waiting for a Lonergan moment in systematic theology has seemed like waiting for Godot (or maybe even Guffman).

But Godot has suddenly, if tardily appeared. The Collected Works of Bernard Lonergan have been completed after thirty years of painstaking effort. New initiatives (and renewed interest in old ones) with Lonergan's work at their center have been started at a diverse array of institutions—from universities and seminaries to pontifical colleges and nursing schools. Major new and ambitious works of explicitly systematic theology have been published and have commanded the attention of the whole theological guild—proving that theology can be more than well-intentioned but amateur efforts at philosophical hermeneutics and critical history.[1] And after decades spent laying the groundwork, Robert Doran has at last begun bringing his systematic theology of the divine missions into print. What the first two volumes of *The Trinity in History* make clear is that while their appearance in Doran's corpus is late, they depend upon and complete ideas that have their origins not only as far back as *Theology and the Dialectics of History*, but indeed, *Subject and Psyche*. They could not have been written any earlier than they were.[2]

But if one follows Doran's paper trail from *Subject and Psyche* to *Trinity in History*, I would suggest that no single text is as illuminating of the whole trajectory as *What is Systematic Theology?* There, Doran indicates the broad outlines and basic anticipations of what a methodical systematic theology would be, and argues that any such theology, even if it effects a synthetic grasp of the whole *nexus mysteriorum*, will be no more than an episode in a cumulative, progressive, open-ended, and collaborative human drama. A fully methodical systematic theology, Doran argues, will be "an ongoing succession of systems genetically related to one another."[3] This successive scheme results in a diachronic theological pluralism, wherein rather than an enduring synthesis, one has an integral plurality, with each successive systematic articulation of the mysteries of faith effecting an intellectual mediation between the Christian religion and its cultural matrix.

In this essay, I will complexify and complement Doran's account of the theology of theologies by showing that his and Lonergan's fundamental position on post-classicist systematic theology entails not only a diachronic pluralism that attaches to the succession or sequencing of systems, but also a synchronic pluralism that results from discrete but contemporaneous

---

1. See especially Sarah Coakley, *God, Sexuality, and the Self: An Essay 'On the Trinity'* (Cambridge: Cambridge University Press, 2013); Katherine Sonderegger, *Systematic Theology, Volume 1, The Doctrine of God* (Minneapolis: Fortress Press, 2015); Katherine Sonderegger, *Systematic Theology, Volume 2, The Doctrine of the Holy Trinity: Processions and Persons* (Minneapolis: Fortress Press, 2020).

2. Robert M. Doran, *Subject and Psyche, Second Edition* (Milwaukee, WI: Marquette University Press, 1994); Robert M. Doran, *Theology and the Dialectics of History* (Toronto: University of Toronto Press, 1990); Robert M. Doran, *The Trinity in History: A Theology of the Divine Missions, Volume One: Missions and Processions* (Toronto: University of Toronto Press, 2012; Robert M. Doran, *The Trinity in History: A Theology of the Divine Missions, Volume Two: Missions, Relations, and Persons* (Toronto: University of Toronto Press, 2019.

3. Robert M. Doran, *What Is Systematic Theology?* (Toronto: University of Toronto Press, 2005), 89.

cultural matrices, each with distinct contexts, situations, and questions that lead to distinct realizations of the systematic exigence, and thus to distinct speculative interventions. Like the diachronic pluralism that Doran outlines, synchronic pluralism invites an authentic, integral relationship among its systems to the extent that those systems and the minds behind them advert to the invariable foundations of human intellectual, moral, and religious dynamism. In what follows, I will indicate the basic features of the theology of theologies as Doran conceives of them, explain how those same features entail a synchronic theological pluralism, and sketch out the main heuristic elements of a methodical speculative pluralism that organizes the data on synchronic theological multiplicity, diagnoses the specific relations between and among the terms of that multiplicity, and dialectically advances positional relations while reversing counter-positional ones.

The Theology of Theologies

As early as his investigations of the development of the doctrines of grace and freedom in the writings of Thomas Aquinas, Lonergan possessed a sharp analytic distinction between the doctrinal context of Catholic belief and its speculative apparatus. By the time of *Method in Theology* (though the basic position is evident much earlier), Lonergan had worked out the functional structure of this distinction, grounding it in the relations that obtain between conscious acts and the dynamic operators of consciousness that drive the subject from one operation to another. Lonergan referred to affirmative judgments by which one says, with the Church, "yes" to this or that matter of belief as "doctrines." He termed the consequent intellectual pursuit of the analogical intelligibility of doctrines as "systematics." The operator that moves the subject along from the rational act of judgment to the intellectual act of understanding is the same spiritual dynamism to which the schoolmen referred when speaking of *fides quaerens intellectum*.

The stability of this distinction in Lonergan's thought, unbuffeted by the many shifts and breakthroughs he underwent in different phases of his career, is remarkable. And yet, while Lonergan's understanding of faith and his phenomenological, intentional theory of *intelligere* are firm fixtures of his thought, his notion of theology changed with two, roughly simultaneous breakthroughs. While the exact order is somewhat ambiguous even in Lonergan's own recounting, it is clear from the material history of his writings that by 1965, Lonergan had worked out the structure of functional collaboration that was to be the central heuristic of *Method in Theology*, and he had abandoned the classicist theory of culture and embraced an empirical one.[4] And though this shift has far-reaching consequences for the relationship between doctrines and systematics, those consequences are not fully articulated within the text of *Method in Theology*. Doran's self-assigned task in *What Is Systematic Theology?* is this fuller articulation. According to Doran, a methodical systematic theology, a theology at the level of our time, places upon the theologian and the theological community three distinct but related demands, each of which concerns one or another element of theological pluralism.

First, Doran argues, theologians must lay bare the structured cognitional and existential ground for the anticipation of "an ongoing genetic sequence of interrelated systematic positions."[5] The foundation for this anticipation is the "*inevitable pragmatic engagement* in certain operations and certain states or dispositions, along with the discovery that there are *norms* for authentic performance of the relevant operations, and *criteria* for discerning authentic and inauthentic states and dispositions."[6] And while these operations and states are activated in and by the theologian anytime his or her mind is engaged in theologizing, there is a difference between the exercise of an operation and the signification that comes with explicit advertence and thematization. A methodical anticipation of the genetic sequence of systems adds this *signato* to the *exercito*, and in so doing, "provides an ever-developing account of the source" of systematic sequencing; namely, the theologian as subject. As the theological subject enquires into the possible intelligibility of Christian constitutive meaning, the understandings effectuated by that inquiry enter into the historical flow of insight and the diachronic sequencing of systems. "The anticipation," writes Doran, "is one of successive systematic expressions of theological understanding, with the later building on and transposing the earlier, and with all of them building on the same engagement in the operations constitutive of cognitional, moral, religious, and affective integrity, and so of the *imago Dei* that we are."[7]

---

4. For the breakthrough to functional specialization, see Lonergan's hand-drawn chart, completed in February of 1965 (file 47200D0E060 / A472 V71 in the Lonergan Archives). While Lonergan claims to have discovered the empirical notion of culture as early as the summer of 1930 with his reading of Christopher Dawson's *The Age of the Gods*, there is little material evidence of this shift in his published writings until much later. His 1964 essay, "*Existenz* and *Aggiornamento*," (CWL 4, 222–231) telegraphs the shift, and 1965's "Dimensions of Meaning" (CWL 4, 232–245) shows it to be a fully functional theorem in Lonergan's thinking. For Lonergan's autobiographical claim regarding Dawson, see "*Insight* Revisited," CWL 13, 222.

5. Doran, *What Is Systematic Theology?*, 78.

6. Doran, *What Is Systematic Theology?*, 78–79.

7. Doran, *What Is Systematic Theology?*, 79.

Second, if a methodical theology recognizes the sequencing of systems that follows upon the ongoing, historical effort of concrete subjects to understand systematically the mysteries made known in faith, it will also anticipate the generation of a set of explanatory and dialectical perspectives on the terms generated by the sequence of systems. As explanatory, it will relate the terms of the sequence to one another. As dialectical, it will sort methodically between and among positional and counter-positional terms. This ontology of meaning will, according to Doran, be the operational instantiation of the functional specialty "dialectics," but it will, more precisely, be the dialectical operation as subordinated to the norms and goals of the functional specialty "systematics." The result will be "a systematic theology of theologies."[8]

Finally, Doran's notion of the theology of theologies anticipates the generation of theological content that would serve an integrating function for positional theologies that at present are related only coincidentally. A theology at the level of our time would demonstrate its timeliness by finding the means of integral relation between these theologies. And that theological ordering would in turn be judged according to the foundations of the theologian as subject.[9] With these three anticipations, Doran indicates the basic heuristic shape of diachronic theological pluralism. He clarifies the goal of systematic theology and shows how that goal is distinct from that of the earlier schoolmen, and how its distinctness owes to the twin breakthroughs of the methodical structure of functional collaboration and the discovery of the empirical notion of culture.

There is another entailment of these anticipations, however. At a formal level, the empirical notion of culture indicates not only that constitutive meanings and values change and multiply over time, but also that there are multiple sets of meanings and values in any age. If theology's charter is the mediation of the significance and role of religion within a cultural matrix, then that charter enlarges in a proportion correlative to the distinct sets of meanings and values to which it must mediate religion's significance. There will be no single synthetic theological mediation because that mediation's *terminus ad quem* is as numerically plural; indeed, as numerous as the stars in the sky. But the theological situation that results from the empirical notion of culture need not be one of unencumbered, relativistic, and incommensurable multiplicity. The functional structure of theology and the invariant cognitional and existential structure on which it rests provide

8. Doran, *What Is Systematic Theology?*, 80.

9. Doran, *What Is Systematic Theology?*, 82.

at least the heuristic tools for the generation of a set of perspectives on synchronic theological pluralism analogous to those Doran offers on diachronic theological pluralism. To those perspectives we now turn.

Speculative Pluralism: A Heuristic Sketch

As Lonergan argues in the opening paragraph of *Method in Theology*, a post-classicist theology mediates between a cultural matrix and the significance and role of a religion in that matrix. But because a post-classicist perspective recognizes a pluralism of cultural matrices, it must recognize, as a consequence, a synchronic pluralism of theological mediations. And if such mediations are the goal of the whole of theology, then systematic or speculative theology has the more exact task of mediating between the concrete religious, moral, and intellectual questions that occasion the speculative exigence's emergence in a particular pattern of cultural making and the transcultural permanence, validity, and personal enactments of religious doctrines.

The result will be a pluralism of speculative theologies, wherein the multiplicity of concrete cultural matrices and the various occasions of their speculative exigence demand a multiplicity of speculative mediations, within which the transcultural elements of the unified dogmatic-theological context and the normative human subject both are a bulwark against radical relativism and make possible an analogical and methodical cooperation among distinct speculative theologies. Such a speculative pluralism has four principle heuristic elements: a material element that pertains to the concrete pluralism that becomes explicit in the shift from classicism to historical mindedness; a subjective formal element that is the pluralism of theologians engaged in the enterprise of mediation between religion and their respective cultural matrices; an objective formal element that is the pluralism of understandings effected through the subjective formal acts of theologians; and a dialectical element that attempts to diagnose the complementary, genetic, contrary, and contradictory relationships between theologies with the goal of coordinating constructive collaboration among them.

The Material Element

Material pluralism is the human situation of the meaningfulness of social living as understood according to the empirical notion of culture. The concrete variety of distinct intellectual, moral, and historical contexts in various stages of development or decay, flowering or decadence, progress or decline set the conditions for distinct trajectories of speculative thought.

This pluralism has both synchronic and diachronic aspects that correlate with the spatio-geographic multiplicity of cultural matrices at a given time, and a tempo-historical multiplicity that results from the development or decline of the organizing meanings and values of particular matrices. And because development or decay both involve a change in the meanings and values (or indeed disvalues) that animate a culture's living, they also indicate a change in the moral and intellectual conditions to which a speculative theology mediates the meaningfulness of the doctrinal confessions of the Christian religion.

While many historical examples of speculative intervention pertain principally to problems in the order of understanding that vexed the medieval mind (e.g., the challenge of reconciling divine simplicity with eternal procession, or human freedom with the gratuity of divine grace), there are also speculative interventions that respond to problems in the order of understanding that result from moral disvalues in a culture and the dissonance they create for grasping the meaningfulness or value of religion. Moral disvalue can create the conditions for distinct emergences of speculative exigence, which in turn commits the resulting speculative theology to mediate the meaning and value of the self-revealing God within the circumstances of moral decay that call the significance of such a God—and even more so the community that confesses him—into question. These situations in which the social surd of objective meaninglessness and the patterned experience of oppression, subjugation, alienation, and the collective suffering they promote condition the speculative exigence no less than those formal intellectual *ambigua* that weighed upon the religious imagination of medieval schoolmen. Thus, synchronic and diachronic variances in the conditions of speculative exigence anticipate synchronic and diachronic variations of speculative understanding.

For example, M. Shawn Copeland's *Enfleshing Freedom* argues that in an American culture partially constituted by the meanings and values of white supremacy and its long history, the embodied experience of black women becomes the locus for the question of the theological understanding of human personhood as reflective of divine dignity, and of incarnation as the union of God with the human.[10] Her speculative reconstruction of

10. M. Shawn Copeland, *Enfleshing Freedom: Body, Race, and Being* (Minneapolis: Fortress Press, 2009). For an analysis of American white supremacy in terms of the empirical notion of culture, see Bryan Massingale, *Racial Justice and the Catholic Church* (Maryknoll, NY: Orbis, 2010), 13–33. Massingale's use of Lonergan, Geertz, and Copeland within his analysis of racism and Catholic social ethics illustrates well both the benefit speculative or theoretical structures can provide, and the contextual character of theoretical applications.

theological anthropology mediates the doctrinal affirmations of creation and incarnation into a cultural matrix organized around the de-humanization and abuse of black women. And while some may be tempted to classify Copeland's efforts as no more than an instance of so-called "contextual theology" at a praxiological remove from the labors of an Aquinas or a Lonergan, it is better to say that hers is a fully post-classicist speculative theology, which eschews the chasm between knowing and doing, responds to the unique ways in which the speculative exigence arises in a cultural matrix constituted by the de-humanization of black women, utilizes the symbols, images, ideas, and organizing meanings of that matrix, and makes use of theoretical technique to render visible the meaning of Christian doctrines through the icon of the experience of black women themselves.[11] And while Copeland's work exemplifies the speculative theological task of mediating the truth of Christian doctrines to the intellectual and moral horizon of a particular culture, it remains that there exists a plurality of cultures and, with it, an exigence for additional speculative mediations. And so, correlative with the material pluralism of cultural situations that follows upon the shift to historical mindedness, there is a formal pluralism that responds to that shift, both a subjective formal element that is the various theologians in their speculative operations, and an objective formal element that is the resulting plurality of speculative theologies.

The Subjective Formal Element

In *Grace and Freedom*, Lonergan elaborates his early theory of speculative form and operation. He defines speculative theology as a modality of theological practice distinct from positive and moral theology, with a unique charter and a specialized technique. By speculative form, Lonergan means a generic orientation of intellectual mentality that is ordered to the pursuit of *intellectum* from within the horizon of *fides*. But such a generic orientation only becomes actualized within specific lines of speculative inquiry that emerge from specific patterns of attention to specific problems in the order of understanding and in specific constellations of meaning and value. As a consequence, the generic form of speculation will be specified differently

11. Copeland's project extends beyond the limited tasks of speculative theology and includes those of historical reconstruction and retrieval, interpretation, dialectical critique, ethical injunction, and communications. But one should not overlook the speculative/theoretical elements and the guiding role of theory in her work out of the assumption that "contextual" or "praxis" theologies are anti-speculative.

in distinct lines of inquiry, as those inquiries interrogate distinct problems of understanding. And while those problems emerge spontaneously in the process of living, the coordination of the activities and practices that meet those problems require what Sarah Coakley calls contemplation or "an attentive openness of the whole self (intellect, will, memory, imagination, feeling, bodiliness) to the reality of God and creation."[12] Specific speculative inquiries, then, even of the most assiduously theoretical nature, emerge from concrete circumstances and respond to those circumstances through the operation of theoretical understanding.

What Thomas Kuhn notes of scientific theory is no less true of speculative theology. He writes, "An apparently arbitrary element, compounded of personal and historical accident, is always a formative ingredient of the beliefs espoused by a given scientific community at a given time."[13] Theoretical understanding, even as it abstracts from the concreteness of common sense in the pursuit of the *soli et omnia*, remains a human enterprise. And as a human enterprise, it remains tethered to the contexts of the minds engaged in the abstraction. Thus, the cultural, intellectual, moral, and religious orientations of theorizers play an essential role not only in the emergence of the speculative exigence, but also in any speculative response. A theory's mobility across the borders of contexts lies in the correspondence between the meaning expressed in the theory and the specific questions of abstractive intelligence posed from within a different context. If a concrete situation of inquiry does not lead to the formulation of the question to which a given theory purports to be an answer, then the theory itself cannot become enacted in that context until the relevant question emerges.

Such orientations, the historical accidents of concrete circumstances, belong to the ordinary constitution of the human subject and the human world. And because there exists a material plurality of such worlds, there will also exist many distinct formal species of speculative theological inquiry that respond to those circumstances by deploying the specialized mentality of theory so as to mediate an understanding of faith back to those circumstances in a way that resolves the ambiguities embedded in them. Further, because all specific speculative inquiries and their answers bear an analogical relationship to the genus of speculative form, they also obtain an analogical relationship to one another. Thus, speculative understandings

---

12. Coakley, *God, Sexuality, and the Self*, 88.

13. Thomas Kuhn, *The Structure of Scientific Revolutions, Third Edition* (Chicago: University of Chicago Press, 1996), 4.

reached in one context may prove to possess adequate mobility to be resituated within another. As analogous classes of speculative questions are asked in different ways at different times and in different places, analogous speculative theories may prove cross-cultural, cross-temporal, and cross-spatial in their significance.

The theologian as subject, in terms borrowed from Michael Novak, "is both social gift and personal achievement: dove and mountain."[14] The cultural situation of theologians is had in the givenness of their histories, but theologians as originating values also contribute to the maintenance and transformation of cultural situations themselves. A commerce obtains between the material context of a cultural matrix and the speculative insights that both arise from it and mediate new meanings and values back into it, transforming the common meanings of the cultural matrix through the process of mediation. The material element and the subjective formal element of speculative pluralism thus exercise a reciprocally conditioning influence on one another that unfolds dynamically in the process of theologizing.

The Objective Formal Element

The commerce that obtains between the material element of speculative pluralism and its subjective formal element includes the formal effects of the subjective acts. These effects are the objective speculative theological mediations between the dogmatic context of a religion and the concrete circumstances of speculative exigence within a cultural matrix. Thus, co-extensive with the subjective formal element of speculative pluralism that is the multiplicity of theological operators, there is the objective formal element that is the multiplicity of theological objects or understandings that result from the theological operations. As Elizabeth Johnson notes, "words about God are cultural creatures, entwined with the mores and adventures of the faith community that uses them. As cultures shift, so too does the specificity of God-talk."[15] Such words are cultural, but they emerge from the intellectual practices of theologians within those cultures. For example, Johnson argues, "Feminist theology results when women's faith seeks understanding in the matrix of historical struggle for life in the face of oppressive and

---

14. Michael Novak, *Ascent of the Mountain, Flight of the Dove: An Invitation to Religious Studies* (New York and London: Harper & Row, 1971), 88.

15. Elizabeth A. Johnson, *She Who Is: The Mystery of God in Feminist Theological Discourse* (New York: Crossroad, 1992), 6.

alienating forces."[16] As such, the formal functions at work in the emergence of a feminist speculative theology, then, are the same functions at work in, for example, the seven-century-long effort of western theologians to reconcile intellectually competing vectors of their Augustinian theological heritage with their own philosophical culture. In a speculative theology, one seeks "a complete vision of Christian doctrine," and such visions "have taken many forms—appropriate to the philosophical, cultural, and political ethos of their times, or sometimes in conscious reaction to the same."[17] This formal diversity, as has already been argued, includes both synchronic and diachronic forms, and as such, "One cannot therefore speak of systematic theology as a fixed or unchanging entity in Christian tradition."[18]

Furthermore, theological objects or productions that result from theological operations enter into the nexus of common meanings and values that organize cultural existence. And when they do, they can lead to transformations and reorientations of cultural circumstances themselves. As Elizabeth Johnson argues regarding the emergence of feminist symbolic speculative discourse, "The symbol of God functions. Language about God in female images not only challenges the literal mindedness that has clung to male images in inherited God talk; it not only questions their dominance in discourse about holy mystery. But insofar as 'the symbol gives rise to thought,' such speech calls into question prevailing structures of patriarchy."[19] In other words, the accumulation of new and transformational meanings and values—even those of a rigorously theoretical nature—can lead to a transformation of culture, for culture itself is but a relatively stabilized nexus of meanings and values.

Taken together, the material, subjective formal, and objective formal elements comprise a situation in which both at any given moment and across time and place, there will be not a single normative speculative theology mediating the Christian faith to a single normative culture, but rather a descriptive, empirical plurality of speculative theologians, speculative theologies, and cultural matrices. The analogical relationship between genus and species suggests a consequent analogical relationship between species themselves. Thus, one can expect a kind of "family resemblance" between distinct speculative theologians and their speculative theologies. But the

16. Johnson, *She Who Is*, 18.

17. Coakley, *God, Sexuality, and the Self*, 40.

18. Coakley, *God, Sexuality, and the Self*, 40–41.

19. Johnson, *She Who Is*, 5–6.

character of that resemblance, because it is analogical and so has difference encoded within it, invites analyses of a more dialectical character. Differences between cultures, differences between theologians, and differences between theologies may be complementary, genetic, contrary, or contradictory. And so, an adequate heuristic structure for speculative pluralism must include a dialectical element beyond these material and formal elements.

The Dialectical Element

In his 1974 essay, "Dialectic of Authority," Lonergan proposes a heuristic structure for understanding the dynamic relationship between authority, power, and legitimacy.[20] Without rehearsing his entire argument, one can say that 1) authority is legitimate power; 2) power is the result of past cooperation; 3) cooperation occurs both diachronically through time and synchronically in the here and now; 4) community carries power along through time; 5) community entrusts power to authorities; 6) the legitimacy of communal power is measured by the authenticity or inauthenticity of the meanings and values that the community holds in common; and 7) the authenticity of meanings and values is a matter of a cumulative process of communal attentiveness, intelligence, reasonableness, and responsibility. Analytically, the diagnosis of authenticity or inauthenticity is fraught and often inconclusive, but synthetically, one can judge the authenticity of authority by its fruits: collective progress indicates authenticity, while collective decline reveals inauthenticity. On its own, the dialectic of authority is a valuable tool for analyzing the state of a culture. But its invocation here is for a different purpose. The basic form of the dialectic of authority can be repurposed as a heuristic structure for understanding the dialectical element of speculative pluralism.

In the dialectic of authority, communal cooperation over time yields power, the community mediates that power as authority and entrusts it to particular authorities, and the dialectic of authenticity or inauthenticity measures the legitimacy of the meanings and values expressed in community, authorities, and those under authorities. In the case of speculative theology, communal cooperation both in and over time consists in what Lonergan calls a functionally specialized method that coordinates the efforts of theologians into a dynamic and intelligible whole of operations, relations, and effects. Embedded within and enabling that methodical

20. Lonergan, "Dialectic of Authority," *A Third Collection*, CWL 16, 3–9.

collaboration is the anterior gift of God's love and human cooperation with that love in the pursuit of theological truth. Coordinated theological collaboration is the source of theological achievements, of an ongoing series of theological judgments that populate and expand into a tradition and, with it, a dogmatic-theological context. Particular cultures carry the meaning of the tradition forward into the realm of speculative understanding. The theologian is the agent of speculative understanding, who, through his or her acts, effectuates objects or theological meanings. Culture, agent, and object form a circle of mutually conditioning relationships in which culture contextualizes the agent in communal meaning, the agent effects objects, and the objects mediate new understanding or meaning back into the common context of a culture.

The dialectic of authenticity measures the legitimacy of this ongoing process. It looks to the progress or decline of the cultural situation as an indication of the authenticity or inauthenticity of the meanings and values that constitute it. It poses itself to the agent in terms of intellectual, moral, and religious conversion, and the presence or absence of distinct differentiations of consciousness. But diagnosing the legitimacy of theological objects requires a distinct criteriological strategy. The speculative understandings that result from the speculative operation of the theologian as agent must be judged in terms of their adequacy to the horizon of meaning and value of the cultural matrix, to the interrogative determinations of the theologian's questions, and to the dogmatic-theological judgments whose meaning they are to communicate. But while the dialectic of authenticity can work out the legitimacy of a set of meanings and values in accord with an analysis of progress or decline, and it can measure the completeness or incompleteness of the theologian's act of understanding through recourse to the transcultural unity of the normative human subject, reaching a judgment about the adequacy of the achieved understanding to the revealed mystery requires a confrontation with the transcultural unity of revealed truth itself. The hypothesis pursued here is that this confrontation is best executed theorematically.

Analogous to the medieval function of theorems in which they serve to establish a framework of mental perspectives that allow relevant theological data to be distinguished from the irrelevant, investigated with rigor, and arranged in thought such that resolutions to received problems become possible, a post-classicist speculative theology invites a theorematic intervention into the dialectical multiplicity of perspectives and realized understandings. Such an intervention has two principle functions. First, it discloses the analogous congruities between complementary, genetic, and contrary theologies. Second, it aids in identifying contradictory viewpoints, and exercises a criteriological operation whereby the positional element of the dialectic of contradictories is distinguished from the counter-positional element.[21] But if the perspective of speculative pluralism is truly post-classicist, and thereby rejects any source of normativity in the contents of a specific cultural matrix, where does the normativity operating in the theorems come from?

While the normativity of the formal element of speculative pluralism lies in the transcultural structure of the human subject as attentive, intelligent, reasonable, and responsible, the normativity of the dialectal theorems is secured in the dogmatic-theological context itself. Theological doctrines disclosed in the narrative universe of biblical revelation and refined through the intellectual and rhetorical process of creedal expression can also be elaborated as theorems, that is, as systematic articulations that can organize whole networks of thinking, that can take on a mobility of application, and so both direct consequent theologizing, and pass judgment on its results.

For any speculative theology, the *via analogia* will be the principle path in which theological insight travels. But speculative pluralism anticipates *viae analogiae*. Thus, a main function of the dialectical element regards discerning legitimate from illegitimate *analogiae*, coordinating the legitimate toward collaborative plurality, while unburdening that collaborative effort from the need to integrate the illegitimate. The structure of this dialectical heuristic is open-ended, and, as such, invites the development of additional theorems in the ongoing process of discernment and collaboration.

Conclusion

This essay has sought to honor Robert Doran's work not only through compliment, but also, and more importantly, through complement. His efforts

21. Lonergan's basic triplet of possible relations includes the complementary, genetic, and the dialectical. For Lonergan, the dialectical is the contradictory relationship between basic terms, as, for example, good's relationship to evil or affirmation's relationship to negation. Doran has argued, however, that there are two forms of dialectical relationship, a dialectic of contradictories as articulated by Lonergan, and a further dialectic of contraries, wherein the basic terms remain linked, but opposed principle of change, but can be held in creative tension with one another. Such a dialect would include, for example, the relationship of limitation and transcendence. They are not contradictory opposites like good and evil, but they also are not straightforwardly complementary. Thus, an integral dialectic of contraries maintains the balanced tension between the two poles without giving sway to one pole or the other. See, Doran, *Theology and the Dialectics of History*, 9–10.

to enrich Lonergan's notion of systematic theology have yielded not only a set of heuristic determinations, but, in recent years, actual systematic theological contents born of those determinations. What this essay has sought to do is draw out further the methodical entailments of Doran's work. It has tried to outline the synchronic complement to Doran's notion of a diachronic sequence of speculative systems. Toward that end, I have highlighted Doran's own account of theological pluralism, indicated the enrichments that account entails, and presented a heuristic structure of elements and relations for a synchronic speculative pluralism. It remains, however, that this presentation is merely heuristic. And as such, it invites verification in particular instances and cases. That work, though, will fall to other occasions. For now, it is sufficient to say that what Doran has achieved has been and will continue to be brought into the service of the projects and endeavors of others, and this fact more than any other exemplifies what it is to labor in the advancement of the Lonergan enterprise.

CHAPTER NINE

ROBERT DORAN, HANS URS VON BALTHASAR, AND POETRY

Anne Carpenter
St. Mary's College of California (Moraga, CA)

One of Robert Doran's great efforts has been to place Bernard Lonergan and Hans Urs von Balthasar in dialogue with one another. This essay is a tribute to that effort by way of a dialogical encounter between Balthasar and Lonergan. Our focus will be, on the one hand, clarifying: we will show how engagement with Lonergan can clarify, can offer further rigor, to the Thomist framework that rests "beneath" Balthasar's theological dramatics. Our focus will also be, on the other, on the contributions each theologian can offer one another with respect to the "drama" of theological personhood. The rapprochement between the two men will be, therefore, constructive rather than conciliatory or adversarial.

Balthasar's "theological dramatics" are an effort to account for the divine economy of salvation primarily in terms of "action." Thus even the "stage"—the context, the location—of this economy is a fundamental part of the drama of Christ. But how Balthasar describes this can often be perplexing to those trained in other fields of theology. We deal in but two of the major areas of confusion: kenosis and person. Lonergan's theology contributes to both theological-dramatic categories through his own theology, and with Doran's help. By the end of the essay, we will come to understand that contingent predication is fundamental to understanding what the drama is, and is not; we will also come to understand the way theological "personhood" is an area for further exploration in *both* Balthasar and Lonergan.

Setting the Stage

It is important to understand that Balthasar is always in dialogue with Thomas Aquinas. I mention this because an essential presumption of the essay that follows is that, because Balthasar maintains his Thomist foundations, an explanatory dialogue with Lonergan is possible. In other words, the background that Balthasar and Lonergan share means that Lonergan really *can* throw light on the ways that a Thomistic background functions, or can function, in Balthasar. I am not the only scholar to highlight these Thomist "bones" in Balthasar.[1] But even after articulating the metaphysical grounds of Balthasar's thought and describing its bounds, several questions remain.

The first question centers on what difference there is between a metaphysical analysis of worldly finality and, in the case of this essay of ours, a theo-dramatic analysis. In other words, why *drama* and why not, say, more straightforward essays on human freedom? This question, in turn, demands a heuristic by which Balthasar's operating metaphysics can be both detected in and distinguished from its dramatic nexus. There are metaphysical (and dramatic, and theological) questions other than these to be asked, but these are the two that will dominate the following essay.

Our focus, both for the sake of length and for the sake of clarity, must be razor-sharp; so, the essay will emphasize Balthasarian dramatics, with key interventions from Lonerganian thought. At a broader level, Robert Doran has described the relationship between the two thinkers in a number of ways, most prominently in a comparison between Bonaventure (Balthasar) and Thomas (Lonergan).[2] The tactic of this essay is not so much on the more global problem of how the two relate to one another, a vision which Doran has already achieved, so much as it is on deploying one theologian (Lonergan) in an attempt to clarify and explain what the other theologian (Balthasar) is doing when he does what he does. If this makes for a rather Lonerganian Balthasar, we are assured that many other Balthasars can and do co-exist. But our interest here is more in understanding the network of ideas in Balthasar, in doing so with Lonergan's help. It is to such an explanation that we now turn.

---

1. Michele M. Schumacher, *A Trinitarian Anthropology: Adrienne Von Speyr and Hans Urs Von Balthasar in Dialogue with Thomas Aquinas* (Washington, DC: Catholic University of America Press, 2014); Angelo Campodonico, "Hans Urs von Balthasar's Interpretation of the Philosophy of Thomas Aquinas," *Nova et Vetera* 8, no. 1 (Winter 2010): 33–53; D. C. Schindler, "Towards a Non-Possessive Concept of Knowledge: On the Relation between Reason and Love in Aquinas and Balthasar," *Modern Theology* 22, no. 4 (October 2006): 577–607.

2. Robert M. Doran, "Lonergan and Balthasar: Methodological Considerations," *Theological Studies* 58, no. 1 (March 1997): 61–84.

Stage and Action: The Balthasarian Transposition

In the second volume of *Theo-Drama,* Balthasar effects a transition from "aesthetics" to "dramatics."[3] But this transition is analogical.[4] This means that the categories established in *Herrlichkeit* continue operating inasmuch as Balthasar's analysis ever passes over them, while his horizon for questions has shifted, demanding new categories and a transposition of inquiry or stance.[5] Thus many of the moves that he makes early in the second volume of the drama mirror positions he has already taken up at the close of the aesthetics, in *Herrlichkeit* volume seven.[6] "We," he says, "are deliberately speaking on several levels at once."[7]

Much has been made, rightly, about the transcendentals that govern each panel in the Balthasarian triptych. Balthasar himself guides readers in this direction.[8] So, *Theodramatik* is a turn to the transcendental of the good. But it is important to remember that each governing transcendental, as in Medieval faculty psychology and in Plato's *Symposium*, draws our sight not only to being but also to particular anthropological qualities that in some way correspond to being. In the case of the good, Western tradition highlights the human will that desires goodness. This human will, too, is Balthasar's concern—but again, the turn here is analogical. For, Balthasar's interest is not quite in willing as such.

Balthasar is concerned with *action*. Much could be said, in another essay, about the Blondelian roots of this interest. For our purposes, we note that Balthasar's other correlates here include *obedience* and *freedom*.[9] These are the major divine and human qualities that guide the subsequent volumes, most of all in the interaction *between* freedoms, an interaction

---

3. All citations from Hans Urs von Balthasar will have to include full bibliographic information in the first instance of each book, followed by an abbreviated form. Thus, *Theo-Drama: Theological Dramatics* [= *TD*]; *Glory of the Lord* [= *GL*]; *Theo-Logic* [=*TL*].

4. Balthasar, *Theo-Drama: Theological Dramatic Theory*, vol. 2: *Dramatis Personae: Man In God*, trans. Graham Harrison (San Francisco: Ignatius, 1990), 29.

5. Anne M. Carpenter, "Analogy and Kenosis," *Nova et Vetera* 17, no. 3 (2019): 811–838.

6. See Hans Urs von Balthasar, *The Glory of the Lord: A Theological Aesthetics*, vol. 7: *Theology: The New Covenant*, trans. Brian McNeil, C.R.V., ed. John Riches (San Francisco: Ignatius, 1989), 202–238.

7. Balthasar, *TD* 2:29. Cf. 28–33.

8. Hans Urs von Balthasar, *The Glory of the Lord: A Theological Aesthetics*, vol. 1: *Seeing the Form*, trans. Erasmo Leiva-Merikakis, ed. Joseph Fessio, S.J., and John Riches (San Francisco: Ignatius; New York: Crossroad, 1982), 18–19.

9. See also Todd Walatka, *Von Balthasar and the Option for the Poor* (Washington, DC: Catholic University of America Press, 2017), 102–130.

that constitutes the very heart of the meaning of the word "drama," and describes as well any "tension" in the drama.[10] In every case, Balthasar is never quite concerned with—in the sense of never quite placing at the center—metaphysics. This is never at any point to say that he loses sight of metaphysics. It is only to say that metaphysics is the frame for the actual center: the meaning of the decisions that are made, on God's part and on human beings.' In other words: the center is action, or history.

"A genuinely human figure," argues Balthasar, "developing over the course of a lifetime, is not something given. It has to be built up through free decisions."[11] Theology must therefore not only apply metaphysical categories to its questions, but must also seek other ones, ones that can address not only *that* freedom makes decisions, but also that decisions have a happening, have taken place, continue to take place, in a range of meanings that must be accounted for. "Drama" is Balthasar's attempt to rise to just this challenge, which at once involves him indirectly in metaphysics, always, and also in "more" than metaphysics (the "more" that is "drama"). Therefore, all the dramatic categories presume metaphysics, but are not identical with metaphysics. So, too, dramatic categories presume history, but are not identical with history.

Balthasar is not concerned with critical history as such. Lonergan can intervene here to provide a definition for what this latter category is: the understanding, through concrete data, of what was "going forward" in a particular time and place and people. By "going forward," Lonergan means that which is not a repetition in a routine. He means the relatively new. "Historical experience is one thing," he explains in *Method in Theology*, "and historical knowledge is quite another. [Historical knowledge] grasps what was going forward, what for the most part contemporaries did not know."[12] Balthasar is, for himself, concerned with what happens when human freedom and divine freedom encounter one another in the person of Jesus Christ. This dramatic encounter is at once critically historical (as what is, concretely, decisively, "going forward"), and it is more than critical history, since its objects (human and divine) are complexly transcendent. Critical history is not a total explanation of such transcendence; it is but one field of inquiry.

10. Cf. Balthasar, *TD* 2:30, 54, 57, 63.

11. Balthasar, *TD* 2:37.

12. Bernard J. F. Lonergan, *Method in Theology*, ed. Robert M. Doran and John D. Dadosky, vol. 14 in *Collected Works of Bernard Lonergan* (Toronto: University of Toronto Press, 2017), 174.

Therefore, two more ideas round out our basic sketch. The first has to do with what we might call the end-point or telos of the drama. Balthasar will depict this end-point from a number of complementary angles. From the standpoint of the dramatic stage itself, he argues,

> Anyone who wishes to be led by God's word into God's truth must open himself to the heaven/earth dimension [of the theo-drama]—which is a better expression than "the beyond" and "the here-and-now." But he must not fail to realize that, while he finds himself on the stage as soon as he comes into the world, he also has a part in shaping it. He does this through the measure of his receptivity, which enables him in an earthly way to receive heavenly things and give birth to them, and through the measure of his freedom to keep the kingdom of heaven away from the earth or, conversely, to cause it to come nearer. Ultimately, therefore, the stage is entirely assimilated into the spiritual dimensions of the actors themselves.[13]

The interpenetration of heaven and earth through free acts of human willing is one angle of the eschatology (the end-point) that is always operating as a through-line in the theological drama at work in Christ. It is accompanied by the second major idea that we must heed, which is that human freedom can and does "make way for" and "prevent" this divine work, the coming of the Kingdom, from taking place. Thus the "stage" of world history is where the Triune God, in Christ, in total freedom, chooses the world, and it is where human freedom, as free, cooperates—or does not. So we have something like a third idea, one that emerges to govern the sense of the other two: God's own action, on the stage of the world, (upon and) in human freedom.

Kenosis, the Economy, and Eternity

Kenosis and obedience are dramatic categories, by which I mean their emphasis is on describing action of one kind or another. Kenosis and obedience not only help frame the drama, but also serve as part of its internal mechanism, since both have to do with wills and willing, that is, with decisions made in history, here in the form of free self-surrender. We need to spend some time with kenosis and obedience, which will then unearth

13. Balthasar, *TD* 2:188.

a latent metaphysical problem—or opportunity—having to do with how these semi-metaphysical categories interact with the difference between God and the world.

Late in *Herrlichkeit*, as Balthasar both concludes the first panel of his triptych and prepares the way for *Theodramatik*, he describes the kenosis and the obedience of the Son in detail. Divine "kenosis," at this angle, is something like selflessness, something like a surrender that enables the freedom of others: first in the divine act of creation, then (more "truly") in the God-man's surrender on the cross.[14] Balthasar insists that the *economic* acts of creation and obedience must have some kind of correlate in the *immanent* Trinity, which Balthasar finds in Bulgakov's description of the eternal "divine selflessness" of the Triune persons.[15] Here the mutual "letting-be" whence the persons eternally come to be is a model both for the great act of creation, which allows finite freedom to really be, and for the great act of obedience on the cross, in which the God-man summatively offers himself back to the Father in solidarity with the world.[16] In this way, Balthasar can say that the economic Trinity reveals the immanent one, since in the economy God acts as God eternally is.

Elsewhere in the trilogy, Balthasar shifts terminology somewhat as he describes not kenosis as an action in creation, but kenosis as "eternal" in the Godhead. Again, the major reference is the "divine selflessness" borrowed from Bulgakov. But we have moved from the economy to eternity. There is "a first, intratrinitarian *kenosis*, which is none other than God's positive 'self-expropriation' in the act of handing over the entire divine being in the processions."[17] Notice from the outset that kenosis is explicitly a way of describing Trinitarian procession. So, it is no mistake that Balthasar associates this divine selflessness "first" of all with the Father, who, in a kenosis (or, in a paternity) that the Father also *is*, brings forth the Son.[18] At its

14. Balthasar, *GL* 7:214.

15. Balthasar, *GL* 7:213.

16. Cf. Hans Urs von Balthasar, *Theo-Drama: Theological Dramatic Theory*, vol. 5: *The Last Act*, trans. Graham Harrison (San Francisco: Ignatius, 1998), 411–424.

17. Hans Urs von Balthasar, *Theo-Logic: Theological Logical Theory*, vol. 2: *Truth of God*, trans. Adrian J. Walker (San Francisco: Ignatius, 2004), 177–178. "The identity of the divine essence is found in the positive self-expropriation of the Divine Persons, which in all three is one, true, and good" (178).

18. Balthasar, *TL* 2:177; cf. idem, *Theo-Drama: Theological Dramatic Theory*, vol. 3: *Dramatis Personae: Persons in Christ*, trans. Graham Harrison (San Francisco: Ignatius, 1991), 153; idem, *Theo-Drama: Theological Dramatic Theory*, vol. 4: *The Action*, trans. Graham Harrison (San Francisco: Ignatius, 1994), 323.

ultimate, Balthasarian circumincession involves the mutual kenosis of the three divine persons, the indwelling of the undivided processions of the Godhead, with the Father as "principle."[19]

But here we encounter an opportunity for confusion, and in two directions. The first has to do with the intra-divine life: if we can speak of the kenosis of the Father, in what respect is the Son also kenotic (and so too the Spirit), without descending into a kind of Sabellian absence of real distinction between the Father, the Son, and the Spirit? If all is kenosis, after all, then how are there—in Thomist terms—still two distinct processions in God? Then, in the economy, in what respect is the kenosis of the God-man not identical with that kenosis of eternity, else-wise we run up against a God of process trapped in the cage of history? We might say, by way of summary, that in both we have the opposite possible problem than that of a Balthasarian tri-divinity.

Balthasar offers certain demarcations, though at various stages of clarity. For example, in *Mysterium Paschale,* a text that predates the dramatics and *Glory of the Lord*, volume 7 (whence kenosis), Balthasar writes,

> By letting go of the "form of God" that was his (and so his divine power of self-disposal) [the Son] willed to become the One who, in a remarkable and unique manner, is obedient to the Father—in a manner, namely, where his obedience presents the kenotic translation of the eternal love of the Son for the "ever-greater" Father.[20]

Here we have a description of economic kenosis (in a reference to Phil 2:7) that supposes some kind of difference from the immanent relation of the Son, though the two remain connected, since the obedience of the economy is a "translation" of the Son's relation to the Father in immanent Trinity. This differentiation is repeated with somewhat more clarity in the later *Theodramatik,* where we see how "this 'kenosis of obedience' ('emptying himself of the form of God': Phil 2:7)" in the economy "must be based on the eternal kenosis of the Divine Persons one to another."[21] Here the difference is clarified inasmuch as the economic kenosis of the Son—as in *Glory of the Lord*, volume 7—is more nearly associated with obedience, whereas the eternal kenosis is not. There, in eternity, Balthasar leans more

19. Balthasar, *TL* 2:137.

20. Balthasar, *Mysterium Paschale: The Mystery of Easter*, trans. Aidan Nichols, O.P. (San Francisco: Ignatius Press, 1990), 90–91.

21. Balthasar, *TD* 5:123.

heavily on language such as divine "letting-be."[22] Such is the admittedly thin ground, based in the term "kenosis," for a differentiation between the economic and immanent Trinities, a difference Balthasar admits as necessary—if vaguely expressed—even in *Mysterium Pascale*.[23]

Balthasar is clearer, at least at this phase of our exploration, with respect to the immanent Trinity. There Balthasar is willing to adopt Thomistic language of procession, where the analogies of the *verbum mentis* and of love (ultimately, Augustine's psychological analogy) govern the distinctions between the persons as relations of mutual opposition. Balthasar shows his understanding of such distinctions most clearly in the *Theologik* panel of his triptych, where he discusses the Thomistic-Augustinian language of procession as a way of denying both quaterity (the divine essence as a hidden "fourth") and Sabellianism.[24]

Balthasar relies on Thomistic language procession despite clear hesitance toward the psychological analogy.[25] So, if Balthasar is consistent, we can charitably conclude that, in the drama, the "gratitude" with which the Son responds to the Father is an expression of a different relation of origin, and is therefore expressive of a different person, than the Father's exultant self-giving that generates the Son.[26] Both are "kenotic," but differently so. Indeed, this difference—cast as distance in *Theo-Drama*—provides the "location" of the world in the Triune God.[27]

The above sketch, combined with the more general view of the dramatics, provides us with the opportunity to begin clarifying and developing qualities of Balthasar in an engagement with Bernard Lonergan and Robert Doran. We begin that now, with an exploration of contingent predication.

Robert Doran, Bernard Lonergan, and Contingent Predication

Essential to Doran's exegesis of Lonergan in *The Trinity in History* is the theory of contingent predication, whereby some contingent effect in

22. See Balthasar, *TD* 2:243–270; *TD* 5:85–93.

23. Balthasar, *Mysterium Paschale*, 35.

24. See Balthasar, *TL* 2:132–135; 157–170.

25. See ibid., 135–138; Idem, *Theo-Logic: Theological Logical Theory*, vol. 3: *The Spirit of Truth*, trans. Graham Harrison (San Francisco: Ignatius, 2005), 131–142.

26. See Balthasar, *TD* 5:83.

27. See ibid., 395; cf. *TD* 4:327, and large sections of *TD* 2, most important for our purposes involving pp. 284–287.

creation is attributable to the eternal God. The change wrought is one wrought in the world, and not in God. Contingent predication thus preserves God's immutability by clarifying "where" the change that is the work of salvation takes place. But this change in creation is also what makes our statements about salvation in Christ true.[28] There must be some real term, after all, that our claims about God's work in history are attached to. Or, to put the matter in Lonergan's own words, "contingent truths imply the existence of an appropriate created term."[29]

With the Incarnation, for example, we are able to ask what is willed and made to be the case in creation, by the Triune God, such that this assumed human nature really is the divine's Word's human nature. This is the reasoning behind Thomas's *esse secondarum,* which is (in Doran's words) "a substantial supernatural act received in Christ's human nature," such that that nature is the Word's, and the Word's only.[30] That is, a contingent act, an act in creation, grounds a relation to an eternal person. "The procession of the divine Word . . . is not contingent," explains Doran, "but the mission of that Word in history is thoroughly contingent."[31]

This leaves us with the further puzzle of the "principle of union," that is, the principle cause of the union of the divine Word to his human nature. The *esse secondarum* explains what contingent act corresponds to the Word's assumption of a human nature; now we must explain what it is in God that brings about this assumption. For Lonergan, it is the divine act of existence itself. In *On the Ontological and Psychological Constitution of Christ,* Lonergan explains, "whatever the triune God . . . can understand and will about himself, God (1) can be, and (2) can be through the divine act of existence."[32] In other words, there is no *new* act in God by which the Word becomes flesh. God becomes man through the pure act that God is.

A Thomistic Dramatics: First Application

What these various Lonerganian-Thomist ideas have to do with Balthasar's *Theo-Drama* will not be, perhaps, immediately clear. But one thing they

28. Cf. Robert Doran, *The Trinity in History: A Theology of Divine Missions, Volume 1: Missions and Processions* (Toronto: University of Toronto Press, 2012), 31, 47.

29. Ibid., 97.

30. Ibid., 52.

31. Ibid., 51.

32. Ibid., 135.

can do is offer a sense for the frame under which the drama might sensibly unfold. If Balthasar considers kenotic obedience to be some kind of "translation" of eternal kenosis into the economy, then not only is he aware of the God-world difference (as we might be wont to put it, in a Balthasarian grammar), but also he is presuming some mode of contingent predication: the event of obedience effects a change, not in God, but in the world. Nevertheless, the one doing the effecting is the same God, the immutable God. The obedience of Jesus, then, is a corresponding term that makes our statements about salvation true, and that makes salvation real.

Whether Balthasar is always this precise or this explicit is somewhat beside the point. We already know, after all, that Balthasar is not directly building a metaphysics in the drama—only indirectly so, and not as his central task. It is too much to ask the drama to suffice as a full systematic theology when it is not one. But our essay is after what this metaphysical indirection might be when made a direct object of inquiry, and not only in its original constraints, but also when more rigorously expressed. So, already, we have observed something like contingent predication functioning in the "background" of the dramatics, which Balthasar's devotion to the *analogia entis* centers as a possibility for explanation.

It might well be argued that it is too much to presume contingent predication of a Balthasar who does not spell out its nature. But to insist this is not to take Balthasar at his word, though it does so in the very shape of his words—and they alone. But to hew to his vocabulary is not necessarily to understand it. For if Balthasar more than once makes a distinction between eternal kenosis and economic kenosis, if he more than once locates obedience in one and not in the other, and if he considers the relationship between kenosis and obedience to be analogical—all of which we saw previously—then the doctrine of contingent predication does nothing but make sense of this nexus of Balthasarian habits. To put the matter more succinctly: it is not *only* the analogy of being constantly operating underneath Balthasar's thinking; it is also analogy's attendant concepts.

Supposing a Thomist sense to the Balthasarian nexus of terms, we might also further it. We can follow Lonergan here to offer something of a clarification that at the same time develops Balthasar. When we ask, therefore, how (in the drama) the Word assumes his human nature, we can refer to his kenosis, and in three simultaneous senses. First, we can say that the economic kenosis of creation, effected by the Trinity "through" the Word, is a contingent term for a contingent act. Second (and similarly), the economic kenosis of Incarnation, effected by the Holy Spirit, is a contingent term for a contingent act. Third, the eternal kenosis, the divine selflessness of the Trinitarian persons, which and by which they always are, is also that by which the Word alone becomes man, without a change in God. This last kenosis is not contingent. If we follow this trifold summary, we can see how following Lonergan's logic gives us a way of differentiating more precisely between one kenosis and another while not vitiating them, nor doing violence to Balthasar's thought. Lonergan also gives us some "guardrails" for what an appropriation of Balthasar in other theologies by other theologians might sensibly mean, and might not mean, at least in a Thomist frame.

It is worth noting that such a frame does not account for every aspect of the Balthasarian Trinity. It is but a rule for how God acts in the world, and for how various uses of "kenosis" and "obedience" might be applied when borrowing from Balthasar. So, for example, there is not really a Thomist account for letting-be or divine selflessness; these are Balthasar's own appropriations from elsewhere. Bulgakov, for example, looms just as large in the Balthasarian Trinity in his own particular way. By no means, then, are these Lonerganian-Thomist guardrails anything save exactly that.

But there are more possibilities at play than a more precise working of kenosis through the mechanism of contingent predication. There is still the matter of understanding the ways that the metaphysical substructure of the dramatics allows for non-metaphysical (in the sense of not directly metaphysical) theoretical work to take place. We have so far focused on the ground for such an inquiry. In what follows, we will study one instance, allowing Lonergan and Balthasar to again engage one another, and in a manner where both contribute.

The Drama of Human Freedom: Balthasar

We have so far clarified Balthasar by way of his own work and that of Lonergan's. That clarification has involved for the most part the difference, we might say, between the dramatic stage of the economy of salvation and the eternal "drama" of the immanent Trinity. Contingent predication allows for a non-mythological grasp of what exactly Balthasar seeks to describe in the economic encounter between God and man in Jesus. But this is only the backdrop to *Theodramatik*, which focuses—as we saw near the beginning of this essay—on the human encounter with God, conceived of through concrete acts of willing, ones that allow the Kingdom of God to draw near—or that do not.

At the heart of the theo-drama is the infinite divine freedom that makes finite human freedom possible. This infinite freedom, God's own, is not only "where" finite freedom emerges from, since God makes it; God's freedom is also the "where" that finite freedom travels toward, in the Medieval model of *exitus* and *reditus*, as finite freedom in its concrete decisions reaches toward the infinite goodness that it desires. "Finite freedom," says Balthasar, "can only be made possible by infinite freedom; consequently it can only fulfill itself, as finite freedom, within infinite freedom. In its finitude it has a 'whence' and a 'whither'; by its very nature it is set [ge-setzt] on a path and pointed in a direction [ge-wiesen]."[33] So Balthasar is able to see freedom not only as a gift to be "had," indeed as always-already possessed as a potency, but is also able to see freedom as a goodness to be developed toward (or against). "While we are free," argues Balthasar, "we are always only moving *toward* freedom."[34] And finally, this "toward" of freedom directs Balthasar (and the free subject) not to the faceless One of Plotinus, but rather it instigates striving toward the eminently free, personal "thou" of the Triune God.[35]

So we are able to grasp how Balthasarian "freedom" is both ecstatic and interpersonal, and in this double sense: as first and primordially Trinitarian in the divine selflessness of the persons, that is, in the freedom of the Trinity; and as *imago Trinitatis*, as ecstatic and interpersonal in finite freedom's engagement with the world, and through the world, with God.[36] In this sense, for Balthasar, "there is no anthropology but the dramatic," which is to say that there is no other anthropology but the real, lived, concrete playing out of human freedom in the world, in all its variety.[37]

Balthasar frames human freedom in Christ through this basic structure (of *ekstasis* and *diastasis*): Jesus' freedom, as divine and human in one subject, as concrete historically, is both the exemplary "site" of all drama *and* is the site of every finite participation in the one theological drama of salvation. The concreteness of Jesus is to be found in his historical, bodily existence; the universality of his work and our ability to participate in it is to be found in his divinity—yet always through his concrete humanity. Jesus' work, especially after the resurrection, is thus not only temporal, but also transtemporal. So the Christian, explains Balthasar, "regards himself

33. Balthasar, *TD* 2:284.

34. Ibid., 208.

35. Ibid., 287.

36. Cf. Balthasar, *TD* 2:290–292, 302; *TD* 5:98.

37. Balthasar, *TD* 3:335; cf. 336.

as involved with the life and work, not of the Jesus *of that time*, but of the Christ who is at work *here and now*."[38]

This "here and now" of Jesus in our time is possible, we must stress, precisely because Balthasar sees Jesus as doubly ecstatic, as infinite God and finite man, accomplishing the one salvation in the theandric unity of his two wills. It is an *ekstasis* that founds human striving and that serves as such striving's goal, one that—because "staged" by an infinite freedom become incarnate—leaves "space" for the self-determination of other finite freedoms, including the Word's own.[39] Human striving is therefore not only graspable in philosophical or even theological terms, but also in Christological terms. Christ "spans" the length of every possibility that the human will can make present to itself, and that God can make present to it, from God-forsakenness to (ultimately) the beatific vision. Christ's "face" is discernible in them all.[40]

What all this means is that the theo-drama is at once an exemplary, original image (*Urbild*) that is in some sense unrepeatable, and an image that must be appropriated according to the infinite varieties of uniquenesses present in each human person who responds to the call of grace.[41] In theo-dramatic terms, Jesus is both "stage" and "actor."[42] But in more general terms, Jesus' obedience to the Father becomes the Christic rule by which human action in the world is ultimately to be judged—not in terms of absolute identity, but in terms of a free act of will, where the human person makes way for God's own will through their (Christological) agreement.[43]

The Drama of Human Freedom: Lonergan and Balthasar

Lonergan also has an ecstatic description of human freedom, one that ultimately occurs thanks to—and under the auspices of—divine freedom, though of course his vocabulary, even the structure of his theological "grammar," here is different. "The rational subject," he explains in *Insight*,

> as carrying out an obligation is not just a knower but also a doer, and his rationality consists not merely in excluding interference

38. Ibid., 127.

39. Ibid., 129–134.

40. Cf. ibid., 162.

41. Cf. ibid., 162–168.

42. Cf. ibid., 531–532.

43. Cf. Balthasar, *TD* 4:317–319.

> with cognitional process but also in extending the rationality of his knowing into the field of doing. But that extension does not occur simply by knowing one's obligations. It occurs just inasmuch as one wills to meet one's obligations.[44]

Lonergan's emphasis on the rational subject is less straightforwardly Christological, though we will fill out how it is Christological below. So, too, Lonergan begins with a Thomist emphasis on the transition from intellect to will. But again we have the insight that human *doing*, that actual acts of willing, introduce to the human subject a further quality, one that—for Lonergan—cannot be encapsulated merely by human knowing—which is that the human subject is not only rational, but also free. Human willing is fundamental to the total dynamism of the individual; willing, willing specifically and concretely in the world, is an *ekstasis* of human being out into the world.

But the case of human freedom is a contingent one, which is to say that human freedom relies not on the contingence of creation *simpliciter*, but on the contingence of context, of decision(s), of imagined options.[45] Whereas God creates and knows the world through the single act of divine self-knowledge that God both "has" and "is," human beings activate their freedom through a bewildering array of places and times, in concrete limitations, and in metaphysical ones. We cannot even say that every act of the human will is free.[46]

Indeed, there must be a willingness to will in the first place, or what might have been willed, so to say, will not be at all. "When antecedent willingness is lacking," says Lonergan, "persuasion can be invoked; but persuasion takes time, and until time is devoted to persuading oneself or to being persuaded by others, one remains closed to otherwise possible courses of action."[47] On this model, what Lonergan calls "basic sin" is neither event nor decision, but is instead the lack of one. Sin not only does not have intelligibility; sin also cannot be willed.[48] But just as seriously, the human being must

44. Bernard J. F. Lonergan, *Insight: A Study of Human Understanding*, ed. Frederick E. Crowe and Robert M. Doran, vol. 3 in *Collected Works of Bernard Lonergan* (Toronto: University of Toronto Press, 1992), 638.

45. Lonergan, *Insight*, 642. "Freedom, then, is a special kind of contingence. It is a contingence that arises, not from the empirical residue that grounds materiality and the nonsystematic, but in the order of spirit, of intelligent grasp, rational reflection, and morally guided will" (642).

46. Ibid., 632.

47. Ibid., 646.

48. Ibid., 689–690.

(we can echo Balthasar here) ever more wholly lay hold of their own freedom, which they do imperfectly, unevenly, authentically, unauthentically.[49] Human *ekstasis*, we might say, is not only troubled, but is indeed profoundly so.

Yet every effective act of finite willing has God as first agent and as final end. In Thomist-Lonerganian terms, "God applies every contingent agent to its operation." Every act of my own willing involves an act of God. And God is not only agent in my own willing, but also is my final cause: "God would be the ultimate final cause of any universe, the ground of its value, and the ultimate objective of all finalistic striving."[50] Here we see an insight that echoes with Balthasar's own, one where God not only "gives" freedom, but also makes freedom effective, and where God is the end toward which all willing strives.

It is within such an ecstatic, Thomistic frame that we can understand a statement from Balthasar himself. "Infinite freedom," argues Balthasar,

> because it is by nature infinite, simply cannot fail to be present wherever finite freedom is. It operates through the latter yet in a latent manner which allows finite freedom to realize itself as genuine decision (for or against its being-in-God). If it decides correctly, it simultaneously chooses both itself (which can only be realized in God) and God; it grasps that God's immanence in it, in grace, is nothing alien (alienum), no more than God himself can ever be a stranger to it (aliud); everything that is relative and created comes to itself in the Absolute.[51]

Though Balthasar does not use Thomas's vocabulary, still it is possible to see his thought present and presumed in Balthasar's logic. God as first agent, as final cause, "makes sense" of Balthasar's argument here; so, though his language is "dramatic," his logic is (at the very least an echo of) Thomas's.

But before we move ahead of ourselves, we need to sketch the Christo-logic of Lonergan's own thought. Here we look briefly toward his Latin work in *On the Ontological and Psychological Constitution of Christ.* In that text, we can see Lonergan thinking through a Christology that can also make sense of Jesus. But here the linchpin is not so much on the theandric willing of Jesus, though that is present, as it is on the fullness of his humanity, which he shares wholly (save in sin) with us.

---

49. Cf. Lonergan, *Method in Theology*, 36–40.

50. Lonergan, *Insight*, 687.

51. Balthasar, *TD* 2:317.

We can begin with the idea consciousness itself. This, Lonergan says, is "a preliminary unstructured sort of awareness that is presupposed by intellectual inquiry and completed by it."[52] Human beings are conscious in this way. God is, as pure act, as "substantial knowing," eminently conscious.[53] God the Son is also, therefore, eminently conscious of his Incarnation. Or, as Lonergan describes the matter:

> The divine persons are conscious in the totality of their being, both absolute and relative; and therefore the hypostatic union, although effected not in a nature or on the basis of a nature but in a person and on the basis of a person, nevertheless was effected in something conscious and through something conscious, for in a divine person there is nothing that is not conscious.[54]

But this introduces the problem of Jesus' human consciousness, and whether he indeed has one. Lonergan's answer to this puzzle is complex. When the theologian asks about Jesus' consciousness with respect to his person, then the answer is that he has *one* consciousness as *one* single subject, the Incarnate Word; when the theologian asks about Jesus' consciousness with respect to his natures, then the answer is that he has *two* consciousnesses, a divine and a human consciousness, just as he has *two* natures. The Incarnation is "in one way both ontologically and psychologically one and in another way [is] both ontologically and psychologically two."[55]

We have here a place of disagreement with Balthasar. But it is not yet prudent to explore this disagreement. First we must emphasize how, for Lonergan, the divine Son in his human consciousness knows himself to be the divine Son. Or, in Lonergan's own words, "*through a consciousness that is truly and properly human, a divine person is conscious of a divine person.* Here is the difficulty! This is the crux of the problem!"[56] So Lonergan's Christology allows him to describe the great mystery of how one of the Trinity is, in his humanity, conscious of himself. It is, then, not just the case that the Triune

52. Bernard F. J. Lonergan, *The Ontological and Psychological Constitution of Christ* [orig. *De constitutione Christi ontologica et psychologica*, 4th ed.], ed. Michael G. Shields, Frederick E. Crowe and Robert M. Doran, trans. Michael G. Shields, vol. 7 in *Collected Works of Bernard Lonergan* (Toronto: University of Toronto Press, 2002), 157.

53. Ibid., 191–193.

54. Ibid., 203. Cf. Robert Doran, "Are There Two Consciousnesses of Christ? Transposing the Secondary Act of Existence," *Irish Theological Quarterly* 82, no. 2 (2017): 153.

55. Lonergan, *The Ontological and Psychological Constitution of Christ*, 221.

56. Ibid., 211.

God is conscious of the Incarnation, nor just the case that the divine Son, as God, is conscious of the Incarnation—though both claims are true—it is also that the Incarnate Word is conscious of himself as Incarnate Word through his humanity.

There is one step more that Lonergan takes, at least for our purposes: he describes the kenosis of the Son as twofold, as ontological and psychological. The Word's assumption of a human nature as really his own is the "first" kenosis; the Word's consciousness of himself as human is the "second." "Hence," says Lonergan,

> as the Son of God is aware of himself in his infinite perfection through his divine consciousness, so also the same Son of God is aware of himself through his human consciousness in the poverty of human nature. As a result, that first, ontological kenosis, brought about by the assumption of a human nature, becomes very evident through the consequent psychological kenosis inasmuch as Christ not only is human but also experiences himself as human.[57]

We can apply Lonergan's logic in order to say that the God-man experiences himself as divine and as human, and yet also it is this same Son of God who is both divine and human, who is not two subjects but one subject.[58] It is important that Lonergan and Balthasar both acknowledge the kenotic nature of the Incarnation, though of course their formulations are distinct. Balthasar "extends" the concept of kenosis to the eternal Trinity, and Lonergan "extends" it in the other direction to Jesus' human consciousness. But this is a consciousness, a double consciousness, that Balthasar is suspicious of. It is to this disagreement that we now turn.

A Thomistic Dramatics: Second Application

Balthasar more nearly associates consciousness with person, and so tends to insist that Jesus had but one consciousness. This leaves Balthasar in partial disagreement with Lonergan, though Lonergan can at least appropriate something like this Balthasarian perspective, since it has to do with person and therefore emphasizes Jesus' consciousness as "one." But the danger here is with respect to person, too, since Balthasar is speaking of "person"

57. Ibid., 223.

58. Cf. Lonergan, *The Ontological and Psychological Constitution of Christ*, 269.

theo-dramatically, and therefore not quite ontologically. Which is to say, both men use the word *person,* but their usage partially overlaps (since in both cases it refers to a subsistent rational nature) and partially diverges (since in one there is the matter of "drama"). We cannot presume a one-to-one relationship between their words.

What Balthasar contributes to the concept of person, or perhaps, how he reframes the meaning of "person," has to do with his understanding of "mission." A person, on this view, is fundamentally one-who-is-sent.[59] So we can again see Balthasar referring his categories back to the drama of salvation, and deriving his meanings and usages therefrom. Person is not *only* a single subjectivity, nor even primarily; person is *also* one who goes forth to partake of the divine drama of the cross and resurrection. We can render this in Lonerganian terms by saying that, for Balthasar, "person" is a special theological category, not a general one. That is to say, "person" is a category used to explain the unique terms of revelation and Christian tradition; it is not one of the more general, philosophical, shared concepts that theology also uses. "Person" does not mean "a rational subject"; Balthasar uses "conscious subject" for that designation. "Person" is one who partakes of the divine mission of salvation.

Jesus is a unique person in the sense that his mission is identical with his person: he is, as divine Son, fundamentally the one who is "sent forth." It means that Jesus always *is* what he *does.* Human persons are first conscious subjects who *then* respond to God's call, even if "only" through baptism. They are not absolutely one with their sending forth into the world. But to say so presents Balthasar with a puzzle. "If," he says,

> Jesus' consciousness of an absolute (divine) mission is to coincide with his I-consciousness, how can the child Jesus ever have awakened to self-consciousness without simultaneously knowing of his mission—at least implicitly?[60]

We are faced with the possibility of a Jesus who does not learn. Or, as is nearer to Balthasar's concern, we are faced with the overly pious work of art that foreshadows the cross over the brow of the small Christ-child. Are these not fanciful imaginings?

But Balthasar does not think these theological ideas are so many ardent nothings. They have content; that is to say, "Jesus' sense of mission has no

59. Balthasar, *TD* 3:208–219.

60. Ibid., 173.

conceivable beginning."[61] Jesus, even as one who must—as man—awaken to himself, awakens always as one-who-is-sent. We might be tempted to impute to Balthasar's Jesus some kind of absolute, total knowledge, as in the Father's, but what Balthasar is saying here is more complex. He means that the whole of Jesus awakening to his "I" is fundamental to his mission, to his being-sent into the world. So, rather than Jesus figuring out who he is and what he is to do at a single flash-point, or through a series of steps, Balthasar deploys the language of "mission" to secure a farther-reaching process, one that takes up the whole of Jesus' life.[62] He is deliberately more heuristic than specific, because for him the keyword for theological study is the "mission" of the Son in the world.

"Person," defined as one-who-is-sent, has more to do with the inclusion of others "in Christ" than it has to do with a description of Jesus' unique subjectivity.[63] Yet personhood is not without this quality, since the Word is always-already one-who-is-sent, and is also always one who knows himself before God (as God). So, again, Balthasar distinguishes between being a conscious subject, which one can be regardless of one's awareness of God, and being a *theological* person. Jesus is the only one who is *always* person, and here is the essential function of this "always": it reveals God to us in Jesus' every action, and it is what allows other persons to become "persons," and in the Son's image.[64] Balthasar is firm on the opinion that, given these categories, Jesus' "I" and his "mission" are *one.*

But this is a dramatic category, one meant to explain action. It leaves Balthasar relatively unclear about whether Jesus, as conscious subject, a conscious subject who is always also a person, *must* absolutely have one consciousness or two, though Balthasar more than once seems to lean toward one consciousness only. This one-ness is not easy to track, however, because Balthasar does *not* mean "consciousness" in Lonergan's sense. That latter sense receives *some* attention as a "historical consciousness," as awareness of an "I," and as "awareness," but these terms are general, with an unfortunate amount of slippage between them. Surely Jesus' God-consciousness and his historical consciousness are not absolutely one. So does that make his consciousness, under this aspect, two? But, again, Balthasar does not quite have the terminology or horizon of inquiry such that we can ask him, at least

61. Ibid., 177.

62. Cf. Balthasar, *TD* 3:179. This is where Balthasar brings up the idea of Jesus learning.

63. Cf. Balthasar, *TD* 3:202–203.

64. Cf. Balthasar, *TD* 3: 230–250; 447–456.

directly (one-to-one, Lonergan to Balthasar), how many consciousnesses does Jesus have?

We will not attempt a total rapprochement, nor force a decision between one theologian or another. Those explorations have already taken place, and those include the further puzzle of Jesus' beatific knowledge. Nor will we leave ourselves only at an awareness that Balthasar and Lonergan ask different theological questions with different theological horizons for answers. That does, however, leave us with the question of what might be left to say.

At one angle, what we have here is an opportunity for further drama in the theo-drama. Rather than critiquing Balthasar's rightness or wrongness, we can say that Lonergan's categories contribute to a description of Jesus' dramatic self-appropriation. In this sense, Balthasar misses the doorway to a further element of the drama of salvation. It is a doorway that Lonergan opens. At another angle, what I have offered is different than an effort from Robert Doran himself. We will spend the space remaining left to us exploring that difference—I will not say disagreement—between Doran on Balthasarian "person" and myself.

In an essay on the consciousness of Christ, Doran—trying to make sense of both Lonergan and Balthasar together—argues,

> The divine consciousness of the incarnate Word, then, would be the consciousness 'on the side of the subject that is the Son in being consciously generated by the Father' as well as 'on the side of the subject that is the Son who with the Father consciously spirates the Spirit.' . . . [The Incarnate Word's] human consciousness, on the other hand, is ontologically grounded in the secondary act of existence that makes it true to affirm that the Second Person of the Blessed Trinity is this man Jesus of Nazareth. This human consciousness is the mission consciousness of the Eternal Word become flesh.[65]

I do not disagree with the logic as a whole, though it is important to see in full here. The question, for this essay, has to do with the last logical flourish in the final sentence: "this human consciousness is the mission consciousness of the Eternal Word."

Doran's review of Lonergan and Balthasar on "person" is decisive here, and theologically and philosophically probative. But it remains incomplete,

65. Doran, "Are There Two Consciousnesses of Christ?," 153.

on the side of Balthasar, in the sense that Doran does not take into account the ways that "person"—in the dramatics at least—has been moved into a new set of concepts ("dramatic" ones), leaving "conscious subject" to carry the less relational concepts Doran criticizes Balthasar for not attending to sufficiently.[66] It may well be the case that Balthasar's account of *persona* is insufficient, and that his reliance on relational categories is also insufficient, to the task of Christology, and of consciousness. But that is not the question here. The question is what those more dramatic, more relational Balthasarian categories are doing. My claim is essentially that they change the meaning of Balthasarian "person" to "one-who-is-sent," such that there is no longer any full coherence with its previous, Latinate meaning. This latter meaning Balthasar ascribes, at least mainly, to subjectivity.

If "person" is "one-who-is-sent," then its primary dramatic meaning is found in the Trinity, with the eternal Son. Here in the Trinity we have an original sending-forth that, while not *simply* the economic mission of the Son, is its unchanging truth in eternity. Balthasar is outright in this claim.[67] He has, therefore, moved the question of person into questions of special theological categories, and he primarily derives the meaning of Jesus' "God-consciousness" in history from the Gospels, especially from John: "As the Father has sent me, so I send you" (John 20:21). It is what has Balthasar so confusingly insisting on the singleness of Jesus' consciousness: it is because his mission-personhood is not an addition to his divine personhood even if its created terms *are* ad extra. Here, at this point in Balthasar's theology, there is no metaphor in Latin theology for what Balthasar is doing, and this is so precisely because all his metaphors are dramatic.

Yet this leads Balthasar to fail to fully account for the drama of Jesus' humanity, and indeed his human consciousness. In this Doran and I are in agreement. We differ on its backdrop, but in either direction—toward Doran's claims or toward my own—Balthasar is opened out into new potential, one in which Jesus' human consciousness is not lost in the wake of dramatic categories, but carried into being by them. Our task has been merely to open the door, and so to show how Balthasar's Thomist background allows for an engagement between him and Lonergan. In the first half of this essay, we saw Thomas and Lonergan clarifying Balthasar's terminology; in this second half, we see Thomas and Lonergan offering a place for further inquiry. Either deployment of the Thomist tradition is both necessary

66. Ibid., 161.

67. See Balthasar, *TD* 5:80–83.

and helpful in the study of Balthasar, and shows how salutary a dialogue between the two thinkers can be.

Conclusion

We have spent our time moving back-and-forth between Lonergan and Balthasar in order to understand aspects of Balthasar's theological dramatics more clearly. In particular, we saw how contingent predication clarifies what Balthasar might mean by (eternal) "kenosis" and "obedience" (or the "kenosis of obedience"). Whether or not Balthasar himself is either clear enough or consistent enough, appropriating him into the wider theological conversation via contingent predication both secures the *truth* of salvation by providing contingent terms for our statements about it, and secures the immutability of the Trinity, since the change that takes place occurs in the contingent world and not in God.

In the second half of the essay, we engaged Lonergan and Balthasar on the topic of Jesus' consciousness. Here our striving unveiled how both men have not only distinctive vocabulary, but also distinctive theoretical frames for their terminology, making direct rapprochement impossible. But we were able to achieve more than a study of two ships passing in the night. Instead of choosing one theologian over the other, we applied each to the other in the frames original to each. Therefore, we saw how Balthasar's linguistic slippage with respect to "consciousness" and "I" prevent him from describing a further quality of Jesus' salvific drama: his self-appropriation of his own humanity through his human consciousness. At the same time we saw how the "performance" of Balthasar's drama, his logic for supporting Paul's "in Christ," provides at least the Latin Lonergan with new categories for investigation, for the playing-out of the Son's self-awareness in salvation history. We thus arrived at something other than a reconciliation: we discovered the ways that questions that are new to theological projects, whether Balthasar's or Lonergan's, allow for the possibility of further clarity and further exploration. In this, we honor—even if only in a shadowy way—one of the major efforts of Robert Doran's long career, in which he has sought not to conclude theological discussion but to continue it. In this great hope, one that embraces Lonergan and Balthasar both, we conclude our essay.

SECTION IV

ECONOMICS OF HUMANE GLOBALIZATION

CHAPTER TEN

WORLD CHRISTIANITY AND THEOLOGY FOR WORLD CULTURAL COMMUNITY

Joseph Ogbonnaya

Marquette University (Milwaukee, WI)

"It is the community of the church as a whole that is to evoke a world-cultural community, by its fidelity to the integral scale of values and its incarnate witness to the mission of the suffering servant of God under the just and mysterious law of the cross."[1]

Introduction

In this paper I argue that decades of cross-cultural encounter and actual practice of contextual theologies have dealt extensively with the issues of religion and culture to an extent the debate between world Christianity and global Christianity is addressed. The question that should be uppermost in our mind as theologians now should be one of the significances of world Christianity in our globalized world. What role should contemporary Christianity play in the world stage in the face of the challenges of globalization? What is the task of theology in evoking alternative communities towards peaceful and mutual coexistence of humankind? And how is theology to accomplish this? I will seek answers to these questions in Robert M. Doran's theology of world-cultural community.

World Christianity or Global Christianity

In the wake of the movement of Christianity to the majority world church, the contextuality of all theology has been emphasized and is

1. Robert M. Doran, *Theology and the Dialectics of History* (Toronto: University of Toronto Press, 1990), 418.

almost accepted by the global church. While Christianity is now comfortable with accommodating cultural diversity as intrinsic to the Christian faith, constructing theology for the world church is a tall order as the question remains which and whose theology serves the global church. Even the terms "world church" and "global church" are problematic as they could either be construed to imply replication of a way of being church and Christian to other parts of the world or understood to emphasize the autochthonous nature of expressions of Christianity among various cultures and peoples. And so, historians and theologians are divided as to whether "World Christianity" or "Global Christianity" is the appropriate description of the worldwide spread of Christianity making it a truly world religion.

"World Christianity" emphasizes the growth of Christianity in places and cultures that were non-Christian in ways unique to those cultures and not necessarily being influenced by the dominant Western Christianity or cultures. World Christianity emphasizes the variety of indigenous responses to the Gospel in the language and culture of people.[2] "Global Christianity" on the other hand, presupposes the adaptation of Western Christianity to non-Western cultures converting to Christianity. It recalls the repeat of the hegemonic imperial triumphalist Christendom supposedly aimed at maintaining the one unified universal Western Christianity applicable to all cultures. It gives the impression that Christianity in the Afro-Asia-Lam countries depend on the Western intellectual tradition as well as economic (capitalistic), info-technological, cultural and social order. "The idea of "Europeandom" captures well the carry-over echoes that have survived under the term "Global Christianity."[3] For this reason, Christianities in the global South ought to be the same or to differ only slightly from Western Christianity.

Philip Jenkins while recognizing the validity of Sanneh's position, prefers to interpret Christianity in the global South from the perspective of Christendom.[4] But, his use of global Christianity resembles Sanneh's criticism of Europeandom—in the original sense of "unity in common

2. Lamin Sanneh, *Whose Religion is Christianity? The Gospel Beyond the West* (Grand Rapids: Wm. B. Eerdmans, 2003), 22.

3. Lamin Sanneh and Michael J. McClymond, "Chapter I: Introduction," Lamin Sanneh and Michael J. McClymond ed., *The Wiley-Blackwell Companion to World Christianity* (West Sussex, UK: John Wiley and Sons Ltd, 2016), Kindle Edition, Loc. 41.

4. Philip Jenkins, *The Next Christendom: The Coming of Global Christianity* (Oxford: Oxford University Press, 2007), xiii.

religious beliefs."[5] Jenkins claim that "debates about "Christendom" have also emerged powerfully in the global South, those regions of the world in which Christianity have spread rapidly in recent decades, especially in Africa and Asia."[6] Face to face with emerging Pentecostalism, Jenkins surmises Latin American Catholic church romanticizes the affinity of church and state in Christendom when the state would have been used to forge unified Christian belief. Jenkins seems unable to study Christianity in the global South outside the purview of Western Christianity. Christianity elsewhere resembles Christianity in Europe and if people are questioning Christianity in Europe, Britain for example, they are questioning it in Africa and Asia. This is the major problem Sanneh is contesting by his insistence on "World Christianity" instead of "Global Christianity." Jenkins asserts: "In other ways too, present day conditions in some emerging Christian churches echo those of older Europe. The growth of Christianity has occurred against a backdrop of economic globalization and political weakness, which challenges the very idea of nation state."[7]

Jenkins fails to reconcile the fact that Christianity was never originally a Western religion. He is struggling to come to grips with the worldwide spread of Christianity and the attendant plurality of Christianity in various cultures. He may be struggling with the thorny question of the form of the relation between Western Christianity and Christianity in the global South. But he could have done this without being stuck to the category of "Christendom." Karl Rahner reminds us how limited such category is in describing the world church: "Everyone knows how great an obstacle the ecclesial division of Christendom also constitutes for the spread of Christianity in all the world, in the so-called "mission countries."[8] But with Vatican II the church officially and fundamentally began to see itself as a world church, conscious of the importance of the inculturation of the faith to variety of ever changing cultures across the globe. Rahner compared the transition from the Western Church to the World Church to the break from the Jewish Christianity to Gentile Christianity launched by Paul.[9] The challenge remains one of the relation of religion and cultures, of Christianity and the

5. Philip Jenkins, "The Legacy of Christendom," in Lamin Sanneh and Michael J. McClymond ed., *The Wiley-Blackwell Companion to World Christianity*, Loc. 221.

6. Ibid., Loc. 218.

7. Ibid.

8. Karl Rahner, "Towards a Fundamental Theological Interpretation of Vatican II." *Theological Studies* 40, no. 4 (1979): 720.

9. Ibid., 716–727.

world cultures into which the faith is to be incarnated. Rahner recognizes this as the central issue tackled in Vatican II and notes the church either stands or falls based on its courage to carry it through.

This, then, is the issue: either the Church sees and recognizes these essential differences of other cultures for which she should become a world Church and with a Pauline boldness draws the necessary consequences from this recognition, or she remains a Western Church and so in the final analysis betrays the meaning of Vatican II.[10]

So, first, underlying the study of world Christianity is the recognition of the growth of Christianity in formerly non-Christian parts of the world. Second is comprehending theologically the distinct nature of Christianity in each culture. Third, articulating the relation of various local churches to one another and to the universal church with emphasis on collegiality. Fourth, determining how world Christianity will impact theology, mission and ministry. Fifth, thinking through the significance of Christianity to development and modernity as well as contributing to social transformation through Christian values.

Thus far, world Christianity as a discipline has concentrated in statistical growth and decline of Christianity in different geographical centers. Pew research centers report clearly the varying figures of this development across various epochs. The arduous contribution of David Barrett's World Christian Encyclopedia, the Atlas of Global Christianity[11] maps the demographic shift in the center of Christianity from the Northern to the Southern hemisphere.[12] Andrew Walls interprets the fluctuation in growth and decline as intrinsic to the very nature of Christianity. Despite some challenges, the progress of theology of inculturation highlights the distinctness of Christianity in various cultures. It is no longer in doubt that Christianity easily translates into the language and culture of each people embracing the faith. Even though the relationship between local churches and the universal churches can be very dicey arising from varieties of the exercise of power, the achievements of Vatican II on the Church as the people of God as well as the labor of theologians on communion ecclesiology with emphasis on collegiality in the exercise of ministry has strengthened the relationship between local and universal churches. In view of the global context of world

10. Ibid., 724.

11. *Atlas of Global Christianity*, ed. Todd M. Johnson and Kenneth R. Ross (Edinburgh: Edinburgh University Press, 2009).

12. Todd M Johnson and Kenneth R. Ross, "The Making of the Atlas of World Christianity," *International Bulletin of Missionary Research*, 34 no 1 Jan 2010, p. 12–16.

Christianity, the focus of the global church should be on the significance of world Christianity to the promotion of "the good human world"[13] in contemporary societies and cultures. That is, the formulation of a systematic theology of history, culture and society for the world church's engagement with the globalized world.

The Global Context of World Christianity

Not only is world Christianity made possible by early forces of globalization that facilitated transportation for the missionaries,[14] Christianity in the remotest part of the world today is affected positively and negatively by the advances in information technology and the ubiquitous transnational corporations made possible by the free trade thanks to neoliberal capitalist market-state spread across the globe.[15] A lot has been written both in support of and critical of globalization. But our focus will be on its impact on evangelization, on world Christianity. Pope Francis *Evangelii Gaudium* warns of "certain present realities [which] unless effectively dealt with, are capable of setting off processes of dehumanization which would then be hard to reverse."[16] While saluting improvements in "people's welfare in areas such as health care, education and communications,"[17] Pope Francis highlights some of the challenges of today's world to God's people and to evangelization attributed to these global changes:

> This epochal change has been set in motion by the enormous qualitative, quantitative, rapid and cumulative advances occurring in the sciences and in technology, and by their instant application in different areas of nature and life. We are in an age of knowledge and information, which has led to new and often anonymous kinds of power.[18]

---

13. Robert M. Doran, *Theological Foundations II: Theology and Culture* (Milwaukee: Marquette University Press, 1995), 27.

14. Richard Baldwin, *The Great Convergence: Information Technology and the New Globalization* (Cambridge, Massachusetts, London, England: The Belknap Press of Havard University Press, 2016).

15. Daniel M. Bell, *The Economy of Desire: Christianity and Capitalism in a Postmodern World* (Grand Rapids, Michigan: Baker Academic, 2012).

16. Pope Francis, *Evangelii Gaudium* no. 51.

17. Ibid., no. 52.

18. Ibid.

Pope Francis goes on to reject the basic tenets of neoliberal capitalism (economic globalization) by his vehement "no to the trickle-down theories of an economy of exclusion and inequality," and the attendant "globalization of indifference;"[19] "no to the new idolatry of money" arising from denial of the "primacy of the human person" leading to the widening gap between the rich and the poor. And finally, "no to a financial system which rules rather than serves; a financial system that rejects ethics and God but is guided by competition and shuns solidarity."[20] These conditions prevail the Pontiff argues, because the global "socioeconomic system is unjust at its root."[21] In *Laudato Si*, the Pontiff paints a clear picture of global social decline caused by the unbridled consumption engendered by the various forms of globalization:

> The social dimensions of global change include the effects of technological innovations on employment, social exclusion, an inequitable distribution and consumption of energy and other services, social breakdown, increased violence and a rise in new forms of social aggression, drug trafficking, growing drug use by young people, and the loss of identity. These are signs that the growth of the past two centuries has not always led to an integral development and an improvement in the quality of life. Some of these signs are also symptomatic of real social decline, the silent rupture of the bonds of integration and social cohesion.[22]

This in brief is the global context of world Christianity. And so, the question should be one of the significance of world Christianity to this global context. What is the task of theology to the global church's contribution to the existence of a good human world?

The Notion of the World-Cultural Community

Robert M. Doran answers these questions by adopting Lewis Mumford's 'World-cultural humanity' as the end goal of humanity and by extension of the Christian community. Mumford as one of the earliest thinkers to

---

19. Ibid., nos. 53 and 54

20. Ibid., no. 58.

21. Ibid., no. 59

22. Pope Francis, *Encyclical Letter, Laudato Si*, no. 46. http://w2.vatican.va/content/francesco/en/encyclicals/documents/papa-francesco_20150524_enciclica-laudato-si.html.

recognize the variety of human cultures explores through ideal-types he develops, the gradual process of human development culminating in appreciation of world cultures.[23] As alternative to the mechanomorphic automaton of the post-historic culture envisioned by the sciences intent on using humans as objects, world culture recognizing cultural differences of diverse peoples, seeks to restore the "unified self"[24] attuned to his biological, organic, intellectual and spiritual selves by paying attention to the hierarchy of values and the interrelationship of those values to one another from above and from below. World culture presupposes integration of the healthy elements of pre-existing cultures in the various historical trajectory and development of humankind. It thrives not in discarding but in integration of various cultures to enhance human holistic development.[25] In other words, according to Mumford, world culture integrates in new and changed forms "the communal polity of Neolithic times, the urban civilization of antiquity and later, the axial and national cultures that succeeded them and the mechanical models of the New World."[26] World culture is an open society to be attained by persons "capable of breaking through the boundaries of culture and history."[27] The ideal of wholeness envisioned by world culture is attained "when every aspect of life is open to cultivation, when the instinctual life is no longer cut off from rational development, and when order and reason are not impoverished by torpid emotions or listless routines or limited purposes."[28] In brief, world culture consists in recognition of the validity of other cultures and readiness to learn from them to enhance the excellences of one's culture and overcome their inadequacies.[29]

> To reach full human stature, at the present stage of development, each of us must be ready, as opportunity offers, to assimilate the contributions of other cultures; and to develop, for the sake of wholeness, those parts of his personality that are weakest . . . He who has reached the level of world culture will be at home in any part of that culture: in its inner world, no less than its outer world.

23. Lewis Mumford, *The Transformations of Man* (Gloucester, Mass.: Peter Smith, 1978).

24. Ibid., 144.

25. Ibid., 154–155.

26. Ibid., 149.

27. Ibid., 169.

28. Ibid., 177.

29. Ibid., 178.

> Everything that he does or feels or makes will bear the imprint of the larger self he has made his own.[30]

The human person is at the center of world culture because he incarnates love, that force able to rescue the earth from forces like hate and violence unleashed against it.

In different occasions in his writings,[31] Doran acknowledges the centerpiece of Mumford's world-cultural humanity in his work. He writes:

> The problem with which I want to come to grips was set by Lewis Mumford nearly twenty-five years ago. In his book, *The Transformations of Man* Mumford employs a series of ideal-types to trace the major developments of human consciousness and of the cultural forms that can be found in recorded history. At the end of this overview of cultural history, he raises the question of where we go from here. He proposes two further ideal-types to help his readers imagine alternative options for human development or regression. The first he calls "post-historic man," and the second, "world-cultural man." Post-historic humanity is one whose neurophysiology, memory, imagination, intelligence, and freedom would become ossified in patterns of behavior or—to use Lonergan's term—schemes of recurrence that have been cumulatively programmed by neural, psychological, social, economic, political, conceptual, and linguistic conditioning. World-cultural humanity, on the other hand, would be the alternative that would emerge if we recognize the gravity of our present situation and move to a major transformation of selfhood. We must take our stand on the crosscultural constituents of genuine humanity and move from these foundations to appropriate and transform the major cultural acquisitions bequeathed us by the previous stages in human development. In this way the human community would be able to move to a new unity.[32]

Doran is convinced Lonergan's work is germane for the emergence of world-cultural humanity.[33] For this reason, he appropriates and advances

---

30. Ibid., 190–191.

31. *Theology and the Dialectics of History* (Toronto: University of Toronto Press, 1990); *What is Systematic Theology?* (Toronto: University of Toronto Press, 2005).

32. Robert M. Doran, *Psychic Conversion and Theological Foundations: Toward a Reorientation of the Human Science* (Chico, California: Scholars Press, 1981), ix.

33. Ibid.

Lonergan's works "not only to specify the foundations of a world-cultural humanity but also to initiate a movement toward the realization of a new human community."[34]

Early Doran's writings were devoted to the establishment of this movement. His 1981 article "Theological Grounds for a World-Cultural Humanity" identifies the good human world to be realized through the global transformation of human consciousness made possible by crosscultural grounding of genuine human authenticity, as "world-cultural humanity."[35] Appropriation of the transcultural roots of this "historic synthesis of faith and culture," of world cultural community presupposes openness to cultural differences as an enrichment to be preserved not one to be homogenized. Primarily it implies genuine respect for peculiar ways of being at the heart of human dignity of people. For, "no empirically given culture is normative for genuine humanity. On the contrary, the constituents of genuine humanity are normative for the genuineness and maturity of a culture."[36] This can only come about by not displacing the tension of limitation and transcendence on either side of the psyche and intentionality. In simple terms, by not disregarding the role of feelings, emotions, aesthetic part of the human person in preference for the intellectual part; by not demeaning the dignity of people closely attuned to nature (cosmological) and exalting those cultures that emphasize human knowledge (anthropological) modes of culture. "This tension [between psychic limitation and intentional transcendence] constitutes the integral dialectic of the subject; it lies at the root of the integral dialectic of community; and it is the key to understanding and appropriating a dialectic of culture out of which the cultural values of a world-cultural humanity can be generated through crosscultural exchange, dialogue, and cooperation."[37] World-cultural humanity is realized through the integrity of cosmological and anthropological constitutive meaning achieved by the soteriological consciousness. Doran's thesis is clear:

> cosmological and anthropological constitutive meanings will constitute an integral dialectic of culture for world-cultural humanity; soteriological differentiation will be the condition of the possibility of the integrity of the dialectic; and by mediating the

---

34. Ibid., x.

35. Robert M. Doran, *Theological Foundations Vol Two: Theology and Culture* (Milwaukee: Marquette University Press, 1995),

36. Doran, *Theology and the Dialectics of History*, 536.

37. Ibid., 484.

> soteriological differentiation with cosmological and anthropological insight and truth, theology will be assuming responsibility for the integrity of the dialectic of culture.[38]

World-cultural community is the alternative Mumford gives to the post-historic community characterized by modernity's scientific disregard of the human sciences emphasis of the integration of the psyche and intelligence.

According to Doran, modernity's option for the practical sciences manifests itself in the two-opposed political and economic systems of socialism and multinational dominated neoliberal capitalism. World-cultural community is to be realized through the integral scale of values, that is, maintaining the taut balance of limitation and transcendence of the dialectics of the subject, the community and culture, and not displacing them on either side. "The ultimate center of the true order of humankind will always be located in the heuristic anticipation of the complete integrity of the scale of values that constitutes the consciousness of the catalytic agents of that order."[39] His "Report on a Work in Progress" of 1984 was beginning a work on a systematics entitled "A Theology for a World-Cultural Humanity."[40] This decision is informed by his observation that the totalitarianisms of the distortion of the post-historic community operative in the modern political economies collapse cultural values to social values and therefore the distortion of the scale of values. It will be necessary to distinguish the infrastructure of culture from its superstructural complexifications in different disciplines. Christian systematic theology to mediate cultures as Lonergan postulates, must do this globally by insisting on the integral scale of values.[41] This is not surprising because history is the integral dialectics of the subject, culture and community.

> In such a conception religious values condition the possibility of personal integrity, personal integrity conditions the possibility of genuine cultural values, such cultural values condition the possibility of a just social order, and a just social order conditions the possibility of an equitable distribution of particular goods. The network of alternative communities arising from the praxis of such a mentality must extend across both cultural and religious boundaries.[42]

---

38. Ibid., 502.

39. Ibid., 131

40. Ibid., 3.

41. Ibid., 26

42. Ibid., 5. See also *Theology and the Dialectics of History*, 476

The theological foundations of world-cultural humanity are the four aspects of conversion: religious, moral, intellectual, and psychic. Doran promises to devote his intellectual energies to working out such a theology "that can mediate Christian faith with the global cultural matrix in such a way as to promote the emergence of a world-cultural community."[43]

Theology for World-Cultural Community

Doran's devotion of his intellectual energies towards theology for a world-cultural humanity came to fruition in *Theology and the Dialectics of History*, (TDH). In Chapter 17 of TDH, he "assembled some of the elements of a world-cultural consciousness."[44] These elements include the implementation of the transcendental precepts: Be attentive, Be intelligent, Be reasonable, Be responsible, Be in love; the differentiations of consciousness (at various levels in society) "an assembly of the realms of meaning disengaged in the course of history: realistic common sense, theory, modern science, art, scholarship, interiority, transcendence, ecological participation in nature, and soteriological experience."[45] And conscious attempts at the level of personal value, a commitment to "refinement, education and purification of consciousness."[46] This in no way means that everybody must attain the superstructural scholarly differentiation of consciousness. But in some sense, the impact of such differentiation on the part of the minority can indirectly affect and influence the infrastructure of culture.

Following Doran, one can say that human flourishing is brought about by authentic persons converted soteriologically, morally, intellectually and psychically governed by differentiations of consciousness who are committed to creating alternative communities to the post-historic mechanical cultures and societies prevalent in our globalized world. Theology does this by rejecting cultural exclusivism and radically affirming and promoting an integral dialectic of culture that makes for a world-cultural community.[47] The task of contemporary systematic theology should be articulating such regulative ideal for the development of such converted persons. Such theology will be based on the integral scale of values. "The task before us is to promote the emergence of a world-cultural community of men and

43. Ibid., 6.

44. Ibid., 529.

45. Ibid., 531

46. Ibid., 537.

47. Ibid., 420

women who acknowledge the intrinsic value of all nine differentiations of consciousness as these have been developed in various cultural traditions, and who leave themselves open to growth in all four dimensions of conversion."[48] It will consist in the self-appropriation of consciousness and in the acknowledgement of the normative scale of values.[49] It will be grounded not in the anthropological and cosmological symbolizations of the experience of life but in the soteriological differentiations of consciousness. Anthropological and cosmological symbolizations are not inclusive of others but exclusive catering only for its members. Soteriological consciousness on the contrary is inclusive of humanity as it is based on the universal salvation of humankind. Contemporary systematic theology so envisioned implies a shift in the understanding of church from a narrow parochial sense to an ecumenic understanding of world church not necessarily in the sense of the church being in all parts of the world but in the sense of the church not just being institutional as being inclusive of humanity standing up against distortions of the dialectic of community. The church is to extend beyond itself to include humanity beyond its boundaries.

World Christianity Towards A World Cultural Humanity

The distinction between world Christianity and Christendom now makes perfect sense. Christianity should be conceived not in the restricted classicist sense of Europeandom, as that will not be respectful of the plurality of cultures, common meanings, and peoples world Christianity represents. World Christianity envisions a world cultural humanity where people's human dignity and personhood counts uppermost as one of the presuppositions of being Christian as revelation and the history of salvation presupposes the human subject exercising the freedom and responsibility of personal relationship with God. This freedom is exercised and expressed in variety of ways in accordance with one's culture. Doran is full of hope:

> Implementing Lonergan's achievements in a systematic theology that mediates in direct discourse from the present into the future entails providing the constitutive meaning of the integral dialectics of community, the subject, and culture, and doing so in such a way as to evoke a world-cultural alternative to the present globally pervasive distortions of these three dialectics. This is the context

48. Ibid., 551.

49. Ibid., 483.

that defines the ulterior finality of the multiform tasks that must be performed if Lonergan's achievement is to be implemented and thus prove ultimately fruitful for the human community."[50]

Achieving such systematic theology means first preference for the term 'world Christianity' instead of 'global Christianity.' Second, the inter-pollination of theological ideas in the world church where the church in the global south and the church in the global north mutually respect and learn from one another. Third, the recognition of and the promotion of theological plurality in the world church. Fourth, the healing of the distorted dialectic of world community broken by the lop-sidedness of the structure that favor the rich at the expense of the poor and hence the promotion of global inequality, worship of profit regardless of human dignity, 'thingification' of the weak and those at the margins of society by a structure that regard others as mere statistics leading to demeaning of the personhood and subjectivity of individual as objects to be used and discarded. Fifth, constructing theology for world Christianity that recognizes the diverse forms of plurality including plurality of cultures, languages, religions, (and hence inculturation of liturgies and ways of being church), scale of values, histories, social, political, economic policies, and legal institutions, etc. Such theology prioritizes human well-being, mutual co-existence and world peace.

Conclusion

Studying Christianity as a belief-system expressed in various cultures in diverse languages and contexts is the hallmark of World Christianity. The differences in Christian practice in various localities does not negate the essential element of Christianity. While any attempt at cultural imperialism must be resisted as evidenced in World Christianity's rejection of Christianity as a Western religion, it is possible to construct systematic theology for World Christianity in the light of the mission and ministry of Jesus Christ, the establishment of the reign of God and the imperative of love as the Magna Charta of Christian faith. Recognizing that such theology could be expressed in diverse ways in the light of various cultures, yet the centrality of the Kerygma makes such theology possible.

Doran's systematics is an example of such a theology. It is based in Bernard Lonergan's invariant dynamic structure of human consciousness emphasizing the unrestricted desire to know common to humanity of all

50. Ibid., 158.

cultures. Hence it is transcultural. It draws on Lonergan's functional specialization of theology, and therefore it upholds the general and special categories and hence appreciates the contribution of the social and human sciences to theology. It addresses one of the most important concerns of the majority world church, of the Afro-AsiaLam countries which insists on the praxis of faith and theology. Systematics for Doran hinges on the integral scale of values, not just religious values of God's grace but the gift of God's love as underlying personal integrity, authentic cultures, sound social order and thus making possible the constant and recurrent provision of the vital needs necessary for human wellbeing in the world. Because of its belief in the common humanity Christians share with people of other religious faith, Doran's systematics takes seriously interfaith relations. It understands the gift of God's love as a universal gift of God to humanity in the light of the universal salvific will of God for humanity. The universality of the gift of the Holy Spirit extends even to religions that may not even recognize it. Such broadening of the horizon of the role of the Holy Spirit it claims is a bonus to Christianity as it opens all religious faith to Christian theology making it possible for building a world church or world theology and hence of promoting world-cultural humanity.

CHAPTER ELEVEN

ROBERT DORAN

The Master Collaborator

Cyril Orji

University of Dayton (Dayton, OH)

A festschrift in itself is an acknowledgment of a scholar's contribution to the field. There is no one template for the honor. The achievement of Robert Doran to Catholic systematic thought and Lonergan scholarship cannot be reduced to single trope. Since other contributors in this volume will all highlight different aspects of Doran's contribution, I take the leeway to describe him with a pair of words that captures both his contribution to Catholic intellectual thought and Lonergan scholarship: master-collaborator. Doran, the master-collaborator, has ensured that Lonergan's work does not remain an "unfinished symphony." Drawing from my own personal context, I argue that the scissors-action metaphor Lonergan made famous in *Insight* hints at Doran's role in bringing the Lonergan project in tune with the realities of the World Church. If Lonergan intentionally left his work unfinished, it was only because he could rely on the collaborative effort of the community of scholars that Doran epitomizes.

A Personal Context

Working on my doctoral dissertation, I wrestled with two-pronged issues: how to bring Lonergan scholarship to bear on World Christianity (which some still abnormally refer to as global Christianity) and the important matter of Catholic Intellectual Tradition (CIT). The distinction between global Christianity and World Christianity comes within the purview of differentiation of consciousness, which Lonergan says is a necessity for theology in the new context. The one who made this Lonergan-esque distinction (though not a Lonerganian) is the Gambian historian of religion,

Lamin Sanneh (1942–2019). Global Christianity is a faithful replication of Christian forms and patterns that have been developed in Europe. But unlike global Christianity, which is one thing (classicist to be blunt), "World Christianity is not one thing, but a variety of indigenous responses through more or less effective idioms, but in any case without necessarily the European Enlightenment frame."[1] Failure to grasp this distinction has led to the continued confusion and conflation of the terms. My context was Catholic Christianity, particularly the expression of this religious faith in the Southern Hemisphere. I was convinced at the time, and even more so now, that Lonergan contributes immensely to the shift in the Christian landscape southward—that his Generalized Empirical Method (GEM) was the much-needed catalyst for both World Christianity and CIT. One only needs to read *Insight*[2] and *Method in Theology*[3] to understand how he effected this massive shift from a Eurocentric to a world vision of the church, hence the neologism World Christianity. Lonergan broadened the scope of theological and historical studies through the transcultural method he delineated in these works to include the cultures and peoples of the Southern Hemisphere—cultures that had hitherto been excluded by a normative classicist thinking that dominated Catholic intellectual thought for a long time. Working on a doctoral dissertation, as I was at the time, and sifting through the Lonergan corpus was daunting. It is one thing to be convinced of an idea (as I was of what Lonergan brings to the table) and another thing to work out the implications of that idea by working through *Insight* on your own. I recall the admonition of Frederick Crowe—that far too many doctoral candidates "ignore the more humble role of a dissertation; they aim at a world-shaking production, only to find in the end that the world remains unshaken, and that they have squandered the best years of their lives on a rather fruitless idea."[4]

Taking Crowe's admonition to heart, I wanted to let Lonergan be the thinker whose ideas I would appropriate for my Catholic and African audience. But Lonergan writes in a technical and language-specific way, which

1. Lamin Sanneh, *Whose Religion is Christianity? The Gospel Beyond the West* (Grand Rapids, MI: Eerdmans, 2003), 22.

2. See Bernard Lonergan, Collected Works of Bernard Lonergan 3: *Insight: A Study in Human Understanding*, eds. Frederick E. Crowe and Robert M. Doran (Toronto: University of Toronto Press, 1992).

3. See Bernard Lonergan, Collected Works of Bernard Lonergan 14: *Method in Theology*, eds. Robert M. Doran and John D. Dadosky (Toronto: University of Toronto Press, 2017).

4. Frederick E. Crowe, *Lonergan* (Collegeville, MN: Liturgical Press, 1992), 47.

is not easy to decode by a novice. How was a graduate student to understand a thinker who, for example, employed scholastic terms but gave to them his own creative meaning? It is undeniable that Lonergan employed terms that were current and gave them "his own personal content."[5] My task was made easier when I discovered *Theology and the Dialectics of History* by Robert Doran.[6] Doran's work elucidated for me my struggles with *Insight*. It also unnerved the tensions of inquiry that had me imprisoned for months of working through *Insight* on my own. I was working at the time to apply Lonergan's notion of bias to the perennial ethnic and religious conflicts in Africa. What Doran calls psychic conversion was quite helpful to my project then (and even more helpful to my project now). I began to understand, as he himself made clear years later, that the mimetic theory of Rene Girard can elucidate what Lonergan means by dramatic bias—that it is the aberration of sensitivity that psychic conversion enables one to acknowledge.[7] Anyone who understands the scale of the Rwandan genocide of the 1990s, the scope of the war in Darfur that began in 2003 with still no end in sight, the magnitude of the seemingly endless war that began in the Congo in 1996, and the sporadic religious tension in Nigeria and other parts of Africa that have brought the continent to its knees, would appreciate what Doran means by the mimetic dimension at the root of human conflicts. In all, Doran helped me with a more manageable reading and understanding of the dimensions of bias and conversion in the Lonergan corpus.

As Lonergan broadened the scope of theological and historical studies through his functional specialization, Doran understands the global vision which Lonergan helps to establish to be, not a finished article, but a process. The process can be attained, not only by Lonergan's intellectual, religious, and moral conversion, but also by a further fourth dimension Doran calls psychic conversion. This fourth dimension of personal transformation, as Doran understands it, is "not specifically included in Lonergan's discussion of intellectual, moral, and religious conversion."[8] By introducing a fourth dimension of conversion process, Doran fully integrates into Lonergan's thinking a transcendental imagination [by no means intended in the twisted Kantian or Heideggerian meaning] Lonergan had already begun

5. Ibid., 125.

6. See Robert M. Doran, *Theology and the Dialectics of History* (Toronto: University of Toronto Press, 1990).

7. Robert Doran, "Two Ways of Being Conscious: The Notion of Psychic Conversion," *Method: Journal of Lonergan Studies* 3 (2012), 1–17, 16.

8. Ibid., 7.

by transcending the limitations of Kant and the Frankfurt School. *Theology and the Dialectics of History* became for me (and as I discovered much later, also for many others) a companion to *Insight* and *Method in Theology*. As I finished my dissertation and began teaching and researching further in the area of Lonergan scholarship, it became evident to me that the perichoresis I found between *Insight/Method in Theology* and *Theology and the Dialectics of History* is not limited to these works. The synchrony extends to the whole of gamut of Lonergan and Doran works.

To Live is to Change

The consciousness that the human species, as a whole, possesses, is potential rather than actual.[9] Lonergan was among the Catholic thinkers who introduced into Catholic theology historical consciousness. Historical consciousness is a counterpoint to elite consciousness that had earlier pervaded Catholic thought. Lonergan taps into the rich resource of the Christian tradition to help Catholicism realize a hidden potential. The phenomenological process he calls intentionality analysis, a key part of GEM, is a procedure Lonergan introduced to help turn potential to actuality. Doran, on his part, always writes to expand, elucidate, and bring forth the rich ideas that Lonergan injects into Catholic theological thought. He underscores the Lonerganian idea that our historical consciousness must include all peoples everywhere. Doran brings out more clearly the transcultural nature of Lonergan's method. It was through Doran's work that I began to understand, very early in my professional career, how the *novum organnum*, which Lonergan labored tirelessly to preserve, can be systematically organized and presented to the World Church in a way that is coherent and meaningful. It was through my reading of Doran that I got to know the more that Lonergan is an inculturation theologian.

Frederick Crowe once wrote, with respect to Lonergan's relation to other thinkers, that Lonergan "was a loner, and must be studied in himself and for his own contribution." It is only when that basis is laid, Crowe continues, that one "could make interesting comparisons with other historical figures."[10] My engagement with Doran's work over the years has made it even more evident that Doran is one whose vocation is to lay the basis of Lonergan's scholarship. He is one who helps other Lonergan scholars

9. William H. McNeill, *The Global Condition: Conquerors, Catastrophes, and Community* (Princeton, NJ: Princeton University Press, 1992), x.

10. Crowe, *Lonergan*, ix.

to connect Lonergan to "other historical figures." One only needs to read some of the editors' note and footnotes of the masterful project of the *Collected Works of Bernard Lonergan* (now in the 25th volume) to see how Doran is making these connections. Where some sadly read Lonergan to search for blemishes in his work,[11] Doran reads Lonergan to learn from him and make available to others a systematic presentation of the mind of a genius. Cardinal John Henry Newman once said, in one of the many adages for which he is known, "To live is to change and to be perfect is to have changed often."[12] As a thinker who kept thinking all through his life, Lonergan's ideas changed somewhat. Doran's task has been to provide a context for understanding these genetic and dialectical changes.

The Scissors-Action Metaphor Applied

Doran's immense admiration for Lonergan cannot be quantified. His project is geared towards advancing Lonergan's work for World Christianity and CIT. In *Insight*, Lonergan introduces a scissors metaphor. He equates the process of attaining insight or rational self-appropriation to the action of a pair of scissors. What he calls the lower blade includes research results and scholarly techniques. The upper blade consists of a heuristic structure, "a set of generalities that is at once universal and concrete."[13] He makes clear that the scissors metaphor should not be mistaken for a way of organizing data. The upward and downward movements of the scissors action are also not to be construed as alternative ways of knowing. The upper blade of scissors action in no way determines the data supplied by the lower.[14] Lonergan locates the "upper blade in the categories and [the] lower blade in the data."[15] He uses examples from physics to illustrate how the principles and laws of physics are not mathematics and data, but the fruit of a genuine interaction between mathematics and data. He envisages theology in a similar way—that it is "neither purely a priori nor purely a posteriori but only

11. Ibid.

12. See John Henry Newman, *Conscience, Consensus, and the Development of Doctrine* (New York: Doubleday, 1992). See Section 1 titled, "On the Process of Development in Ideas."

13. Donna Teevan, "Albert Einstein and Bernard Lonergan on Empirical Method," *Zygon* 37 (2002): 873–90, at 882.

14. Fredrick E. Crowe, "Rhyme and Reason: On Lonergan's Foundations for works of the Spirit," in *Developing the Lonergan Legacy: Historical, Theoretical, and Existential Themes*, edited by Michael Vertin (Toronto: University of Toronto, 2004), 314–331, at 323.

15. Bernard Lonergan, *Method in Theology* (Toronto: University of Toronto Press, 1996), 293.

the fruit of an ongoing process that has one foot in a transcultural base and the other on increasingly organizing data."[16] What he calls the upper blade and the lower blade operate in parallel ways, the data of the lower blade has its own source and its own autonomy; it is not determined by the upper blade. When the upper blade joins itself to the lower, it does not destroy it in any way, shape, or form, but to sublate it. The two (the sublated and the sublating) are like two disparate factors (objectivity-subjectivity) that work harmoniously together to produce result.[17] The upper blade is prior intellectual achievements a person attains. It is the genuine objectivity that proceeds as the fruit of his or her authentic subjectivity. The upper blade shows that even in our differentiated universes of discourse, "objectivity can be achieved, and dialogue can become fruitful where authentic personal and collective subjectivity is operating in a more explicit manner."[18]

A great deal of what Lonergan says about intellectual development can be interpreted biographically. The scissors action metaphor can be applied to Lonergan and Doran in tandem—Lonergan being the upper blade and the Doran the lower blade. The one does not destroy the other. Also, the two work harmoniously to aid human achievement, human development, and higher viewpoints.[19] Where Lonergan makes allusions without developing them or broaches a subject with many ramifications, Doran helps develop them with a certain freshness. It is fascinating to see how Doran at times goes back to courses Lonergan himself gave on different subjects to enrich Lonergan's own published works. For instance, from 1959 to 1962, Lonergan gave a series of courses on method at the Gregorian University where he enumerates, among other things, the problems that give rise to method. Doran has been integrating Lonergan's notes on these courses in the *Collected Works*. The same applies to Lonergan's work in Christology. For reasons relating to health, Lonergan did not develop his Christological treatise. Doran has been refining and developing that treatise.

Dialectics and the World Church

I have always been convinced that a proper understanding of what Lonergan means by interiorly differentiated consciousness will yield to

16. Ibid.

17. Crowe, "Rhyme and Reason," 322.

18. John C. Haughey, *Where is Knowing Going?: Horizons of the Knowing Subject* (Washington DC: Georgetown University Press, 2009), 92.

19. See discussion of "higher viewpoints" in Lonergan, *Insight*, 37–38.

a method that can serve World Christianity. The language of interiority needs to be transposed and further developed, in the light of the realities of the World Church, because, as Doran has shown, there is more to what Lonergan means by interiority than is apparent in *Method in Theology*. This is not the place, however, for that much-needed transposition. It is a project I have in the pipeline for World Christianity in the light of insights Doran sheds on the subject.

In discourse on the World Church, a distinction has often been made, as it should be, between the realities of the churches of the Northern Hemisphere and the realities of the churches of the Southern Hemisphere. Unfortunately, these realities are at times spoken of in a way that seems to pit them against each other, as if they are perennially opposed. What Lonergan calls "Dialectics" can offer a rapprochement. The functional specialty, Dialectics, (together with Foundations) is one of Lonergan's ways of bringing the Church to the level of the times.[20] Our time is a time of World Christianity, not global Christianity or Christendom. The creation of dialectic (and foundations) was meant to replace the old appeal to proof-texts that served Christendom.[21] It has no basis in World Christianity. Dialectics deals with conflicts of opposing viewpoints. It clarifies opposition through a careful, deliberative, and evaluative process. The conflicts that dialectic deals with may be overt or latent, known or unknown. They may even be conflicts that are hidden in the historical traditions, or religious imaginations of a people. Lonergan sees the basic conflict in human development to be one between positions and counter positions, two contradictory abstractions that need to be resolved if human development is to become a reality. What Dialectics does, therefore, is help reveal that not all differences are dialectical and that while opposing viewpoints may in fact be contraries, they are not all necessarily contradictories.

Doran develops Lonergan's idea further and distinguishes between what he calls the dialectics of contradictories and the dialectics of contraries. "There are opposites that are contraries. Such as matter and spirit, consciousness and unconscious, the masculine and the feminine dimensions of the psyche, the ego and the personal shadow [technical terms in Jungian psychology] as victim of social and personal history. Between such

---

20. Frederick Crowe, "Lonergan's Vocation as a Christian Thinker," in *Developing the Lonergan Legacy: Historical, Theoretical, and Existential Themes*, ed. Michael Vertin (Toronto, ON: University of Toronto Press, 2004), 16.

21. Frederick Crowe, "All my Work has been Introducing History into Catholic Theology," in *Developing the Lonergan Legacy*, 95.

opposites there can be established a dialectical integration, a creative tension that constitutes personal integrity."[22] There are also opposites that are contradictories, such as good and evil, progress and decline. Dialectics of contradictories are those opposite poles at odds with each other. A dialectic of contradictories cannot be resolved by integration, but by good reasoned decisions.[23] Following Doran's distinction, the churches of the Northern Hemisphere and those of the Southern Hemisphere are not to be conceived as dialectical (dialectics of contradictions). "The point of the dialectic is not to choose one over the other but to assure that they are working harmoniously with one another. And so, I came to call the respective poles of the dialectic, not contradictories but contraries. To regard them as contradictories is to head toward personal disaster."[24]

Doran introduces the category of the dialectics of culture—that the dialectics of culture is a dialectics of contraries.[25] To be found in the dialectics of culture is a tension between cosmological meanings and values and anthropological meanings and values constitutive of that culture.[26] The cosmological and anthropological meanings are meanings by which various peoples express their experience of the search for meaning and direction in the movement of life.[27] Dialectics of culture is a corrective to a disjunctive approach to culture that was inspired by the Cartesian and Hegelian dualism that thinks in terms of either-or, not both-and. Dialectics of culture moves towards a holistic worldview, creating a balance between two seemingly opposing cultural viewpoints.[28]

Lessons Moving Forward

When I got my first job after my doctoral studies and started teaching, it did not take long to discover how difficult it is to get articles on Lonergan published in certain journals. As I began to talk to colleagues about frustration of anti-Lonergan bias in certain journals, I began to discover that the

22. Doran, *Theology and the Dialectics of History*, 349.

23. Ibid.

24. Doran, "Two Ways of Being Conscious," 9.

25. Doran, *Theology and the Dialectics of History*, 503.

26. Ibid.

27. Ibid., 505.

28. See Tae-Seop Lim and Seokhoon Ahn, "Dialectics of Culture and Dynamic Balancing between Individuality and Collectivity," *Journal of Asian Pacific Communications* 25 (2015), 63–77.

problem is even more widespread. There are many reasons for this. Understandably, not everyone is well disposed to Lonergan's ideas. One cannot fault a journal that has a specific focus for not being receptive to Lonergan's ideas. There is also some anti-Lonergan bias stemming from the fact that some may have been rubbed the wrong way by some Lonergan enthusiasts. It was impressed on me, by some colleagues aware of the situation, that the best way to get a Lonergan article published in journals without specific focus on Lonergan's ideas is to identify a theological problem and attempt to use Lonergan to resolve it. I tried it, but only with a limited success. It was not until I read Doran that I discovered the limitations of this action plan. For the young and upcoming Lonergan scholars out there who may be facing the same dilemma I faced early in my professional career, Doran has a much better action plan. Doran's plan is a more reason-based and pragmatic action plan to follow, if one wants to get one's work out in top tier journals. One of the limitations of Lonergan students in their engagements with other thinkers, Doran writes, is that they tend to be "one way streets," in their engagement with other thinkers. Doran finds this "one way street" to be antithetical to Lonergan's own way of reading other authors. Lonergan's own way of reading other thinkers and his interlocutors, according to Doran, is not to sniff out counter-positions, but to make them better than they really are.[29] Doran cites, as an example of how Lonergan makes his interlocutors better than they are, the case of Kant, who purportedly claimed to have destroyed metaphysics. Rather than make Kant worse than he really is, Lonergan interprets "Kant's transcendental imagination as inquiry transforming mere experiencing into the scrutiny of observation, trying to promote something imagined into something intelligible."[30] Herein lies Doran's reason-based pragmatic action plan for Lonergan students: in engaging other thinkers, avoid the old temptation of sniffing out counter-positions in these thinkers, and be brave and creative enough to make the position of these thinkers better than they really are. That was what Lonergan did, that is what Doran is doing, and that is a lesson for young Lonergan scholars.

29. Doran, "Two Ways of Being Conscious," 3.

30. Ibid., 4; see footnote 5.

CHAPTER TWELVE

CAPITALISM, REFORM IT OR REPLACE IT?

The Encounter of Ethics and Economics in Current Ecological Debates

Gerard Whelan, S.J.

An increasing number of students of Bernard Lonergan are recognizing the relevance of his thought for reflection on ecology. In particular, his cosmology of an emergently probable universe is recognized as a rich resource upon which to ground the necessarily interdisciplinary nature of reflection on the environmental crisis.[1] In this article, I illustrate this point by focusing on one of the interdisciplinary tensions being experienced within the ecological movement—that between economists and some ethicists. I proceed in two steps. First, I outline the thought of two authors who represent both sides of this tension. I note that differences often revolve around what emphasis to place on policies of carbon pricing as a strategy for mitigating climate change. Next, I offer a dialectical analysis of the thought of these authors. I side primarily with the argument of the economists that favors carbon pricing. However, I also recognize much value in the wider ethical arguments being offered, suggesting that, in part, they represent an expression of the "cosmopolis" that Lonergan and Robert Doran believe will be necessary to offer cultural support for rational and responsible economic policies.

1. See, Joseph Ogbonnaya and Lucas Briola, ed., *Everything Is Interconnected: Towards a Globalization with a Human Face and an Integral Ecology* (Milwaukee, WI: Marquette University Press, 2019), especially the entry by Paul St. Amour, "A Heuristic for the Critical Analysis of Globalization," 3–22; Cynthia Crysdale and Neil Ormerod, *Creator God Evolving World* (Minneapolis, MN: Fortress, 2013); Janna Metcalfe Rosales, *Method in Ecology* (Newfoundland, Canada: Memorial University of Newfoundland Press, 2002); Ann Dalton, *A Theology for the Earth: The Contributions of Thomas Berry and Bernard Lonergan* (Ottawa: University of Ottawa Press, 1999).

The Economic Perspective: Ottmar Edenhofer and Carbon Pricing

Ottmar Edenhofer is a German economist who is a member of the International Panel for Climate Change (IPCC).[2] He has philosophical interests and attends interdisciplinary academic conferences, which include ethicists who do not agree with him. He is associated with a think tank, based in Berlin, that held a conference in September 2019, "Divergent Values in Sustainability Assessments." The term "sustainability assessments," here, refers to technical questions of evaluating levels of carbon in the atmosphere and policies needed to mitigate the increase of these. The organizers of the conference note that such technical questions also involve ethical questions:

> Conflicting values are increasingly understood to be a considerable challenge for sustainability governance in general and integrated assessment processes in particular. But how can international (e.g., IPCC, IPBES, etc.) or domestic science-policy interfaces explicitly consider divergent normative viewpoints, including, for example, different interests, ethical principles, different framings of sustainability, as well as the various policy goals underlying climate change mitigation, biodiversity protection and sustainable development?[3]

Before discussing the ethical debates which this conference encourages, it is important to understand the technical insights that underlie them.

Edenhofer outlines how the response to the ecological crisis developed at the level of international governance.[4] He explains, how an initial

2. A description of the history and purpose of the IPCC is offered on the next page. Ottmar Edenhofer is Director and Chief Economist of the Potsdam Institute for Climate Impact Research as well as Director of the Mercator Research Institute on Global Commons and Climate Change (MCC) and Professor of the Economics of Climate Change at the Technische Universität Berlin.

3. Conference of the "Mercator Research Institute on Global Commons and Climate Change "(MCC), Berlin, September 2019, "Divergent values in sustainability assessments: love them, leave them, or change them?" https://www.mcc-berlin.net/en/valuesconference.html (accessed November 2019).

4. Explaining the perspective of the IPCC to a non-economist audience, see Ottmar Edenhofer and Michael Jakob, *Klimapolitik: Ziele, Konflikte, Losungen* (Munich: C.H. Beck, 2017). There are plans to publish an English translation of this book. See also a lecture by Edenhofer on the notion of the carbon budget and climate change, accessed November 2019, https://www.youtube.com/watch?v=XrQHKyqDWxw&t=1432s.

awareness of the ecological problem emerged during the 1960s, with 1972 witnessing the convoking of a United Nations Conference on the Human Environment and the founding of the United Nations Environment Programme (UNEP). In 1988, UNEP combined with the World Meteorological Organization to establish the IPCC, defined as "an intergovernmental body of the United Nations dedicated to providing the world with an objective, scientific view of climate change, its natural, political and economic impacts and risks and possible response options." The IPCC published a First Assessment Report[5] in 1990 and this led directly to a meeting in Rio de Janeiro in 1992 entitled the "United Nations Framework Convention on Climate Change" in order to produce an international agreement based on its conclusions. The aim of this convention was "to stabilize greenhouse gas concentrations in the atmosphere at a level that would prevent dangerous anthropogenic [i.e., human induced] interference with the climate system."

The first "Earth Summit" of 1992 produced much good will but had limited results, with parties to the convention making only limited promises on the key issue of reducing carbon emissions so as to mitigate climate change. The parties to the convention agreed to form a "Conference of Parties" (COP) which would meet annually and see if more radical commitments were possible. The insights of the First Assessment Report of the IPCC have been confirmed and deepened by the IPCC in subsequent years, culminating in the Fifth Assessment Report in 2014. COP meetings have been informed by these documents and parties to the covenant have been significantly increasing the promises they make about carbon emissions. In this process, the Paris gathering, "COP 21," held in 2015, was significant. Commentators suggest that one influence that helped government leaders to make relatively generous offers was the fact that the encyclical of Pope Francis, *Laudato si'*, had recently helped to mobilize world public opinion.[6]

Most of what Edenhofer presents at interdisciplinary conferences is a summary of the insights of the IPCC reports. Each of the assessment reports treat the key areas outlined in the mandate given to the IPCC. The first and second areas involve "providing the world with an objective, scientific view of climate change, its natural, political and economic impacts

5. IPCC, "First Assessment Report," accessed November 2019, https://www.ipcc.ch/report/ar1/wg3/.

6. A representative of the Holy See to COP 21 expressed his opinion that *Laudato si'* contributed positively to the success of COP 21. See, Paolo Conversi, "COP 21 e Laudato Si,'" in *Laudato si': linee di lettura interdisciplinari per la cura della casa comune*, editor Humberto Miguel Yáñez sj, (Roma: G&B Press, 2017.)

and risks." Here the panel concludes that there has indeed been human-induced climate change with negative results for the environment, and that far worse results are in prospect. It explains that climate change has been primarily caused by the emission of carbon dioxide into the atmosphere, with the result that heat from the sun is retained in the atmosphere rather than being reflected back into space. It states that, while "anthropogenic interference with the climate system" is already upon us, this has so far amounted to less than an increase of one degree centigrade in the average temperature of the atmosphere. However, it notes that the consequences of anthropogenic interference are likely to accelerate.

Edenhofer acknowledges that debates about the causes of climate change can become complex. However, he stresses that, at their heart, there is a simple insight. He points out that, once emitted, carbon remains in the atmosphere. Consequently, a study of anthropogenic causes of climate increase needs to study the accumulation of carbon in the atmosphere from the beginning of the industrial revolution. Furthermore, he notes that the IPCC speaks about the probability that when carbon in the atmosphere reaches a certain level, a kind of saturation will occur which will have an accelerating effect on the absorption of heat from the sun and, consequently, on climate change. He therefore stresses how important it is that the atmosphere not reach that level of carbon saturation. He speaks of a fixed "carbon budget" that is available to the human race which the human race has already gone a long way toward consuming.[7]

The third question that the mandate of the IPCC allows it investigate is what "possible response options" are available to humanity to control climate change. Here the IPCC reports have maintained an optimistic tone. They state that it is possible for humanity to remain within its carbon budget and to "mitigate" the climate change that has already begun. However, they warn that, given how much of the carbon budget humanity has already consumed, world economies will need to reduce carbon emissions to zero by the year 2050. They state that this could limit the increase of world temperature to between 1.5 and 2.0 degrees centigrade. They acknowledge that, already, such climate change will still bring major negative consequences but describe how world economies may be able to adapt to such changes. Consequently, a terminology of "mitigation" and "adaptation" becomes key to IPCC reports.

---

7. For further analysis of the carbon budget, see the web-page of the Mercator Research Institute, of which Edenhofer is director: https://www.mcc-berlin.net/en/research/co2-budget.html (Accessed April, 2020.)

Edenhofer suggests that key proposals of the IPCC concerning mitigation appertain to policies of carbon pricing. He explains that policies of carbon pricing are based on a principle in economics called "externalities." This principle acknowledges that many industrial activities do not have to pay for all the inputs that contribute to their profit-making and that this justifies the role of government taxation. The IPCC applies the principle of "the polluter pays" to carbon emissions at the global level. It proposes that it is appropriate that such activities be taxed as a means of reducing such emissions as well as funding other mitigating measures to reduce carbon emissions. Two main lines of approach are proposed. The first is a direct tax on those who emit carbon, one that will be sufficiently high to discourage continuing emissions. The second involves a "tradable permit programme." Here, nations are allotted a permitted level of carbon emissions. Those (usually poorer nations) who do not need to use their quota can sell rights to it to other (usually richer) nations.

The Christian Ethics of Michael Northcott

Edenhofer has attended conferences with the Christian ethicist Michael Northcott and the differences of approach between these two is striking.[8] Northcott criticizes the proposals of the IPCC concerning carbon pricing, suggesting that these depend too much on market mechanisms within the capitalist system. He proposes instead a more radical break with this system itself.

Northcott is an English Anglican priest who was a missionary in Indonesia in the 1980s. There he was so scandalized by the behavior of big-business and government in degrading the natural environment that he decided to dedicated himself to an academic life that would seek to redress such evils. In 1996 he published *The Environment and Christian Ethics*, which established him as an important voice in his field; and he has been a prolific author ever since.[9] Northcott is familiar with ethical arguments, which emerged in the 1960s and 1970s, that placed much of the blame for the ecological crisis on a cultural "anthropocentrism" that is characteristic of the culture of the West

8. Edenhofer contributed a conference at which Michael Northcott also spoke, "Creatures, Radical Ecological Conversion After Laudato Si,'" held at the Pontifical Gregorian University, 7–8 March, 2018. The differences of ethical perspective became a focus of debate among conference participants.

9. Michael S. Northcott, *The Environment and Christian Ethics* (Cambridge: Cambridge University Press, 1996).

and has its origins in Christianity.[10] He expresses sympathy for such arguments, but seeks to primarily shift the blame for Western anthropocentrism onto the thinkers of the European Enlightenment, who often understood themselves to be separating themselves from Christian influence.

Northcott identifies three tendencies in Enlightenment ethics: utilitarian (David Hume), consequentialist (John Stuart Mill) or deontological (Immanuel Kant). He cites Elizabeth Anscombe, in her criticism of consequentialism and deontological ethics as well as Val Plumwood who criticizes most modern ethicists for conducting "a quest for a logical, abstract and universal moral discourse of contracts and absolute forms of norms and responsibilities" which, at the same time, "eschews the normal human discourses of love and care, reciprocity, emotional attachment and familial concern."[11] He acknowledges that recent years have witnessed an increase in the number of ethicists reflecting on the environmental crisis. However, he notes that most of these adopt either consequentialist or deontological forms of reasoning and concludes that their arguments are doomed to failure.[12]

Northcott next declares his own preference is for a "communitarian ethics." He turns to Alasdair MacIntyre to suggest that ethical enquiry should be conducted in the context of "the particularity of specific religious traditions and cultural identities."[13] He avers that the reversal of the environmental crisis, "will only come about when we recover a deeper sense for the relationality of human to particular ecosystems and parts of the biosphere."[14] In this respect, he advocates that modern cultures retrieve insights and values from "those surviving indigenous communities on the frontiers of the juggernaut of modernity."[15] He states that it is in such cultures that one finds preserved, "those virtues of justice and compassion, of care and respect for life, human and non-human, of temperance and prudence in our appetites and desire."[16]

---

10. Northcott refers often to a famous author, Lynn White, who cites the work of Max Weber, who speaks of a so-called "Protestant ethic" as forming the basis of modern capitalism. See "The Historical Roots of Our Ecologic Crisis," Science 155 (March 1967): 1203–1207, and found also at, file:///C:/Users/W/Downloads/HistoricalRoots_of_EcologicalCrisis%20(2).pdf (accessed October 2019).

11. Northcott, *The Environment and Christian Ethics*, 117.

12. Northcott, *The Environment and Christian Ethics*, Chapter 3, "The Turn to Nature," 86–123.

13. Northcott, *The Environment and Christian Ethics*, 121–123.

14. Northcott, *The Environment and Christian Ethics*, 123.

15. Northcott, *The Environment and Christian Ethics*, 123.

16. Northcott, *The Environment and Christian Ethics*, 122.

Northcott pays considerable attention to medieval European philosophical traditions. He notes the way philosophers such as Thomas Aquinas developed the thinking of Plato and Aristotle on natural law, and finds a resource here to avoid the disincarnated rationalism of modern philosophy. He advocates an "ecological repristination of natural law ethics,"[17] and explores how current discoveries by moral and evolutionary psychologists can help to expand our notion of what is natural. He notes that studies have been made of "sensory experiences related to breast-feeding, touch, nutrition and the visual and auditory environment of home," and that most of these factors are established as "crucial determinants of moral flourishing and empathic capacities in growing children and young adults." He adds that the studies also reveal "the potential for denatured urban environments and industrialised foods to arrest or depress the development of creative, empathic and morally sensitive individuals."[18] On a similar line, he speaks of the importance of a sense of place for cultivating ecological virtues and laments the way that urbanisation has undermined such a sense. He adds, "resistance to corporate power is an essential tactic in the recovery of place, and that religious tradition is a potentially powerful source of such resistance."[19]

Northcott's more recent writings explore the theme of a sense of place. In *A Political Theology of Climate Change*,[20] he explores the thought of a German philosopher, who wrote in the 1930s and had Nazi sympathies, Carl Schmidt.[21] He distances himself from various opinions of this thinker but notes that various political philosophers are rediscovering Schmidt, who introduces a sense of place into political philosophy, criticizing the globalizing tendency associated with "international capital" and stressing national sovereignty and the protection of borders from outsiders. He compares Schmidt to the more left-leaning Alasdair MacIntyre:

> MacIntyre's critique of the democratized, emotivist, liberal self is the analogy in philosophical liberalism to Schmitt's account of the dehistoricised, despatialised, and despiritualised nation in political liberalism and international relations. Both discern a conflict

---

17. Northcott, *The Environment and Christian Ethics*, 309,

18. Northcott, *Place, Ecology and the Sacred*, Kindle locations, 2045, 3861–3874.

19. Northcott, *Place, Ecology and the Sacred: The Moral Geography of Sustainable Communities* (London, Bloomsbury Publishing. 2015, Kindle Edition), Kindle locations 378–379.

20. Northcott, *A Political Theology of Climate Change* (London: SPCK, 2013).

21. A key work of Carl Schmidt is, *The Concept of the Political*, trans. George D. Schwab (Chicago: University of Chicago Press, 1996 [orig. 1932]).

> between the liberal account of the autonomous individual, and the familial, geographical, historical, national, and religious contexts of individuals gathered into political collectives.[22]

In *Place, Ecology and the Sacred*, Northcott builds on such insights, offering an analysis of how a sense of place was lost in early modernity and describes a series of current initiatives to recreate a sense of place, both in rural and in urban living.

Northcott's books never confine themselves to philosophical argument. In addition to reflecting on natural law and political philosophy, he devotes considerable time to reflecting on the ethical teaching of the Christian Bible. This includes noting how the gift of the land of Israel to the Hebrew people represents a key dimension of the Hebrew Scriptures. He also notes how often Jesus contrasts the values of the reign of God with values of financial greed and the pursuit of power.[23]

Northcott is clear that reflection at the level of ethics should culminate in concrete proposals for government policies that will mitigate the environmental crisis. However, he is skeptical about the potential of IPCC proposals to achieve this end. He discusses at length how the attempts at carbon pricing adopted by governments after various COP meetings have enjoyed only limited success. He suggests that this has happened because such policies imply a confidence in the capitalist system that is misguided. He attributes much of the ecological crisis to "the philosophical emptiness of the positivist legal conception of private property" that underlines the capitalist system. He speaks of "the intrinsic relationship between capitalism and fossil fuels,"[24] and adds "there is a conflict between the global form of industrial civilization and the health of human and species communities in both rural and urban areas, and the health of the planet as a whole."[25] He notes with approval that "radical ecological thinkers argue that a deeper turn from present-day capitalism is needed before global atmospheric greenhouse gas emissions will begin to come down," and insists that "so long as nations severally can choose to continue to sell goods and services to

---

22. Northcott, *A Political Theology of Climate Change*, 250–251.

23. See Northcott, *The Environment and Christian Ethics*, Chapter 6. "Creation, Redemption, and Natural Law Ethics," 199–256. See also, ibid., *A Moral Climate*, Chapter 7, "Mobility and Pilgrimage," Chapter 8, "Faithful Feasting," 213–266; ibid., *Place, Ecology and the Sacred*, Chapter 6, "Food Sovereignty from Joshua to La Via Campesina," Kindle locations, 2937–3303.

24. Northcott, *A Political Theology of Climate Change*, 133, 143.

25. Northcott, *Place, Ecology and the Sacred*, at Kindle location 3335.

other nations in a world trading system without regard to climate change, cheating will always undermine efforts."[26]

Northcott echoes the thinking both of Carl Schmidt and of various current expressions of political populism when he suggests that the best way to oppose the dominance of the international capitalist system is for nation-states to assert their sovereignty and to break away from transnational trading blocks. He then proposes that governments initiate major interventions in their national economies, including: expropriating land from private owners; the creating of new community ownership structures; and the promoting of self-sustaining, local economies.[27]

I turn now to offer a dialectical analysis of the arguments outlined above employing the thought of Lonergan and Doran.

Lonergan and Carbon Pricing

Lonergan lived in an era prior to the spread of ecological awareness, but he was deeply concerned with questions of ethics and economics. A major influence on his intellectual development was his experience during the 1930s of the Great Depression. He was convinced that key causes of the stock market crash of 1929, and the Great Depression that followed, were misguided economic policies which had been proposed to governments by economists who, in turn, had employed faulty macroeconomic theory. In response to this, Lonergan recalled the teaching of a lecturer he had during his philosophical studies in England, who declared that what was needed was a Catholic response to Karl Marx. This lecturer had spoken of a kind of genius at work in Marx who had recognized the need first to develop an overall theory of history, and secondly a theory of economics.[28]

Regarding the first challenge, Lonergan worked on a series of essays that explored how epistemology should be based on intellectual conversion and how a consequent "metaphysics of history" could be based on three heuristic categories, or "vectors," of "progress," "decline," and "redemption."[29] Regarding the second challenge, he began studying economics, and in the depth of

26. Northcott, *A Political Theology of Climate Change*, 142–143.

27. Northcott, *Place, Ecology and the Sacred*, Chapter 8, "Re-placing Ethics in the City and in the Countryside," Kindle location, 3908–4524.

28. The lecturer in question was Fr. Lewis Watt, S.J.. See, William A. Mathews, *Lonergan's Quest: A Study of Desire in the Authoring of* Insight (Toronto: University of Toronto Press, 2005), 32–64.

29. Michael Shute, *The Origins of Lonergan's Notion of the Dialectic of History: A Study of Lonergan's Early Writings on History* (Lanham, MD: University Press of America, 1993.)

World War II, would produce two manuscripts on macroeconomic theory, *Toward a New Political Economy* (1942), and *An Essay in Circulation Analysis* (1944).[30] These manuscripts were a prescription for how to pursue a line of progress in history, assuring that economic growth proceeds in a way that is free from recession and depression. Lonergan's thought can be understood as broadly Keynesian.[31] A central characteristic of his theory is that government should employ monetary and fiscal instruments to intervene in the economy in different ways according to the stage of a cycle of economic growth in which the economy finds itself. This, in turn, requires that the government appeal to its citizens to exhibit different social virtues at different times. On occasion, they should accept that a period of "belt tightening" is needed; at other times, they should insist on a redistribution of wealth from the rich to the poor.[32] A series of short articles and book reviews Lonergan wrote during the 1940s illustrates this point. In "Savings Certificates and Catholic Action," he encourages Canadian Catholics to buy war bonds. He points out that not doing so would make it difficult for the government to finance the war effort and would lead to inflation at home. Implicitly, he is employing his macroeconomic theory to suggest that investment in armaments, etc., constitutes the phase of capitalist expansion at the beginning of a wave of growth, which requires a period of belt-tightening on the part of the citizenry. Switching to an exhortative tone, he states that the voluntary acceptance of citizens to buy war bonds is the sort of responsible exercise of economic freedom that represents progress in history: "If we take this opportunity seriously and make the most of it, we are making here and now the greatest possible contribution we can to the development of a democratic technique that can confront and solve any economic problem."[33]

In an article written toward the end of his life, Lonergan would articulate the general principle of how ethics should relate to economics that influenced his writings in the 1940s:

---

30. Bernard Lonergan, *For a New Political Economy*, ed. Philip J. McShane, vol. 21 in *Collected Works of Bernard Lonergan* (Toronto: University of Toronto Press, 1998); ibid., *Macroeconomic Dynamics: An Essay in Circulation Analysis*, ed. Frederick G. Lawrence, et al., vol. 15 in *Collected Works of Bernard Lonergan* (Toronto: University of Toronto Press, 1999). An impressive overview of Lonergan's theory of macroeconomics is provided by Frederick G. Lawrence, "Editor's Introduction to Volume 15," xxv–lxxiv.

31. See, Mathews, 109–130.

32. Lonergan, "Savings Certificates and Catholic Action," *Shorter Papers*, ed. Robert C. Croken, Robert M. Doran and H. Daniel Monsour, vol. 20 in *Collected Works of Bernard Lonergan* (Toronto: University of Toronto Press, 2007), 68–73.

33. Lonergan, "Savings Certificates and Catholic Action," 73.

> Two requirements must be met. The first regards economic theorists, the second regards moral theorists. From economic theorists we have to demand along with as many other types of analysis as they please, a new and specific type that reveals how moral precepts have both a basis in economic process and so an effective application to it. From moral theorists we have to demand along with their other various forms of wisdom and prudence, specifically economic precepts that arise out of economic process itself and promote its proper functioning.[34]

Lonergan's thinking about economic growth did not extend to the question of the degree to which economic growth produces carbon emissions that are harmful to the environment. However, his thought can easily be extended to such problems. His contribution to macroeconomics lies in his analysis of timely government intervention in the economy and how such intervention requires the readiness of a culture to support such interventions. It does not require an exaggerated leap of logic to suggest that the proposals of the IPCC concerning carbon pricing involve just the kind of interface of economic and ethical insights of which Lonergan would approve.[35]

Cosmopolis and the Environment

If a Lonergan-based approach tends to support the argument of Edenhofer, what then is to be said about the arguments of Northcott? One, unavoidable, conclusion is to regret that the ethical reflection of Northcott did not produce a more robust support for carbon pricing, which I judge to be a rational and responsible policy proposal. One has to recognize elements of counterpositional ethical reasoning in the manner in which Northcott engages with this question. On the other hand, there is also much positional thinking in Northcott. A basis for a balanced dialectical analysis of Northcott is found in a book, *Globalization and the Mission of the Church*, written in 2009 by Neil Ormerod and Shane Clifton.[36] These authors conduct an

34. Lonergan, "Healing and Creating in History," in *A Third Collection* (Mahwah, NJ; New York: Paulist, 1985), 100–109, at 108.

35. Paul St. Amour makes a significant technical contribution to Lonergan's notion of progress by integrating an ethic of ecological responsibility into Lonergan's notion of emergent process in economic systems, "A Heuristic for the Critical Analysis of Globalisation," in Joseph Ogbonnaya and Lucas Briola (editors), *Everything is Interconnected : Towards Globalisation With a Human Face and an Integral Ecology* (Milwaukee, WN: Marquette University Press, 2019), 3–22.

36. Neil J. Ormerod and Shane Clifton, *Globalization and the Mission of the Church* (New York: T&T Clark, 2009), 134.

analysis of current literature on globalization employing heuristic categories taken from Robert Doran. A major conclusion of the book is that rapid technological change has led to globalization at economic and political levels with little control by cultural values. They speak of the urgent need for a development from above, representing a cosmopolitan exercise of the superstructure, that can help reverse decline and promote progress at the level of infrastructure.

Illustrating their point, the authors note a relative paucity of literature on cultural and ethical dimensions of globalization. Within the literature that exists, they note that a good deal represents a neo-liberal argument that they consider to be mostly inauthentic—defending a status quo that in fact represents the capturing of the superstructure by special interests within the infrastructure. On a more positive note, they identify two cultural forces that are already exercising a redemptive role: the human rights movement and the ecological movement. They find both position and counterposition in each of these movements, but suggest that the Churches have been over-cautious in affirming and advancing what is positional in these. Regarding the ecology movement they state: "Of itself, it may at times appear naïve, anti-progressive, romantic and idealizing, but in terms of our present context of global warming and widespread pollution affecting all parts of the globe, it is a voice that desperately needs to be heard."[37] Applying this broad attitude to the thought of Northcott, I notice three counterpositions and three positions in his thought.

A first counterposition of Northcott appertains that his philosophical thinking is incomplete and has characteristics that Ormerod and Clifton describe as "naïve, anti-progressive, romantic, and idealizing." It is striking how, while Northcott is able to identify dimensions of progress, decline, and redemption in cultures prior to modernity, he seems to identify only decline in modernity. The contrast with Lonergan becomes evident when Northcott quotes the historian of science, Herbert Butterfield, who is often quoted by Lonergan. Lonergan supports Butterfield's praise for the emergence of the "new thinking cap" in the modern era that culminated in the empirical method of Isaac Newton. For Lonergan, this represented a valuable differentiation within the second stage of meaning, which would help inaugurate a process toward the application to human affairs of empirical method and the eventual emergence of a third stage of meaning based

37. Ormerod and Clifton, 134.

on intellectual conversion. By contrast, Northcott sees only decline in the developments that Butterfield documents. He focuses exclusively on how the "mathematization of the universe" described by Butterfield as central to empirical method led to a break with the human ability to empathize with nature, leading eventually to a desire to manipulate it, and to the destructive behavior of the capitalist system.[38]

Northcott falls short of the insight that the way to exercise an "ecological represtination of natural law ethics" is to pass through intellectual and psychic conversion and to employ a metaphysics based on emergent probability. Cynthia Crysdale seems to echo Northcott when she draws on Lonergan to state: "a revised natural law is both possible and imperative." However, she differs from Northcott when she adds, "it must further locate itself in an analysis of history that is critical and normative, but that grounds its critical stance in the norms constitutive of human intelligence."[39]

A second counterposition in Northcott follows from the first. Northcott tends to make illogical leaps from cultural analysis to proposing government policies. His argument often proceeds from describing some of the worst aspects of decline in the modern economy, to describing idyllic, non-capitalist communities of virtue, and concluding to the need for draconian government intervention in the economy (e.g. regarding land ownership). This method of ethical argument has characteristics of what Alasdair MacIntyre calls "emotivism."

A third counterposition of Northcott relates to the way he blends philosophical reasoning with reference to the Bible. It becomes clear that the economic conclusions at which he arrives are at least as much generated by Biblical reflections as by philosophical ones. One commentator suggests that Northcott does not always make it clear what audience he is addressing: a secular one, for whom his communitarian ethics is most accessible; or a Christian one, for whom reference to the Bible is persuasive. He explains that "Northcott's appeals to systematic and moral theology, however, remains relatively thin," and adds, "his basically allegorical reading of Scripture offers paradigms of social criticism and moral outrage."[40]

---

38. For the reference to Herbert Butterfield, see Lonergan, "Questionnaire on Philosophy: Response," in *Shorter Papers*, 353, and Northcott, *A Political Theology of Climate Change*, 189.

39. Cynthia S. W. Crysdale, "Revisioning Natural Law: From the Classicist Paradigm to Emergent Probability," *Theological Studies* 56 (1995): 464–484, at 484.

40. Anthony Egan, review of *A Moral Climate*, by Michael Northcott, in *Theological Studies* 70 (2009): 492. See also, Holmes Rolston, review of *The Environment and Christian Ethics*, in *Theology Today*, 54 (1998), 549–550; Fergus Kerr OP, review of *The Environment and Christian Ethics* in *New Blackfriars*, 79 (1998), 105–107.

Having outlined counterpositions in the thought of Northcott, one can also recognize at least three positions. First, Northcott is to be admired, simply for recognizing the importance of ethical reflection for producing proposals at the level of economics. Here his thought converges with that of Lonergan who appeals for "a cosmopolis that is neither class nor state that stands above all their claims, that cuts them down to size, that is founded on the native detachment and disinterestedness of every intelligence, that commands man's first allegiance."[41]

A second position in Northcott lies in his desire to invoke religious values as well as philosophical reasoning in addressing the environmental crisis. Here one recalls what Doran describes, how in the later chapters of *Insight*, Lonergan conducts a theological transposition of the notion of cosmopolis.[42] This involves identifying the phenomenon of moral impotence and the need for a divine solution for the problem of evil. Again, however, what is positional in Northcott's thinking here stands in need of considerable advancing. Central to such advancement would be introducing a distinction between general and special theological categories, and a firm grasp that when one is engaging with a non-religious audience one confines one's argument to general theological categories.[43]

A third position in Northcott lies in what can be explained as his promotion of cosmological values in modern culture. Here his thought converges with that of Doran, who insists that we respond to cultural value in a dialectical way that requires us to find a *via media* between anthropological and cultural values. Doran seems to echo Northcott when he states, "An exclusively anthropological determination of culture is productive of that distortion of the dialectic of culture that is internally constitutive of modern imperialism."[44] Ormerod and Clifton are alert to this positional aspect of ecological ethics and explain: "the environmental movement is not just a corrective to anthropological culture," but rather, "it is the genuine promotion of the alternative cosmological pole of the cultural dialectic, notably evident in its evoking of the 'natural' order and its respect for indigenous cultures."[45]

---

41. Lonergan, *Insight*, 263.

42. Robert M. Doran, *Theology and the Dialectics of History* (Toronto: University of Toronto Press, 1990), 199.

43. On general and special theological categories, see Lonergan, *Method in Theology*, ed. Robert M. Doran, John D. Dadosky, vols. 14 in *Collected Works of Bernard Lonergan* (Toronto: University of Toronto Press, 2017), 267–273; and Robert M. Doran, *What is Systematic Theology?* (Toronto: University of Toronto Press, 2005), Chapter 4, "Categories," 42–52.

44. Doran, *Theology and the Dialectics of History*, 479.

45. Ormerod and Clifton, 133–134.

However, it must be noted that Northcott seems to so emphasize the importance of cosmological culture as to negate the role of anthropological culture. Here one needs to recall that it is primarily by an appeal to anthropological values—and the metaphysics of an emergently probable universe that is associated with this—that one can make a link from the super-structural reflection on values to the nuts and bolts of an economic system. This was how Lonergan believed he could appeal to moral theorists to produce "specifically economic precepts that arise out of economic process itself and promote its proper functioning."[46]

Finally, I would like to come to a similar conclusion regarding Northcott as did Lonergan regarding George Boyle, author of a book *Democracy's Second Chance.* Lonergan reviewed this book, written toward the end of World War II.[47] As described by Lonergan, Boyle suggests that abuses of democracy and of capitalism contributed to the outbreak of the war. Boyle then points to the cooperative movement as providing a model of economic behavior based on cooperation and community-building and suggests that such an approach to economics should provide the basis for the democratic systems that emerge after the war. Lonergan is full of praise for this argument. He states: "Undoubtedly there has to be a rebirth of rural living," and adds, "Undoubtedly the organic and integral mentality fostered by a life in touch with nature has to spread through the whole fabric of society and completely oust the mechanist and fractional thinking that has landed us where we are."[48] At the same time, Lonergan chides Boyle for making utopian statements that indicate a limited understanding of economics. He quips, "One might be inclined to ask whether our economic and social structure is not rather a sick man needing treatment than a dying man awaiting burial."[49]

---

46. Lonergan, "Healing and Creating in History," in *A Third Collection*, 108. Here it is worth noting that one Lonergan scholar, Kenneth Melchin, debates whether communitarian ethicists who are discovering cosmological values will ever be capable of integrating anthropological values. He suggests that there may be greater hope of advancing the position among Kantian ethicists, including followers of John Rawls, and helping them recognize that intellectual conversion should be the basis of thinking about human rights (Melchin, "What Is a Democracy, Anyway? A Discussion Between Lonergan and Rawls," *Lonergan Workshop 15,* ed. Fred Lawrence (Boston: Boston College, 1999), 99–116.

47. Lonergan, "Review of George Boyle, *Democracy's Second Chance*," in *Shorter Papers*, 157–159.

48. Lonergan, "Review of George Boyle," *Shorter Papers*, 158.

49. Lonergan, "Review of George Boyle," *Shorter Papers*, 158.

Conclusion

In this article I sought to explore the relevance of the thought of Lonergan and Doran to current debates within the ecological movement. I focused on a tension that exists between economists and some ethicists. I have noted that Lonergan did not directly address the ecological crisis at any length, but was keenly aware of the difficulty economists and ethicists were having in relating to each other in his own day. I noted how he anchored his writings in economics in an attentiveness to the importance of the intellectual and moral conversion for all those working in the human sciences and, in consequence, of the relevance of a cosmology of an emergently probable universe for relating questions of economics and ethics. I suggest that this has direct relevance for debates between ethicists and economists today and I also note how Doran's expansion of Lonergan's notion of the dialectics of history has a relevance to the way current ecological ethicists speak about the importance of retrieving the wisdom of indigenous cultures. I now conclude with one more reflection on how commentators today recognize that the way Catholic thinkers relate ethics to economics is emerging as a key question.

In late 2019, *The Economist* magazine ran a feature article where the author discusses a conference, "The Economy of Francesco," which was being planned for 2020, in Assisi, Italy.[50] The author notes that the conference is organized by the Vatican and that participants include some world-famous economists. The author states, "at a time when the world is an unholy mess, even asking basic questions about the purpose of business has some virtue." He describes Pope Francis as "having a knack for catching the zeitgeist," and identifies two main reasons why world leaders need to listen to him. First, he states that the encyclical on the environment, *Laudato Si'*, "sums up as eloquently as anything written so far the pressure from runaway growth on resources.;" second, "the pope makes an argument about individual morality" and the necessary link of this to economics. He quotes with respect a conference organizer who states that trying to separate ethics from economics is like "teaching about sex purely in biological terms." However, the article concludes with a warning. The author suggests that there are diverse tendencies within Catholic social teaching. Firstly, "faced

50. Brett Ryder, "Popenomics: What Sermons Business Should and Should not Heed from a Leftist Pontiff," The Schumpter column (no author given), *The Economist*, September 7, 2019. https://www.economist.com/business/2019/09/05/popenomics (Accessed, April, 2020). This article discusses a forthcoming conference "The Economy of Francesco," see, https://francescoeconomy.org.

with climate change and inequality the temptation is to call for draconian top-down measures to throttle economic activity." On the other hand, he notes that there are indications that Catholic social teaching is also taking a more pragmatic turn, one that respects the fact that government interventions in the economy must respect market mechanisms. He concludes by speaking of the value of a Catholic influence in helping economic and political leaders "to behave as responsible citizens, corporate or otherwise." Lonergan and Doran would concur.[51]

51. *The Economist*, "Popenomics."

SECTION V

SYSTEMATIC THEOLOGY

CHAPTER THIRTEEN

BIAS, CONVERSION, AND GRACE IN THE TIME OF A PANDEMIC

Cecille Medina-Maldonado

Marquette University (Milwaukee, WI)

Introduction

Late in 2019, a novel virus was discovered in Wuhan, China with pneumonia-like symptoms rumored to be linked to Severe Acute Respiratory Syndrome (SARS).[1] The virus spread quickly, with most infected persons experiencing acute respiratory symptoms including fever, a dry cough, and shortness of breath, among many other complications. Between the end of 2019 and early 2020, the virus spread through Wuhan and eventually to other regions of China. Within weeks, the virus had spread outside China's borders,[2] and by the end of February 2020, the United States witnessed its first fatality from the novel virus.[3] By this point it was renamed COVID-19, shorthand for coronavirus disease 2019.[4]

In the months that followed the onset of the disease caused by the novel coronavirus, particularly in the United States, myriad responses, opinions, and solutions regarding COVID-19 met one another with suspicion and vitriol. The highly politicized atmosphere of an election year in the

1. "Chinese officials investigate cause of pneumonia outbreak in Wuhan," Ed. Tony Munroe and Gerry Doyle *Reuters.com* 31 December 2019.

2. Geddie, John. "Coronavirus outbreak 'just beginning' outside China, says expert," Ed. Nick Macfie. *Reuters.com* 12 February 2020.

3. Borter, Gabriella and Steve Gorman. "Washington state man becomes first U.S. coronavirus fatality." Ed. Daniel Wallis and Paul Simao. *Reuters.com.* 29 February 2020.

4. Nebehay, Stephanie and Emma Farge. "Coronavirus emergency is 'Public Enemy Number 1': WHO." Ed. Alex Richardson, Nick Macfie and Philippa Fletcher. *Reuters.com.* 11 February 2020.

U.S., in addition to the racial justice movements in the wake of instances of police brutality,[5] combined with the stress and anxiety from an unknown illness, created a national crisis of unrest and less-than-civil discourse. Startlingly, the very same issues plaguing the general public made their way into religious circles. Catholic leaders and laypersons across the United States varied widely in their responses to the pandemic. Parishes, dioceses, and indeed even the United States Conference of Catholic Bishops (USCCB) struggled to find agreement on appropriate responses to the novel coronavirus. What led to these disagreements across these various structures of society? Is reconciliation possible in any of these structures, and if so, how can we come to it?

In order to answer these questions, I turn to the thought and theology of Robert M. Doran, S.J., and his work on expanding the teachings of Bernard Lonergan, S.J. I employ Doran's work on the psychic conversion and social grace as avenues for reconciling and indeed *improving* discourse and action in the United States in the context of COVID-19. *First,* I explore the role of Lonergan's biases in the U.S., with a particular emphasis on dramatic bias, as demonstrated by the complications of the COVID-19 pandemic. *Second,* I argue that psychic conversion is key to transforming the conflicts that result from dramatic bias. I argue that psychic conversion both "from below" and "from above" are necessary to overcome dramatic bias, particularly with this bias's tie to communal meanings and values. *Finally,* I conclude that supernatural grace, poured out on humanity through the gift of the Holy Spirit, serves as the catalyst behind psychic conversion, and can contribute to progress in combating the disagreements of the U.S. response to a massive health crisis by imbuing communities with social grace, showing the dynamic reality of the Trinity in modern history.

A Global Pandemic

The effects of COVID-19 were still relatively unknown by the time it arrived to the United States. This led to recommendations and measures to attempt to slow the spread of the illness. The rapid uptick in cases in early March 2020 led many cities, counties, and states to implement social

5. The death of George Floyd, a Black man in Minneapolis, led to widespread protests and movements decrying the injustices faced by Black communities in the United States, primarily from excessive police force. For further readings, see Hiller, Jennifer and Gary McWilliams. "George Floyd hailed as 'cornerstone of a movement' at funeral; family calls for justice." Ed. Frank McGurry, Howard Goller, Cynthia Osterman, and Lincoln Feast. *Reuters.com.* 9 June 2020.

distancing guidelines, restrictions on use of public spaces, and limitations for social gatherings. The Center for Disease Control (CDC) of the U.S. recommended mask wearing for all individuals earlier on in the disease's hold,[6] when there were just over a million confirmed cases of COVID-19 in the United States.[7] Some cities, counties, and states began mandating restrictions, including mask wearing, in public spaces; at the same time, many other leaders refused to issue any guidance surrounding mask wearing or public restrictions. In many areas, determined anti-lockdown activists publicly decried and protested the mask wearing mandates or other restrictions aimed at slowing the spread of COVID-19.[8] Many of these activists protested against the restrictions citing violations to personal liberty and freedom.[9]

Despite the overwhelming scientific support and evidence demonstrating the effectiveness of mask wearing,[10] social distancing, and restrictions on public gatherings, many people in the U.S., continued to disbelieve their effectiveness or value in reducing the spread and impact of COVID-19, in part fueled by popular, non-vetted news or information sources.[11] In some

6. Holland, Steve and Gabriella Borter. "Americans urged to wear masks outside as coronavirus pandemic worsens," Ed. Dan Whitcomb. *Reuters.com.* 2 April 2020.

7. Dong E, Du H, Gardner L. "An interactive web-based dashboard to track COVID-19 in real time." Lancet Inf Dis. 20(5): 533–534. doi: 10.1016/S1473–3099(20)30120–1.

8. Chiacu, Doina and Barbara Goldberg. "More U.S. protests call for lifting coronavirus restrictions as governors push back." Ed. Daniel Wallis and Lincoln Feast. *Reuters.com.* 19 April 2020.

9. Ibid.

10. An early study submitted in March 2020 and published in June 2020 states, "Overall, in the current COVID-19 outbreak, wearing suitable type of masks to prevent COVID-19 is truly necessary and limits the infection of the influenza virus…It is truly important to wear and remove masks correctly to reduce the person-to-person transmission of COVID-19 as well as to ensure correct fit of the mask so that it covers the nose and mouth properly" (p. 199), in Thi Sinh Vo, Tran Thi Thu Ngoc Vo, and Tran Thi Bich Chau. "Coronavirus Infection Prevention by Wearing Masks." *Eurasian Journal of Medicine* 2020, 52(2): 197–201. doi: 10.5152/eurasianjmed.2020.20056.

11. The first major publication of non-vetted informational sources was the viral video, *Plandemic,* which amassed millions of views on various social media platforms. The video was largely discredited by the vast majority of the scientific community, as reported by Scott Neuman, "Seen 'Plandemic'? We Take a Close Look at the Viral Conspiracy Video's Claims," *NPR.com,* 8 May 2020. A second major publication of non-vetted informational sources was viral video by journalist Ben Swann, uploaded to social media outlets in July 2020. A fact check through The Annenberg Public Policy Center confirmed Mr. Swann's incorrect use of scientific data that misrepresented the value and effectiveness of wearing masks, as reported by Saranac Hale Spencer, "Video Misrepresents the Science Behind Face Masks," *Factcheck.org.* 24 July 2020.

cases, guidelines such as mask wearing are no longer a public health matter, but a political issue, despite scientific data supporting the effectiveness of wearing masks.[12] These issues did nothing to improve consensus in social, cultural, and civic circles.

As of July 21, 2020, COVID-19 had claimed the lives of over 600,000 people globally; U.S. fatalities accounted for nearly 25% of the global deaths.[13] In nations where masks, social distancing, and restrictions to public gatherings were mandated, the spread of the disease slowed significantly, leading to fewer hospitalizations and fewer fatalities. Nations such as the United States, which experienced uneven COVID-19 restrictions, did not fare as well: a slight plateau in cases was observed as a result of lockdown or shelter-in-place mandates between March and April 2020, and yet when the restrictions were lifted early in certain states, the case numbers began to increase dramatically in the early summer.

The United States' response to COVID-19 is bewildering to many.[14] A sizable bloc of citizens in the U.S. denied the reality or severity of the disease, blaming media outlets, politicians, and global health organizations with fabricating or grossly exaggerating[15] the effects of the illness. Social media and news outlets' stories depicting the frontline experiences of healthcare and essential workers were discounted as fake or overblown.[16] Vast evidence in support of restrictions to curb the spread of COVID-19 was either discarded or ignored in favor of arguments supporting personal freedoms and liberties, with opponents citing mask mandates as unconstitutional,[17] or as attacks on freedom and personal liberty. Despite the best

---

12. Hansen, Sarah. "Masks Help Stop the Spread of Coronavirus, Studies Say—But Wearing Them Still a Political Issue." *Forbes.com.* 13 June 2020.

13. Dong E, Du H, Gardner L. "An interactive web-based dashboard to track COVID-19 in real time." Lancet Inf Dis. 20(5): 533–534. doi: 10.1016/S1473–3099(20)30120–1.

14. A video by *The New York Times* interviewing people from around the world shows negative opinions regarding the U.S. response to COVID-19. The video is by Brendan Miller and Adam Westbrook, published online under the title "'That's Ridiculous.' How America's Coronavirus Response Looks Abroad," on 27 July 2020 via www.nytimes.com.

15. Mitchell, Amy, Mark Jurkowitz, J. Baxter Oliphant, and Elisa Shearer. "Three Months In, Many Americans See Exaggeration, Conspiracy Theories and Partisanship in COVID-19 News." *Pew Research Center* via journalism.org. 29 June 2020.

16. Gross, Jenny. "Nurses Who Battled Virus in New York Confront Friends Back Home Who Say It's a Hoax." *The New York Times.* 7 July 2020. Accessed online 20 July 2020 via https://www.nytimes.com/2020/07/07/us/coronavirus-nurses.html.

17. Trotta, Daniel. "U.S. divided over masks, schools as coronavirus cases rise by over 70,000 again." Ed. Rosalba O'Brien, Cynthia Osterman, and Lincoln Feast. *Reuters.com.* 17 July 2020.

efforts by public health officials, government leaders, and community liaisons to counteract misinformation, a vocal bloc of U.S. citizens, including high-ranking government officials,[18] continued to ignore scientific suggestions, data, and evidence that had mitigated the spread of the disease in other nations.

These broad positions and counterpositions, coexisted simultaneously and combatively, among those in the United States. Some positions acknowledged the presence and severity of COVID-19 in the U.S.; adherents of these positions supported mask wearing, restrictions on public gatherings, and social distancing as *beneficial* to the health of the community, despite the inconvenience or discomfort of such measures. Counterpositions either disbelieved or downplayed the presence and severity of COVID-19 in the U.S.; adherents of these positions protested mask wearing, restrictions on gatherings, and social distancing as *detrimental* to the freedom and liberty of the individual, despite the *perceived* possible (or non-existent) benefits to public health. These various positions and counterpositions were in tension, yet is it possible to reconcile them and make them better through listening? What biases are at play in these positions? How can grace help us progress to prevent further death as a result of a deadly disease?

Biases in the Midst of a Pandemic

In order to determine the possible responses and interventions for the disagreements regarding the U.S. response to COVID-19, it is necessary to study the biases at play, as they are one of the biggest dilemmas in solving the COVID-19 pandemic. First, dramatic bias involves a blind spot or scotosis which arises from the psyche. Upbringing and life circumstances heavily shape how data, including emotional reactions, arise within an individual, shaping one's dramatic bias. Psychological formation, whether positive or negative, plays a particularly important role in shaping dramatic bias. The sorts of emotions and reactions that rise from dramatic bias indicate something deep in the psyche whether or not the subject is aware of it. Second, individual bias involves self-interested desires that intentionally prevent the subject from an insight. Individual bias involves emotions and reactions that urge one to focus on one's own interests. Self-interest and

18. McKay, Rich and Gabriella Borter. "U.S. elected leaders clash over masks as new COVID-19 cases set another record." Ed. Howard Goller, Rosalba O'Brien, and Cynthia Osterman. *Reuters.com.* 16 July 2020.

self-preservation prevent authentic insights. Third, group bias involves a community, society, or nation's bias; this kind of bias is shaped by the collective attitudes and beliefs held by a particular group, often in response to another group. A group that holds majority power and influence over another group is likely to experience unpleasant attitudes, beliefs, and emotions in response to a minority group. Group bias can influence the members of that group to false or incomplete insights, preventing progress and authentic human development. Finally, general bias involves biases that rise from common sense, or the "stuff" of "how things get done." General bias can conjure reactions, attitudes, beliefs, actions, and emotions that occur when there is pushback or challenges to common sense. The refusal or delay to implement new methods and practices can lead to decline. The prioritization of independence and self-direction in the United States, for example, has caused feelings of confrontation, imposition, and disagreement from those who feel that the current COVID-19 practices are un-American.[19] The pushes to change common sense in response to a particular situation—that of a global health pandemic—demonstrate the power of general bias in preventing insight and progress. These misperceptions prevent insights from forming, thus leading to deterioration and decline. The four types of biases are behind many of these issues, leading the United States in struggling to find a way to deal with COVID-19 on a national scale.

One of the largest challenges to the COVID-19 response is dramatic bias, because it is one of the least understood and identified biases. The particular issue of dramatic bias is censorship of the subject. The censorship is unknown and unintentional to the subject. The censorship can be a result of individual trauma or conditioned by social or cultural circumstances. In the case of COVID-19, the various types of biases seep into dramatic bias without the consent or knowledge of the subject. The individual subject may have their own form of dramatic bias through childhood or adult trauma that effectively rewires their ability to experience, understand, judge, or make decisions in an authentic way. The individual subject may have a form of dramatic bias that is inculcated within them due to the society in which they are born. This is distinct from group bias; the bias inherited from the culture that is present in dramatic bias is one that is handed down from unchecked ordinary meaningfulness, in what Doran describes as "sedimented communal meanings and values" that we receive 'from above

19. Vince, Gaia. "Why it's so hard to be rational about Covid-19." *BBC Future: Comment & Analysis.* 6th May 2020. Accessed online on 6 May 2020 via https://www.bbc.com/future/article/20200505-why-its-so-hard-to-be-rational-about-covid-19.

downwards.'[20] These are meanings and values that have been affirmed and accepted by previous generations that have shaped the context into which one is born; these are *cultural values*.[21] This is the move from original to ordinary meaningfulness. When the way of doing things is changed and affirmed, original meaningfulness becomes ordinary meaningfulness. When original meaningfulness prohibits or does not check the insights from previous subjects, the ordinary meaningfulness itself is skewed. Thus, while group bias creates the biases present when two ethnic groups, class, or two nations, and so on, dramatic bias "from above" as Doran reiterates, does not actively come from one group against another but rather from one group against itself, its values, and its future.

Dramatic bias "from above" creates the opportunities for individual subjects to have skewed forms of entering into the levels of consciousness, out of no reason except that they were born in a particular time, place, and context. Again, this differs from group bias in that it transcends one particular group. It is handed down from one generation to another, usually in a particular context, and left unchecked by the meaningfulness that is passed on from generation to generation; it is the meanings and values that are collected, shaped, and transformed by peoples over time according to various contexts. Meanwhile, dramatic bias "from below" creates the opportunities for individual subjects to have skewed forms of entering into the levels of consciousness from events, contexts, and instances that are unique to those individuals. These are not effects that are handed down from generation to generation but ultimately come from individual instances that shape the subject's way of thinking. It is akin to the soldier who experiences the tragedies of war and develops post-traumatic stress disorder (PTSD). While many soldiers absolutely experience the trauma of war, only certain ones develop PTSD. This is an instance of dramatic bias from below.

However, dramatic bias from above might be from the way a particular culture passes on knowledge and practices from one generation to another. A particular example of this in the context of the United States is the emphasis on freedom and liberty. The general ideals of freedom and liberty are enshrined in the Constitution of the United States and are frequently invoked among citizens of all walks of life as reasons for their expression of rights and privileges; they are very much two of the main cultural values in the United States. However, the overemphasis of values such as freedom and liberty,

20. Doran, Robert M. *What is Systematic Theology?* Toronto: University of Toronto Press, 2005. pp. 126.

21. Ibid, 177–8.

inculcated and enshrined in this context, create dramatic bias for those who are born into the culture. Freedom and liberty are values that are imbued with meaning, the very meaning of what it means to be a citizen of the United States. Anything that goes against these values of freedom and liberty—or what is perceived to be against these values of freedom and liberty—are considered anathema and antithetical to the "American" value system.

This type of dramatic bias from above, again, is to be distinguished from group bias. The emphasis on liberty and freedom as the foundations of American living are interpreted differently depending on one's group within the borders of the United States. For example, those who are members of the NRA, the National Rifle Association, equate the highest form of liberty and freedom to the preservation and support of the second amendment—the right to bear arms. Alternatively, the NAACP—National Association for the Advancement of Colored People—equates the highest form of liberty and freedom to the preservation and support of equal rights and access for persons of color, protected by all the amendments that would prevent persons of color from being discriminated against in seeking jobs, housing, goods, and services. The group bias would prioritize the group expressions of the values of freedom and liberty; the dramatic bias comes from the very prioritization of freedom and liberty across all contexts.

Freedom and liberty are the particular values that are most difficult to reconcile with respect to the COVID-19 pandemic in the United States. Differing ideals of what freedom and liberty mean for those in the United States have created roadblocks to insights and progress to prevent the spread of the disease. Many of these roadblocks are supplemented by individual bias, group bias, and general bias. In turn, these biases prevent insight and authenticity in the levels of consciousness, which rely on each other to form true progress and prevent deterioration and decline. As an example, the individual who owns a restaurant may be against social distancing guidelines and outdoor-only seating because it negatively impacts their revenue stream. This individual bias prevents them from actively listening to sources that suggest the importance of social distancing and preventing indoor gatherings, such that the individual disbelieves or downplays the risks to their restaurant's patrons out of their own self-interest. Their ability to receive data is impacted by their individual bias, which in turn affects understanding, judgment, and decision.

This individual may not be alone in their assessment, of course. The restaurant owner may be part of a group of restaurant owners, such that the group has a bias against anything that might impact their revenues. The group of restaurant owners may be motivated by political concerns, adding to the amount of group bias that prevents authentic insight and decision making. The political group that they are a part of may be part of a greater nation or culture that is affected by general bias, or the bias against progress, innovation, and change. The biases work together and contribute to each other. Some biases stay and are passed on from one generation to another generation, such that they contribute to censorship at the point of dramatic bias. In fact, precisely because dramatic bias can originate in the meanings and values of previous generations and a community context, it is crucial that the integrity of society and culture be upheld for the good of all in the social order. Unfortunately, as Doran observes, "The insistence that intellectual and cultural integrity are required for the well-being of the social order runs counter to the pragmatic orientation even of most American intellectual life."[22] The hyper-focus on the individual and their freedom and liberty, the basis for American life, is both the source of inspiration and decline, particularly in the face of a national health crisis.

Thus dramatic bias becomes a very dangerous point for those seeking to remedy the issues in the COVID-19 pandemic. However, it is not the *only* bias. Biases of every kind are present in the health crisis; as dramatic bias has two sources, it becomes especially challenging for those wishing to overcome it, especially when the bias is a form of censorship that the subject is unlikely to be aware of in the first place. Dramatic bias is in a unique position in that it is in part formed by communal meanings and values. Without identification of some of these cultural values—and the steps necessary to discern whether these cultural values are authentic—there simply is no way to work towards an improvement of the social crisis that COVID-19 has wrought upon the United States, let alone the world. These deep problems with the identification and transmission of cultural values depends on individuals' self-transcendence, which depends on overcoming dramatic bias. The only clear remedy to dramatic bias, to enable such self-transcendence, is psychic conversion.

Psychic Conversion as Remedy

Psychic conversion is the process by which dramatic bias is overcome so that the subject can more authentically live the four levels of consciousness, leading to greater human authenticity (and community progress). Doran defines it as "the process of changing the direction of one's orientation

---

22. Doran, Robert M. "Lonergan's Ethics and Ignatian Election," *Theoforum* 45 (2014), pp. 133–156. P. 135.

through conversion, so that the psychic component of the repressive censorship becomes constructive. It thus establishes, or helps to establish, the integral dialectic of the subject."[23] Psychic conversion can be achieved in one of two ways, seeking that dramatic bias arrives in one of two ways. The first of these is dramatic bias at the level of the individual subject, such that psychic conversion comes "from below" to uncover the censorship in the individual psyche. Such an approach would consider psychotherapy, counseling, and possibly psychiatry as paths to psychic conversion. The individual subject who has experienced trauma may need to rely on the wisdom and training of another to overcome dramatic bias and realize the unwitting censorship within their own psyche. This results in psychic conversion from below.

Psychic conversion from above arrives through the avenue of the supernatural. The supernatural interacts with and inspires the natural; that is, the supernatural can be seen at work through the actions of the natural. The natural avenue for psychic conversion from above is through original meaningfulness. This occurs when an individual subject is the catalyst for change in ordinary meaningfulness; the catalyst subject observes a problem with the way ordinary meaningfulness plays a role in their culture or context and so inspires a change to correct or improve the ordinary meaningfulness. Such an example, in the context of the United States, is Martin Luther King, Jr. His emphasis on the equality, dignity, and personhood of Black persons provided original meaningfulness to the ordinary meaningfulness of general liberty and freedom for Americans. He qualified, improved, and expanded the notions of freedom and liberty with an emphasis on the personhood and equality of Black persons. Such an example of original meaningfulness through a natural source, in the estimation of the theologian, arrives through the supernatural intervention and inspiration in the life of an individual.

In the context of the COVID-19 pandemic in the United States, dramatic biases obviously exist. These dramatic biases occur both in the individual subject from below and from ordinary meaningfulness from above. From below, it may be that an individual has had a particularly traumatic health or persona experience through wearing a mask or practicing social

---

23. Doran, Robert M. *Theology and the Dialectics of History*. Toronto: University of Toronto Press, 1990. p. 75. Doran provides a further qualified definition for psychic conversion in *What is Systematic Theology?*, which includes the role of dramatically patterned consciousness: "Psychic conversion is the transformation of the censorship exercised by dramatically patterned intentionality over the neural infrastructure of the aesthetic dimension, a transformation from a repressive to a constructive functioning." P. 168.

distancing. Perhaps an individual with a pre-existing health condition, wearing a mask, has experienced adverse health effects. This trauma of distress may impact their willingness to wear a mask or their perception to mandates to wear masks, because this individual subject fears that others will experience similar negative effects.

More importantly, however, is the dramatic bias that stems from the ordinary meaningfulness of the United States, particularly with the emphasis of values such as freedom and liberty. Freedom and liberty, being such strong values in the United States, are unsurprisingly interpreted in various ways that clash with one another. This is where we might see Doran's thought of dialectic of contraries versus the dialectic of contradictories. The dialectic of contraries, in the context of COVID-19, might be the dialectic of whether a cloth face mask or a plastic face shield is more effective or useful for a particular demographic at preventing the spread of COVID-19; all, in this scenario, agree that face coverings are important, but the manner in which the face is covered differs. The dialectic of contradictories is more pressing with the matter of face coverings; this dialectic cannot agree on whether or not faces should be covered at all.[24] Based on scientific evidence, it is obvious that faces should be covered to prevent the spread of COVID-19; such a dialectic of contradictories suggests that only *one* of these positions should be upheld if the goal is to prevent the spread of disease.

More broadly speaking, the position and counterposition of whether or not face masks should be used, mandated, or necessary to prevent the spread of a disease is not exactly the true dialectic of contradictories that is behind dramatic bias "from above," with respect to the cultural values of freedom and liberty. It may very well be that those against mask mandates acknowledge and respect the scientific findings of the usefulness of preventing COVID-19 through face coverings. The true roadblock that forms the dramatic bias is whether or not such face coverings should be mandated, in terms of how the individual perceives the role of liberty and freedom with such a mandate. If the individual understands freedom and liberty on a very individual scale—that is, the individual is free to do whatever they choose—then a mask mandate is clearly in violation of such

24. I base this thought on whether or not it is authentically human to choose to wear face coverings during the time of a pandemic, in which research shows the effectiveness of masks as a means to prevent spread of the disease. In general, in my estimation, it appears to be acting authentically when wearing a face mask as it supports the best available science and morality to prevent the spread of disease; it returns good (protection of human life) for evil. I draw the definition of the divide between authenticity/inauthenticity from Doran, *Theology and the Dialectics of History*, p. 74.

values. However, if the individual understands freedom and liberty on a communal scale—that is, the individual is restricted from impugning on the rights of others to life and their own liberty—then it is very much in line with the cultural values of freedom and liberty to mandate mask wearing, as it upholds the right to life and liberty for everyone in all spaces.

The dramatic bias coming "from above" with respect to the cultural values of freedom and liberty in the context of the United States and COVID-19 is the importance of these values and the hyper-focus on those values as guiding principles for the response to COVID-19. Freedom and liberty as values are entrenched in the American experience as a form of dramatic bias; they dramatically pattern American intentionality. How these cultural values are understood to play a role in shaping American politics is highly dependent on individual, group, and general bias. Psychic conversion, in response, goes beyond the individual, group, and general views of liberty and freedom to the greater question of whether freedom and liberty are *the* guiding principles for American politics; are they authentic? Psychic conversion uncovers the ordinary meaningfulness that is passed along from one generation to another to see if that meaningfulness ought to remain ordinary.

Psychic conversion is vehemently resisted, due to the very same dramatic biases that psychic conversion can address. The resistance to examine one's own thinking is itself clouded by the insistence that one's own thinking cannot possibly be flawed, particularly if the thought is inspired by and inundated from individual, group, and general biases. The greatest difficulty in this resistance to psychic conversion is the role it plays in self-transcendence of the individual, which leads to the betterment of the community. Dramatic bias, coming from both above and below, clearly affects the individual. The individual who is unable to overcome dramatic bias will develop flaws at the four levels of consciousness, which turns the individual away from human authenticity and contributes to overall deterioration and decline. The deterioration and decline are passed onto the next generation, furthering the effects of dramatic bias and the desperate need for psychic conversion. Faced with such bleak prospects, how is it possible that psychic conversion can enter into our lives?

Social Grace and a Pandemic

Psychic conversion is not merely psychic in nature; it is very much spiritual and requires a spiritual origin, as Doran writes, "The bias of the egoist and the bias of common sense against theoretical pursuits, ultimate questions, and long-range solutions are spiritual in origin and tone, with psychic resonances but not psychic origination."[25] The spiritual origin of the solution to overcoming biases is through the Trinity. The supernatural avenue for psychic conversion occurs through grace, poured out on a community. Just as there is communal sin, so too there is communal grace. Communal sin became more understood in the latter half of the twentieth century, when structures of sin were exposed—these sins, such as systemic poverty, racism, sexism, were best observed in the sinful structures that produced them.

Psychic conversion, however, shows us that communal structures of grace exist too. These communal structures of grace are those that have been inspired by the work of the Holy Spirit, infusing individuals and their communities with the habit of charity. Thus, groups of people, communities, are avenues for psychic conversion from above. These movements reform and reshape the dramatic biases that are passed on from one generation to another by uncovering and removing the censorship laid down by previous generations and the issues that lie in their ordinary meaningfulness. As Doran affirms, "As one moves from dramatic bias through group bias to the individual bias of the egoist and the general bias of common sense against theoretical pursuits, ultimate questions, and long-range solutions to human problems, the center of the bias's gravity, as it were, moves more and more from being psychic to being spiritual, to being rooted in the abuse of human freedom."[26] The precise manner in which grace flows from the supernatural to the human person and their community occurs through the Trinity.

The outpouring of grace through the working of the Holy Spirit is constantly inviting *all* persons to the inner life of the Triune God and thus work with the Trinity to expose the flaws, shortcomings, and aberrations of ordinary meaningfulness that is passed from one generation to the next. The grace that is poured out on all persons operates within us so that we can respond to it and act in accordance with it. It is grace that inculcates us with the habit of charity, a created external term that allows us to participate in the life of the Triune God. I quote Doran at length here:

> The transformation of cultural values, in turn, depends on people striving for self-transcendence in all they do, and such consistent

25. Doran, Robert M. "The Nonviolent Cross: Lonergan and Girard on Redemption," 60.

26. Doran, Robert M. "The Nonviolent Cross: Lonergan and Girard on Redemption," *Theological Studies* 71 (2010), pp. 46–61, p. 59–60.

> self-transcendence is not possible without God's grace, in fact without the grace that enables the return of good for evil. Conversely, then, *it is the gift of God's grace that alone can meet the underlying difficulties*. Grace is the condition of sustained personal value, which itself conditions the emergence of the genuine cultural values that in turn are required for a just social order assuring the equitable distribution of vital goods to the entire community. The gift of God's grace that is the ultimate base is understood in terms of the created participations in and imitation of the triune God that occur in sanctifying grace and the charity that flows from it, that is, in terms of the mission and gift of the Holy Spirit, both *in and beyond the boundaries* of the Christian communions.[27]

This grace is given to *all* persons, and in such a way that inspires each individual to respond and thus grow in love with God and one another. Grace, therefore, is the key to psychic conversion and transformation of the community.

Grace works at the level of the individual to enable the individual to strive for self-transcendence. The individual, striving for self-transcendence, in turn works at the level of the community to transform the community. This transformation of the community is critical for the betterment of the social good. As Doran has affirmed, per Lonergan, the dialectic of community takes relative primacy over the dialectic of the subject, as "it is the community that sets the stage for the subject's dramatic pattern of experience."[28] Thus in such a way structural, social sins can become structures of grace. Social grace is imparted when individuals respond to God's grace and experience conversion that allows them to be more authentically human. That is, a human being is a being who is inspired and filled by the love of God, to in turn love neighbor, community, and God in return.

The social reality of grace that Doran proposes flows from the gift of the Holy Spirit. This social reality of grace "is an articulate set of cultural values that arise from the collective discovery, expression, validation, criticism, correction, development, [and] improvement of the formulations of the judgments of meaning and value that flow from the gift of God's love."[29] This is the Trinity in history that Doran writes of in his two

---

27. Doran, Robert M. *The Trinity in History: A Theology of the Divine Missions vol. 1, Missions and Processions*. Toronto: University of Toronto Press, 2012. p. 84. Emphases added.

28. Doran, *What is Systematic Theology?*, p. 126.

29. Doran, *The Trinity in History vol. 1*, p. 89.

volumes, *The Trinity in History: Missions and Processions* and *The Trinity in History: Missions, Relations, and Persons*. This is the Trinity in history that creates the category of social grace:

> The category of social grace refers to the cultural transformation of the meanings and values that inform human living, as well as the transformation of social, economic, and political structures. It refers to the cumulative and transforming effect of the divine missions in the realms of cultural and social values, precisely through the agency of converted subjects working together on mission from the Word just as the incarnate Word was on a mission from the Father.[30]

When human persons act and respond to the movement of the Holy Spirit, human communities move forward in progress and cumulative social good. I suggest that we can observe the Trinity in history and the Spirit at work within our communities when we hear the voices of those crying for social change, for the protection of the lives of the vulnerable, and for policies that ensure the betterment and health of the community. The moments of grace in the midst of a pandemic can be seen, from the grassroots movements of homemade, donated masks to large-scale fundraisers and donations to food pantries for those suffering from food insecurity. Despite the tremendous negativity, and indeed evil, present in the face of such a historic situation, we can see the work of the Holy Spirit in the actions of all those who return good for evil. This is grace, charity, and the love of God at work in lived human history.

Conclusion

In this essay, I described the health crisis of COVID-19 in the United States and its unintended consequences on the social order, particularly with respect to the questions surrounding American cultural values. I identified dramatic bias as the most important form of bias to tackle in order to promote the social good and progress at a time of a global health crisis. Dramatic bias, being shaped by communal meanings and values, in conjunction with the "relative primacy" of the dialectic of community over the dialectic of the subject, indicate a need to reshape the values that censor

30. Doran, *The Trinity in History: A Theology of the Divine Missions vol. 2 Missions, Relations, and Persons*. Toronto: University of Toronto Press, 2019. p. 36.

the individual's ability for self-transcendence. Psychic conversion is the path to transforming this censorship and constructing a way to authentic self-transcendence; individuals' efforts at self-transcendence, furthered by psychic conversion, helps to transform the cultural values that both hinder and help the U.S. response to COVID-19. Finally, the gift of grace, poured out on all humanity through the Holy Spirit, is absolutely necessary in order to bring about psychic conversion to overcome dramatic bias. This social grace not only prompts psychic conversion but in turn transforms and elevates all the values in the sociocultural milieu. Grace transforms the individual and the community, and can be seen in the movements of individuals towards social improvement and the defense of the dignity and value of human life. By intentionally and cautiously reviewing the meanings and values of one's culture brought on through ordinary meaningfulness, with the help of God's grace, one can transform the community and join in the healing mission of the Word.

CHAPTER FOURTEEN

TRANSPOSING *IN PERSONA CHRISTI*

Toward a Theology of Priestly Ministry for the Third Millennium

Joseph C. Mudd

Gonzaga University (Spokane, WA)

Introduction

Theological questions emerge in contexts. The proximate context of the present question is the history of clergy sexual abuse and cover-up that has led many to ask, "why priests?"[1] Some have concluded from this appalling history that priesthood is a failed institution to be consigned to the dustbin of ecclesiastical history.[2] Others cast the crisis as the fruit of an ecclesial phenomenon that has been given the name "clericalism."[3] Still others suggest that the crisis reveals the influence of secular culture, especially the moral laxity of the 1960s, and the "sexual revolution."[4] In each case these views express deep feelings of anger and regret, of sadness but also of hope. Clearly, the status quo is unacceptable. The Body of Christ has suffered unspeakable trauma. The questions that confront the faithful are heart-wrenching. One wonders, how did we get here? What is the

1. See, for example, Gary Wills, *Why Priests? A Failed Tradition* (New York: Viking, 2013)

2. See James Carroll, "Abolish the Priesthood," *The Atlantic* (June 2019), available at https://www.theatlantic.com/magazine/archive/2019/06/to-save-the-church-dismantle-the-priesthood/588073/.

3. See Thomas P. Doyle, "Clericalism: Enabler of Clergy Sexual Abuse," *Pastoral Psychology*, vol. 54, no. 3 (January 2006): 189–213. See also, Mary Gail Frawley-O'Dea, *Perversion of Power: Sexual Abuse in the Catholic Church* (Nashville: Vanderbilt University Press, 2007).

4. See, for example, the essay of Pope Benedict XVI, "The Church and the scandal of sexual abuse" published by *Catholic News Agency*, available at https://www.catholicnewsagency.com/news/full-text-of-benedict-xvi-the-church-and-the-scandal-of-sexual-abuse-59639.

priesthood for? How is it that priests and bishops covered up such heinous crimes, abetting the perpetrators in the process? Can the priesthood be saved? How have I been complicit in this history of violence? Can the church be saved?

In this chapter, I face the questions provoked by the present crisis by returning to the theology of priesthood. The crisis in the Catholic Church is not only one of horrific sexual violence, but also of the near total collapse of authority of a massive institution. In that regard, the crisis in the church is part of a larger crisis of authority found in other sectors of culture. At bottom the crisis is one of meaning. The fissures revealed in the church by the crisis reveal a breakdown in common meaning. I examine this crisis of meaning in relation to the theology of priesthood. I begin with a consideration of the phenomenon of clericalism, in dialogue with Bernard Lonergan's incisive analysis of the dialectic of authority. Then, I turn to a brief overview of contemporary theological and church doctrines on priesthood before articulating a critical-realist metaphysical analysis of priestly identity. Next, I rehearse to Robert Doran's elaboration of dramatic bias and psychic conversion in relation to ecclesial ministry. Doran's work enables us to diagnose the disease plaguing the church and to move toward a theology of priestly ministry for a healing church. Finally, I situate priestly ministry in trinitarian theology. I argue that the abuse crisis is attributable to clericalism, that clericalism is an instance of dramatic bias, and that any resolution of such a crisis of meaning will have to attend to psychic conversion.

Clericalism, Authority, Dramatic Bias

In his essay "The Dialectic of Authority," Bernard Lonergan offers a series of distinctions that can help frame the crisis of priestly authority in the church.[5] On Lonergan's analysis, authenticity gives power the prestige of authority.[6] Without authenticity, authorities function with the cool efficiency of bureaucrats concerned solely with adhering to policies and getting things done. Lonergan's description clarifies the way clerical authority tragically slides into bureaucratic power and efficiency on its way to clericalism.

Clericalism is a slippery term. For some it pertains to any exercise of priestly authority. For others it is as innocent as a free round of golf, or a complimentary dinner. In his 2018 letter to the faithful on the abuse crisis,

---

5. Bernard Lonergan, "The Dialectic of Authority" in Collected Works of Bernard Lonergan, eds. Robert M. Doran and John D. Dadosky (Toronto: University of Toronto Press, 2017)

6. Lonergan, "The Dialectic of Authority," 7.

Pope Francis defines clericalism as "an approach that 'not only nullifies the character of Christians, but also tends to diminish and undervalue the baptismal grace that the Holy Spirit has placed in the heart of our people.'"[7] He continues, "Clericalism, whether fostered by priests themselves or by lay persons, leads to an excision in the ecclesial body that supports and helps to perpetuate many of the evils that we are condemning today. To say 'no' to abuse is to say an emphatic 'no' to all forms of clericalism."[8] In another letter, Francis explains, "Clericalism, far from giving impetus to various contributions and proposals, gradually extinguishes the prophetic flame to which the entire Church is called to bear witness in the heart of her peoples. Clericalism forgets that the visibility and sacramentality of the Church belong to all the People of God (cf. *Lumen Gentium*, nn. 9–14), not only to the few chosen and enlightened."[9] Clericalism refers to all the ways in which authority exercised in the church is employed to diminish the people of God. In this sense clericalism is perpetuated by clergy and laity alike. What is at issue is a lack of authenticity and the resulting loss of authority.

Lonergan's elaboration of the dialectic of authority captures the dynamics at work in these ways of distorting ministry in the church. In the absence of authenticity, power becomes bureaucracy. Indeed, one of the greatest scandals of the sad history of recent decades has been the revelation of the attempted bureaucratic management of abuse cases—the relocation of sexual predators, the financial settlements used to silence victims, and the management of "public relations." The slide into bureaucratic thinking reveals the sickness beneath the veneer of competence—the abuse crisis exposes clerical power. Lonergan writes:

> Authenticity makes power legitimate. It confers on power the aura and prestige of authority. Unauthenticity leaves power naked. It reveals power as mere power. Similarly, authenticity legitimates authorities, and unauthenticity destroys their authority and reveals them as merely powerful. Legitimated by authenticity authority

7. Pope Francis, "Letter of His Holiness Pope Francis to the People of God," 20 August, 2018, available at http://www.vatican.va/content/francesco/en/letters/2018/documents/papa-francesco_20180820_lettera-popolo-didio.html#_ftn3.

8. Ibid.

9. Pope Francis, "Letter of His Holiness Pope Francis to Cardinal Marc Ouellet President of The Pontifical Commission for Latin America" 19 March, 2016, available at https://w2.vatican.va/content/francesco/en/letters/2016/documents/papa-francesco_20160319_pont-comm-america-latina.html.

> and authorities have a hold on the consciences of those subject to authority and authorities. But when they lack the legitimating by authenticity, authority and authorities invite the consciences of subjects to repudiate their claims to rule. However, subjects may be authentic or unauthentic. Insofar as they are authentic, they will accept the claims of legitimate authority and legitimate authorities, and they will resist the claims of illegitimate authority and illegitimate authorities. On the other hand, insofar as they are unauthentic, they will resist legitimate claims and they will support illegitimate claims.[10]

What Lonergan's analysis adds to our understanding of clericalism is the criterion of authenticity. Power itself is not unauthentic. Power survives on consent. Clericalism refers to a distortion of power that operates at the level of imagination. It might best be explained as an instance of dramatic bias.

To be sure, some examples of clericalism reveal individual and group biases, but these are relatively easy to identify and cause relatively little difficulty. The more intractable form of clericalism in the church, the one that wreaks havoc over history, lies in the imagination. It assumes that the priest, qua priest, is closer to God, more holy, and more powerful. The most tragic instance of this kind of clericalism as dramatic bias is found among parents who could not believe their own child's accusations against a priest.

Dramatic bias is the most difficult to understand of the four biases Lonergan describes in *Insight*. Put very compactly, dramatic bias has to do with feelings. More specifically it regards the way in which affect laden images or symbols function in the psyche either in eliciting or suppressing questions and insights. Robert Doran has written extensively on the topic of dramatic bias and the need for psychic conversion in conversation with Jungian analysis. His recent works on the *Trinity in History* move Rene Girard's analysis to the center of his treatment of dramatic bias. In *Trinity in History, Volume 2* Doran admits that "the vagaries of mimetic desire to which Girard's gives us entrance" are principle instances of what Lonergan calls dramatic bias.

In thesis 40 of *Trinity in History, Volume 1*, Doran turns to Girard in order to clarify what Lonergan means by "dramatic bias," by distinguishing between two ways of being conscious. Doran writes, "distinguishing and negotiating the two ways of being conscious calls for what Christian

10. Lonergan, "The Dialectic of Authority," 7–8.

spiritual tradition has called discernment."[11] Girard's analysis helps clarify what Lonergan means when he refers to this "first way" of being conscious, i.e., the sensitive, psychic dimensions of consciousness. Given certain conditions, the first way of being conscious supports the second way, as Lonergan explains in *Insight* in terms to the role of the psychic censor.[12] But, as Doran notes, "those optimal circumstances are rare indeed, and to the extent that they do not obtain, we can speak of a statistical near-inevitability of distortion precisely in the spiritual dimensions of human operation."[13] The distortion to which Doran refers takes the shape of what he calls a "radical ontological sickness" that Girard elaborates in terms of the deviated transcendence of mimetic rivalry. Doran explains:

> The individual is at some level painfully aware of his or her own emptiness, and it is this that leads the individual to crave so desperately the fullness of being that supposedly lies in others. The figures onto whom such desire is projected mediate being itself for us. It is via them that we seek to become real, and it is through wanting their very being that we come to imitate them. The wish to absorb, or to be absorbed by or into, the substance of the other implies an insuperable revulsion for one's own substance. Such metaphysical desire is masochism or pseudomasochism, a will to self-destruction in becoming something or someone other than what one is . . . One may even become the tormentor, torturing others as one was oneself tortured, and so masochism is transformed into sadism.[14]

This "radical ontological sickness," this "insuperable revulsion" at one's own being that manifests in acquisitive desire and deviated transcendence, clearly stands in need of healing grace. Of course, in Christianity the grace of forgiveness is intended to affirm the objective lovableness of every sinner in God's eyes. In the imagination of clericalism, however, forgiveness is a matter of power. This leads to a twisted logic wherein lay people of a clericalist bent see themselves as unlovable in comparison to a priest, who God must love more. Some priests are more than willing to play along

11. Doran, *Trinity in History*, Volume 1: 201.

12. See Bernard Lonergan, *Insight: A Study of Human Understanding*, CWL 3 (Toronto: University of Toronto Press, 1992) 214ff.

13. Doran, *Trinity in History*, Vol. 2, 21.

14. Doran, *Trinity in History*, Vol. 2, 23.

with these distorted set of images, setting themselves up as superior in all respects. The metaphysical desire of some laity for the being they believe priests have creates a situation of rivalry that manifests on the one side as obsequious deference to clerical authority, hoping to bask in the priest's reflected glow of holiness, and on the other as derisive mockery of clergy and of priesthood. More fundamentally, seeing oneself as wholly unlovable can have profoundly distorting effects on the religious imagination, especially one's ability to imagine the God of Jesus Christ who addresses the church through the sacramental ministry of priests. It may even lead one to indulge images of God that are Satanic, in which God becomes the accuser, the enemy, rather than the defender of human nature, in which, in the imagination of a masochistic psyche, the abusive priest is justified in his violence toward sinful nature.

Clericalism, then, takes us to the depths of psychic dis-ease. It torments the faithful, especially those who have been traumatized by clergy sexual abuse. It reflects a kind of distorted sacralization that afflicts the religious imagination of many, if not most, Catholics and many theologies of priesthood. In the confrontation with clericalism, the stakes are high because nothing less than the Catholic sacramental economy is at stake. To redress the evils of clericalism, therefore, requires a scalpel and not a hammer. The issue is theological, not political or rhetorical. It demands that we reconsider our theologies of priesthood.

Contemporary Doctrine on Priesthood

A complete history of priesthood is beyond the scope of this essay, but a review of the contemporary magisterium on priesthood will indicate the roots of the breakdown of common meaning today.[15] According to the Second Vatican Council, the priest acts *in persona Christi* in the exercise of his apostolic ministry. *Lumen Gentium* states plainly, "Acting in the person of Christ, he brings about the Eucharistic Sacrifice, and offers it to God in the name of all the people."[16] The document goes on to clarify that this identity extends not only to the exercise of the priestly office in the liturgy and sacraments, but

15. See Kenan B. Osborne, *Priesthood : A History of Ordained Ministry in the Roman Catholic Church*. (New York: Paulist, 1989). See also Matthew Levering, *Christ and the Catholic Priesthood: Ecclesial Hierarchy and the Pattern of the Trinity* (Chicago: Hillenbrand Books, 2010); Maty Gautier, et al, *Same Call, Different Men: The Evolution of the Priesthood Since Vatican II* (Collegeville, MN: Liturgical Press, 2012)

16. Vatican Council, "*Lumen Gentium*, Dogmatic Constitution on the Church" 10.

to the whole ministry of the priest in teaching, governing, and sanctifying. The council's Decree on the Ministry and Life of Priests, *Presbyterorum Ordinis* affirms, "By the sacrament of order priests are made in the image of the Christ the priest as servants of the Head."[17] The decree invokes the image of the Good Shepherd as the preeminent model for priestly ministry, saying, "As they direct and nourish the People of God, may they be aroused by the example of the Good Shepherd that they may give their life for their sheep."[18] Priests are not to be mere bureaucratic functionaries, but models of Christian virtue. Therefore, the decree recommends that priests cultivate those qualities "which are rightly held in high esteem in human relations, qualities such as goodness of heart, sincerity, strength and constancy of mind, careful attention to justice, courtesy, and others found in the letters of Paul."[19] Furthermore, the council assigns to priests the ministry of unity saying, "Theirs is the task, then, of bringing about agreement among divergent outlooks in such a way that nobody may ever feel a stranger in the Christian community."[20] In brief, conciliar doctrine grounds priestly identity primarily in terms of Eucharistic sacrifice, while also affirming that from that center, the priest must tend to the needs of the flock in a ministry of unity and love as a shepherd who is willing to lay down his life for his sheep.

Of course, the Second Vatican Council also famously stressed the baptismal priesthood of all believers, as well as a universal call to holiness, inaugurating a renewed theology of the laity.[21] Both these factors enabled a massive growth of lay ecclesial ministries in the church in the second half of the twentieth century. The resulting situation raises new theological questions about ministry that several theologians have attempted to answer by both returning to the sources and broadening out the classical theology of priesthood.[22] Consequently, theologies of ministry from the post-conciliar period tend to emphasize the community as the foundation for ministry. These theologies respond to a context in which the laity increasingly serve in ecclesial ministries that had previously been reserved to seminarians or

17. Vatican Council, "*Presbyterorum Ordinis*, Decree on the Ministry and Life of Priests," 12.

18. Ibid., 16.

19. Ibid., 3.

20. Ibid., 9.

21. See *Lumen Gentium*, 11.

22. See Edward Schillebeeckx, *Ministry, Leadership in the Community of Jesus Christ* (New York: Crossroad, 1981) and *The Church with a Human Face: A New and Expanded Theology of Ministry* (New York: Crossroad, 1985). See also, Kenan Osborne, *Orders and Ministry: Leadership in the World Church* (Maryknoll, NY: Orbis Books, 2006).

the ordained—lectors, acolytes, catechists, and so on. As a result, theological doctrines developed that identified ministry as the work of the community, furthering the kingdom inaugurated by Christ and handed over to the whole church. On this account, all ministry derives its power from the community; the whole church is ministerial. These theologies distinguish between ministry and office with the purpose of highlighting the ministerial work of the whole church on behalf of the kingdom. The result of this reorientation of the theology of ministry in regard to priesthood was to interpret priesthood primarily, even exclusively, in terms of function. The priest, like all the baptized, performs a ministry, but the primary responsibility of the priest is to serve the baptized, and to promote their ministerial works. This reorientation of priestly ministry in the church led some to argue that the offices of priest and bishop ought to be filled by members of the local community through something like a democratic process.[23] The 1990 synod on priesthood responded to these trajectories in contemporary theologies of ministry by defending the central role of ordained clergy in the church and the episcopal character of apostolic succession, while broadening the ecclesial imagination regarding priestly identity to include the priesthood of all believers.[24]

For the most part, contemporary papal teaching interprets conciliar doctrine in terms of the priests' pastoral leadership as shepherds. Recall, for example, Pope Francis's consistent refrain that priests acquire the small of the sheep, but also of the primary image of John Paull II's exhortation, *Pastores Dabo Vobis*, in which the pope casts the ministry of priests in the image of a shepherd tending the flock. That document, however, also highlights the "ontological bond" that connects the priest to Christ. This bond does not exist in isolation from the whole body of believers, for "The new priestly people which is the Church not only has its authentic image in Christ, but also receives from him a *real ontological share* in his one eternal priesthood, to which she must conform every aspect of her life."[25] Indeed, it is on account of the priestly identity of the whole church that the ministerial priesthood

23. See for example, Eugene Bianchi and Rosemary Radford Ruether, *A Democratic Catholic Church: The Reconstruction of Roman Catholicism* (New York: Crossroad, 1993). These sorts of theologies, especially as expounded in various works of Edward Schillebeeckx prompted the Congregation for the Doctrine of the Faith to issue the letter "Sacerdotium Minsteriale" in 1983 and a subsequent notification in 1986 on the Dutch version of Schillebeeckx's *The Church with a Human Face.*

24. See John Paul II, *Pastores Dabo Vobis, Post-synodal Apostolic Exhortation.* See also Thomas P. Rausch, "Forming Priests for Tomorrow's Church: The Coming Synod" *America*; New York Vol. 162, Iss. 7, (Feb 24, 1990): 168–172.

25. John Paul II, *Pastores Dabo Vobis, Post-synodal Apostolic Exhortation,* 13.

has its identity in the ministry of Christ the head and shepherd.[26] John Paul II fully embraces the conciliar image of the priesthood of the faithful and grounds his theology of priesthood in the priestly identity of the whole ecclesial body. Furthermore, he describes the relationship between the ministerial priest and Christ as follows: "In this bond between the Lord Jesus and the priest, *an ontological and psychological bond, a sacramental and moral bond*, is the foundation and likewise the power for that 'life according to the Spirit' and that 'radicalism of the Gospel' to which every priest is called today and which is fostered by ongoing formation in its spiritual aspect."[27] Notice that the bond is ontological *and* psychological as well as sacramental and moral. By introducing the category of psychology into a discussion of priesthood, John Paul goes beyond the strictly moral and juridical categories that dominated pre-conciliar theological and church doctrines.[28] Subsequently, programs of priestly formation have added an element of "human formation" to promote the emotional maturity and psychological health of seminarians. This does not mean that the theology of the priest as *in persona Christi* has waned—far from it. However one interprets the phrase *in persona Christi*, it remains the principal theological claim that establishes priestly authority in the church. Priestly power derives neither from public mandate nor personal excellence; rather, it is granted solely by the power of Christ passed down to the apostolic group and their successors, the bishops.[29] While some critics of priesthood claim this is a relatively late development of church doctrine that constitutes a deviation from New Testament descriptions of the ministry of elders or presbyters, recent critical historical scholarship shows that the reality was more complex than that popular narrative allows.[30]

To summarize, in this brief survey of the present context of doctrines on priestly ministry, we can see that, following the council, theologies of priesthood tend in one of two directions. One approach interprets priestly ministry through the functions the priest performs in the church and emphasizes

26. See *Presbyterorum Ordinis*, 2.

27. *Pastores Dabo Vobis*, 72.

28. See Pius XII, *Sacramentum Ordinis* and *Mediator Dei*

29. See *Presbyterorum Ordinis*, 2.

30. See G. Pierre Ingram, CC, "The Representation of Christ by the Priest: A Study of the Antecedents of in persona Christi Theology in Ancient Christian Tradition," a dissertation of St. Paul University, Ottawa, Canada (April 2012) The popular narrative identifies the shift from elder to priest as a relatively late change. Ingram, however, narrates an organic development of the priesthood that has its origins in the apostolic period.

the priestly and apostolic character of the whole church which grants to certain persons the authority to stand on behalf of the whole community, thereby representing the head *in person Christi capitis* as well as the body *in persona Christi corporis*. Another approach emphasizes priestly identity in terms of an ontological distinction from the priesthood of the baptized. While emphasizing the priestly identity of the baptized and a universal call to holiness, the council nevertheless retains a distinction between ministerial and baptismal priesthood that some post-conciliar theologies of ministry tended to downplay in favor of more democratic images of the church. The papal magisterium of the last forty years, on the other hand, has held to a theology of priesthood that begins by identifying priestly ministry with the ministry of Christ the Good Shepherd, Priest and Victim. The unique conformity to Christ given to the priest at ordination endows him with specific powers related to his office. The power of ordination, in this analysis, derives from the apostolic authority possessed uniquely by the bishops as successors of the apostles, not to the more generic apostolic authority of the community.

The phrase *in persona Christi* can therefore be taken in two senses. In one sense it refers to the role or *function* the priest performs in his ministry, in another sense it refers to his *identity*. These theologies offer apparently dialectically related views of priestly authority. Those theologies that emphasize the priest's function in the community tend to cast priestly authority in more democratic terms that emphasize collaboration and synodality. Those theologies that emphasize the unique identity of priests in the categories of ontology, tend to portray priestly authority in terms of an apostolic mandate and sacred power. There result diverging sets of images connected to priestly ministry and ecclesial authority from the imaginations of the faithful who relate to clergy according to the images they receive. These diverging images are further complicated by the cultural contexts in which clergy exercise their authority today. For example, in cultures that have made self-government a preeminent value, clerical assertions of authority or sacred power, no matter how elevated the language, cannot be but alien languages. For example, dramatic levels of disaffiliation among younger Catholics in the United States might reveal a near total collapse of religious authority, especially as it regards the priestly mediation of sacramental reconciliation.[31] The present breakdown of common meaning

31. See Mark M. Gray and Paul M. Perl, "Sacraments Today: Beliefs and Practices Among U.S. Catholics" publication of The Center for Applied Research in the Apostolate, Georgetown University, 2008.

regarding priestly authority suggests that we reinterpret the phrase *in persona Christi* in terms of a critical-realist metaphysics.

Priestly Ontology in Critical Metaphysics

Historically ecclesial authority was cast in terms of certain sacred powers, or *potestates*—a category borrowed from medieval jurisprudence—delegated to clergy by a divine mandate. The medieval ontology of priestly authority invested certain persons with power, solely on the basis of office. The resulting theology of sacramental causality identifies the effect of the sacramental action in the nexus between the sacred power given to a priest at ordination and the material elements of the rites of the church. Central to that understanding was the priest's power from Christ to confect the sacrament of the altar.[32] Later medieval theologies of ministry develop this theology of clerical power in terms of a metaphysical analysis of priestly identity that obtains in sacramental theology into the present, namely the notion of sacramental character.

In much contemporary sacramental theology, sacramental character is normally left out of the analysis for a variety of reasons mostly to do with a desire to move away from scholastic categories. In the theology of priestly ministry, however, it is often foregrounded in terms of the aforementioned ontological bond between the ordained and Christ. The doctrine of sacramental character can provide a legitimating theological justification of clerical power.[33] Of course, this raises questions about authenticity and holiness that have a long history in the western church, dating back to the Donatist controversy. Nevertheless, one might reasonably wonder whether this theology of priestly sacramental character increases the probability of unauthentic exercises of power in the church and ends up undermining the legitimate exercise of authority on which such a vast community depends. I am suggesting that while sacramental character and ontological distinctions

---

32. See Saint Thomas Aquinas, *Summa Theologiae*, III, q. 82, a. 1. See also *Summa Contra Gentiles*, Book IV, ch. 74, no. 6.

33. The *Catechism of the Catholic Church* affirms "The sacrament of Holy Orders communicates a "sacred power" which is none other than that of Christ" (no. 1551). Sacred power, however, is to be distinguished from temporal power. Clericalist attitudes blur this distinction. Donald Gelpi explains, "Clericalism…transforms clergy into a power elite. Power elites use positions of authority for self-aggrandizement or in order to oppress rather than to serve those they govern." See Donald L. Gelpi, S.J., *Committed Worship: A Sacramental Theology for Converting Christians, Volume II: The Sacraments of Ongoing Conversion* (Collegeville, MN: Liturgical Press, 1993), here at 124.

ought to be retained in a theology of the priesthood for today, they need to be transposed into the categories of critical-realist metaphysics. It is manifestly the case that the ordained are those who have been uniquely marked by a rite and endowed thereby with an office that exercises certain powers within a human community constituted by meaning. Using the elements of a critical-realist metaphysics, I would identify priestly power as conjugate potency, priestly identity as conjugate form, and priestly ministry as conjugate act. Transposing metaphysical elements into categories of meaning will further clarify that priestly identity can be understood in terms of Lonergan's categories of constitutive and incarnate meaning, and finality.

Sacramental ordination is a concrete historical event. No one has laid hands on me and commissioned me by the Holy Spirit to exercise the office of priesthood. Those are not among my conjugates. This does not mean that those in whom these conjugates inhere are a different kind of being than me. This is very important: ordination does not change the ordinand's *nature*. That is not how sacramental grace works. Sacramental grace, like all graces, has to do with the ways created realities relate to the Triune God and to history. The sacrament of ordination mediates a change in the way ordinand relates to God and to the church. The ordained person relates to the church and to God in a different way than I do as a lay person. That difference is a *real* difference. It is an *ontological* difference within a world mediated by and constituted by meaning. But the change is a change in the conjugates. When we transpose Lonergan's elements of metaphysics into categories of meaning, we can understand changes in the world constituted by meaning as changes of constitutive meaning. The constitutive meaning of a person, their incarnate meaning, refers to the totality of the various intentional states that constitute a life—feelings, values, imagination, thoughts, judgments, and decisions. These intentional states knit together the various exterior, historical occurrences and events that shape human biographies—festivals, harvests, work, family meals, friendships, births, deaths, and so on. The reality of person is all these intentional and historical events taken together and placed in the horizon of vertical finality. Finality adds a further clarification to the theology of priesthood.

To put the matter in terms of finality, we might say that both the priest and I are horizontally ordered to sacramental worship because of the baptismal character or conjugates we share that grant us the power to worship.[34] In addition, we are both vertically ordered toward the beatific vision

34. Lumen Gentium, 11. See also Saint Thomas Aquinas, *Summa Theologiae*, III, q.63, a.2.

which the sacramental economy mediates symbolically in history, and by which we are healed and elevated in our natures by grace to become partakers of the divine nature.[35] But, we are differently horizontally ordered as it regards our fulfillment of the sacramental economy in the church. As I noted above, this distinction leads some to claim that the priesthood is merely functional. A critical metaphysical analysis shows, however, that the difference in function already indicates an ontological difference, while locating that difference in conjugate potency, form, and act.

To clarify in relation to authority, one can find in some Catholic theologies of priesthood a persistent mystification regarding the ontological change of ordination. These theologies employ the categories of ontology to legitimate power in the manner of mythic consciousness. Image and affect predominate in these theologies, even if the language sounds metaphysical. I should aver that this deployment of the language of ontology by mythic consciousness is often sincerely trying to get at the genuine religious experience of priestly ministry as personally and communally transformative in the concrete lives of the faithful. But the terminology reflects a patterning of religious experience that sets the church on a collision course with reality when the language of ontology no longer provides power with the legitimating aura of authority. Our present crisis of authority, in no small part, reflects the demise of these mythical ways of imagining clergy. Over and over again, power, as exercised in the church, has been exposed as mere power exerted by perpetrators of sexual violence, those who cover up their crimes, and those who look the other way. Does this mean that we ought not speak of character or ontology in relation to the priesthood? Not necessarily. While the terms bear the heavy weight of recent history, they still capture genuine insights into the theology of ordained ministry. If general categories derived from Lonergan's elements of metaphysics can clarify ontological change, Doran's analysis of psychic conversion identifies the foundations of a renewed theology of priesthood in interiorly and religiously differentiated consciousness.

Psychic Disfunction and the Priesthood

In the aftermath of revelations of clerical sexual abuse, some bishops preferred to speak about the crisis as one of moral degeneracy, *not* clericalism. But, in truth, clericalism *is* a kind of moral degeneracy. While the term

35. *Catechism of the Catholic Church*, 1129.

'clericalism' can be thrown around far too easily, the reality to which the notion points, as indicated above, is a psychic disorder plaguing the church. The elaboration of psychic conversion is one of Robert Doran's major contributions to Lonergan studies and to theology, for it takes us to the root of distortions of subject and community such as clericalism. Without attending to the symbolic level of consciousness, our diagnoses of clericalism will inevitably miss the mark. In this section, I turn to Doran's *Theology and the Dialectics of History* to develop the basic foundations for a theology of ministry for the third stage of meaning.

A theology of ministry for today begins with a consideration of the work of the church in history. In *Theology and the Dialectics of History,* Doran explains that work of the church in history is the praxis of the reign of God that "enables ecclesial ministry of whatever kind to be a catalytic agent of the transition from the prevailing situation to an alternative situation that approximates more closely the rule of God in human affairs."[36] The work of systematic theology is therefore, in part, to evoke the "constitutive dimension of the church's inner spiritual life and external structure and ministry."[37] The constitutive dimension of ministry, that which makes the church a "living sacrament of God's catalytic agency," is nothing other than the paschal mystery of Jesus Christ.[38] Embodying the just and mysterious law of the cross in history, ecclesial ministry, including the ministry of theology, advances a transformation of the prevailing situation into one more closely approximating the reign of God. Insofar as the church in its various ministries fails in this regard, it finds itself collaborating, often unwittingly, with the forces of victimization and violence that constitute the reign of sin. Sin and evil reveal the repeated and systematic failures of self-transcendence that constitute the histories of the shorter and longer cycles of decline. Evil, therefore, includes the breakdown in the integral and normative scale of values.

On Doran's analysis, fidelity to the normative and integral scale of values, in order, includes psychic self-appropriation. Psychic conversion identifies the transition from the repressive functioning of the psychic censor to a constructive one; it "allows access to one's own symbolic system and through that system to one's affective habits and one's spontaneous apprehensions of possible values."[39] The psyche operates on symbols, "on images and their

36. Robert M. Doran, *Theology and the Dialectics of History*, (Toronto: University of Toronto Press, 1990) 109. Hereafter *TDH.*

37. *TDH,* 109.

38. *TDH,* 110.

39. *TDH,* 61.

concomitant affects."[40] These symbols can orient us toward the universe of being, or they can be the symbolic expression of mythic consciousness that confine wonder to the readymade world of myth and magic.[41] By attending to patterns of behavior indicative of clericalism we can glimpse the operative symbols that animate the clericalist psyche. What is often revealed, as indicated above, is a deviated transcendence—an idolatrous worship of clerical power. A church undergoing psychic conversion, on the other hand, consistently attends to the cross.

Only through the cross does the sacramental economy of the church avoid falling into bureaucracy and clericalism. Lonergan places the law of the cross at the center of the Christian theology of redemption and the center of the life of the church.[42] If the sacramental economy derives its power from Christ's passion,[43] then it too is a mediation of the law of the cross in history. This is revealed symbolically and sacramentally in the continual re-inscription of Christian bodies with the sign of the cross. Furthermore, as Doran points out, "without participation in the law of the cross, the ministry of anyone, even one with the fulness of orders, is ministry only in the attenuated sense of merely *ex opere operato* in those limited areas where such an understanding of sacramental grace is applicable."[44] In order to move beyond such an attenuated way of construing priestly ministry, a theology of the priesthood for the third millennium would begin with a reconsideration of the theology of redemption, for it is here that so much goes array at the level of image and affect. It is in preaching and teaching about redemption that sadistic images of an angry god visiting justice on an innocent child enter the psyche of too many Christians. Lonergan's treatise on redemption, on the other hand, identifies the cross as the transformation of evil into good, and clarifies that the mission of the God-man is to mediate friendship to God's enemies.[45]

---

40. *TDH*, 60.

41. Lonergan elaborates on mythic consciousness in *Insight*. See Lonergan, *Insight*, CWL 3 (Toronto: University of Toronto Press, 1992) 560.

42. Bernard Lonergan, *The Redemption*, CWL 9 (Toronto: University of Toronto Press, 2018) 197ff.

43. See Saint Thomas Aquinas, *Summa Theologiae*, III, q. 62, a. 5.

44. *TDH*, 122. A fuller account of priesthood would affirm that "The ability to assent to such participation in the law of the cross and the exercise of that ability in the actual performance of the demands of life constitute the apex of a person's religious, moral, and psychological development." (idem.)

45. Lonergan, *The Redemption*, 631.

Priesthood and Participation in Trinitarian Relations

In the background of theologies of priestly ministry that emphasize the ontological difference of priests lie a range of assumptions regarding how the church relates to the Trinity. Lonergan's systematics of the Trinity, and Doran's further elaborations, offer important clarifications regarding our participation in the Trinitarian life, toward which the whole sacramental economy and priestly ministry are ordered. If it is true that the priest acts *in persona Christi*, in a functional and therefore an ontological sense, his ministry can be understood in terms of a created participation in the Trinitarian relations Lonergan identifies in his treatise on the Trinity in terms of the four-point hypothesis.[46] Specifically, we can think of priestly ministry as a participated likeness to the relation of paternity. This is not to say that the priest participates in the secondary act of existence of the Incarnation which belongs uniquely to Christ—the theology of *in persona Christi* does not make the priest Christ, but an *alter Christus*. It is rather to affirm that the *totus Christus*, head and members, participates in the relation of paternity through its acts of meaning that continue to mediate the Word to the world. Central to those acts of meaning is the ecclesial sharing in the Paschal Mystery, symbolized in the church's liturgical life and by its incarnating the law of the cross in history. As ministers of the church's liturgy and proclaimers of God's outer word of love, priests bear a special likeness to the Son. Preeminently, in the sacrificial offering of the altar and the act of absolution, the priest symbolizes God's grace in the world in imitation of Christ's human historical life of healing, forgiving, and self-offering, and in his Spirit of love for his friends.

Anointed with the same Spirit, priests offer a sacramental embodiment of the intelligibility of redemption Lonergan identifies as the law of the cross. Of course, all Christians, indeed all people, are called to embody the law of the cross in history, but priests in liturgical offering and in the offering of their lives, embody the law *sacramentally*. That is to say that clergy mediate the law of the cross through sacramental symbols. Through the priest's sacramental/symbolic dramatization of sorrow over sin in a life of *misericordia*, the evil of guilt is awakened and potentially transformed into the good of forgiveness and restoration of spiritual integrity. The catastrophe of clerical sexual violence and corruption, on the other hand, heaps evil on top of evil. It is properly described as Satanic, because it symbolizes

46. Bernard Lonergan, *The Triune God: Systematics*, CWL 12, eds., Robert M. Doran and Daniel Monsour, trans. Michael Shields (Toronto: University of Toronto Press, 2007).

the meanings and values of the accuser—the diabolical dynamic of pride and shame, in which shame leads to rationalization and pride to reveling in one's wicked ways.

Crucially, the priest reveals a created participation in paternity not as a mere cipher, but in the fullness of his humanity. While some theologians so emphasize the self-effacing character of priesthood that the subjectivity of the priest must be wiped out entirely and replaced by the subjectivity of Christ, a Lonerganian approach would emphasize personal priestly authenticity and a clerical culture of ongoing conversion in which the priest enacts the dramatic artistry of imitating Christ while remaining fully himself. The priest is simply not able to empty himself of all subjectivity.[47] This would amount to a kind of psychic suicide. It is the obverse of Paul's evocation, "no longer I, but Christ lives in me." Rather, the properly supernatural element of acting *in persona Christi* has to do with what is disproportionate to the end of a human person, namely, to mediate the presence of a divine person. Does the priest lose his human personhood when he acts *in persona Christi*? Clearly not. This would be to mistake the enactment of the ontological change of ordination in act as central act, rather than as conjugate act. Ordination is not a transubstantiation. The priest retains his subjectivity, even while he acquires a new conjugate potency, as grace does not destroy nature. Rather than eliminate his historical particularity, his subjectivity, the priest who wishes to imitate Christ needs to embody the "mind," the *psyche*, of Christ, Paul refers to in Philippians 2 by taking the form of a slave, living and dying the law of the cross.

Conclusion

The foregoing outline of elements for a renewed theology of the priesthood highlights the important role psychic conversion plays in overcoming the culture of clericalism. Like religious, moral, and intellectual conversion, psychic conversion is a matter of psychic self-appropriation. Psychic self-appropriation entails attending to and scrutinizing the symbols that mediate one's experience of the world; "it allows access to one's own symbolic system, and through that system to one's affective habits and one's spontaneous apprehensions of possible values."[48] Critically, for our

47. For instance, interpretations of John 3:30—"He must increase and I must decrease."—in relation to priestly ministry can function symbolically in the psyche in a repressive and masochistic way.

48. Doran, *TDH*, 61.

purposes here, attention to psychic conversion allows us to probe the depths of contemporary ecclesial suffering and to identify a possible long-term solution in the renovation of the church's theology of ministry.

The tendency of some theologies of ministry toward the mythical deployment of metaphysical diction does not negate the real and verifiable difference ordination makes. On a critical-realist account, however, one can preserve classical insights regarding the unique relation between the ordained minister and Christ while at the same time affirming that the priest's identity derives from the function he performs in the community. At the heart of priestly identity is the law of the cross, the pursuit of which gives priestly power the authority of authenticity. The contemporary magisterium's emphasis on the priest's role as shepherd highlights the need for authenticity among the church's ministers. Similarly, John Paul II's evocation of the psychological bond the priest shares with Christ can be elaborated in terms of the law of the cross. Priests formed under this theology of priesthood will have a better sense of the function of ecclesial ministry in history as the praxis of the reign of God that transforms histories of decline in the church and in culture by resisting imperialist temptations through embodying the law of the cross.

CHAPTER FIFTEEN

HISTORICAL SOTERIOLOGY AND THE SCALE OF VALUES

Ellacuría and Doran in Dialogue

Andrew T. Vink

Boston College (Chestnut Hill, MA)

In Chapter 13 of *Theology and the Dialectics of History*, entitled "Theology, The Church, and Liberation," Doran engages Latin American liberation theology (LALT) through the work of Juan-Luis Segundo's *The Liberation of Theology*. While Doran's reading and analysis of Segundo's work is sound, there are other figures in the Latin American liberation theological tradition that share a great deal more of Doran's commitments, one such example being the Jesuit martyr Ignacio Ellacuría (1930–1989). In the following essay, I argue that Ellacuría's theological perspective, focusing on historical soteriology and the incorporation of grace via the church of the poor as the historical sacrament of the poor, provides a fruitful complement to the way Doran implements the integral scale of values in light of the preferential option of the poor.[1]

Situating a Liberation Theology in the Scale of Values

Doran's engagement with liberation theology in Chapter 13 comes from the need for theology to engage with a culture that distorts the various levels of the integral scale of values.[2] Since the church is meant to be a

1. There is a case to be made that this analysis would also fit with Doran's later project *The Trinity and History* and its discussion of the visible and invisible missions of the Son and the Spirit. Ellacuría's historical-soteriological focus could provide valuable insights into the missions and how they are carried out in light of a unified, historical reality. Such a project, however, would go well beyond the space provided in this volume and is an area for further research.

2. Doran, Robert M. 1990. *Theology and the Dialectics of History*. Toronto: University of Toronto Press, 418.

community that is fully in line with the scale of values, theology dictates that the church must be a community of resistance that, through its ministry, creates a further community of resistance in the form of a world-cultural humanity. As a part of this world-cultural humanity, theology then must engage the cultural particularities of a community so that the church can understand what the community needs the church to contribute.[3] What Doran describes is, in essence, the work of liberation theologies; a liberation theologian seeks to understand the context of the suffering of a particular community so that one can recognize what a community needs from the Gospel to restore hope and be energized by God's self-giving love through the church.[4]

When this concept of liberation theology is put in conversation with a global political, economic, and technological order mentioned in the first paragraph of Chapter 13, one can understand how liberation theology fits into the integral scale of values. Considering how corruptions of social, cultural, and personal values can eventually lead to the maldistribution of vital goods, one function of liberation theologies is to critique and heal social, cultural, and personal values by way of articulating the voice of the marginalized communities.

The core of Doran's argument in this chapter is that the framework of the integral scale of values provides a theoretical framework that complements the praxis-framework of liberation theology, which responds to liberationist critiques that transcendental methods do not sufficiently address the concrete realities upon which political and liberation theologies focus.[5] Throughout section 2.1, Doran articulates how the framework of the scale of values and his conception of the distortion of values overcomes those critiques, showing that with proper application, transcendental methodology leads to privileging the position of the victims and making the preferential option for the poor the organizing principle for the ministry of the church.[6]

Given this argument, along with the development of Doran's thought since 1990, it is clear that Doran's work seeks a dialogue partner who is

---

3. Doran 1990, 421.

4. It is important to note that the idea of context is not an element of only Latin American liberation theology, or other "contextual theologies," but of all theologies and the theologians associated with them. To paraphrase one of M. Shawn Copeland's adages to her students, even Aquinas had a context. The emphasis on context in this instance is to emphasize that instances of suffering are unique to each context and must be respected as such. A universal approach in light of these instances would only show a lack of attentiveness to the needs of a community.

5. Doran 1990, 422.

6. Doran 1990, 423–4.

methodologically rigorous, historically minded, and seriously engages the Christian tradition in its prophetic nature to engage the distortions of social, cultural, and personal values. One opportunity for dialogue comes in the work of the Jesuit martyr Ignacio Ellacuría.

Ellacuría: Liberation Theologian and Philosopher of Historical Reality

Ellacuría's philosophical and theological work provides an excellent dialogue partner for Doran's liberative approach, complementing Doran in a way that few others in the LALT tradition can, primarily due to his nuanced understanding of history, philosophically oriented methodological rigor, and recognition of the primacy of the poor and marginalized in the form of the crucified peoples. This section will start with a brief biographical note on Ellacuría, followed by discussion of his definition of liberation theology. This definition is then fleshed out in Ellacuría theory of historical reality, methodological thinking, and finally, his reflection on the privileged role of the poor and marginalized in theology, through his understanding of the crucified peoples and the church as historical sacrament of the poor.

Ellacuría, a native Basque, spent the majority of his life living among and serving the people of El Salvador. After joining the Society of Jesus at 16, Ellacuría was sent to El Salvador in 1948, followed by his early intellectual formation in Quito, Ecuador, where he learned the Thomistic tradition as well as explored the work of José Ortega y Gasset.[7] After returning to El Salvador for three years to teach in a diocesan seminary, Ellacuría went to study under Karl Rahner in Innsbruck from 1958–1962. After completing his theological formation at Innsbruck, Ellacuría wrote his three volume dissertation under the philosopher Xavier Zubiri (1898–1983) entitled "La principialidad de la esencia en Xavier Zubiri."[8] After completing his doctorate, Ellacuría returned to El Salvador, serving as professor and eventually rector of the Universidad Centroamericana "José Simeón Cañas" (UCA) in San Salvador. He also worked with Jon Sobrino, among others, as theological advisors to Archbishop St. Oscar Romero, as can be seen in Romero's Second Pastoral Letter, entitled "The Church, The Body of Christ in History." Ellacuría stood as a champion of the poor during the Salvadoran Civil War, following the example of St. Oscar Romero, and taking on the

7. Burke, Kevin F. 2001. *The Ground Beneath the Cross: The Theology of Ignacio Ellacuría*. Washington, D.C: Georgetown University Press, 15.

8. Burke 2001, 35.

mantle after Romero's martyrdom. Ellacuría was assassinated on November 16, 1989 along with five other Jesuits, their housekeeper, and the housekeeper's daughter in a planned attack by the Salvadoran military.

While his life was cut short, Ellacuría provided a philosophically robust theology of liberation, making use of his extensive training under Zubiri. Given that Lonergan and Zubiri shared areas of interest, it follows that students of both thinkers such as Doran and Ellacuría should have ample room for dialogue. Ellacuría's liberative philosophy and theology can help further articulate how the critical element of the integral scale of values parallels Ellacuría's concerns. Ellacuría's theology, then, can provide one way of understanding how a concrete expression of the integral scale of values may manifest.

To begin, we must look to Ellacuría's definition of liberation theology to understand how Ellacuría sees the starting point of the theological task. In his seminal essay "The Church of the Poor, Historical Sacrament of Liberation," Ellacuría provides a detailed definition of what he understands as the theology of liberation:

> The theology of liberation understands itself as a reflection from faith on the historical reality and action of the people of God who follow the work of Jesus in announcing and realizing the Reign of God. It understands itself as an action by the people of God in following the work of Jesus and, as Jesus did, it tries to establish a living connection between the world of God and the human world. Its reflective character does not keep it from being an action, and an action by the people of God, even though at times it is forced to make use of theoretical tools that seem to remove it both from immediate action and from the theoretical discourse that is popular elsewhere. It is, thus, a theology that begins with historical acts and seeks to lead to historical acts, and therefore it is not satisfied with being a purely interpretive reflection. It is nourished by faithful belief in the presence of God within history, an operative presence that, although it must be grasped in grateful faith, remains a historical action. There is no room here for faith without works; rather faith means being drawn into the very force of God that operates in history, so that we are converted into new historical forms of that operative and salvific presence of God in humanity.[9]

9. Ellacuría, Ignacio. 2013. *Essays on History, Liberation, and Salvation*, edited by Michael E. Lee. Maryknoll, NY: Orbis Books, 228.

While pages of ink could be spilled diving into the depths of this definition, there are a few important elements that need to be drawn out for our purposes. First, Ellacuría's theology of liberation rests squarely on the foundation of a theory of history. He understands theology's task as one shaped by the historical reality human beings inhabit, and it cannot be abstracted from that historical reality. Second, the theology of liberation is a concrete action carried out by the people of God in response to the call to follow Jesus' work and ministry. This is an action that is required by the needs heard in the cry of the poor, always moving beyond complacent reflection. Finally, this action is driven by faith. This implies faith is not simply something to be received without response. Faith is what allows one to cooperate with God's action in history. Ellacuría's allusion to the assertion in James 2:20 that faith without works is barren reiterates his emphasis that faith is not merely about showing up to Mass every Sunday and putting a few dollars in the collection basket. Instead, faith requires one to challenge the structural injustices that systemically dehumanize vulnerable members of the community. For Ellacuría, Christian faith is a dynamic faith that serves as a prophetic call to action that makes God's presence tangible and apparent to all of humanity. Ellacuría's primary example of this is St. Oscar Romero, a martyr for the people of El Salvador. After Romero's martyrdom, Ellacuría said, "With Monseñor Romero, God passed through El Salvador."[10] Faith is exemplified by the blood of the martyrs, who stand with those who cannot. With this understanding of the theology of liberation, we can move forward to see how this definition forms the rest of Ellacuría's philosophical and theological work.

The next aspect of Ellacuría's thought that must be considered is his theory of history, or, more accurately, his theory of historical reality. Building on Zubiri's concept of reality as a dynamic unity of distinct elements that human beings are situated in, Ellacuría argues that this human reality must also be grounded in history, moving away from the idea that the human person could be grounded outside of history. For Ellacuría, the human person is essentially historical. In *Filosofía de la realidad historical* (*FRH*), Ellacuría's posthumously published philosophy monograph, he describes the unique historical nature of human reality in the following way: the human experience of reality is radically distinct from the experience of other animals because of the necessity for human beings to choose a way to engage reality from among many. A cat can only exist in reality as a cat, while a human being can choose from a plethora of options for humans to exist in

10. Ellacuría 2013, 285.

reality. One can live a life as a scholar, a husband, a father, a friend, or even a combination of these categories to name a few. Each role brings particular insights and connections to reality and allows for a unique understanding of a situation. It is how one engages with reality, the desire to act at the heart of human nature, that provides the distinction. Ellacuría expounds on this in his conclusion to *FRH*, writing: "The truth of reality is not what is already done; that is only part of reality. If we do not turn to what is being done and what is to be done, the truth of reality escapes us. One must make the truth, which does not mean primarily to implement or realize what is already known, but to make that reality in which the interplay of praxis and theory is shown as true. That reality and truth must be made and discovered, and that they must be made and discovered in the collective and successive complexity of history, of humanity, is to indicate that historical reality can be the object of philosophy.[11] Ellacuría's commentary provides an anthropological note that helps to elucidate the concept of historical reality: human beings are praxis-oriented beings, and the historical reality human beings create is shaped by praxis. This is why Ellacuría's focus is on the making of truth in history as truth in history must be made manifest by action. As will become evident below, the truth of divine revelation comes in the historical reality of the cross, and salvation is inherently tied to that action of the cross inserted into history.

The second aspect of Ellacuría's thought that is significant for conversation with Doran's work is the focus on understanding what makes a LALT methodologically unique. Given his training under Zubiri, the most significant aspects of Ellacuría's methodological thinking are the philosophical elements. In an address given at the *Conference on Latin American Theology* in 1975, Ellacuría lays out his methodological reflections by first articulating the significance of LALT's understanding the methodological task as a posterior one, asking the question of how one accomplishes a task successfully so that it may be repeated.[12] Fundamental method, which is Ellacuría's primary concern in this lecture, is defined in the following way: "Fundamental method is the very manner of thinking, and this very manner of thinking is only realized and verified when in fact it has produced a thought. In reality, it involves all of that thought as the ultimate foundation of what, from another point of view, appears as method. From this perspective, method is nothing but the critical and operative aspect of a

11. Ellacuría, Ignacio. 1990. *Filosofía de la realidad histórica.* San Salvador: UCA editores, 599. Translation mine.

12. Ellacuría 2013, 64.

system of thought, considered reflexively."[13] This is key to recognizing the focus on praxis for Latin American theological reflections. Ellacuría offers two concerning extremes into which Latin American theological reflection could fall. The first is an overemphasis on method, leading to a failure to ask questions of content and praxis; the second is an uncritical praxis that cannot provide an explicit account of its justification.[14] The goal, then, must be to find a third way that properly balances the tension of methodological clarity and a full engagement in praxis.

Ellacuría's proposed solution to this issue begins with a question very familiar to those working in the Lonerganian context: one understands the moment of knowing in theology by asking what precisely does it mean to know "x."[15] He answers this question by providing an overall structure of human knowing that takes into account various levels this structure has. The first aspect of the structure Ellacuría describes is the biological element, meaning that human knowing and intelligence serves a biological function.[16] In other words, human intelligence exists because it helps the human person to survive in a way that animals do not need, meaning it is a necessary function for humans but not for animal life.[17] This implies that human intelligence has a proper structure that must be understood thoroughly to make sense of how human reality is differentiated.

This structure and differentiation, according to Ellacuría, is focused not on being or meaning but on the apprehension of reality. The language of reality comes from Zubiri's understanding of the philosophical project. Burke concisely describes Zubiri's project in the following way: "The Zubirian critique focuses not only on modern philosophy, but on the entire history of Western philosophy insofar as that history manifests a proclivity for an idealism that is reductionistic. Stated simply, idealism becomes reductionistic when knowing is separated from sensing."[18] Reality, on the

13. Ellacuría 2013, 64.

14. Ellacuría 2013, 64.

15. Ellacuría 2013, 75.

16. Ellacuría 2013, 79.

17. In a rather amusing anecdote, Ellacuría drives the point home: "Zubiri used to say that a species of idiots is not biologically viable, even though a species of superior animals without intelligence is perfectly viable" (Ellacuría 2013, 79). While animals can be unintelligent by comparison to humans, they do not actually need intelligence to consume nutrients and reproduce, therefore perpetuating the species. Human beings, on the other hand, require intelligence to do these things because we are social, political animals, which assumes intelligence. For a reflection on how Ellacuría makes further use of the Zubirian concept of intelligence, see Burke 2001, 44–48, and, for a more condensed reflection, Burke and Lasalle-Klein 2005, 18–22.

18. Burke 2001, 45.

other hand, serves as the condition for the possibility to understand being and comprehend meaning. Reality provides context that prevents idealistic abstraction. The engagement with reality has three elements that flesh out the structure of human intelligence. The first is becoming aware of the weight of reality, which means one is present to reality and the context it provides.[19] This awareness entails an attentiveness that avoids reductionism. The second element is shouldering the weight of reality.[20] The act of shouldering points to the ethical nature of human intelligence, implying a responsibility towards reality. The final element, taking charge of the weight of reality, emphasizes human intelligence as committed to praxis, that knowing implies action within reality.[21] Since reality has priority to both being and meaning, changes in either of the latter concepts implies a change in reality. This means that the apprehension of reality is the condition for the possibility of human life. Only by engaging reality, and recognizing the realm of reality one is investigating, can a proper method be developed.[22]

Moving to theological method, Ellacuría first establishes theology as a social activity; without recognizing this social element, theology can easily become distorted.[23] He then offers three reasons for the importance of the social element to theology. First, Ellacuría claims theology is intimately connected to an ecclesial institution, which is always in the context of a society with a particular history that configures said institution.[24] This means that one cannot consider the theological task without considering the ecclesial community in which the theological activity is taking place, as to consider its emphases, biases, and major figures. Second, recognizing that no theoretical resource is perfect, theological activity must use the tools provided by these emphases, biases, and major figures, even if such resources are formed by an imperfect ideological process.[25] This means the theologian's tools will always be imperfect, and the theologian must be aware of the unintended slants her theoretical tools may imply. Finally, theological activity, as an activity that occurs in sphere of human reality,

19. Ellacuría 2013, 80.

20. Ellacuría 2013, 80.

21. Ellacuría 2013, 80.

22. Ellacuría 2013, 84.

23. Ellacuría 2013, 85.

24. Ellacuría 2013, 85–6.

25. Ellacuría 2013, 86.

has a historical character and responds not only to individual options, but formally social ones.[26] It is through these primary methodological foci that a theology can then take on a character representative of the concrete situation of the theological community engaged in that activity.

For Ellacuría and the Latin American liberation theological context, the subtext of this methodological discussion points to the use of Freudian and Marxist analyses that go back to Gutiérrez's *A Theology of Liberation*.[27] While there is a tendency to rely on such methodological tools, Ellacuría's concern is that one loses the tradition and graces that come from the Christian faith when one uses methodological tools from Freudian and Marxist analysis uncritically. Instead, Ellacuría argues that a Marxist critique of Christianity must be accompanied by an authentically Christian critique of Marxist methodology.[28] By holding this critical tension, Ellacuría argues that Marxist analysis, which is unavoidable given the intellectual history of Latin America, can provide LALT with theoretical tools without allowing the ideological aspect of Marxism to change the Christian message.[29] By developing a grounded theological method that can critically appropriate theoretical tools, Ellacuría provides an alternative method that can make use of Marxist and Freudian theoretical tools without committing to positions contrary to the Gospel that those theories entail, such as the necessity of violent revolution to bring about a truly egalitarian society.

From this methodological framework, Ellacuría offers various theological concepts in light of the major foci in systematic theology, but two stand out in light of an engagement with Doran's project. The first of these, and perhaps the most significant for Ellacuría's thought as a whole, is historical soteriology. In one of his four major essays, entitled "The Crucified People: An Essay in Historical Soteriology," Ellacuría claims historical soteriology is essential to understanding how the salvation of all humanity comes from the person of Jesus of Nazareth, defining the term in the following way: "Historical soteriology here means something referring to salvation as it is

26. Ellacuría 2013, 86.

27. Gutiérrez, Gustavo. 1988. *A Theology of Liberation*. Translated by Sister Caridad Inda and John Eagleson. Maryknoll, NY: Orbis Books, 19–22.

28. Ellacuría 2013, 88.

29. Ellacuría finds Marxism unavoidable in Latin American given the inroads of Marxist political movements in the Global South during the latter half of the twentieth century in countries such as Cuba and Nicaragua. From Ellacuría's perspective, attempting to engage in conversation over philosophical and theological methodology without addressing the Marxist perspective would be a non-starter.

presented in revelation. But the accent falls on its historical character in a double sense: as the realization of salvation in the one and only human history, and as humankind's active participation in that salvation, in this case, the participation of the poor."[30] For Ellacuría, it is important to understand how human beings participate in their salvation, especially those who continue to be oppressed. A significant part of understanding the concept of historical soteriology is understanding how the marginalized and downtrodden, to whom Jesus ministers in the Gospel accounts, are linked to the salvific activity that moves throughout history.

To answer this question, Ellacuría begins with the passion of Jesus, but emphasizes the grounded, historical reality of Jesus as a first-century Palestinian Jew. Jesus of Nazareth was executed in the manner of a political criminal during the *Pax Romana* over a spiritualized account of the passion, which can allow the details of the socio-political reality to be overshadowed by the transcendent elements of Christ's death and resurrection. If the spiritualizing approach to the passion of Jesus allows one to evade the commitment of Jesus' mission to bring about the Reign of God leading to his persecution and death, says Ellacuría, then it is necessary to revisit the circumstances of Jesus' death to help one reflect on the plight of the oppressed.[31] Part of the answer to this question comes in recognizing Jesus as a part of the prophetic tradition. The prophetic role requires one, following a positive response to God's word, to resist and speak truth to sinful reality that is in contradiction of the Reign of God. Since Jesus' earthly ministry took the form of preaching the coming of the Reign of God to the poor and marginalized, in stark contrast to the reign of sin around them, the necessity of Jesus' death follows given the socio-political context. Ellacuría writes, "The reason could not be clearer: If the Reign of God and the reign of sin are two opposed realities, and human beings of flesh and blood are the standard bearers of both, then those who wield the power of oppressive domination cannot but exercise it against those who have only the power of their word and their life, offered for the salvation of many."[32] There is victory over the reign of sin, however, as Jesus' death is not the end of his ministry. The miracle of resurrection and the mission of the Church allow for the continuation of Jesus' ministry by his followers, working together to bring about the Reign of God.

30. Ellacuría 2013, 196.

31. Ellacuría 2013, 203.

32. Ellacuría 2013, 204.

The question that follows is its application to the crucified people who are oppressed throughout the world. In one way, one must understand that the continued oppression of the innocent among so-called Christian nations is a scandal, and it is this scandal that requires the prophetic tradition to continue. This, however, is not enough. According to Ellacuría, the crucified people are not only the victims of the world, but also the bearers of the world's salvation.[33] Just as the Christian narrative cannot end on Good Friday and must continue to Easter Sunday, the victimization of the crucified people is not the end of their journey. When they rise up in resistance to this oppression, they, in imitation of Christ, show that the power of death and violence has no purchase on them. While the reign of sin seeks to deprive the crucified people of their human dignity, the crucified people have their dignity not only affirmed but also celebrated in their membership in the people of God.[34] It is in this Easter moment for the crucified people that one can have genuine hope.

The second concept relevant to a discussion of Doran's work is the way the church of the poor is a channel of grace for salvation in a unified historical reality. In the essay "The Church of the Poor: Historical Sacrament of Liberation," Ellacuría defines salvation as an activity in need of an object; someone needs to be saved, namely human beings.[35] This salvation is God's gift to humanity, negating a need in the fallible human condition. This leads Ellacuría to consider a tension between the two different emphases on the nature of salvation in the Christian scriptures: the historical salvation of the Hebrew Scriptures and the mystical salvation of the New Testament. The historical salvation of the Hebrew Bible, starting with Exodus and moving through the prophetic tradition, shows God's active work in the materiality of the history of the people of Israel, leading them to the Reign of God, which Ellacuría defines later in the text as taking away the sin-of-the-world and "making the incarnate life of God present in human beings and human relationships."[36] The mystical salvation arising from the New Testament comes from Pauline language, such as being baptized in Christ, which stands in contrast to the very concrete liberation and flight from Egypt.[37] These different emphases can appear to lead to conflicting

33. Ellacuría 2013, 223.

34. Ellacuría 2013, 224.

35. Ellacuría 2013, 229.

36. Ellacuría 2013, 235.

37. Ellacuría 2013, 232.

views of the Body of Christ, but Ellacuría argues that each emphasis actually requires the other. The historical Body of Christ cannot be a channel for God's gracious gift of salvation without the mystical, revealed truths that name all as one in Christ. Likewise, the mystical Body of Christ cannot make that gift visibly present and effectively realized without concrete, historical grounding, which emphasizes the need for prophetic action.[38] This is because the various levels of reality in which creation operates are a unity without loss of distinction. This reality is historical, as human beings have concrete histories that cannot be pushed aside by abstraction and instead must be considered carefully.

Ellacuría pulls together the various strands of his argument in understanding the exemplar of the unity of the mystical and the historical in the person of Jesus of Nazareth. Jesus, Son of God, second person of the Trinity, cannot be fully understood without a recognition of the fact of His incarnation: the act of God becoming incorporated[39] and entering into history. Without this incorporation, salvation and the mission of the Son would not be possible. It follows, therefore, that the church must likewise be incorporated to be the Sacrament of Liberation from sin that the Reign of God represents.

Historical Soteriology and the Scale of Values

At this point, we can now turn to how Doran and Ellacuría's theological methods and concepts can work together to provide a fuller picture of what actions need to be taken to, in Ellacuría's language, bring about the Reign of God. There are three points of cooperation between Doran and Ellacuría that can be seen from data at hand: 1) Ellacuría's understanding of the church of the poor is a concrete articulation of that community of resistance Doran mentions in Chapter 13 of Theology and the Dialectics of History. 2) Ellacuría provides a substantial theory of history in his conception of historical reality that, as Doran claims, is necessary for systematic theology; and 3) the definition of the Reign of God in Ellacuría's work provides a point of transposition that allows Doran's appropriation

38. Ellacuría's emphasis on prophetic action is not as strong in this essay as it is in other essays. For one of Ellacuría's longer discussions of propheticism in translation, see "Utopia and Propheticism: An Essay in Concrete Historical Soteriology" (Ashley et al. 2014, 7–56).

39. Ellacuría uses this term to define an event in which something that is not historical, such as God, is historically embodied and adheres to the single body of history (Ellacuría 2013, 230).

of Lonergan to enter into conversation with a wider conversation in Latin American liberation theology.[40]

An opening point of conversation between Doran and Ellacuría is about the church of the poor as a community of resistance. When Doran writes of the church as a community of resistance, he does not elaborate on what that looks like beyond the following: ". . . the resistance of the church cannot be understood as a withdrawal into pietistic self-satisfaction, a retreat to the margins of society, an abdication of worldly responsibility. Ecclesial resistance is rather transformative agency in mediating a community that extends far beyond the church's own explicit boundaries."[41] This leaves a great deal of room for one to interpret what is required of this community of resistance so long that it is engaged with the wider global community and expands beyond the church itself and the wider human community.[42] Ellacuría's understanding of the church as the historical sacrament of liberation provides a fleshing out of the concrete praxis of these ecclesial communities. By engaging in the fullness of historical reality, the church of the poor is able to bring about liberation, the historical form of salvation for Ellacuría, as all liberation is liberation from sin.[43] This liberation that comes from a faith-inspired praxis motivated by following the concrete example of Jesus' ministry to and preference for the poor.[44] Ellacuría's interpretation of ecclesial resistance, therefore, is able to expand upon Doran's ecclesial community of resistance in a way that fits a wider theological structure and context.

The second point of conversation is that Ellacuría provides a substantial theological theory of history that a contemporary Catholic systematic theology requires. While this formulation appears in Thesis 1 of *The Trinity in History*,[45] the necessity of a theological theory of history is what grounds Doran's project in the earlier work. As Doran writes in the introduction to

---

40. The goal of these brief descriptions is not to delve deeply into what could be potentially several research projects, but rather offer sketches for what those projects would eventually entail. These three topics have enough depth to them that they could develop into individual articles or book chapters, and the space here does not permit further exploration. I therefore admit that what follows are sketches of these interrelated projects that will be developed further at a later date.

41. Doran, *Theology and the Dialectics of History*, 418–9.

42. Doran, *Theology and the Dialectics of History*, 419.

43. Ellacuría 2013, 244.

44. Ellacuría 2013, 248.

45. Doran, Robert M. 2012. *The Trinity in History, Volume 1: Missions and Processions* (Toronto: University of Toronto Press), 10.

Theology and the Dialectics of History, a contemporary Christian systematic theology must first require one "to generate the categories that will enable systematic theology to be a theory of history: categories that will allow a systematic understanding of the positions one espouses to be expressed in terms of a heuristic structure of historical process."[46] As shown above, Ellacuría's theory of historical reality is not only open to the idea of transcendence and theological concepts that allow the work of systematic theology to continue, but also a further theory of reality that can concretely situate human understanding and praxis historically, supporting Doran's argument for the necessity of historicity in theology. The further strength for Doran engaging Ellacuría's project is that the metaphysical realism of Ellacuría can be traced back to the same Thomistic metaphysics that served as the foundation for Lonergan and Doran's understanding of metaphysics. By using Thomas to connect both Ellacuría and the Lonergan/Doran project of bringing historicity to bear on classical metaphysics, one can see them as complementary theories for such a project.

Third and finally, Ellacuría's definition of the Reign of God presents an opportunity for Doran's understanding of the integral scale of values to enter into discourses of justice and action in Latin American liberation theology. Since the Reign of God seeks to make God's presence known and felt in human beings and their relationships, and God is inherently just, then it follows that the Reign of God seeks to bring to justice into every human life and relationship. This is, of course, very abstract, and the Latin American liberation theologian is able to concretize it by emphasizing a justice for the poor and marginalized, or the "crucified people needing to be taken down from the cross," to paraphrase Jon Sobrino's addition to Ellacuría's phrase.[47] The question that follows is how one goes about providing for the needs of these groups in a sustainable way that respects the inherent dignity of each member of the group. The integral scale of values offers a series of questions that allows for clarification and plan of action. The distinction between vital, social, and cultural values and how these values build upon one another can help to articulate the values needed to ensure the equitable distribution of vital goods, especially to those who have been deprived of the ability to have their basic human needs met. Both Doran and Ellacuría, while articulating the ideas differently, are advocating for the core theological principle of the preferential option for the poor. This

---

46. Doran *Theology and the Dialectics of History*, 5

47. Sobrino, Jon. 1994. *The Principle of Mercy: Taking the Crucified People from the Cross.* (Maryknoll, NY: Orbis Books), vii.

places them at the table of conversation on one of the central themes of Latin American liberation theology, allowing for a spirit of collaboration that stems from the heart of the liberationist's concerns.

By way of conclusion, it is important to emphasize that Doran's emphasis on historical mindedness that stands at the core of the theological projects that span his career offers a great opportunity to engage with liberation theologies of all contexts, not just that of Ellacuría's El Salvadoran context. Doran helps to push Lonergan's project in a way that makes it conversant with liberation theologies and open to their insights. By opening the door to collaboration, Doran has made genuine strides towards creating a truly global theological project.

CHAPTER SIXTEEN

HISTORY ILLUMINED BY DISCERNMENT

Gordon Rixon S.J.

Regis College, University of Toronto

In a discussion of the challenges of discerning the authenticity of civil authorities, individual citizens, and the formative traditions in which they participate, Bernard Lonergan proposes an alternative synthetic viewpoint focused on evaluating the historical outcomes of social movements.[1] Rather than pursuing solely an assessment of individuals and traditions in the measure that they exhibit and foster authentic self-transcendence—that is to say, the extent to which they are or encourage being attentive in experience, intelligent in understanding, critical in judgment, and responsible in the deliberation of value-guided action—Lonergan redirects his readers' attention to the more evident fruits of the three vectors of progress, decline, and redemption shaping social movements. Whereas the direct analysis of authenticity risks becoming mired in problematic attributions of motivation, the data assessed by the three vectors are more accessible and the criteria for their evaluative interpretation can be debated transparently in a public forum that itself cultivates the shared experience, common understanding, conjoint judgment, and collegial deliberation required for social cooperation. Yet, as evidenced amply in the overall development of Lonergan's corpus, both approaches—fostering responsible personal and collective authenticity and discerning participation in social action and history—remain significant and mutually advising. As this festschrift celebrates Robert Doran's lifework of preserving, promoting, developing, and implementing Lonergan's work, I address this interrelation of authenticity and the discernment of the three vectors shaping social movements.

1. Bernard Lonergan, "Dialectic of Authority" in *A Third Collection*, volume 16, *Collected Works of Bernard Lonergan*, eds. Robert M. Doran and John D. Dadosky (Toronto: University of Toronto Press, 2017), pp. 3–9.

I focus my remarks through Doran's engagement of the *Spiritual Exercises* of Ignatius of Loyola, the sixteenth-century founder of the international Jesuit religious community, to which Doran and Lonergan both belong.[2] This performative, rhetorical guide to a structured series of mental prayer activities cultivates the ongoing development of heightened self-awareness, affective freedom, and intellectual flexibility required to promote a potent interweaving of ever emerging personal authenticity and the discernment of social movements.[3] Drawing on an earlier essay in which Doran discusses themes drawn from the *Spiritual Exercises*, I focus on the three times of making a decision (##175–178) as I elucidate the contribution of Doran's recent constructive trinitarian theology. My thesis here is that locating the Ignatian character of Doran's constructive interpretation of his fellow Jesuit's work cultivates a privileged vantage from which to parse effectively their complementary contributions to the interrelation of developing authenticity and the discernment of the vectors constituting social movements in history.

I begin by developing an extended analogy between spiritual movements and the three times that Ignatius identifies for making a decision. Locating the first analogue, we observe that spiritual movements have a source, a development and, hopefully, a fruitful end that confirms the validity of the source and development. The source exhibits some complexity, which our discussion below of Doran's treatment of *memoria* brings into helpful relief. As a first approximation, however, we could consider how an infant's emerging orientation to the world through identity and desire is shaped by attachment to a primary caregiver. The infant receives its initial identity by learning to imitate a parent's loving face-to-face gaze and

---

2. References will be to Ignatius of Loyola, *The Spiritual Exercises of St. Ignatius: Based on Studies in the Language of the Autograph*, trans. Louis J. Puhl (Chicago: Loyola Press, 1951). I focus my remarks on the Ignatian themes identified in Robert M. Doran, "Ignatian Themes in the Thought of Bernard Lonergan: Revisiting a Topic that Deserves Further Reflection" in *Lonergan Workshop* 19 (2006), pp. 83–106.

3. The text of the *Spiritual Exercises* is a resource for spiritual guides as they accompany the existential prayer exercises and practical discernment of practitioners. The text draws upon, collates and develops the medieval, monastic adaptation of the principles of Ciceronian rhetoric in the practice of mental prayer. Assisted by a spiritual guide, practitioners gather the resources of Scripture and Tradition (*inventio*) as they journey (*dispositio*) in evolving love and affective freedom (*elocutio*) to create sacred meaning in the everyday events of their lives (*memoria*). These exercises are rhetorical rather than didactic in the sense that, assuming the prior conveyance of content oriented catechetical instruction, they foster performative spiritual engagement as practitioners create personal faith narratives and participate in the creative remembering of the communal Christian story. See Gordon A. Rixon, "Transforming Mysticism: Adorning Pathways to Self-Transcendence," *Gregorianum* 85 (2004), pp. 719–34.

proto verbal interactions. Orientation to further objects beyond the parent is shaped by the parent's desires and aversions. Deep patterns of psychic orientations becoming the source of future affective movements that figure perception, contour action, and are subsequently continuously resolved and refined through reflection and self-modifying existential choices. Passive imitation anticipates and leads to active participation in a community of meaning. Figuratively, but truly vulnerably, we are spoken before we speak, and when as spoken we speak, we reveal the depth of source memories affirming our identity and expressing desires and aversions that regard, organize, and evaluate the world about us.[4]

Much as Aristotle would differentiate a power by its object, a mature movement is defined by the fruit it produces or obtains. In part, the maturity of the movement is evidenced through cognitive clarity, articulate expression, and responsible evaluation. Beyond clear, articulate affirmation of the fruit, the movement is further confirmed through the affirmation of the one who genuinely understands, articulates, and evaluates the movement, its source and its fruit. Although the evidence for evaluation is most apparent in the fruit born by a mature movement, the criteria for evaluation touch no less upon the source and the development. Typically, positive fruit does not emerge from an evil source or corrupted development. In the throes of life, unfolding the evaluative complex of source, development, and fruit is clouded by confusion and contestation. Indeed, in the contemporary transnational and multicultural context, there is little or no agreement about the basic characteristics of a just society, the appropriate range of persons whose interests should be considered, or even how to establish the political process required to develop social consensus.[5]

---

4. For a discussion of the early psychic development that precedes and accompanies the development of language see Charles Taylor, *The Language Animal: The Full Shape of the Human Language Capacity* (Cambridge, MA: The Belknap Press of the Harvard University Press, 2016). See also, Judith Butler, "Rethinking Vulnerability and Resistance" in Judith Butler, Zeynep Gambetti, and Leticia Sabsay, eds. *Vulnerability in Resistance* (Durham, NC: Duke University Press, 2016), pp. 12–27, especially at p. 16. Lonergan addresses similar issues in his discussions of intersubjectivity and the distinction of original and ordinary meaning. See, for instance, Bernard Lonergan, *Method in Theology*, volume 14, *Collected Works of Bernard Lonergan*, eds. Robert M. Doran and John D. Dadosky (Toronto: University of Toronto Press, 2017), pp. 56–58, 238–241.

5. For a discussion of the breakdown of the what, who and how of justice adjudication, see Nancy Fraser, "Abnormal Justice" in *Critical Inquiry* 34/3 (2008), pp. 393–422. Lonergan identifies a similar pattern of social malaise as the longer cycle of decline arising from a loss of confidence in the intelligibility of social institutions and human reason. See, Bernard Lonergan, *Insight: A Study in Human Understanding*, volume 3, *Collected Works of Bernard Lonergan*, eds. Frederick E, Crowe and Robert M. Doran (Toronto: University of Toronto Press, 1992), pp. 252–67.

The contemporary person confronts a complex ethical landscape. Leaving aside the vestiges of a classical confidence in a closed correlation between the logic of language and the intelligibility of world process, the present challenge eclipses the Aristotelian paradigm of a virtuous person applying abstract rules in concrete circumstances.[6] While we admit that established patterns of desires and aversions serve as the prima facie criteria for deliberative evaluation, we must also acknowledge that the affective dispositions of the most virtuous persons are no less ordered in social, cultural, linguistic, and political constellations of valuation that beg further discernment. As Lonergan suggests, an authentic person may genuinely appropriate an unauthentic tradition bound in some measure by group bias and discouragement in the face of the surds of history.[7] Confronting such an imbroglio of attractions and aversions, how are we to espouse a credible confidence in the potential of human desire to identify and pursue the good, the true and the beautiful?

Reflecting an implicit confidence in the ultimate integrity of the human person's self-transcending desire, Ignatius proposes a performative Foundation Exercise (#23) to surface and evaluate the de facto affective orientations contouring a person's value horizon. A religious meditation that evokes and assesses the person's acknowledgment or resistance to their creaturehood, spiritual detachment from gifts and talents and commitment to praise, reverence and serve God.[8] Pervasive perseverance in gratitude, and a joyous freedom to use oneself and one's resources in a spirit of service, are evidence of a normative and well-disposed value horizon focused on participation in a transcendent project. Entitlement, envy, jealousy, and a desire to spend oneself and one's resources in self-promotion and self-protection are evidence of an anti-normative and ill-disposed value horizon centered upon the self and its appropriated possessions. Referring to this basic orientation of a person's affectivity and value horizon, as either a consoling movement towards greater union with God or a desolating movement to further distance and alienation from God, Ignatius proposes rules to discern the positive or negative valence of persons' further

6. Aristotle, *Nicomachean Ethics*, II. 9.

7. Lonergan, *Method in Theology*, pp. 77–78.

8. Puhl refers to this foundational exercise as the "First Principle and Foundation." Elsewhere, and notably in the first guides to the use of the *Spiritual Exercises*, known collectively as the "directories," Ignatius and other early authoritative practitioners refer simply to the "Foundation," which serves as a primary reference point in the process of discernment. For examples, see Martin E. Palmer, ed., *On Giving the Spiritual Exercises: The Early Jesuit Manuscript Directories and the Official Directory of 1599* (St. Louis: Institute of Jesuit Sources, 1996).

responses as they contemplate any particular potential course of action. As proposed in the First Week Rules (##313–327) for discernment, a person resolving the specific affective orientations of an anti-normative value horizon in the Foundation Exercise would be counseled to resist what is attractive and potentially pursue what is disturbing. While a person resolving the specific affective orientations of a normative horizon might be counseled to test their inclinations further, they would be encouraged to generally trust the prima facie evidence that delight accompanies inclinations to positive actions and disquiet accompanies inclinations to negative actions. A person demonstrating an affective orientation generally consistent with grateful acknowledgment of creaturehood, freedom in the use of gifts and talents and commitment in praise, reverence and service, would be encouraged to employ the Second Week Rules (##328–336) to assess their inclinations further as they strive to choose the greater good when confronted by choices between praiseworthy options.[9] In every case, discerning a person's specific orientations helps to chart a path through existential choices that confirm or reshape the spontaneous expression of desire, but also raises a reflective question about the implicit possibility and nature of an underpinning primordial desire, that itself motivates formative reflection about the orientation of the spontaneously expressed value horizon.

In the absence of clarity about the mature fruit of historical movements, thus, the affective dispositions advising movements can still be resolved and evaluated, and serve to guide faithful decisions and actions toward uncertain outcomes. Dispositions resonating with a normative value horizon—gratitude, freedom, and a spirit of service—indicate, but do not guarantee, movement toward a consoling fruit. Dispositions resonating with an anti-normative value horizon—entitlement, possessiveness, and a spirit of self-promotion—indicate and almost guarantee movement toward a desolating outcome. Through resolving reflection, consoling dispositions can be confirmed and strengthened subsequently by resonant, coordinated decisions and actions. Desolating dispositions can be reformed by existential decisions and actions that deliberately resist and even contradict ill-shaped desires oriented toward self-promotion. While the practitioner's spiritual

9. The Foundation Exercise helps practitioners resolve the general orientation of their value horizon by eliciting affective responses to its presentation of stipulated normative claims and dispositions, affective movements which then become available to the retreatant and spiritual guides as matter for further reflection, and, thereby, establishing a basis to apply the rules for discernment and from which to move forward into the remaining exercises. For a discussion of the role of the Foundation Exercise, see Juan Alonso de Vitoria's account of the Ignatius' directives, Palmer, *On Giving the Spiritual Exercises*, pp. 21–22.

desire for the true, the good, and the beautiful remains the self-transcending foundation for discernment, the Foundation Exercise provides a sounding board that facilitates the discerning resolution and refinement of a person's established value horizon shaped by specific social, cultural, political, and personal patterns of affective response, perception, and activity.

These dispositions may be concretely mediated by iconic representations that eventually bear witness to their effectiveness in fruitful practice. For instance, the recent statement of universal apostolic preferences by the Jesuits could be understood as spiritual dispositions guiding social, cultural, ecological, and ecclesial action in diverse contexts and settings in an uncertain world. Showing the way to God, walking with the excluded, journeying with youth, and caring for our common home remain goal oriented dispositions as they abstain from espousing determinate objectives.[10] In *Querida Amazonia*, the recent post-synodal apostolic exhortation on the Synod on the Pan-Amazon Region, Pope Francis reflects on the interconnection of analogous dispositions as he reflects on four dreams addressing the social, cultural, ecological, and ecclesial aspirations of indigenous peoples.[11] He remarks on patterns of social injustice and cultural oppression suffered by the poor and witnessed by ecological degradation before exploring the spiritual dispositions that guide restorative responses to otherwise confining imbroglios. In each instance, engaging the struggles of history and peoples through the cultivation of spiritual dispositions overflows in practical action stemming in faith from a transcendent source and advancing in hope toward an indeterminate goal.

The extended analogy per se arises by correlating the three dimensions of a spiritual movement with the three times for making a decision. Correlated with the source of a movement, we propose the first time for decision that arises when ". . . our Lord so moves and attracts the will that a devout soul without hesitation, or the possibility of hesitation, follows what is manifest to it" (#175). Correlated with the dispositions accompanying the development of a movement, we associate the second time that is characterized by the light and understanding derived "through experience of desolations and consolations and discernment of diverse spirits" (#176). Finally, correlated with the cognitive and affective clarity accompanying

10. Arturo Sosa, S.J, "Universal Apostolic Preferences of the Society of Jesus, 2019–2029," 19 February 2020, https://jesuits.global/en/documents/send/8-uap-docs/63-universal-apostolic-preferences, accessed 9 March 2020.

11. Pope Francis, "Querida Amazonia: Post-Synodal Apostolic Exhortation on the Synod for the Pan-Amazon Region," 2 February 2020.

reflection about the fruit of a movement, we ally the third time marked by a "time of tranquility" when "the soul is not agitated by different spirits, and has free and peaceful use of its natural powers" to consider its purpose to praise God and serve the Lord for its salvation (#177).

These three correlations, in effect, generate two different types of analogy. On the one hand, we identify three analogies of attribution whereby a focused quality is understood somewhat differently in each of the two distinct but related contexts. The first quality is the intimate attraction that characterizes the source of a movement and the first time for decision-making. Here, we think of the intimate, receptive imitation of the Father that precedes actively discerned participation in the mission of the Son. The second quality is the contention of attractions and aversions that is the signature of the development of a movement and the second time for decision. Here, we heightened our awareness of the self-implicating discernment of affective movements as intentional responses to value, which resolves merely imitated responses and engages personal freedom in choices among alternative paths.[12] The third quality is the affective tranquility and cognitive clarity that marks the fruit of a movement and the third time for decision. Finally, we observe the wisely ordered integration of truth and goodness that is charity infused understanding, and accompanied by the recognition of the transparent beauty of creation, praise of the creator present in all things, and the confirmation of the self-transcending desire of the decision-maker.

On the other hand, we might consider two analogies of proportionality, where not the two sets of three terms are compared, but the two sets of interior relations defining the three moments of a movement and the three times for making a decision. Thus, one analogy is between the relation of source and dispositions of a movement and the relation of the first and second times for decision-making. The second analogy is between the relation of the dispositions and ripened fruit of a movement and the relation of the second and third times for decision-making. In each case, we might begin to think of analogous processions from act to act, whereby, in the limit case, a principle act is preserved and transformed by an ensuing second act. As the source is preserved and expressed in the positively discerned

12. See Doran's discussion of autonomous spiritual processions, Robert M. Doran, *The Trinity in History: A Theology of the Divine Mission, Volume 1: Missions and Processions* (Toronto: University of Toronto Press, 2012), pp. 183–187 and Robert M. Doran, *The Trinity in History: A Theology of the Divine Mission, Volume 2: Missions, Relations and Persons* (Toronto: University of Toronto Press, 2019), pp. 15–20.

dispositions advising a movement, intimate attraction is resolved in the similarly discerned opposition of attraction and aversion. As the constructively discerned contending dispositions of a movement yield a matured fruit of cognitive clarity and affective transparency, the opposition of affective responses yields love charged wisdom of responsible reason.[13]

In each instance, we think of the relation between an act as preserved and the same act as transformed through a shift in context. As the source of a spiritual movement is preserved and transformed in the positive dispositions of gratitude, freedom, and self-transcending service, the immediate union of the first time is preserved and transformed in the discernment of attraction and aversion of the second time. As the positive dispositions of a spiritual movement are preserved and transformed in the fruit of affective delight and cognitive clarity, the discernment of the affective attractions and aversions of the second time is preserved and transformed in the reasoned assessment of the third time. The value of these two different analogies is elucidated by comparing them with aspects of the psychological analogy for the Trinity developed by Augustine, Aquinas, and Lonergan but, for our present purpose, especially in light of Doran's recent discussion and elaboration of the relation of trinitarian theology with history. Recalling Lonergan's discussion of two relevant Thomist distinctions helps to locate our appreciative discussion of Doran's contribution and illuminates the distinction we have introduced between analogies of attribution and analogies of proportionality. We recall first the distinction between *actus perfecti* and *actus imperfecti* and then between *processio operati* and *processio operationis.*[14]

The first distinction addresses the relation of an action to its terminal object. An *actus imperfecti* is a motion or *kinêsis* toward a term that remains in act only in so far as the motion itself has not yet attained its object. Inquiring proceeds until understanding emerges, but as soon as one understands inquiry per se ceases. Desiring a good proceeds until the good is enjoyed as obtained or produced, but once one enjoys the desired good, desiring per se ceases.

---

13. For a discussion of the distinction between analogies of proportion and analogies of proportionality and a discussion of the limitations of a "theory" of analogy, see David Burrell, *Aquinas: God and Action*, third edition (Eugene, OR: Wipf & Stock, 2016), pp. 62–65.

14. My treatment of *actus perfecti, actus imperfecti, processio operationis* and *processio operati* passes over a complex and sometimes controverted development in the thought of Aquinas. For detailed discussion, see Bernard Lonergan, *Verbum: Word and Idea in Aquinas*, volume 2, *Collected Works of Bernard Lonergan*, eds. Frederick E. Crowe and Robert M. Doran (Toronto: University of Toronto Press, 1997), pp. 107–116.

An *actus perfecti* is an operation or *energeia* that coincides with its end or terminal object. Although inquiring is an *actus imperfecti*, understanding is an *actus perfecti*. Although desiring a good is an *actus imperfecti*, enjoying a good is an *actus perfecti*. Understanding or enjoying a good ceases when the object is no longer produced or obtained. In each case, though limited by its terminal object, the act is in complete possession of its end. Admittedly, understanding and enjoying a good are finite, human examples of an *actus perfecti*. The notion of an *actus perfecti* is most appropriately applied to a divine, unbounded act of understanding that comprehensively and equally expresses truth, goodness and beauty. Application of *actus perfecti* to human understanding and enjoying presents an analogy of attribution, where the difference remains infinitely greater than any similarity.

The second distinction refines the first by highlighting the relation of the act to its principle. A *processio operationis* is an act that proceeds to its term from a potency as its principle. For instance, acts of understanding and acts of remembering proceed from a potency to understand or remember. One potentially understands and then actually understands. One potentially remembers and then actually remembers. A *processio operati*, in contrast, is an act that proceeds not from potency, but from another act as its principle. The act of judging about the adequacy of understanding or remembering proceeds from the act of grasping the sufficiency of relevant evidence. Significantly, the act of judgment is a consequent term that preserves and transforms the act of grasping the adequacy of the evidence, but as act from act, not as act from potency. Likewise, in the Thomist metaphysics of knowledge, the act conceiving the act of understanding (terminal object or inner word) proceeds from the act of understanding determined by a proper object.[15]

Notice that an *actus imperfecti* is necessarily a *processio operationis* but an *actus perfecti* is not necessarily a *processio operati*. Discursive inquiring is a *processio operationis* and an *actus imperfecti*. Likewise, recalling—discursive self-interrogation about something previously understood or known—moves from potency to act but only remains in act so long as its object is not obtained. In contrast, understanding is an *actus perfecti* that, unlike a *processio operati*, moves not from act to act, though still from potency immediately to perfect act. Similarly, remembering moves from potency to act but only when its object is completely obtained. One does not understand and then does understand, one does not remember

15. For a succinct discussion of the interrelation of the multiple objects of the act of *intelligere* in the Thomist metaphysics of knowledge, see Patrick H. Byrne, *The Ethics of Discernment: Lonergan's Foundations for Ethics* (Toronto: University of Toronto Press, 2016), pp. 139–142.

and then does remember. Each is in act only in so far as it instantly and completely obtains its term. Each is an *actus perfecti* but neither proceeds as act from act, the hallmark of a *processio operati*. In contrast, while a *processio operati* is evidently associated with *actus perfecti*, beyond co-existing with its transforming term, a *processio operati* proceeds from and preserves its source act. Transforming act proceeds from preserved act. Conception proceeds from and preserves understanding. Judgments of fact or value proceed from and preserve grasping the adequacy of evidence.

In his explorations of trinitarian theology, Doran affirms that the most adequate analogues for the processions of the truly divine *actus perfecti* arise from the processions in human cognitive operations that are not only *processio operati*, but specifically those engaging the self-present, self-implicating, existential activities such as valuation and decision-making.[16] Referring to such existential *processio operati* as autonomous spiritual processions, Doran retrieves Augustine's notion of *memoria* to elaborate the later Lonergan's account of a psychological analogy for the two trinitarian processions; Lonergan's account pivots on the generating procession from the evaluative grasp of evidence (paternity) to the expressed judgment of value (filiation) and the proceeding procession from the expressed grasp of evidence in the judgement of value (active spiration) to the responding avowed love expressed in decision and action (passive spiration).

Doran associates *memoria* ("sanctifying grace as it affects consciousness"), the recalled reception of the gift of God's love, as grounding the expression of a set of judgments of value (faith), which he clarifies together establish a relation to the indwelling Holy Spirit and a response of love (charity), participating in the Holy Spirit, that creates a relation to the mutually indwelling Father and Son. "Memory and faith combine to imitate and participate in active spiration and charity imitates and participates in passive spiration."[17]

Before returning to parse the significance of Doran's elucidation of Lonergan's development of the psychological analogy for our discussion the interrelation of the three moments of a spiritual movement and the three times for decision-making, we offer three observations. First, as the *recalled* reception of a divine gift of love *memoria* is an *actus perfecti* but not the end term of a *processio operati*.[18] As Lonergan implies in *Method in*

16. Doran, "Thesis 36," vol. 2, *The Trinity in History*, p. 201.

17. Doran, "Thesis 34," vol. 2, *The Trinity in History*, p. 198.

18. John Dadosky offers a similar observation, see John Dadosky, "God's Eternal Yes! An Exposition and Development of Lonergan's Psychological Analogy of the Trinity," *Irish Theological Quarterly* 81/4 (2016), n. 23, p. 402.

Theology, years of spiritual discipline may proceed the appropriation of a hitherto real, conscious but unarticulated undertow of divine love.[19] *Memoria* is a perfect act that obtains its term immediately and completely but only as it proceeds from potency, not as act proceeding from act. Yet, insofar as it refers to a divine gift that affects consciousness (sanctifying grace), *memoria* refers to a real, natural, conscious act proceeding ultimately from a divine act. Second, as an *actus perfecti* recalling the evidence of God's gift of love, *memoria* is the source principle of a *processio operati*: the judgment of value that is expressed as the affirmation of faith. Third, recalling our previous discussion of the two types of analogy, subject to the limitations discussed below, as we extend our consideration of a spiritual movement and the times for making a decision to take account of Doran's elucidation of the psychological analogy, we expect to identify analogies of attribution among the principles and terms and analogies of proportionality among the processions within not just two but three sets of analogues.

We could now refine our understanding of the intimate attraction of the first time as the recalled gift of divine love and the source of a spiritual movement. Rooted most immediately in the imitation of the attractions and aversions of caregivers and friends, this memory grounded source is founded ultimately in a transforming imitation of and participation in divine love, and impels self-transcending desire. A founding that presents intimate attraction, *memoria,* and the source of self-transcendence as analogous attributes across the initial members of the three analogous sets of terms.

The discernment of the attractions and aversions of the second time is guided by the judgments of value advising avowals of faith. Proceeding from the recollection of the gift of divine love, faith appropriated judgments of value enliven the emergence of self-transcending dispositions. As we have discussed above, the cultivation of the specific dispositions of gratitude, freedom in the use of resources and talents, and commitment to praise, reverence and serve God redirects the focus of human activity in the service of a divine project. A cultivation that is nurtured by the formative discernment of received attractions and aversions, the faith avowal of judgments of value and the development of foundational dispositions, which are analogous attributes across the medial members of the three sets.

Beyond the analogous resonances among these first two sets of attributes, we also note the analogy of proportionality among the three processions, as each medial term preserves and transforms each initial term. Here

19. Lonergan, *Method in Theology*, p. 109.

we observe the constructive discernment of attractions and aversions that proceeds from intimate attraction, the affirmation of faith that proceeds from the recalled gift of divine love, and the development of foundational dispositions that proceeds from the source of the movement. Of course, these processions are analogous. Only the divine relations of paternity and filiation and active and passive spiration are truly perfect acts that are distinguished solely by their relations of opposition. Only the judgment of value grasping the evidence afforded by the recollection of the gift of divine love and expressed by the affirmation of faith proceeds as a *processio operati*. Although neither the development of authentic dispositions nor the discernment of attractions and aversions could claim to be a *processio operati*, insofar as they do proceed as act from act, they preserve and transform more fully and appropriately their intimate imitation and participation in the divine well-spring.

The peacefully reasoned decisions of the third time turn on the imitation and participation in charity infused actions, that yield delightful and transparent fruits in history. Here reason and love intermediate as they imitate and participate in divine providence preserving the integrity of the cascading natural, social, and cultural ecologies of the cosmic order that not only express but are drawn freely into the transforming wisdom of the divine economy. An intermediation that presents peaceful reasoning, imitation and participation in charity and beautiful fruits of wisdom as analogous attributes across the final members of the three sets of analogues.

Again, we note an analogy of proportionality among the three processions as each final term preserves and transforms each medial term. Wise actions in a troubled world proceed from the dispositions of gratitude, freedom and service. Charity as gift and response proceeds from the recollection of the divine gift of love and the affirmation of faith. Grace-filled fruits proceed from the development of spiritual movements that could not anticipate their providential outcomes.

None of our observations, of course, can adequately articulate the intermediation of the providential intelligibility and love suggested by such analogical exploration. Each analogy, whether of attribution or proportionality, serves only to develop the fuller, spiritual sense of theological discourse by tensioning metaphoric appositions, which present symbolic references to the realities preserved and transformed as our limited human projects and all of creation are drawn ever more deeply into the love relations of the Trinity. As Aquinas observed, our most precious theological reflections must be packed carefully in straw.

CHAPTER SEVENTEEN

LAW OF THE CROSS AND THE MYSTICAL BODY OF CHRIST

Jeremy Blackwood

To join the mystical body of Christ is to become one with Christ crucified, entering into the paschal mystery and allowing one's own life to become an extension of Christ's work in the world. Bernard Lonergan's law of the cross expresses the divine meaning delivered into history by the life, death, and resurrection of Christ, the divine meaning into which human persons are drawn in our participation in the mystical body of Christ, and Robert M. Doran has begun to develop the law of the cross and the mystical body in terms of a full ontology of meaning and value. As a step in the direction of that fully methodical account, in this article I affirm that the meaning expressed by the law of the cross is the meaning of the mystical body of Christ, and that that meaning becomes constitutive for the members of the mystical body.

The law of the cross is a centerpiece of the first two volumes of Doran's *Trinity in History*. His interpretation has three mutually penetrating aspects: understanding the law of the cross in terms of Girardian mimetic analysis, emphasizing the concrete effect of the actions of Jesus of Nazareth in history, and specifying the social deformities that the law rectifies. While Girard has become important for Doran as perhaps the key way to understand what exactly it is that psychic conversion heals, and therefore what the law of the cross is effecting and how that radiates into the larger social ills, that element is less important for our purposes here.[1]

1. Robert M. Doran, *The Trinity in History, Volume 1: Missions and Processions* (Toronto: University of Toronto, 2012), 236, also see 255. While for Doran Girardian analysis specifies much of the concrete evil to be transformed, I am more concerned with the intentional rather than the affective in this piece. I hope to pursue in the future a larger argument that takes more from the Girardian aspect into account.

The first and second sections of this article will establish important characteristics of Lonergan's theology of the cross and his understanding of the mystical body of Christ. The third and fourth sections will examine Doran's theological use of the law of the cross and the account he provides of the new community centered around the meaning that law expresses. A final section will focus attention on the connection between the divine redemptive meaning expressed by the law of the cross and the mystical body of Christ. The article concludes with the affirmation expressed above—namely, that the mystical body of Christ embodies the meaning expressed by the law of the cross as it becomes constitutive for the members—and suggests questions that will move the analysis forward toward a fully methodical account of the mystical body.

I. Lonergan on the Law of the Cross

The key point in Lonergan's law of the cross is that "redemption is accomplished, not by doing away with evils through power but by submitting to those very evils and, by the grace of God and by good will, transforming them into good."[2] God does not wipe evils away, but acts in a way that is continuous with the order of the universe, permitting the evils and fostering their transformation into greater good.[3] This account of redemption relies on the notion that evil is a privation of the good. For Lonergan, this point is necessary: without the notion of evil as privation, one thinks of evil in terms of positive being, coequal ontologically with the good. In that case, one risks missing the point that the roles of Judas, Pilate, and the Pharisees, on the one hand, and those of God and Jesus of Nazareth, on the other, are not equally constitutive of the redemption wrought through the passion, death, and resurrection of Christ.[4] In fact, God the Father and Jesus the Son are infusing meaning into the surds created by the failures of Judas, Pilate, and the Pharisees to choose the good and/or to avoid evil. The very point of the redemption is this process of turning around the lacunae objectified by the culpable evils (*malum culpae* in the *Redemption* text, called basic sin in *Insight*) and perpetuated as the evils of punishment (*malum poenae* in the *Redemption* text, called moral evil in

2. Bernard J. F. Lonergan, *The Redemption*, trans. Michael G. Shields, ed. Robert M. Doran, H. Daniel Monsour, and Jeremy D. Wilkins, vol. 9 in *Collected Works of Bernard Lonergan* (Toronto: University of Toronto, 2018), 203.

3. Lonergan, *The Redemption*, 221.

4. Lonergan, *The Redemption*, 263.

Insight).[5] As the former are committed, they give rise to the latter, while the latter "incline" persons toward the commission of further instances of the former. This is in fact how human society comes to be deformed in ways that we would now identify as systemic injustice and social sin:[6] the surds that are individual failures to choose the good or avoid evil malform the intelligible interrelations that constitute our societies, instantiating further, larger, objective surds that become the bases of persons' future actions as well as future persons' actions. This in turn leads to additional individual failures, further disrupted relations, further solidified or additional objective surds, additional individual failures, disruptions, surds, and so on. Here, then, is the concrete situation of the "matter" of the economy of salvation:[7] the economy of salvation stands to "the human race infected by original sin, burdened by actual sins, enmeshed in the penalties of sin, estranged from God, and divided within itself both individually and socially," as the work of the builder stands to the material on which he or she operates, while the law of the cross is that work in operation.

Lonergan identified three steps to that work: "the progression from culpable evil to the evil of punishment," "the voluntary transformation of punishment into good," and "the blessing of this transformation by God the Father."[8] While Christ is the "agent" of the economy of salvation, the one enacting it, this law that is the operation of that economy appears differently in him than it does in the rest of humanity.[9] In sinners, the law of the cross appears "as the matter to be redeemed."[10] In other words, the mass of human sinners is defined relationally by the law of the cross as *that which is to be saved*. We saw above how the surds of sin metastasize into objective failures of intelligibility and value, distorting our social orders and fostering further surds. Because it is we who perform the acts by which the surds are instantiated, objectified, and grown, we justly suffer their consequences. This leaves us with no other path than to turn away from evil and toward the good.[11] Yet the means for us to do so do not fall within our own power.

---

5. Lonergan, *The Redemption*, 199. On Lonergan's transpositions of culpable evil and evil of punishment in *Insight*, see Bernard J. F. Lonergan, *Insight: A Study of Human Understanding*, ed. Frederick E. Crowe and Robert M. Doran, vol. 3 in *Collected Works of Bernard Lonergan* (Toronto: University of Toronto Press, 1992), 689–691.

6. Lonergan, *The Redemption*, 199.

7. Lonergan, *The Redemption*, 219.

8. Lonergan, *The Redemption*, 203.

9. Lonergan, *The Redemption*, 223.

10. Lonergan, *The Redemption*, 205.

11. Lonergan, *The Redemption*, 239.

Instead, we must be united to Christ "as rational material that has to learn and believe, that out of charity gladly feels together with Christ, lives in Christ, works through Christ, is one with Christ, so as to be assimilated and conformed to Christ in his dying and rising."[12] This we do through the sacraments, avoidance of sin, and living by the Spirit, by which we bear a daily cross characterized by loving our enemies. Such practices form us according to the pattern of Christ's life, passion, and death, but they do not leave the resurrection behind. Instead, our daily cross is carried toward a destination, a promised blessing for those who suffer for Christ that is a transformation that does not leave the material body behind.[13]

The law appears differently in Christ. There, it appears "as in the redeeming principle."[14] That is, whereas the mass of sinners is defined in relation to the law of the cross as that which is to be saved, Christ is *that which saves*. Since he did not sin, there was no punishment owed to him.[15] Instead, he accepted the evil of punishment willingly, an acceptance by which he, individually, as a human being who suffered and died, transformed it.[16] Lonergan also described the way in which, not just an individual human being but as "the Head of his body the church," Christ made satisfaction for all sinners. Expressed in the manner appropriate to his context then, Lonergan explained that satisfaction in relation to God's permission of evils in light of the fact that humans sin and deserve their punishment. By this same permission, God allowed the evils even as they were applied to Christ, and by suffering them, Christ took on what was due to us.[17]

We can reformulate this in more contemporary terms by affirming that Christ's acceptance of the suffering redefined it, changing its meaning from an evil into a good. In taking on the punishment not owed to him and thereby redefining the meaning of those actions, Christ changed forever the concrete meaning—or lack thereof—of objective surds. In this sense, then, "the death of Christ is an example for us to imitate."[18] We are to

12. Lonergan, *The Redemption*, 205.

13. Lonergan, *The Redemption*, 227–9.

14. Lonergan, *The Redemption*, 205.

15. Lonergan, *The Redemption*, 237–9.

16. Lonergan, *The Redemption*, 205. See also 225–227, where Lonergan cites John 10:18; Phil 2:8–9; Heb 2:9; Matt 26:38–44 and 26:45–27:50.

17. Lonergan, *The Redemption*, 203. See also 225–227, where Lonergan cites Gal 4:4; Rom 5:19, 8:3; Mark 10:45; Matt 20:28; and Eph 5:2.

18. Lonergan, *The Redemption*, 229.

accept the evils of punishment instantiated in our civilizations as a result of our (collective) sins, an acceptance that puts us at odds with those civilizations insofar as they are characterized by those sins and their effects. Herein is the division "between the flesh and the spirit, and between the wisdom of this world and the wisdom of the Spirit of God."[19]

Yet not only the death of Christ, but also his resurrection, is an example for us.[20] The grace of Christ by which we enter into his resurrection does not simply *replace* the evil with something new—it *transforms* the evil into something new, not only for Christ, but for those who are saved.[21] Here we see the fundamental import of Christ's transformation of the meaning of the suffering. Whereas before, suffering was the effect of our sins to be endured justly because of our responsibility for it, it becomes through Christ the means by which such evil is undone, by which such surds are made meaningful. This is, then, the process by which human evils are transformed into the supreme good that is "the whole Christ, Head and members."[22] This is the "end" of the economy of salvation. When Lonergan speaks about this in *Redemption*, he intends "end" in the sense of "the form that is to be produced in the matter," although since form here is distinct from end, it seems that what he means more specifically is what we might call the enmattered form.[23] That is, the end is the form *as instantiated in* the matter, as concretely realized. In principle, the end of the economy of salvation is both God (the extrinsic end that is the good by essence) and the realization of the intended order of the created universe (the intrinsic end). However, because this end is not simply the end of "matter that is inert or merely biological or only sensitive," but rather the end of a created order that includes rational and free beings, it requires components suited to that matter.[24] While the end must be something reached, in part, through human reason and will, the attainment of their full end exceeds the reach of those faculties. To meet their end, human reason and will are given supernatural aid insofar as the extrinsic end is *communicated to* the human in (1) the hypostatic union, (2) the gift of the Spirit, and (3) the beatific vision. Likewise, the intrinsic end is not an impersonal order, but rather an

19. Lonergan, *The Redemption*, 231.

20. Lonergan, *The Redemption*, 231.

21. Lonergan, *The Redemption*, 225.

22. Lonergan, *The Redemption*, 199.

23. Lonergan, *The Redemption*, 219.

24. Lonergan, *The Redemption*, 205.

"order of persons brought about through charity and a wisdom that is, in this life, faith, and in the life to come, the vision of God."[25] In other words, the communicated extrinsic end brings human beings to their intrinsic end, that for which they are ordered and which fulfills and finalizes their intelligible order.

Finally, what is the intelligible "form" that is realized in this end? Here we return to "the whole Christ":

> The form in the economy of salvation is the whole Christ, head and members. For in the whole Christ we grasp both the threefold communication of the divine good and the order brought about among persons in this communication of the divine good through the wisdom of apprehension and charity of will, whether in the stage of this life or in that of the life to come.[26]

Lonergan states that this form includes God; the threefold gifts of Christ, the Spirit, and the divine essence; and a good of order that includes a "complex of potencies, habits, interpersonal relationships, arrangements, [and] cooperative efforts."[27] This "complex" is, when it comes down to it, that into which the distorted relations that are the consequences of human sin are transformed in the economy of salvation.

II. Lonergan on the Mystical Body of Christ

Lonergan's perspective on the "whole Christ" affirms that this is the Mystical Body of Christ. He discussed the mystical body most directly in a series of exhortatory talks given to his Jesuit brothers in Canada, and in those we see that his understanding of the mystical body centers around four main points. First, the mystical body is a union of God with human beings.[28] The indwelling of the Spirit, the coming of the Son in the incarnation, and the vision of God the Father grasped initially in faith, but fully in the beatific

25. Lonergan, *The Redemption*, 221.

26. Lonergan, *The Redemption*, 221.

27. Lonergan, *The Redemption*, 199, citing Bernard J. F. Lonergan, *The Triune God: Systematics*, trans. Michael G. Shields, ed. Robert M. Doran and H. Daniel Monsour, vol. 12 in *Collected Works of Bernard Lonergan* (Toronto: University of Toronto Press, 2009), 422–5 and 490–9.

28. Bernard J. F. Lonergan, "The Mystical Body of Christ," in *Shorter Papers*, ed. Robert C. Croken, Robert M. Doran, and H. Daniel Monsour, vol. 20 in *Collected Works of Bernard Lonergan* (Toronto: University of Toronto press, 2007) 106–111, at 106, 107–108.

vision, constitute a gift that, while not hypostatic for each and every individual human being, are in fact the telos of human beings coming to us for the sake of union with us.

Secondly, the mystical body is also a union of human beings with one another.[29] As the threefold gift unites us, not only to God, but to one another, first insofar as we are linked through the God who has given each of us this gift, but also more directly as we begin to participate in the relations that the Trinitarian persons *are*.[30] For example, the gift of the Spirit in sanctifying grace sets up a relation to the Holy Spirit. For Lonergan, that relation participates in the relation of the Father-and-Son-as-one-principle to the Holy Spirit which is called active spiration. But the charity that comes forth from this indwelling is a loving response to the gift of the Spirit from the Father-and-Son-as-one-principle, which means it participates in the Holy Spirit's relation to the Father-and-Son-as-one-principle that we call passive spiration. This, in turn, characterizes our relations to other human beings so that those relations participate in the overarching participation in passive spiration. In other words, our participation in passive spiration is not monadically centered on the Father-and-Son-as-one-principle, but includes—in fact, requires—a corresponding relation to other human beings. The relation to God therefore effects not only a union with God, but a union with other human beings, as well.

Thirdly, love grounds this union.[31] Both metaphysically, in terms of love as the Holy Spirit and of love as the presence of the beloved (human beings) in the lover (God), and also relationally, in terms of providing the intelligible ordering between the (human *and* divine) persons, love is the key to the union.[32] As love unites human persons to one another, their relations correspond to and participate in the relation of love between the Father and the Son that is the Holy Spirit. Moreover, the relations of love are ordered accordingly, so that the threefold divine self-gift, as Lonergan would put it a few years later, sets up a further good of order in this world, which is the mystical body of Christ and his church. So, just as this self-giving of God is something that lies beyond any possible exigence or conclusion, any possible exigence of human nature or conclusion of man's

29. Lonergan, "The Mystical Body of Christ," 106.

30. Lonergan, *The Triune God: Systematics*, 470–473.

31. Lonergan, "The Mystical Body of Christ," 107–108.

32. On love as the presence of the beloved in the lover, see Lonergan, *The Triune God: Systematics*, 677.

thinking about the world, . . . so this mystical body of Christ is a further, higher integration of human living. It is the transition from the *civitas terrena* that can be constituted by a pure desire to know, to the *civitas Dei* that is founded on the love of God and the self-revelation of God.[33]

Fourthly, Lonergan understands this union as including not only those who sacramentally participate in Christ, but also at least some beyond those bounds.[34] For him, the gift of God sets up a new order that is "the mystical body of Christ *and* his church"; Christ "is one with the victims of persecution, just as he is one with the hungry and the thirsty, just as he is one with the naked and the sick, just as he is one with those that eat his Body."[35]

III. Doran on the Law of the Cross

Where Lonergan understood history in terms of progress, decline, and redemption, Doran affirms this basic structure and "complicates [it]," to argue

> that being intelligent and reasonable on a communal or collective level means the integral functioning of the scale of values, that the spread of bias leads to a breakdown in the relations among the various levels of the scale, and that the gift of God's grace affects not only the individual in his or her intelligent, reasonable, and responsible living out but, through the scale of values, the entire community in its collective responsibility for a good of order that is truly good for all and not only for some.[36]

This gift of God's grace prompts people toward charitable conscious-intentional operation, which Doran understands to mean a nonviolence that will repay evil, not with evil, but with good.

In the second volume of *The Trinity in History*, Doran notes that Jesus understood that he was the Messiah and that the new covenant would be mediated through the Messiah's death.[37] This point built on his affirmations

33. Bernard J. F. Lonergan, *Understanding and Being: The Halifax Lectures on* Insight, vol. 5 in *Collected Works of Bernard Lonergan* (Toronto: University of Toronto Press, 1990), 381.

34. Lonergan, "The Mystical Body of Christ," 119.

35. Lonergan, "The Mystical Body of Christ," 119.

36. Doran, *The Trinity in History, Volume 1*, 85–86. For Lonergan on progress, decline, and redemption, see Bernard J. F. Lonergan, "Mission and the Spirit," in *A Third Collection: Papers by Bernard J. F. Lonergan, S.J.*, ed. Frederick E. Crowe (New York: Paulist, 1985), 23–34 at 31–32.

37. Robert M. Doran, *The Trinity in History: A Theology of the Divine Missions, Volume 2: Missions, Relations, and Persons* (Toronto: University of Toronto Press, 2019), 168.

in the first volume that the meaning of the messianic mission had a historical locus in Jesus's beatific knowledge, a locus that corresponded to and was appropriated and expressed within a tradition slowly unveiling that same meaning.[38] Together, the two volumes affirm that the divine meaning mediated by the Hebrew-Israelite tradition was, in fact, the notion of messianic redemption and its nature and further, that Christ both revealed and enacted that meaning.[39] Lonergan transposed his earlier language in *Redemption* in the later "The Mediation of Christ in Prayer," in which he stated that "absorbing the evil of the world by putting up with it, not perpetuating it as rigid justice would demand, . . . acts as a blotter, transforms the situation, and creates the situation in which good flourishes."[40] Doran is attempting a similar and complementary effort to articulate the meaning of the revealed truth about suffering, evil, and their solution. The bulk of his discussion of the law of the cross takes place in Chapter 10 of the first volume of *The Trinity in History*, where he emphasizes that Jesus's revelation and enactment of the redemptive meaning in history changes the concrete relations that constitute human societies.[41]

As with Lonergan, so with Doran, the law of the cross appears in Christ and in all other human beings in different ways.[42] In each case, however, relevant suffering is not masochistic submission to the old relations, but a submission that commences something new.[43] The old relations are deformed by "all defects of the good in the concrete determinations and relations of human life,"[44] which Doran identifies as systems of injustice

38. Doran, *The Trinity in History, Volume 1*, 98. See Charles Hefling, "Revelation and/as Insight," in *The Importance of Insight: Essays in Honour of Michael Vertin*, ed. David S. Liptay and John J. Liptay (Toronto: University of Toronto Press, 2007), 97–115, as well as Doran, *The Trinity in History, Volume 2*, 168.

39. Doran, *The Trinity in History, Volume 2*, 168: there this meaning consisted in the fact that "expiatory suffering mediates redemption for those affected by the disorder that led to the suffering itself."

40. Bernard J. F. Lonergan, "The Mediation of Christ in Prayer," in *Philosophical and Theological Papers: 1958–1964*, ed. Robert C. Croken, Frederick E. Crowe, and Robert M. Doran, vol. 6 in *Collected Works of Bernard Lonergan* (Toronto: University of Toronto Press, 1996), 160–182, at 182, quoted in Doran, *The Trinity in History, Volume 2*, 164.

41. Doran, *The Trinity in History, Volume 1*, 237.

42. See Doran, *The Trinity in History, Volume 1*, 237–238. Briefly, in Jesus as an individual, it appears in his transformation of evils into good by suffering them before receiving the blessing of the Father. In him as head of the new community, it appears as the initiation of this new community. In the members, it appears insofar as they are being drawn into the new community through suffering.

43. Doran, *The Trinity in History, Volume 1*, 240.

44. Doran, *The Trinity in History, Volume 1*, 234.

and the elevation of various forms of bias into norms for our behavior.[45] Yet, whereas relations malformed by sin only offer us the options of fleeing or responding in kind, God puts forward another possibility through the law of the cross. Through God's gift, the old relations can be changed into new relations, transforming from objective surds into newly intelligible relationships.[46]

Because they are concrete human relationships, they are historical, unfolding, and change in them requires not only God's gift of grace, but also collaborative efforts among humans and "with divine creativity itself."[47] The change occurs as human beings come to learn about the fundamental message of revelation, to believe in that message and its messenger, and to consent to a life lived in it, embodying the law of the cross and "assimilated and conformed to him in his dying and rising."[48] In this sense, the change in relationships is "catalyzed," as Doran puts it, by Christ's concrete historical revelation and his enactment of the solution to the problem of evil.[49]

These changes are grounded in the gift of God's self to human beings. For Lonergan in *Redemption*, this gift is threefold. Christ is given in the incarnation, the Holy Spirit in sanctifying grace, and the Father in the beatific vision.[50] In his Trinitarian systematics, however, Lonergan laid this out as a fourfold gift, and it is this version that Doran relies on.[51] There, the Christological element is found in the secondary act of existence of the incarnation, the pneumatological element is found in sanctifying grace and the habit of charity, and the patrological element is found in the light of glory. Each of these grounds a relation to a Trinitarian person: the secondary act establishes a relation of all human beings to the Son through our shared human nature; sanctifying grace establishes relations from individual human beings to the Holy Spirit; the habit of charity establishes

---

45. Doran, *The Trinity in History, Volume 2*, 43.

46. Doran, *The Trinity in History, Volume 2*, 42. See also *The Trinity in History, Volume 1*, 234, Thesis 46.

47. Doran, *The Trinity in History, Volume 1*, 240.

48. Doran, *The Trinity in History, Volume 2*, 43.

49. Doran, *The Trinity in History, Volume 2*, 44. When Doran speaks of this, however, his language is metaphysical: "formal effects," "remote proportionate principle," "created communications of the divine nature," "secondary act of existence," etc. Although Doran's metaphysics is clarified by and grounded in cognitional-intentional analysis and therefore moves part of the way toward a full ontology of meaning and value, it remains to complete the passage to an ontology of meaning and value with respect to the new community. (See, for example, Doran, *The Trinity in History, Volume 2*, 43–44.)

50. Lonergan, *The Redemption*, 221, quoted above.

51. The two versions are roughly contemporaneous, with both published in 1964.

relations from individual human beings to the Father and Son as the one originating principle of the gift of the Spirit; and the light of glory establishes relations from individual human beings to the Father. Each of these relations, as relations to Trinitarian persons, participates in the relations that the Trinitarian persons are: as establishing a relation to the Son, the secondary act sets up a participation in paternity, the relation to the Son that is the Father; as establishing a relation to the Holy Spirit, sanctifying grace sets up a participation in active spiration, which is the relation to the Holy Spirit that the Father and Son are, together as one principle; as establishing a relation to the Father and Son as one principle, the habit of charity sets up a participation in passive spiration, which is the relation to the Father and Son as one principle that the Holy Spirit is; and as establishing a relation to the Father, the light of glory sets up a participation in filiation, the relation to the Father that the Son is.

At this point, the immediate significance of this Trinitarian gift is that the four supernatural realities (the secondary act of existence of the incarnation, sanctifying grace, the habit of charity, and the light of glory) constitute fundamental constituents of the constitutive meaning of the church. Doran notes this fact, and that they have each been affirmed to varying degrees: "the Trinity with the 'consubstantial' of Nicaea, the Incarnation with the 'one and the same' of Chalcedon, the gift of the Holy Spirit with the medieval theorem of the supernatural, and the promise of eternal life with the original message itself, located by Lonergan in 1 Corinthians 15:3–5, with its proclamation of the resurrection and the promise of eternal life."[52] At the same time, his language overall is not that of constitutive meaning, but metaphysics, leaving the full turn to an ontology of meaning still to be effected.

IV. Doran on the New Community

An additional significance of the gift is that in virtue of their status in terms of constitutive meaning, these realities ground the new community. Doran notes in metaphysical terminology that this new community is "grounded in the church's participation in the divine missions and measured by the Law of the Cross."[53] It is the "supreme good" that was for Lonergan the end of the economy of salvation, the "whole Christ, Head and members,

52. Doran, *The Trinity in History, Volume 1*, xii. See also 6.

53. Doran, *The Trinity in History, Volume 1*, 57.

whether explicitly Christian or not, in all the concrete determinations and relations constitutive of this community."[54] For Doran, the key is to identify this supreme good as concretely as possible.[55]

As Lonergan held, it is the form of the economy of salvation that informs the matter comprising the human race under sin. The intelligibility of the informing is statistical, unfolding according to probabilities, requiring a distinction between the end as fully realized—a destination not yet reached—and the emerging intelligibility of the form.[56] Human reason and freedom are the loci of this emergence,[57] with Doran identifying the key points as an initial refusal to respond to evil in kind, followed by forgiveness, love, or an actual return of good for evil, with the eventual end of reconciliation.[58] The new community so constituted and enacted is not simply identifiable with the church. The core of the "whole Christ, Head and members" is not a hierarchical structure of human beings, but God's fourfold gift to us. Doran notes Lonergan's statement that "what distinguishes the Christian . . . is not God's grace, . . . but the mediation of God's grace through Jesus Christ our Lord."[59] More fully, Doran explains that specific to Christianity are the incarnation and the Trinity, which include the concrete historical revelation and enactment of the law of the cross,[60] and he states that without those, hierarchical structures have lost their true reason for being and "all magisterial teaching is sounding brass and tinkling cymbal."[61]

This is a central point in identifying the supreme good. For Doran, two negative markers are key: the institutional church is authentic to the supreme good only insofar as it remains faithful to the law of the cross, and the supreme good is not bounded by the institutional church. On the first point, for Doran the authority of the church is authentic to the extent that the hierarchy is authentic to the original deposit of faith, which for Doran centers around the law of the cross. This rules out what he terms

54. Doran, *The Trinity in History, Volume 1*, 231, Thesis 45.

55. Doran, *The Trinity in History, Volume 1*, 232.

56. Doran, *The Trinity in History, Volume 1*, 233.

57. Doran, *The Trinity in History, Volume 2*, 41, quoting Lonergan, *Insight*, 720.

58. Doran, *The Trinity in History, Volume 1*, 233.

59. Doran, *The Trinity in History, Volume 2*, 39, citing Bernard J. F. Lonergan, "The Future of Christianity," in *A Second Collection: Papers by Bernard J. F. Lonergan, S.J.*, ed. William F.J. Ryan and Bernard J. Tyrrell (Toronto: University of Toronto Press, 1974), 149–164, at 133.

60. Doran, *The Trinity in History, Volume 2*, 39.

61. Doran, *The Trinity in History, Volume 1*, 66.

both "the deviated transcendence of darkly sacrificial religiosity . . . [and] the false mantle of authoritarian preaching masking itself as proclamation of the gospel."[62]

With respect to the second marker, in line with Lonergan's position, Doran affirms that the law of the cross "has been operative whether the name of Jesus has been known and invoked or not."[63] The law of the cross is not restricted to the Israelite and Christian scriptures or tradition, but is also found elsewhere. While he acknowledges that "the significance of this pattern is a matter of Christian revelation," that does not mean that the pattern itself is only present in Christianity and its Israelite roots.[64] Instead, where Matthew 25 lays out a concrete pattern of life built on responding to societal evils with good, Doran notes that "no sacramental incorporation" is necessary in order to fulfill those requirements and any such incorporation that is used to get around those central demands is illegitimate.[65] At the same time, no matter where the pattern is found, it "is the central manifestation of the gift of the Holy Spirit."[66] Those who respond to the gift, in whatever concrete context, share a common root of religious experience and are therefore at least in potential to the new community.[67] On the one hand, these positions allow us to think about the supreme good, the new community, in broader terms than would be possible if we could only identify that supreme good with the church. On the other hand, it leaves us with the task of working out the common meanings and values of that community.

We can approach closer to those common meanings and values by attending to Doran's effort to outline Lonergan's heuristic anticipation of the new community in terms of sacralization and secularization. According to Doran, the law of the cross can be used to specify sacralizations and secularizations to be opposed or encouraged.[68] To be opposed are any attempts to use "the name or word of God or any other sacral trappings" to justify

---

62. Doran, *The Trinity in History, Volume 2*, 39–40. See also 41.

63. Doran, *The Trinity in History, Volume 2*, 39. See also *The Trinity in History, Volume 1*, 66.

64. Doran, *The Trinity in History, Volume 1*, 66.

65. Doran, *The Trinity in History, Volume 2*, 40–41.

66. Doran, *The Trinity in History, Volume 1*, 66.

67. Doran, *The Trinity in History, Volume 2*, 53–54.

68. Doran, *The Trinity in History, Volume 1*, 227, Thesis 44, and 228–230. He pairs the law of the cross here with Girardian analysis, but as was stated above, we are prescinding from mimetic analysis as much as possible in this work.

natural or moral evils and any efforts to attack carriers of the authentic message about the pattern of the law of the cross—in whatever tradition it may appear—or to proclaim that ultimate human authenticity is found elsewhere than in that pattern. To be encouraged are performances of that pattern—again, in whatever context they may appear—as well as efforts to maintain that the natural human orientation to meaning, truth, value, and the beautiful has its legitimate autonomy, even if sustained fidelity to it is possible only within the redemptive pattern. A proper discernment of these social components requires a consciousness that is informed by the law of the cross. That law is "the key to discerning the genuine sacred in human history," even insofar as it informs "a praxis that works strenuously to implement the integral scale of values . . . [and] the realms of cultural and social values."[69] In other words, the law of the cross is not only the key to a religious impact on human community, but it is also the key to the full range of human meaning and value.[70]

V. The Law of the Cross, the New Community, and Meaning

For Doran, the new community is brought about by the fourfold gift, in which "the justifying gift of God's love, a created participation in and imitation of divine active spiration, starts into movement the immanent constitution of life in God, the indwelling of the three divine persons."[71] In Doran's understanding, on an individual level divine constitutive meaning comes to characterize our self-presence (*memoria*), and then out of that are generated a set of judgments of value on the goodness of God's gift. This *memoria*-judgments complex gives rise to a response to the good gift, known as charity, which is personal values affecting and effecting cultural and social values.[72]

I would affirm nearly everything that Doran says on this front, although I would further nuance Doran's discussions of the gift of grace in volume 2. There, he states that the gift of grace establishes the fifth level of consciousness.[73] I would instead affirm that there is a proportionate

69. Doran, *The Trinity in History, Volume 2*, 38.

70. See Doran, *The Trinity in History, Volume 1*, 248.

71. Doran, *The Trinity in History, Volume 2*, 63, Thesis 66.

72. Doran, *The Trinity in History, Volume 2*, 58.

73. Doran, *The Trinity in History, Volume 2*, 53–54.

fifth level, proper to the human and an aspect of the spirit that is oriented toward meaning, truth, value, and beauty, and that grace effects an enlargement of the horizon of the whole range of human conscious intentionality. This enlargement is a methodical, conscious-intentional way of speaking about what Aristotle identified as the formal object.[74] That is, the gift raises or enlarges that toward which a faculty (in a metaphysical faculty psychology) or operation/co-operation (in a methodical theology) is oriented. Alternatively, in a mode of expression that avoids the spatial metaphor altogether, the gift makes possible questions and answers that previously were not possible, questions and answers that were, indeed, out of the reach of a human consciousness operating without an active intervention from, in the limit, one constituted by an infinite range of intelligible answers, value, and beauty.

Within this larger horizon, the interpersonal relations already partly constitutive of the human at the fifth level of consciousness are conjoined to the relations that the Trinitarian persons are. This takes place through the fourfold gift: the relations of humans to the Son, the Spirit, and the Father are established by the secondary act of existence of the incarnation, sanctifying grace, the habit of charity, and the light of glory, respectively, and as these are experienced consciously in changed *memoria*, judgments of value, and charitable conscious performance, transcendent meaning is concretely realized within the world of human meaning.

To the extent that this ripples into the larger society, graced change is possible on a social level, issuing forth when religious value influences personal values as they affect and effect cultural and social values. In light of this analysis in terms of the scale of values, Doran affirms both the necessity of the religious for the authenticity of the human and the legitimate autonomy of the human in its proper proportion. This affirmation maintains the link between the values structured as understood in the scale and the meanings developed and grasped at lower levels of human consciousness. Insofar as it is grace, religious value is linked to the specifically transcendent meaning that is delivered into the world of human meaning by revelation.

The key here is that "once meaning is acknowledged as constitutive of the real world in which human beings live and know and choose and love," we can understand revelation as the entry of divine meaning into this world

74. Bernard J. F. Lonergan, "Georgetown University Lectures Notes, 1964: Differentiation of Methods I," in *Early Works on Theological Method I*, ed. Robert M. Doran and Robert C. Croken, vol. 22 in *Collected Works of Bernard Lonergan* (Toronto: University of Toronto Press, 2010), 395.

of human meaning.[75] The core component of that transcendent meaning is the redemptive intelligibility expressed by the law of the cross, the performance of which presupposes the fourfold gift. When that law is performed, persons quite literally go through a concrete series of actions that make their lives conform to the meaning of the crucified Christ—that is, they accept the consequences of evil, releasing their own efforts at self-preservation (they die to themselves) and entering into the new community founded on the Trinitarian relations in a concrete, historical manner that goes beyond thin notions of metaphor or symbol.

When this happens, the divine constitutive meaning becomes the meaning of the members of the new community, with membership in that community establishing that constitutive meaning as constitutive also for the meaning of each member. This, in part, is the sense in which we can understand Lonergan's affirmation that, whereas in other bodies, the members are for the body, the mystical body "is for the members, the members are for Christ, and Christ is for God."[76] The members do not cease to be who they are, but who they are no longer belongs to them, and to reach that point they must die to themselves. In doing so, they take on God's constitutive meaning as their own meaning and become instruments of the change in human relations that moves toward the new community. In fact, discernment in light of the law of the cross makes it possible to identify "the presence of divine Truth and Love in cultural forms and social structures."[77] Yet, while the cruciform imitation of Christ takes place in those who are to be redeemed, it is not itself redemptive in their performance in the way that Christ's performance of the law was redemptive. The law is not present in them as it is in him. Instead, when those who are to be redeemed enact the steps of the law of the cross, that is their participation in what is to be redeemed—it is their movement from potency to act, from possibly participating in the community of the redeemed to real, concrete participation. Only by being part of that community is their effort redemptive for others, and in that case, it is not they as individuals, but Christ in them, insofar as they are in him, that is doing the redeeming.

This functions because the meaning of Christ, the Son, the Second Person of the Trinity, and thus the meaning of the Trinity, has become the meaning of the members of the body. While the fourfold gift offers to us

75. Doran, *The Trinity in History, Volume 2*, 57.

76. Lonergan, "The Mystical Body of Christ," 109.

77. Doran, *The Trinity in History, Volume 2*, 57.

the constitutive meaning of the church, and each of these four is an aspect of divine constitutive meaning, they are notional, particular to Trinitarian persons, and so not simply meanings common to the three Persons. Yet the law of the cross expresses something that the Son came to express, something that therefore is the meaning of the Son, but within the fact that the Son is the Word who expresses the meaning of the Father. The Son, who is the expression of the Father's meaning, incarnately expresses the law of the cross. This suggests that the meaning expressed by the law of the cross is not personal to the Son, but is common to both the Father and the Son. Moreover, one could argue that this meaning is common to all three Persons insofar as they exhibit a kenotic relationship to one another: paternity is a kenotic self-expression in the Son, filiation is a kenotic reception of all that another is giving, and those together are a kenotic expression of love that is the spiration of the Spirit.

This meaning can become salvific insofar as it changes the ultimate meaning of a person from the definitive "no" of someone unauthentically affirming themselves and their autonomy or being caught up in mimetic currents to the definitive "yes" of someone becoming an authentic interdividual in relationship with a transcendent God and with others in that God.[78] Living out the law of the cross concretizes this change in history. Therefore: the fourfold gift is the metaphysical prerequisite of the divine constitutive meaning entering history; Doran identifies the conscious-intentional transpositions of those prerequisites; and in noting the centrality of redemptive suffering in divine constitutive meaning's entry into and effect on history, Doran points toward the fact that the most succinct, focused expression of the divine meaning itself is the law of the cross.

VI. Conclusion

In Revelation 5:6–13, Christ is portrayed as a slain lamb. I often ask my students whether or not Christ is shown in this fashion because he was crucified. Most of them reply in the affirmative initially, but they grow hesitant after a moment. Whether this is because they're having genuine second thoughts or because they've learned that I tend to have ulterior motives when posing probing questions, in either case they realize that it isn't quite right to say that Christ is portrayed this way because he was crucified.

78. Although I have reworked his point to fit the argument with which I'm concluding this article, it is based in Doran, *The Trinity in History, Volume 2*, 57.

Scripture depicts God as God eternally is. Although in Revelation 5, Christ is worthy to open the scroll because he "purchased for God" numerous people with his blood (Rev 5:9), there is no indication that his depiction as a lamb is because he was slain. Rather, it is more accurate to say that the Second Divine Person has the character of a slain lamb from all eternity, and this is why his life took the pattern it did upon his entrance into history. In other words, it is not the case that contingent history is the ring and Christ's eternal meaning is the wax in which it makes an impression; rather, divine eternal meaning is the ring, and contingent history receives its impression. This accords with an exchange that Lonergan had.[79] He was asked whether our suffering makes a difference to God, and in reply he affirmed that it indeed does, but not in the sense that there is a change in God upon the occasion of our suffering. Instead, Lonergan replied, "it makes an eternal difference" to God—that is, God always already is a God for whom our suffering matters. It matters to God before it happens to us. That is the eternal character of God, the eternal divine constitutive meaning, that Jesus performed and revealed, and into which sinners are drawn when they—when we—imitate the self-sacrificial attitude of Jesus.

From this much, it is clear that without Doran's efforts to explicate the relevance of the law of the cross for human meaning and value, we would not be in a position to advance to such a final point in the future. Standing on his shoulders, however, we find a point of departure for future efforts to deepen a theology of the mystical body in terms of an ontology of meaning.

---

79. See Robert M. Doran, "Reflections on Method in Systematic Theology," *Lonergan Workshop* 17 (2002): 23–51, at 50. Although Doran recounts this as having been communicated by a pair of letters, I have a memory of encountering it in the audio of a question and answer session during my dissertation research. However, I have been unable to locate the exchange. In any case, this position falls within good Trinitarian theology and seems to accord with Lonergan's understanding of the relation between necessary and contingent realities.

CHAPTER EIGHTEEN

TRINITY, ELEMENTAL MEANING AND PSYCHIC CONVERSION

A Pastoral Consideration

Darren J. Dias

University of St Michael's College (Toronto, Ontario)

The essay lies somewhere between a thought experiment and a practical pastoral consideration of Robert Doran's groundbreaking work on elemental meaning and psychic conversion, with a consideration of sexist and gendered speech about the Trinity. There is a need for creative ways to speak about God that take into account people's diverse experiences and situations in order to foster affectivity and symbols that promote deeper relationality, and meanings and values consistent with the Reign of God preached by Jesus. Until now new speech about the Triune God has identified only the need for lexical expansions but I argue that the grammatical dimension of language is also an effective aspect of speech that can result in new images and insights. Feminist scholars raised the issue of gendered speech more than thirty years ago,[1] and their insights and orientations

1. See for example, Mary Daly, M. *Gyn/Ecology:The Metaethics of Radical Feminism* (Boston: Beacon Press,1978); Elizabeth Schussler Fiorenza, *Bread Not Stone: The Challenge of Feminist Biblical Interpretation,* 2nd ed. (Edinburgh: T&T Clark, 1990); Carter Heyward, *Our Passion for Justice—Images of Power, Sexuality, and Liberation* (New York: The Pilgrim Press, 1984); Elizabeth A. Johnson, E. A. *She Who Is: The Mystery of God in Feminist Theological Discourse* (New York: Cross Road, 1996); Sally McFague, "God as Mother," in *Weaving the Visions: New Patterns in Feminist Spirituality* ed. C. P. Christ & J. Plaskowski (San Francisco: Harper, 1989) 139–150; Rosemary Radford Ruether, *New Woman New Earth: Sexist Ideologies and Human Liberation* (East Malvern: Dove, 1975); Letty Russell, *Human Liberation in a Feminist Perspective: A Theology* (Philadelphia: Westminster Press, 1974); Dorothy Soelle, *The Strength of the Weak: Towards a Christian Feminist Identity.* (Philadelphia: Westminster, 1984); Phyllis Trible, *God and the Rhetoric of Sexuality* (Philadelphia: Fortress, 1978).

are still timely. In this essay I will revisit some language and imagery that continue to challenge prevalent patriarchal, sexist language and imagery. By referencing more recent empirical studies I demonstrate that the concerns raised in decades past remain live issues still to be addressed. Further emerging discussions around language raised by the LGBTQI community raises new possibilities for thinking about the capacity of how the Triune God can be spoken about and imagined.

This essay draws out the concrete implications of Doran's extremely important work on elemental meaning and psychic conversion by exploring gendered speech for the persons of the Triune God. I begin by situating language, images and symbols within the theoretical frame of elemental meaning and psychic conversion. I will then explore the reality of elemental meaning and psychic conversion through empirical studies that illustrate the connection between language, images, affect, values and gender. After re-visiting feminist critiques on the doctrine of the Trinity, I will survey gendered and transgendered language models for speaking about the Triune God. I will conclude with the suggestion that language practices, including grammatical dimensions, are powerful habits that can shape, re-shape, and liberate consciousness from the negative repression of and flight from potential insights.

Elemental Meaning and Psychic Conversion

One Sunday at the celebration of the Eucharist, I noticed the altar server sitting under a large painting of the Trinity—two bearded, white men and a dove. The homily, delivered by a sympathetic older man, used the traditional language of Father, Son and Holy Spirit. There was nothing wrong with the scene—it was in every way normal and ordinary. Yet I wondered how that young girl imagined God, if she imagined herself in the male God's image and likeness, and what kind of relationship with "Him" could she conceive? Qualitative research has demonstrated the struggle that members of the LGBTI community have in coming to terms with their own self-image and sexualities because of the inherited imaginaries of God in the Catholic tradition.[2] However, in the process of self-discovery and self-affirmation, LGBT participants in one study were capable of destroying false, and often

2. Angele Deguara, "Destroying False Images of God: The Experience of LGBT Catholics," *Journal of Homosexuality* 65 (2018) 317–337. See also, Perry N. Halkitis et. al., "The Meanings and Manifestations of Religion and Spirituality among Lesbian, Gay, Bisexual and Transgender Adults," *Journal of Adult Development* 16 (2009) 250–262.

harmful, images of God moving away from "the image of God as a bearded old man and father of creation . . . toward a conception of God as love."[3]

The Pew Research Forum reports that only 17% of Americans "nones" believe in the "God of the Bible" (i.e. an old, bearded white man).[4] Of the "nones," those whose religion is "nothing in particular," 78% had been raised in a religiously affiliated household.[5] While reasons for disaffiliation vary, it is clear that the religious language and imagery of previous generations no longer resonate with this rapidly growing segment of the population.

These three examples have theological implications: when language and imaginings about God become fossilized and static, then conceptions of God may become idolatrous, since God is always beyond language and image. Furthermore, on a pastoral-experiential level, male-only symbols of God drawn from patriarchal culture do not necessarily respond to large segments of the population anymore. What happens when symbols cease to function in meaningful ways? Or worse, what if they function in ways that block spiritual growth and meaning?

Like all language and images, those that speak about the Triune God are bounded by the history, culture and tradition out of which they emerged. Language and images about the Trinity are not literal representations but analogical and metaphorical. Thus, they function powerfully in people's experience and imaginings of God. Even before consciously embarking on a quest for knowledge of God, believers receive from the community and tradition meaning about God through scripture, liturgy, art, preaching, etc. Doran names this process the reception of elemental meaning that shapes affect, image, feeling, and symbol. Patriarchal and sexist language and images of God are determinants of elemental meanings received from the tradition. Trinitarian language and images "are already invested with meaning that is a function of . . . personal and communal history."[6] According to Doran, "this received meaning functions effectively and constitutively in the lives to whom it occurs."[7] What is received may be insightful and

3. Deguara, 317.

4. Pew Research Forum, "When Americans Say They Believe in God, What do They Mean?" https://www.pewforum.org/2018/04/25/when-americans-say-they-believe-in-god-what-do-they-mean (accessed February 20, 2020).

5. Pew Research Forum, "Why American 'Nones' Left Religion." https://www.pewresearch.org/fact-tank/2016/08/24/why-americas-nones-left-religion-behind (accessed February 20, 2020).

6. Robert M. Doran, *What Is Systematic Theology?* (Toronto: University of Toronto Press, 2005) 129.

7. Ibid., 130.

intelligent or may be biased. What is received in one generation may give rise to challenges and questions in another.[8]

Speaking creatively about the Triune God can also liberate subjects from the very language that functions to restrict the psychic dimension of consciousness. Doran's development of psychic conversion provides critical insight into the relationship between affect, feelings, symbols, and values. For Doran, following Bernard Lonergan, a symbol of something, real or imagined, evokes and is evoked by feelings, and values that are apprehended by feelings.[9] One's moral and religious knowledge is informed and determined by the "psychic self-appropriation, the appropriation of one's life of feeling." Lonergan's transcendental precepts—be attentive, be intelligent, be reasonable, be responsible—accompany each level in his theory of human development from experience to understanding to judging and finally deciding. Without psychic conversion, a subject cannot be attentive to the data of experience. In this sense Lonergan says we are conscious in a way that is "rather passively [in] what we sense and imagine," unlike "through our intellectuality."[10]

According to Doran, "Psychic conversion is a transformation of the censorship exercised with respect to the entire field of what is received in empirical consciousness . . . psychic conversion is a transformation of that censorship from a repressive to a constructive exercise as one engages in the delicate artistry of producing 'the first and only edition' of oneself."[11] Psychic conversion entails the self-appropriation of psyche that "consists in the sensitive flow of sensations, memories, images, conations, emotions, associations, spontaneous intersubjective responses, bodily movements, and received meanings and values."[12] Images and affects condition a subject's self-constitution and that of their world of constitutive meanings.

Language about God functions as a powerful censor, often in unintentional ways. At the same time, speech about God can challenge static patriarchal imagery, not only by expanding the theological lexicon, with

8. For a helpful discussion of ordinary meaningfulness, see Doran, *What is Systematic Theology?* 132–133.

9. Robert M. Doran, "Two Ways of Being Conscious: The Notion of Psychic Conversion" (2011) 10. https://www.lonerganresource.com/pdf/lectures/2003-Doran-Reception_and_Elemental_Meaning.pdf. (Accessed February 20, 2020).

10. See, Bernard Lonergan, *Triune God: Systematics*, ed. Robert Doran and H. Daniel Monsour (Toronto: University of Toronto Press, 2007) 139.

11. Doran, *What Is,* 110.

12. Doran, *What Is,* 111.

new words and analogies, but in a consideration of the structure of speech, its very grammar. Thus, I argue that the use of epicene—gender neutral—pronouns to refer to the persons of the Trinity is both timely and apt.

Empirical Studies

Charles Taylor[13] claims that language determines the way in which its speakers think and act. Thought, language, and culture are so deeply interlocked that each language also constitutes a world-view.[14] Language has the power to encode and so linguistic coding may even "produce differences in experience."[15] Taylor points to "fluidity and change"[16] in contemporary language occasioned, for example, by challenges to hierarchical relations or boundaries in multicultural societies. He writes: "Rules are creatively broken. The system is constantly in some degree of flux."[17]

Empirical studies demonstrate that there is a clear correlation between language, gender, and images of God among English speakers.[18] A 2004 study of English speaking children ranging from the ages of four to eleven showed that both girls and boys overwhelmingly conceptualize God as male, whether as an old man in heaven for many girls, or a superhero for boys. Only 6.1% of girls conceptualized God as female compared to 0% of boys.[19] A survey of German-speaking children aged fourteen to sixteen related the conceptualization of God according to four categories: polysexual (4%), female (6.7%), male (33%), and asexual (57%).[20] While English does not have grammatical gender, German has masculine, feminine and neuter. A 2009 study revealed that the belief that God is beyond gender correlates with images of God as mother, alternate names for the persons of the Trinity, and God as "fatherly mother" and "motherly father."[21] The study

13. Doran engages Taylor's disjunctions that refer to gender, sexuality and hierarchy, see Robert M. Doran, *The Trinity In History: A Theology of the Divine Missions, vol. two, Missions, Relations and Persons* (Toronto: University of Toronto Press, 2019) 59–61.

14. Charles Taylor, *The Language Animal* (Cambridge: The Belkap Press of Harvard University Press, 2016), 320.

15. Taylor, 324.

16. Taylor, 331.

17. Taylor, 330.

18. Mark J. Cartledge, "God, Gender and Social Roles: A Study in Relation to Empirical-Theological Models of the Trinity," *Journal of Empirical Theology* 22 (2009) 136.

19. Cartledge, 125.

20. Cartledge, 125.

21. Cartledge, 133.

also demonstrated that language about God corresponds to social values. For example, participants that subscribe to hierarchal, top-down leadership associate positively with the image of God as "father" but not with God as "mother" or "motherly father/fatherly mother."[22] The study concluded that there is a clear "association between gender-specific language for God and social roles and values."[23]

God-Talk: Feminist Critiques and Trinity

Some feminist critiques, like that of Mary Daly, suggest that the doctrine of the Trinity is irredeemably patriarchal, the basis of exclusion, oppression, inequality, and the divinization of the male and should, therefore, be done away with. Contrarily, Janet Martin Soskice claims that Trinitarian doctrine "preserves the otherness of God . . . from gross anthropocentrism;" protects against "covert monarchianism", the lonely and aloof divinity indifferent to creation; "endorses the fundamental goodness and beauty of the human being" because of the Incarnation; and moves beyond "philosophies of the One" where otherness is reduced to the same, beyond the binarism of "the one and the other, the higher and the lower, the male and the female."[24] Preserving the doctrine of the Trinity, however, does not mean preserving static, gendered language and imagery. Thus, Gail Ramshaw Schmidt concludes, "despite its problematic terminology, trinitarian doctrine is Christianity's strongest defense against classical patriarchal monotheism."[25] The challenge is for meaningful and theological speech that "neither parrot the past nor jettison the Trinity."[26]

Liturgical theologian Gail Ramshaw Schmidt's work is a reminder that all language about God is metaphorical and analogical. Metaphor is the tool that humans use when "straining to say new things, to speak of realities that escape our current labels and reach beyond purely personal expression."[27] Metaphor changes perceptions and makes new mental realities. Metaphoric talk in theology is simultaneously talk about the human

22. Cartledge, 133.

23. Cartledge, 136.

24. Janet Martin Soskice, "Trinity and Feminism," in *The Cambridge Companion to Feminist Theology*, ed. Susan Frank Parsons (Cambridge: Cambridge University Press, 2002) 139–140.

25. Gail Ramshaw Schmidt, *God Beyond Gender, Feminist Christian God-Language* (Minneapolis: Augsburg Fortress, 1995) 84.

26. Ramshaw Schmidt, *God Beyond Gender*, 76.

27. Gail Ramshaw, *Reviving Sacred Speech: The Meaning of Liturgical Language* (Akron: OSL Pulications, 2000) xi.

and divine that uses human or bodily categories and language.[28] Metaphoric talk is "open to associations, which encourages insight and facilitates disclosure by its linking of disparate things."[29] Metaphoric talk must always be subject to the principal of *contradictability*: God is a rock, but God is not a rock; God is a father but a father who lets his son die.[30] This extends to pronouns where the test of *contradictability* remains: God is he, God is not he.[31]

Analogies[32] are "those verbal expressions by which we are trying to say what we mean."[33] Analogy functions by affirming similarity between two things but even greater dissimilarity between analogues. Furthermore, even in the realm of similarity, there is distance (of degree) between the analogues.[34] When dissimilarity and distance collapse then analogy and its constitutive language becomes literal and personal (God is Father, a male parent). God's unfathomable mystery, utter transcendence, and total otherness give way to a static image, an idol. Trinitarian doctrine offers the resources that challenge patriarchal, exclusionary, unequal, totalizing, anthropocentric, domesticating discourse that it also ironically encodes when its everyday language is understood as literal and personal instead of analogical and metaphorical.

Gender

Gendered language to refer to God speaks to the deeply personal dimension of God. According to poet and liturgist Janet Morley, "since we have no experience of persons who are ungendered, it is virtually impossible (and equally undesirable) to envisage one."[35] Analogic and metaphoric language is enriched by gendered speech because it is drawn from human experience. However, if gendered language is to be meaningful in its creative potential,

28. Ramshaw Schmidt, *God Beyond Gender*, 119.

29. Ramshaw Schmidt, *God Beyond Gender*, 119.

30. Ramshaw Schmidt, *God Beyond Gender*, 120.

31. Ramshaw Schmidt, *God Beyond Gender*, 121.

32. I am using analogy as an aspect of speech and thought, not in the precise and technical theological manner in which Doran would define the "psychological analogy" for understanding the Trinity.

33. Ramshaw Schmidt, *God Beyond Gender*, 121.

34. Gerard Loughlin, "Sexing the Trinity," *New Blackfriars* 79 (1998) 18.

35. Janet Morley, "I Desire Her With My Whole Heart," in *Feminist Theology: A Reader*, ed. Ann Loades (London: SPCK, 1990) 158.

it must eschew singular, binary and literal discourse. Static binary biological conceptions of gender are fairly recent developments,

Until the 18th century, Western thought held there was one normative sex (male) with the potential of another (female) to develop from the male. Men and women shared a common biology and differences were a matter of degree and not kind.[36] Referring to Aquinas, Adrian Thatcher described the belief that just as God is the principle of the universe, so too is man the principle of the human race.[37] Although Aquinas speaks of two sexes, the female sex is merely defective or lacking male body.

In the 18th century, the notion of two distinct and opposite sexes arose. The two-sex model posited incommensurable opposition between men and women based on biological difference.[38] Concomitant to biological sexual difference, rooted in cells, was different social roles. The two-sex model eventually replaced the one-sex model of "embodied souls ordered along a continuum on the basis of proximity to the divine."[39] The two-sex model posited inequality between the sexes and the subordination of female to male.[40] Adrian Thatcher suggests a retrieval and modification of the earlier single-sex model to think about gender today. This modification considers the "gradation of perfection, the gender slide, the hierarchical ordering of relationships" between men and women as baseless and oppressive.[41] However, the advantage of the more traditional single-sex model is that it emphasizes the unity of humankind, sexual similarity instead of exaggerated sexual differences that normalize conflict.[42]

Thatcher does not ignore biological difference as these differences enable humans to "share with God in the work of creation and reproduction."[43] He argues for "gender realism" grounded in bodies. Gender realism is based on "different relationship *of possibility* to biological reproduction."[44] There is no single way to relate to this possibility. Instead, gender is a single

36. Adrian Thatcher, *Redeeming Gender* (Oxford: Oxford University Press, 2016) 13.

37. Thatcher, 47.

38. Loughlin, 21.

39. Mary Hawkesworth, "Sex, Gender and Sexuality: From Naturalized Presumption to Analytical Categories," in *The Oxford Handbook on Gender and Politics*, ed. Georgina Waylen et. al. (Oxford: Oxford University Press, 2013) 33.

40. Thatcher, 138.

41. Thatcher, 138.

42. Thatcher, 139.

43. Thatcher, 139.

44. Thatcher, 173.

continuum, a spectrum that avoids hierarchy, binarism, and essentialism. Gender, related to bodily potential, results in multiple and various, sometimes new and seemingly strange, ways for people to relate to their own bodies and to one another, and ultimately God.

God-Talk: Gendered and Transgendered Models

Gendered Models

In her influential 1992 book, *She Who Is,* Elizabeth Johnson summarizes three ways to expand language about God "by uttering female symbols into speech about divine mystery."[45] One way is to image feminine characteristics in a predominately masculine God.[46] Johnson critiques this as counter-productive to realizing the potential of a divine image because the feminine-maternal characteristics simply serve to complete the "wholistic male."

A second way is to emphasize a feminine dimension in the Triune God in one of the persons, usually the Holy Spirit. Luce Irigaray believes that the feminine Spirit present in the life of Jesus completes the Incarnation that is otherwise masculine.[47] In view of the exclusive maleness of language and images of the Trinity, Irigaray demands that there be a female god and suggest that this be the Holy Spirit.[48] Whether Irigaray ascribes gender to the eternal Son is unclear.

Johnson critiques this proposal as the Christian tradition, however unintentionally, subordinates the person of the Holy Spirit, often assigning it an inferior role to that of the Father and the Son. Irigaray's proposal is problematic not only in its understanding of the relations and persons of the Trinity but because it assigns sexual difference in the Trinity that becomes two-thirds male and one third female. Her proposal fails to "emphasize that God is beyond human gender limits, in other words [God] does not lack gender, but surpasses it, and therefore each of the three persons can be described with both male and female imagery."[49]

45. Elizabeth A. Johnson, *She Who Is: The Mystery of God in Feminist Theological Discourse* (New York: Cross Road, 1996) 45.

46. Johnson, 48.

47. Soili Haverinen, "Trinity, Embodiment and Gender" in Embodied Religion, ed. P. Jonkers, & M. Sarot (Utrecht: Igitur: Utrecht Publishing & Archiving Services, 2013) 243.

48. See Luce Irigaray, *Sexes and Genealogies* trans. Gillian C. Gill (New York 1993) 62. Irigary notes that the gender of the noun for Spirit in Hebrew and Syriac is feminine and the notion of the Spirit as feminine is found in the early Syraic tradition.

49. Haverinen, 244.

Johnson's preferred approach to speaking about the Trinity "proceeds with the insight that only if God is so named, only if the full reality of women as well as men enters into the symbolization of God along with symbols from the natural world, can the idolatrous fixation on one image be broken and the truth of the mystery of God, in tandem with the liberation of all human beings and the whole earth, emerge for our time."[50] Johnson avoids the dangers of a binary approach to God, by promoting only female names for the persons of the Trinity: Mother-Sophia, Jesus-Sophia, and Spirit-Sophia. Though Johnson's analogy neither falls into the trap of gender dualism nor does she introduce sexual difference into the Trinity, it still operates within a binary understanding of gender that runs the risk of becoming exclusive, personal and literal.

Transgendered Models

Julian of Norwich employs gender-bending language to speak about the Trinity. In reference to the divine name found in Exodus 3, Julian writes:

> As truly as God is our Father, so truly is God our Mother, and he revealed that in everything, and especially in these sweet words where he says: I am he.[51]

Since motherhood can be applied to the whole Trinity, Julian applies it to the Son by appropriation:

> And so in our making, God almighty is our loving Father, and God all wisdom is our loving Mother, with the love and the goodness of the Holy Spirit, which is all one God, one Lord.[52]

Julian speaks of Father, Son and Spirit as Father, Mother and Lord respectively. She claims that in praying to the Son we are "mightily praying to our Mother for mercy and pity, and to our Lord the Holy Spirit for help and grace."[53] God's motherhood is expressed in creation, incarnation, and grace. Julian employs the evocative image of the pelican to describe Jesus' relationship to humanity:

---

50. Johnson, 56.

51. Julian of Norwich, *Julian of Norwich Showings, The Classics of Western Spirituality Series,* ed. Edmund Colledge and James Walsh (New York: Paulist Press, 1978) 295, quoted in Anne Hunt, *The Trinity: Insights From the Mystics* (Collegeville: Liturgical Press, 2010) 116.

52. Julian of Norwich, *Julian of Norwich,* 293, quoted in Hunt, 115.

53. Julian of Norwich, *Julian of Norwich,* 296, quoted in Hunt, 116.

> The mother can give her child to suck of her milk, but our precious Mother Jesus can feed us with himself, and does, most courteously and tenderly, with the blessed sacrament, which is the precious food of true life; and with all the sweet sacraments he sustains us most mercifully and graciously.[54]

Julian inserts female language and imagery into what is most "male" in the Trinity, the bodily Incarnation of the Son. She speaks of Jesus' body as female, of his labor pains on the cross that give birth to new life. God the Father-Mother has generative qualities, but it is in the Incarnation of the Son "who can truly be characterized as mother because procreative pain is biologically female."[55] Julian connects the Incarnation in the historically real body of Jesus with the historical and real body of woman.[56] Jesus' body is the womb for the new humanity symbolized in the wound in his side.[57] For Julian, God is incarnate in a male-female body.[58]

Hans Urs Von Balthasar uses transgendered language and imagery to speak of the relations and persons of the Trinity. He posits that the Father is (supra-) masculine as "the begetting origin-without-origin"; the Son as begotten and receptive is (supra-)feminine as "begotten and thus receptive"; the Father and Son together spirating the Holy Spirit are (supra-) masculine, making the receptive Spirit (supra-)feminine; but the Father allows himself to be (supra-)feminine in the return of his spirating and begetting.[59] Thus, masculinity is associated with giving, begetting, generating, while femininity with receiving and receptivity.

Von Balthasar's is not an analogy drawn from human operations but a "parody" of insemination and fertilization.[60] The masculine and feminine located in the Trinitarian relations render the Trinity "a self-inseminating, self-fertilizing womb."[61] In Balthasar's image of the Trinity there

---

54. Julian of Norwich, *Julian of Norwich*, 298, quoted in Hunt, 117.

55. Kathryn L. Reinhard, "Joy to the Father, Bliss to the Son, Unity and the Motherhood Theology of Julian of Norwich," *Anglican Theological Review* 89 (2007) 635.

56. Reinhard, 635.

57. Reinhard, 637.

58. Reinhard, 639.

59. David Schindler, "Catholic theology, gender, and the future of Western civilization," *Communio* (Summer 1993) 206; reference to Hans Urs Von Balthasar, *Theodrmatik* IV (Einsiedeln: Johannes Verlag, 1983) 80.

60. Loughlin, 23.

61. Loughlin, 23.

is a gendered hierarchy not based on biology but on relations of origin. In biological terms, the Father and Son are portrayed as hermaphrodites, having both feminine and masculine characteristics. Von Balthasar's creative imagery is interesting because it is God's relationality that gives meaning to gender. Some obvious questions arise: why is generativity associated with the Father masculine and receptivity of the Spirit as feminine? Why are these asymmetrical? Is the Holy Spirit only different from the Son because the Spirit is feminine? Although David Schindler claims that this concept of gender is "integral" and "not fractional,"[62] the notion of masculine-feminine gender complementarity in the Trinity inescapability tends to dualism and hierarchy.

The creative and rich images for the Trinity that have emerged in contradistinction to the patriarchal and exclusive language of the tradition reveal the challenges inherent in any meaningful and accurate speech about God. Adding feminine names to balance the masculine may simply preserve patriarchal, hierarchical patterns, and sanction new forms of exclusionary language and images.[63] Exclusively female language may avoid inserting gender difference into God, but could become static. Transgendered language and imagery may express the persons in relations of origin in highly imaginative ways, but risks inserting hierarchy and dualism. Speech about God can reflect the richness of the Trinitarian symbol, using meaningful language and images within the limits of the English language, but certain challenges and pitfalls will always remain. Perhaps some of these may be addressed through linguistic practices that center not only on the lexical, but on the grammatical.

Epicene Pronouns

An epicene pronoun (or common or gender-neutral pronoun) can refer to both a male or female antecedent, or else to a non-gender specific antecedent. In English this has significance for third person, singular pronouns. These pronouns are limited to "he" and "she" for masculine and feminine antecedents respectively, and "it" for gender neutral, inanimate antecedents. In English, it is the antecedent noun that determines the pronoun. Unlike other languages, words themselves are not assigned either gender or neutrality to determine pronominal use.

62. Schindler, 223.

63. Rosemary Radford Ruether, *Sexism and God-Talk: Toward a Feminist Theology* (Boston: Beacon Press, 1993) 66.

Epicene pronouns are not new to English. Until the 19th century "they" was used as an epicene plural and singular pronoun. In the late 18th century there was some discomfort among grammarians of "forcing a plural pronoun to agree with a singular referent."[64] An 1850 Act of Britain's Parliament put an end to the practice of using "he or she" as a referent of ambiguous gender stating ". . . in all acts words importing the masculine gender shall be deemed and taken to include females."[65] Thus the practice of employing gender neutral/inclusive pronouns dissipated for a century.

In North America, grammarians and linguists attempted to rationalize the use of epicene pronouns. As early as 1850 the use of *ne, nis, nim* was suggested as a third person, singular common pronoun.[66] In the year 1884 alone a series of articles in *The Current*, *The Literary World*, and *The Critic* made such suggestions as *thon, thons; hi, hes, hem; le li, slim; unus; talis; hiser, himer; ip, ips*; etc.[67] Although these proposals lacked the feminist motivations of recent years, the reaction against them "reveal a spirit of antifeminism."[68]

The lack of epicene pronouns and the practice of using "he" as a generic pronoun for the third person singular was most recently challenged by feminist writers beginning in the 1970s. They successfully demonstrated that "he" could no longer be understood as a generic third person singular pronoun since "man" could no longer be substituted for all humankind.[69] Attempts to redress sexism inherent in English language use and grammar resulted in more suggestions for epicene third person, singular pronouns—*she, heris, herm; ve, vis, ver; tey, ter, tem; shis, shim, shims, shimself; ze, zim, zees, zeeself; per, pers; ne; nis ner; sheme, shis, shem;heshe, hisher, himmer; em, ems*—to name but a few proposed between 1970–1977.[70] The following are some possible examples, certainly not exhaustive, of what epicene pronouns might look like:

64. Caleb Everett, "Gender, pronouns and thought: The ligature between epicene pronouns and a more neutral gender perception," *Gender and Language* 5 (2011) 134.

65. Everett, 134.

66. Denise E. Baron, "The Epicene Pronoun: The World That Failed," *American Speech* 56 (1981) 88.

67. Baron, 90–91.

68. Baron, 87.

69. Mark Balhorn, The Epicene Pronoun in Contemporary Newspaper Prose," *American Speech* 84 (2009) 391.

70. Baron, 93–95.

He/She	Him/Her	His/Her	His/Hers	Himself/ Herself
Zie	Zim	Zir	Zis	Zieself
Sie	Sie	Hir	Hirs	Hirself
Ev	Em	Eir	Eirs	Eirself
Ve	Ver	Vis	Vers	Verself
Tev	Ter	Tem	Ters	Terself
E	Em	Eir	Eirs	Emself

In the absence of epicene pronouns, North American English has resorted to using either "they" or else "it" to refer to a non-gender specific noun as "he" or "she." "They" has entered common speech as well as writing to usually refer to a generic antecedent.[71] The Chicago Manual of Style, 17th edition, substitutes "they" for the once generic "he" in speech and informal writing. Likewise it commends "they" for persons who do not identify with a specific gender. However, it remains silent on the use of epicene pronouns.

Linguistic studies have demonstrated that the use of "he" as an epicene "bias subjects in favor of masculine interpretations."[72] "The biasing effects of images called up by different pronouns and the association of such pronouns to stereotyped sex roles certainly make a compelling argument against the use of the epicene *he*."[73] Gendered pronouns have "strong cognitive effects."[74] While the use of gender inclusive language has been a significant achievement, "pronomial usage is probably even more destructive to concept development than continued use of . . . sexist lexical items."[75] Anthropologist Caleb Everett concludes "the absence of an epicene pronoun in a given language results in a generally more male-biased construal of neutral stimuli . . . even [when not presented] with an androcentric stimulus."[76] There are yet few studies on the effect of epicene pronouns

71. Balhorn, 399.

72. Michael Newman, *Epicene Pronouns: The Linguistics of a Prescriptive Problem* (London: Routledge, 1996) 25.

73. Newman, 28.

74. Newman, 31.

75. Newman, 32.

76. Everett, 137.

on referents with unknown or ambiguous gender. "The data are consistent with the suggestion that epicene pronouns allow for a more gender-neutral perception of gender-neutral stimuli."[77] Non-epicene languages, such as English, tend to androcentric construal of gender-neutral stimuli.[78]

Pronouns are not semantically empty substitutes that refer simply to an antecedent. They can supply information about the referent independent of the antecedent.[79] Linguist Michael Newman demonstrates that pronouns are "dynamic referring devices . . . capable of influencing the interpretation of a referent."[80] Insignificant as they may seem, pronouns reflect the role that language plays in social struggle and change.[81] Unlike lexical elements of speech, pronouns as grammatical elements are considered "grammatically constrained" and "difficult to change."[82]

The introduction of epicene pronouns to refer to the persons of the Trinity would not be the first time that new words have been appropriated into Trinitarian theology. For example, the word now translated as "person" was appropriated by the early church as the most appropriate word to answer the question: three *what* constitute the Trinity? Although "they" is gaining popularity to refer to non-gendered stimuli, its use to refer to the Trinity may connote tritheism. The use of epicene pronouns for the persons of the Trinity could be used in any context whether in theological reflection, faith sharing, or even liturgical prayer. Epicene pronouns would not replace the traditional male names for the persons of the Trinity found in the liturgy (Father and Son), but would function as a reminder to the assembly that while God is Father, Son, and Spirit, God is always not father, son, and spirit as we conceive them. Thus, the doxology might read: "Through ver, with ver, in ver, in the unity of the Holy Spirit, all glory and honor are yours almighty Father."[83] Just as prepositions were important in the formulation of doxologies in the post-apostolic period, so too are pronouns today.

The use of epicene pronouns would preserve the contradictability of metaphoric talk and the dissimilarity and distance of analogy by shattering any static notion or imagining that God is gendered in a limiting way.

---

77. Everett, 149.

78. Everett, 148–149.

79. Newman, 204.

80. Newman, 94.

81. Newman, 11.

82. Newman, 11–12.

83. In 2017, the students in my Trinity class decided to use epicene pronouns to refer to the persons of the Trinity. This doxology is an example.

An epicene pronoun reminds us that even when we refer to the antecedent "father" or "mother," it is not a literal or personal term as we understand our mother or father to be. Parental qualities that many have experienced in their mothers or fathers may be ascribed to God who is simultaneously not mother or father, male or female. In God there are relations of origin and generation *like* that of a parent to a child. The moment we name God in gendered terms, the use of the epicene pronoun is a reminder that God is all and beyond gender, with an incomprehensible and inexhaustible relational capacity.

Conclusion

The proposal to use epicene pronouns to refer to the persons of the Trinity encodes the contradictability, dissimilarity and distance necessary in speech about God in linguistic practice. Such practice, whether referring to non-patriarchal, transgendered or traditional liturgical Trinitarian language, is a reminder that the Triune God exceeds speech in every case. If this linguistic practice accepted language, images and symbols that become fossilized, or hegemonic, or less meaningful are challenged.

Language, including and especially its grammatical aspects, leaches into the reception of elemental meaning as a carrier of meaning of a community and tradition, in turn affecting images, symbols, feeling and values, whether preserving or transforming them. Epicene pronouns to refer to the persons of the Trinity could, in fact, be central to "the psychic dimension, with symbolic structures that precede, feelings that accompany, and interpersonal relations that overarch the intentional operations."[84] Thus, small personal pronouns can become an occasion for liberating the richness of images and symbols for God needed to build personal and communal relationships.

84. Robert M. Doran, *The Trinity In History: A Theology of the Divine Missions, vol. one, Missions and Processions* (Toronto: University of Toronto Press, 2012) 311.

SECTION VI

THE ONGOING APPROPRIATION OF DORAN'S WORK

CHAPTER NINETEEN

PSYCHIC CONVERSION AND THE LEGACY OF JULIUS K. NYERERE IN TANZANIA

Josephat Rugaiganisa OFM

In this article I reflect on the life and thinking of the first President, Julius K. Nyerere, of my country, Tanzania. Nyerere held office from 1964 to 1985. He is widely considered to have articulated a political philosophy of abiding value that still has influence in East Africa and beyond. I employ the thought of Robert Doran to illuminate the value of the thought of Nyerere, expanding this analysis to a reflection on what should be the practice of the Church in the region, finding much of theological value in this political philosophy.

Julius Nyerere: His Political Philosophy and Practice

Julius Nyerere was born in 1922 in the north of what was then Tanganyika, near the borders with Kenya and Uganda. He was the son of the fifth wife of a chief of the Zanaki ethnic community, who had twenty-two wives. He was raised in the practice of the traditional religion of that community. It was the policy of the British colonial administration at that time to educate the sons of chiefs, and they supported him in gaining an elementary education in a nearby Catholic school. He displayed academic excellence and won scholarships which helped him further his education. He completed training as a teacher in Uganda, during which time he became baptized as a Catholic. He became fascinated by questions of politics, reading papal encyclicals as well as the the philosophy of Jacques Maritan and John Stuart Mill. While still a student, he published an article which stated that capitalism is alien to Africa, that "the African is by nature a socialistic being," and that the educated elite among Africans should work to develop an original form of political organization, which he called "African socialism."[1] He returned to his native area as a teacher, becoming involved in the early movement for national independence immediately after World War II and onward.

Tanganyika, like many African countries at the time, was structured in the form of an alienated multitude of small welfare and tribal organizations. There was no general economic organization or social system which might form the basis for a political movement for national independence. Fortunately, for the movement for national independence, there had been few real sympathizers with colonial masters who had ruled the region for 76 years, and few privileged groups gaining precedence over others by virtue of religion or ethnic identity. Another advantage for the movement for national independence was that a single African language, the artificially created trading language, Swahili, was widely spoken and would be suitable as a national language. These were tools and advantages that Nyerere would use to create and organize a self-independent country; independence was granted to Tanganyika in 1961. Nyerere was appointed the first President of this new nation-state and already at this early stage, was recognized by outsiders to have some exceptional qualities. Richard Turnbull, the last British governor of Tanganyika, described Nyerere as having "a tremendous adherence to principle" and exhibiting "rather a Gandhian streak."[2]

Now, the task for Nyerere was to build a sense of national unity and direction among the people he led. Few of the citizens of this new country had needed persuading that *Uhuru* (freedom) from colonial masters was desirable. On the other hand, few understood in any detail what it might mean to become a self-governing, modern state. The first leader of the state had much to do in explaining the relevance of the state to the lives of ordinary people. This he would attempt to do through formulating national economic plans and regular speeches to explain a new national political philosophy.[3] He employed the means of radio to have his speeches broadcast throughout the country.

Some constant characteristics of Nyerere's speeches quickly emerged. *First*, he spoke of the essential equality of all citizens of the new state. This

---

1. Thomas Molony, *Nyerere: The Early Years* (Woodbridge UK: James Currey 2014) 68–69.

2. J. Roger Carter, (1995). "Preface " in Colin Legum and Geoffrey Mmari (eds.) *Mwalimu: The Influence of Nyerere* (London: Britain-Tanzania Society 1995) vii–viii.

3. Julius K. Nyerere, "Nyerere on Socialism:" Collections of Nyerere's Speeches (Dar es salaam Government of Tanzania 1979).

was an important message to people who had suffered deeply first from the violence of Arab slavers, and more recently from a form of colonialism that was evidently racist. *Second*, he acknowledged that recent history had led to a psychic-suffering in the culture that still endured. He stressed that the task of nation-building must above all avoid violence, noting how much violence had been experienced by the people in recent centuries. Apart from the long tradition of slavery, he recalled the *Maji-Maji War*, in which people of the region had fought against Germans, and which had claimed 75,000 lives.[4] He also noted that more recent struggles against British colonialists had included violence.[5]

Third, Nyerere noted that threats of division in the new state came from various sources. He acknowledged that his country shared with other African countries the threat of ethnocentrism. However, he also noted that his region was even more vulnerable than most to religious tension. This was due to the presence of Muslims, who formed a significant proportion of the population, while Christians and those who continued to practice traditional religions tended to form an opposing block. This situation was compounded by the fact that, off the shore of Tanganyika lay the large island, Zanzibar. This island had a complicated history, having been the center of regional slave trade and witnessing class-conflict between an Arab ruling elite and a majority population of African descent.[6] These two entities only united, under the leadership of Nyerere in 1964.[7] *Fourth*, with such challenges to unity being evident, Nyerere placed great stress on promoting a national political philosophy of *Ujamaa* (togetherness) and *Undugu* (brotherhood). *Fifth*, as a means of creating national unity, Nyerere created a political party, TANU, which he called a "national movement" and in which he tried to include representatives of different enthic communities and religions. TANU established a one-party state, with Nyerere explaining that a country as new to both modernization and to statehood needed this structure to promote national development.

Sixth, from an early stage, Nyerere acknowledged that a one-party state lent itself to political corruption. He tried to oppose this in the usual way of

4. Bees, (1967) "The Organisation of Maji-Maji Rebellion" In *Journal of African History* vol. 8 No. 3, 495–512.

5. Redmond, "Maji Maji in Ungoni: A reappraisal of Existing Historiography," in *International Journal of African Historical Studies* vol. 8 No. 3, (1975), 407–424.

6. Schacht, "Notes on Islam in East Africa," in *Studia Islamica* No. 23 (1965), 91–136.

7. Bates, "Tanganyika: the Development of trust Territory" in *International Organization* vol. 9 No. 1 (1955), 32–51.

promulgating anti-corruption laws, investigating, and dismissing offending politicians. However, he also noted that the poverty of the national education system inevitably resulted in poorly educated politicians who were more susceptible to corruption. This was one reason why a central part of his message was the importance of education.

Seventh, the call for a universal primary education became a hallmark of Nyerere's thinking. He stressed the need for modernization and the practical purpose of education for members of the traditional cultures of Tanzania:

> The first job of education is to give us the ability to reject bad houses, bad *jembes*, and preventable diseases; it must make us recognize that we have the ability to attain better houses, better tools and better health . . . how to bring about improvement in their lives, . . . that dirty water makes their children ill, and that they can avoid such sickness by working together to bring clean water in their village, or even just by boiling water before drinking.[8]

Nyerere hoped that building a strong system of universal primary education would provide the basis for developments at secondary and tertiary educational levels. He became well-known for his saying: *elimu haina mwisho* (education has no end)[9] and people began to give him the honorary title, *Mwalimu* (teacher.)

Eighth, much of Nyerere's reflection on the need for education took on a dimension of psychological commentary. He spoke often of the need for education to restore self-confidence in Tanzanians who had both experienced violence and who had even internalized the racist criticisms of colonialists. Here he spoke of the need to overcome the "African weakness" which tended to be typical of his people. He hoped that his political philosophy—as well as practical initiatives in education and economics—would help to heal this weakness. To illustrate what he meant by African weakness, he described what he had witnessed in the U.S.A. during visits he had made there. He suggested that African Americans carried the psychic wounds of their past as slaves, internalizing racist attitudes and experiencing self-hatred. He offered an example from mixed-race children:

> Many Africans were sent to America in millions of numbers. Millions died in the Atlantic, and millions died during the wars to

8. E. Lema, (et al), *Nyerere on Education, Collections of Nyerere's Speeches Volume 1* (Dar es salaam, Government of Tanzania 2006), 86–87.

9. Nyerere, *Nyerere on Education*, vol. II, 86–97.

> capture them from the African soil; but the fact is that millions reached America. But even in a case where one is born of a European father and African mother, the mother (slave) and the child are despised because they have African blood. The two cannot be accepted in that society because they are Negroes. Even when the Negro is white in color they try to trace his [distant] origin that is Africa, and despise him accordingly. Because of this the Negroes refuse to be called Africans. They do not want to be reminded that they came from Africa, let alone being called Negroes or Africans because to be called African means you have consented to be despised. To be called an African or Negro is a reason for being denied one's rights and equality. To be reminded of Africa is a dirty thing. You are being reminded of poverty, stupidity, and weakness. Africans have nothing.[10]

Ninth, as previously mentioned, since his days as a student, a core conviction of Nyerere had been that a capitalist economic system was not best suited to the Tanzanian people. He hoped for an economic system that combined an African approach to communitarianism with aspects of capitalist efficiency. He summarized his position:

> By the use of the word "*Ujamaa*," therefore, we state that for us socialism involves building on the foundations of our past, and building also to our own design. We are not importing a foreign ideology into Tanzania and trying to smother our distinct social patterns with it. We are deliberately deciding to grow, as a society, out of our own roots, but in a particular direction and towards a particular kind of objective. We are doing this by emphasizing certain characteristics of our traditional organization, and extending them so that they can embrace the possibilities of modern technology and enable us to meet the challenge of life in the twentieth century world.[11]

The political structure of the *Ujamaa* system began with a political position, the *Balozi wa Nyumba Kumikumi* (the head of each ten-houses).[12]

---

10. Lema, *Nyerere on Education/Nyerere Kuhusu Elimu*, Vol. II, 77–81.

11. Nyerere, *Nyerere on Socialism*, 28.

12. Stanley Dryden, *Local Administration in Tanzania* (Dar Es Salaam: East African Publishing House, 1968), 1.

That meant that there were representatives of the people from the most basic level, and it was on the basis of these figures that the system built up higher levels of governing responsibility. Nyerere also redrew internal political boundaries within the country. The Europeans had divided the African continent to settle their competitive colonial tensions, without considering the long term consequences for the African people. What resulted, within colonial states as well as between them, were conflicts that grew from the essential irrationality of these divisions. Nyerere sought to correct this tendency by reorganizing Tanzanian regions according to the natural division of the already existing tribal land, respecting the authority and ancestral rights. The criteria for these political sub-divisions were: *name, land, and language*.[13]

Beyond this issue of respecting customary land ownership and laws, there remained, in fact, a good deal of land that was left to the supervision of local government authorities as common land (*Mali ya Serikali.*) This land was considered appropriate for economic development, providing a basis for an agriculture-based industrialization. Here the socialist principles of Nyerere came in, as such initiatives were owned and controlled by local authorities. Nyerere did not encourage private ownership of small entrepreneurial enterprises, nor did he encourage a free market in all goods and services at national level.

Evaluating a Political Career

In addition to listing these eight characteristics of the political philosophy and action of Nyerere, it is necessary to evaluate his effectiveness. As the decades of his leadership progressed, Nyerere's policies met partly with success and partly with failure. He retained a high degree of credibility as a leader of integrity. Also, without doubt, he created one of the most united and least violent societies in Africa. However, he also experienced some major setbacks. To a considerable degree, these setbacks were caused by factors beyond his control: the Cold War and the struggle against apartheid in South Africa.

Regarding the Cold War, during the 1960s and 1970s, the monetary donor countries of the Global North insisted that countries of the Global South identify clearly with one or other side of a seemingly bipolar world. Nyerere by no means identified with the communism of the Soviet Union

13. Dryden, *Local Administration in Tanzania*, 1–3.

or China, but the countries of the West believed that he was leading a socialist country which must necessarily be allied with the Soviet bloc. These donor countries largely refused him the kind of financial aid they bestowed on neighbors, such as Kenya. Nyerere was obliged to identify publicly with countries of the communist block, which resulted in many problems. Similarly, his years of governance largely coincided with the struggle against apartheid rule by the majority African population in nearby South Africa and Rhodesia. Nyerere considered it the moral duty of Tanzania to support these liberation struggles, and he did so at considerable cost to the national economy.

However, not all Nyerere's failures can be attributed to external causes. With the passing of the years, it became obvious that his approach to communitarian economics—with a strong role played by local government and the state—produced major inefficiencies. Tanzania remained an impoverished country during the 1970s and 1980s, when a number of neighbor nation-states experienced economic growth (if not always political stability). Nevertheless, the sincerity of Nyerere's political vision was demonstrated when, in 1984, he stood down as President and allowed the election of a successor, the Muslim Ali Hassan Myinyi, who would remain in office for the next ten years. He remained active in politics as a chairman of the governing political party. By 1994, he accepted that it was time to introduce a multi-party political system. He believed that much had been achieved in the realm of national unity (and, to a considerable extent, in primary education) and that it should now be possible for the spirit of *Ujamaa* and *Undugu* in political culture to prevail in a context of such democracy.

Relating Doran to Nyerere

In terms of a vocabulary coined by Bernard Lonergan, Nyerere was a proponent of a move towards "self-appropriation for social transformation." Lonergan already gives us an account of both aspects of this duality. At the level of self-appropriation, he describes a threefold conversion—religious, moral, and intellectual. At the level of social transformation, he explains how these conversions enable societies to "intelligently direct history" conducting redemptive efforts to reverse decline and promote progress. To this set of philosophical and theological foundations, Doran adds that there must be too, the "affective and psychic conversion." He makes it clear that such an expansion of Lonergan's notion of self-appropriation has consequences for one's commitment to redemption in history:

> Psychic conversion is thus foundational for the categories of theology of history, precisely because the psyche, and even more radically the neural demand functions that reach their higher integration in consciousness psychic representation, in image and feeling constitute the source or principle of limitations in the three dialectics of community, the subject and culture.[14]

It is a central point of this present reflection, that the expansion that Doran adds to Lonergan is of particular value to understanding the dialectics of African history. Similarly, one can recognize how many aspects of the thought of Nyerere are compatible with the notion of the redemption of history outlined by Doran.

As mentioned above, Nyerere spoke often of how Africa had been the victim of many forces of decline, producing what he called, "African weakness." Similarly, he spoke of how Africans had a communitarian approach to culture—a sense of solidarity with each other—which must be a central resource in any effort to overcome the victimhood of their past. This was the heart of Nyerere's philosophy of *Ujamma* and *Undugu*. While Nyerere was determined to establish a secular state in which Muslims, Christians, and believers in traditional religion would be equally at home, he was himself a man of faith and convinced that religious motivation could contribute positively to national unity and development. Consequently, he would have been in agreement with the following theological statement offered by Doran:

> Through intellectual and psychic conversions a solidarity base is established for the derivation of many of the categories of systematic theology that would proceed with the aid of an understanding of history; for history is the process constituted by more or less integral or distorted dialectics of the community, subjects, and culture, and the opposite poles of each of these dialectics, in one way or another, are a function, respectively, of the psyche and of intentionality.[15]

For Doran, the notion of national development is intimately related to the process of promoting the integral dialectic of community, subjects, and culture. Next, Doran's analysis of victimization and imperialism has

---

14. Doran, *Theology and the Dialectics of History* (Toronto: University of Toronto Press, 1990), 443.

15. Doran, *Theology and the Dialectics of History*, 443.

a particular relevance to Africa. One of the most original aspects of the political philosophy of Nyerere was his reference to "African weakness," and how his principles of *Ujamaa* and *Undugu* were efforts to redress this problem. Doran's analysis helps to offer an explanation of the phenomenon of "African weakness" and of what restoring national development to a line of authentic progress might mean in this context. Doran first explains victimization in terms of the individual subject. Subsequently, he shifts to the social and cultural realm and describes imperialism as causing the victimization of whole peoples.

According to Doran, religious conversion and the subsequent process of healing of subjectivity has a great deal to do with the psyche. In this way, he expands considerably on what Lonergan has to say about "development from above." In exploring this insight, he introduces a notion of the "victimization" of the psyche, which is close to the notion of negative, or pathological complexes of Carl Jung. Doran reminds us that the psychic censor should normally play a positive role in consciousness, aiding suitable images to arrive in consciousness and further supporting the workings of the pure desire to know and authentic self-transcendence. However, he acknowledges that it is all too common that the psyche of many people exists in a state of what he calls "victimization." He insists that, to differing degrees, virtually all individuals carry some degree of victimization. He also insists that "psychic spontaneity as such is not morally responsible for its own disorder."[16]

Doran therefore suggests that, in spite of the *unfreedom* involved, it is possible for individuals to employ their intentional self-transcendence, such as it is, to recognize that "something is wrong" and to seek help. On this issue, he praises a certain approach to psychotherapy:

> First, one can recognize that the complex is a victim . . . next, one can adopt an attitude of compassion in its regard. And finally, one can allow there to emerge from the recognition and the compassion and willingness to cooperate with whatever redemptive forces are available to heal the disorder of darkness and to transform the contorted energies.[17]

However, Doran adds that, consistently, questions of *moral impotence* afflict even those efforts to find healing through these psychotherapeutic means.

16. Doran, *Theology and the Dialectics of History*, 232.

17. Doran, *Theology and the Dialectics of History*, 239.

He suggests that a vicious circle easily emerges between "the willingness to negotiate emotional darkness," and the fact that we will need to employ resources that are being blocked by this emotional darkness if we are ever to gain insight into it. He concludes that, easily, "the power of the complex negates the possibility of self-transcendent behavior."[18]

It is over and against this moral impotence that Doran begins to explain the healing influence of religious conversion. Echoing Lonergan's explanations in *Insight* of the need for a supernatural solution to the problem of evil, he asserts: "The freedom to deal compassionately with our own darkness must be given to us. We cannot find that freedom in the creative vector of our own consciousness." He then goes through some pains to explain the details of this healing process which functions "by moving from above downwards in consciousness."[19]

Doran introduces his account of *God's grace* by describing how the love of a fellow human being can produce healing by helping victimized individuals to address their emotional darkness with compassion. He suggests that the people with victimized psyches put up any number of resistances to believing that the love of another is sincere; he adds that, often, what finally convinces such people is when one who loves them is prepared to enter into the "private hell"[20] of their suffering and to suffer with them: "Healing will frequently be mediated precisely in and through the suffering of the lover due to the darkness of the beloved ."[21] After first describing such love in terms of human interaction, he insists that, ultimately, love like this is "beyond human capacity."[22] Consequently, he claims that even if immediately some human beings experience another human being as healing them, it does not require a lot of investigating for those with eyes to see to find that, in fact, God's grace has usually been at work in the life of that other human being.

On this matter, Doran suggests that the symbol *par excellence* of a readiness to suffer for others is the cross of Jesus Christ and that, consequently,

18. Doran, *Theology and the Dialectics of History*, 241.

19. Doran, *Theology and the Dialectics of History*, 241–2.

20. Doran states: "John Dunne has distinguished two types of human suffering. There is the hell of the night of private suffering, the suffering of isolation and victimization; and there is the night of the suffering of compassion and forgiveness. . . . The hell of the night of private suffering is not redemptive. The night of the suffering of compassion and forgiveness is redemptive" (Doran, *Theology and the Dialectics of History*, 114.)

21. Doran, *Theology and the Dialectics of History*, 243–244.

22. Doran, *Theology and the Dialectics of History*, 243–244.

"Christianity has some genuine universal significance."[23] He adds that a Christian will mostly find the ability to love selflessly if he or she relates personally and explicitly to the symbol of the cross and so to exercise a "participation in the specifically paschal dimension of 'what Jesus did.'"[24] He insists that it is only because of the divine intervention in history, completed in the self-sacrificing act of Jesus Christ (and the resurrection that followed it), that our damaged psyches find healing:

> Love alone releases one to be creatively self-transcendent . . . then life begins anew, everything changes, a new principle takes over . . . we are lifted above ourselves and carried along as parts within an ever more intimate and ever more liberating dynamic whole.[25]

Next, Doran elaborates on a point already made by Lonergan, that an initial experience of religious love is followed by the sometimes slow process of "development from above" where individuals begin to experience a release in their capacity for self-transcendence at each of the levels of consciousness, beginning with a transformation of the subject's ability to respond *affectively* to value. Like Lonergan, he suggests that this transformation occurs in an order that is "from above," starting with a transformation of religious values and following with transformations in personal, cultural, social, and vital values. He adds that this happens because "the divinely originated solution to the mystery of evil" now "penetrates to the sensitive psychic dimensions of the persons who allow it to become the principal feature of their own development."[26] He explains that this development in fact represents the phenomenon where individuals begin to share an attitude towards others that is in "fidelity to the just and mysterious law of the cross."[27]

On this issue, Doran suggests that the graced individuals begin to recognize how bad behavior of one kind or another on the part of other individuals is often the product, at least in part, of a prior victimization. Spontaneously, individuals who have been receiving healing desire to pass this healing onto others by returning good for evil. So it is that a process

23. Doran, *Theology and the Dialectics of History*, 108.

24. Doran, *Theology and the Dialectics of History*, 121–122.

25. Doran, *Theology and the Dialectics of History*, 41.

26. Doran, *Theology and the Dialectics of History*, 127–128.

27. Doran, *Theology and the Dialectics of History*, 124–125.

begins whereby the part of one's own healing process becomes the effort to assist in the healing of others. Doran suggests that one needs to take care to be realistic about just who can be helped and who cannot. However, he concludes:

> Perhaps one knows oneself to be healed only when precisely the same material dynamics of victimization that once drove one into the hell of private suffering now can be responded to with compassion and forgiveness.[28]

Having offered this profound analysis of both victimization and healing at the level of the subject, Doran now pursues the same question at the level of community and culture. Regarding the dialectic of community, he is able to draw on what Lonergan wrote in *Insight*:

> Social events can be traced to the two principles of human intersubjectivity and practical common sense. The two principles are linked, for the spontaneous, intersubjective individual strives to understand and wants to behave intelligently; and inversely, intelligence would have nothing to put in order were there not the desires and fears, labours and satisfactions, of individuals.[29]

However, when Doran turns to the question of culture, he does not find many resources in Lonergan to explain how this might also be dialectical. On this matter, he turns to the work of the political philosopher and historian of culture, Eric Voegelin. He notes that Voegelin describes three different "modes" or "realms" in which culture manifests itself: "the cosmological, the anthropological, and the soteriological dimensions of the truth about existence."[30] Doran postpones a discussion of the third of these and first explores the meaning of the first two notions. Concerning what Voegelin means by anthropological culture, Doran suggests that this is more or less the same as what Lonergan meant by it: the way in which ideas and values appeal to spirit. By contrast, Doran finds in Voegelin's account of cosmological culture something that is lacking in Lonergan. He insists that "the integrity or authenticity of culture lies in the integral unfolding of

---

28. Doran, *Theology and the Dialectics of History*, 245.

29. Bernard Lonergan, *Insight: A Study of Human Understanding*' edited by Frederick E. Crowe and Robert M. Doran, Volume 3, *Collected Works of Bernard Lonergan* (Toronto, University of Toronto Press, 1992), 218.

30. Doran, *Theology and the Dialectics of History*, 215.

cosmological and anthropological constitutive meaning."[31] Elaborating on the meaning of each of these poles, he states:

> Cosmological truth is the discovery that direction in the movement of life lies in a harmony between human decisions and actions, on the one hand, and the rhythms and processes of nature, on the other hand, that is, in a synchronicity between culture and nature. Anthropological truth establishes by a more specialized reflection that the ultimate measure of human integrity is a reality beyond the cosmos.[32]

Doran recounts how Voegelin explores the meaning of each of these poles by studying how they emerged in the history of civilizations. Voegelin points out that the place where anthropological notions of culture emerged most clearly was within ancient Greece. There it emerged from within a culture that was primarily characterized by a cosmological notion of culture that Voegelin suggests characterizes all primal societies. He notes that older cultural form resisted the challenge of anthropological ideas and values (referring to the death of Socrates) and further notes, with regret, that when anthropological notions of culture began to win approval within Greek and Roman culture it tended to reject and played down cosmological values (pointing out how in ancient Greece the "philosophers" were considered opposed to the "poets"). Doran suggests that this rejection identified by Voegelin constituted a tilting of the dialectic of culture in Western history toward a dialectic of contradictories, asserting: "An exclusively anthropological determination of culture is productive of that distortion of the dialectic of culture that is internally constitutive of modern imperialism."[33] Doran adds that, in both Marxism and capitalism resemble each other in the tendency to favor practical intelligence at the expense of culture:

> The exigencies of intersubjective living are subordinated in both systems to the policies and planning of the social engineers and managers. Whether the bureaucracies be capitalist or socialist, the structure of the distortions and displacements is the same. . . . The corrective lies in identifying the basic social dialectic, not within practicality, but between practicality and intersubjectivity.[34]

31. Doran, *Theology and the Dialectics of History*, 503.

32. Doran, *Theology and the Dialectics of History*, 216.

33. Doran, *Theology and the Dialectics of History*, 479.

34. Doran, *Theology and the Dialectics of History*, 413.

Doran points out that any effort to promote authentic progress in history will find itself confronted by a reality where culture and social structures have strong characteristics of decline. He explains decline in terms of dialectics of contradictories existing at the levels of community and culture. His attentiveness to the imperialistic tendencies of Western culture alert us to the fact that this dialectical imbalance often involves an over-emphasis on the pole of transcendence at the expense of respect for the pole of limitation. The value of this analysis for understanding the challenges faced by Nyerere is high.

Proposals for Integral Development: Nyerere and Doran Combined

We have explored Doran's notion of development in terms of integral dialectics of community, subject, and culture, and decline as often involving an over-emphasis of the transcendent pole of the dialectics, as well as the subordination of the dialectic of culture to a distorted notion of the dialectic of community. This allows us revisit some of Nyerere's political philosophy and to find remarkable convergences. I now offer a set of principles that employ Doran's thought and operate in the spirit of Nyerere. They outline principles that need to be recalled by wise political leadership and point out the role the Church can play in acting as a catalyst for the redemption of history of Tanzania.

First, concern for national development in a country like Tanzania, requires that one pays careful attention to questions of realms and stages of meaning. As Lonergan explains:

> In the first stage conscious and intentional operations follow the mode of common sense. In a second stage besides the mode of common sense there is also the mode of theory, where the theory is controlled by a logic. In a third stage the modes of common sense and theory remain, science asserts its autonomy from philosophy, and there occur philosophies that leave theory to science and take their stand on interiority.[35]

Doran has something significant to add to this analysis of the third stage of meaning. It must involve a promoting of integral dialectics at the levels

35. Bernard Lonergan, *Method in Theology*, *Collected Works of Bernard Lonergan*, edited by Robert M. Doran and John D. Dadosky, Volume 14, (Toronto: University of Toronto Press, 2017 [original edition 1972]), 82.

of community, subject, and culture. How does one apply this to Tanzania? One should recall that Nyerere recognized that Tanzania needed to modernize. High as his respect was for traditional African culture, he was aware of the value of developing a capacity for the self-transcending exercise of spirit of practical intelligence, and of an anthropological notion of culture.

> The traditional order is dying; the question which has yet to be answered is what will be built on our past and, in consequence, what kind of society will eventually replace the traditional one. Choices which involve clashes of principles must therefore be answered in the light of the kind of society we want to create, for our priorities now affect the attitudes and institutions of the future.[36]

Here one recalls that the kind of education so energetically proposed by Nyerere was primarily the kind of education known in Western culture, with its full emphasis on mathematics, science, and so forth.

Second, one must recognize the particular profile of decline in African culture and what damage was done by the way in which the second stage of meaning was introduced to these primal societies. Modernity was introduced in a violent and racist manner, at first by Arab slave traders, and then by European imperialists. Here the account of "African weakness" conveys impressively the analysis that Doran offers of victimization and imperialism. In light of Nyerere's thought, we might add that attempts to propose the entry into the third stage of meaning for Tanzanians, without adding psychic conversion to intellectual conversion, risks failing to recognize the wounds produced in the African psyche and offering an analysis of the situation that over-emphasizes the transcendent pole of the dialectics of community, subject, and culture. This runs the danger of not speaking to the reality of Tanzanian culture and repeating at a level of academic understanding the damaging oversights of imperialism.

Third, such analysis should not romanticize an African past and should state clearly the need for progress in Tanzanian community and cultural dialectics. It is clear that African cultures often remained in a first stage of meaning while others spent centuries struggling with the consequences of living in the second stage of meaning. Africans want to catch up with the benefits of modernity, increasing their capacity to operate at the theoretic realm of meaning. They wish to exercise a sophisticated practical intelligence, as well as respecting intersubjective bonds. They also wish to

36. Nyerere, *Nyerere on Socialism*, 8–9.

recognize and adhere to anthropological-cultural values, as well as respecting cosmological values. The dilemma for Africa today is that these goals involve a complexity that needs to be met by entering into a third stage of meaning. In some respects, then, citizens of countries like Tanzania need to leap from a first stage of meaning to a third stage of meaning.

Fourth, the exigence of progress requires an exercise of moral responsibility on the part of Africans, something that is often culpably absent. Nyerere's analysis of "African weakness" by no means led him to think that Tanzanians were always merely victims and not responsible for problems that they had created for themselves. At times he could be merciless in his criticism of his fellow Africans. One of his favorite targets was the type of national leader who had emerged from pre-independence nationalist movements—as he had done—and who abandoned the people who had supported him as soon as he gained the reins of power. He spoke of how such leaders sought only to substitute the oppression of colonial leaders with their own:

> hence corrupting, the upper reaches of the administrative structures, while allowing the mass base of their movements to wither and decline to the point that they can only be used to put on ritualistic demonstrations at times of 'elections' or when foreign visitors needed to be impressed.[37]

Similarly, Nyerere by no means let his lesser-educated and less powerful listeners be blameless. He regularly rallied against a litany of social diseases: *rushwa, umasikini, udini, ukabira, na unyonge* (corruption, poverty, religionism, tribalism or familism and "African weakness.")[38] Nor did he always criticize the foreigner. He noted that, on occasion, generous and sincere efforts by donor countries could be misused by locals: "The mindset of the people of Tanzania and their leaders has succumbed to donor dependency and has resulted in an erosion of initiative and lack of ownership of the development agenda."[39]

Fifth, integral development in Africa needs to be guided by a notion of cosmopolis. This insight grasps what Doran describes as the priority of the cultural superstructure (the dialectic of culture) over the infrastructure of social structures (the dialectic of community.)

37. Swerdlow, (ed.), "The Political Context of National Development" an essay in *Development Administration Concepts and Problems* (Syracuse 1963.)

38. Nyerere, *Nyerere on Socialism/Uhuru na Ujamaa*, 44, 49–52.

39. Planning Commission: *The Tanzania Development Vision 2025*, 8.

Lonergan's account of cosmopolis appears first in Chapter 7 of *Insight* and describes how a cultural elite can help a society to move to the third stage of meaning and to do so with as little decline as possible:

> For man can discover emergent probability; he can work out the manner in which prior insights and decisions determine the possibilities and probabilities of later insights and decisions; he can guide his present decisions in the light of their influence on future insights and decisions; finally, this control of the emergent probability of the future can be exercised not only by the individual in choosing his career and in forming his character, not only by adults in educating the younger generation, but also by mankind in its consciousness of its responsibility to the future of mankind. Just as technical, economic, and practical development gives man a dominion over nature, so also the advance of knowledge creates and demands a human contribution to the control of human history.[40]

African societies that struggle to enter the stage of meaning characterized by theoretic differentiation of consciousness would do well to listen to Lonergan's criticism of general bias:

> But if the need of some cosmopolis makes manifest the inadequacy of common sense to deal with the issue, on a deeper level it makes manifest the inadequacy of man. For the possibility of a cosmopolis is conditioned by the possibility of a critical human science, and a critical human science is conditioned by the possibility of a correct and acceptable philosophy.[41]

As with other aspects of Lonergan's thought, the addition of a notion of psychic conversion to intellectual conversion expands upon the responsibilities of those who participate in the cosmopolitan community. These must understand the dialectic of culture as being comprised of a cosmological as well as an anthropological approach. They must never compound "African weakness" by exhibiting disrespect for the cosmological pole of culture. At the same time, they must frankly acknowledge that Africans experience a challenge of developing their notion of and loyalty to the anthropological values that are included in a modern way of life.

40. Lonergan, *Insight*, 252–253.

41. Lonergan, *Insight*, 712.

Sixth, our notion of cosmopolis must undergo "a religious and theological transformation."[42] Lonergan implicitly takes this step in Chapter 20 of *Insight*, and it remained for Doran to make this insight explicit and to deepen it. Reflecting on this point, we move beyond a discussion of the political philosophy of Nyerere. Rather, our reflection becomes explicitly theological and regards the role that Christianity can play in trying to promote the reversing of decline and the promoting of progress in society. Still, even on matters such as these, the legacy of Nyerere can help give flesh to our notion of the meaning of the redemption of history in East Africa.

Regarding the theological nature of cosmopolis, Doran draws on an article by Lonergan, "Praxis and Theology." There Lonergan criticizes notions of praxis that are rooted in Hegel and Marx that focus only on action to transform social structures. By contrast, Lonergan states that the most important form of praxis is to work on one's own character and to undergo the three conversions, religious, moral and intellectual. He insists that this can help one engage in the cosmopolitan task of redeeming history. Doran explains that this approach reverses the Marxist notion that changing the infrastructure (dialectic of community) holds priority over changing the superstructure (dialectic of culture.) Rather, Doran asserts:

> The praxis of theology, I have concluded, is proximately the transformation of culture, of constitutive meaning, as the condition of the possibility of the transformation of polities, economies, technological structures, and intersubjective communities.[43]

This insight is consistent with the ceaseless practices of Nyerere to offer speeches, on radio and otherwise, about *Ujamaa* and *Undugu*. He was trying to influence the cultural superstructure, "creating this new nation from old culture."[44]

Seventh, this theological notion of cosmopolis extends to employing notion of praxis as including the "Law of the Cross," considering the Church as the "suffering servant of Yahweh," and looking toward the establishment of a "world-cultural community." Space does not allow an exploration of Doran's understanding of these terms, nor how they are compatible with the thought of Nyerere. A few of excerpts from Doran's work must suffice for now. He states, "intellectual ministry, like all other ecclesial

42. Doran, *Theology and the Dialectics of History*, 356.

43. Doran, *Theology and the Dialectics of History*, 12.

44. Nyerere, Nyerere *and Socialism*, 3.

ministries, will be constituted by the Law of the Cross." He explains that all such ministry seeks to mediate the good news of the divine solution to the problem of evil to the world and will often meet with misunderstanding and rejection.[45] Similarly, he speaks of how cosmopolis today needs to work toward a "world-cultural community" that entails, "the building of a crosscultural communitarian alternative" to the present world situation which is characterized by a "post-historical humanity" that seeks to "lock our psyches and imaginations and questioning spirit into ever more rigid straitjackets."[46] He adds,

> It is the community of the church as a whole that is to evoke a world-cultural community, by its fidelity to the integral scale of values and its incarnate witness to the mission of the suffering and risen servant of God under the just and mysterious law of the cross.[47]

Finally, Doran insists, in a manner similar to Lonergan, that any discussion of the redemption of history must be rooted in the conversion of individuals:

> The challenge of generating and sustaining crosscultural understanding can be met only by differentiating the crosscultural constituents of personal integrity as these are specified in explanatory fashion in science of interiority. And the freedom to live on the basis of such crosscultural authenticity will depend on an articulated partnership with God of all people and nations acting to renew the face of the earth.[48]

Conclusion

The title of this article speaks of the "legacy of Nyerere" and promised to employ the thought of Doran in analyzing this. In what unfolded, we explained how this legacy has at least two dimensions, political and theological. At the political level, Nyerere continues to be invoked in Tanzania as a founder of a national political philosophy. Our conclusion is that this is rich resource for political culture in Tanzania. Nevertheless, questions

---

45. Doran, *Theology and* the *Dialectics of History*, 356–7.

46. Doran, *Theology and the Dialectics of History*, 37.

47. Doran, *Theology and the Dialectics of History*, 418.

48. Doran, *Theology and the Dialectics of History*, 496.

remain regarding just how this philosophy can be translated into concrete decision-making today. Similarly, it is important not to idealize this first President of Tanzania nor to ignore the failures that also characterized his governance. For example, his failures in the realm of economic policies can raise questions about just how clear-minded he was on the appropriate balance to strike between practical intelligence and intersubjectivity in the dialectic of community. Nevertheless, one can recognize that many aspects of his teaching and political actions were impressive efforts at promoting the integral dialectics of community, subject, and culture.

Employing Doran's thought to study Nyerere inevitably draws us to some theological reflections that cannot be limited to reflecting on one political leader or how a political philosophy can best serve the interests of a single nation. Indeed, the thoughts of Nyerere himself at times seem to stretch beyond what is practical in the political realm and take on a theological significance. Engaging with the thought of Nyerere can help theological reflection on the ideal of cosmopolis in culture as well the nature of what a world-cultural community might mean. I conclude with a citation from Nyerere that indicates why his is a thought that is destined to maintain significant influence.

> By the use of the word "*Ujamaa*," therefore, we state that for us socialism involves building on the foundations of our past, and building also to our own design. . . . We are deliberately deciding to grow, as a society, out of our own roots, but in a particular direction and towards a particular kind of objective. We are doing this by emphasizing certain characteristics of our traditional organization, and extending them so that they can embrace the possibilities of modern technology and enable us to meet the challenge of life in the twentieth century world . . . There is, in fact, no substitute for the individual moral courage of men and women; everything ultimately depends upon the determination of the people to be judges over those to whom they have entrusted positions of responsibility and leadership.

CHAPTER TWENTY

JOHN COURTNEY MURRAY AND THE SITUATION AS SOURCE OF THEOLOGY

John P. Cush

PONTIFICAL NORTH AMERICAN COLLEGE (VATICAN CITY)

Robert Doran, in his text, *What is Systematic Theology?* (2007) makes the following statement:

> I do not believe that *Method in Theology* provides explicit materials for the operations, methodological understanding of the kind of development that John Courtney Murray achieved in the church's teaching on religious liberty. Murray was working as a systematic theologian in dialogue with his culture, and his work entailed a mutual self-mediation between that religiously pluralistic cultural matrix and the significance and role of his own religious community within that matrix. His work involved more than the operations that Lonergan would include in the functional specialty 'communications.' For out of that dialogue he developed a new doctrine regarding religious liberty, and he certainly could be called systematic. His new doctrine called for a change in the church's official teaching. After some severe opposition from church authorities, his doctrine became, at the Second Vatican Council, the official teaching of the church . . . In all of this, I suggest, he was doing the work of the systematic theologian. But I do not believe that this particular type of set of operations is adequately accounted for or at least sufficiently stressed in Lonergan's work.[1]

1. Robert Doran, *What is Systematic Theology?*, Toronto: University of Toronto Press, 2006, 58. (Hereafter abbreviated as *WST?*)

This essay seeks to explore Doran's contention, namely that one can greater understand the achievement of John Courtney Murray and his tremendous theological triumph, not only through Lonergan's functional specialties, which Lonergan discusses in *Method in Theology*[2] but also through Doran's completion of Lonergan's theory of conversion: intellectual, moral, and spiritual. Doran, in his text, *Theology and the Dialectics of History* (1990)[3] adds an additional, necessary conversion: one that is psychic.[4] This additional analysis of Murray through not only the perspective of Lonergan, but also the lens of Doran, can greatly aid in the appreciation of Murray's theology, most particularly in Doran's understanding of "Situation as Source of Theology." Doran states: "Situations are constituted by meaning and a change in constitutive meaning is in the long run the most effective form of praxis."[5] The dialectics of culture and community can only be transformed by the communication of values and meanings that reflect soteriological realities and help the transformation of the situation to "more resembling the reign of God on Earth."[6]

John Courtney Murray: Theologian in Context

To begin, we need to first ask who was John Courtney Murray and also strive to understand the context in which he lived. Born in New York City on September 12, 1904 to immigrant parents, Murray's upbringing was rather similar to many other young people at the turn of the Twentieth Century. Murray grew up with a sense of America as a "land of the free and the home of the brave." America was a place with a special dignity and a special role to play in the world, to be a beacon of freedom, hope, and opportunity to the entire world. This concept would later be described by Murray as "the American Proposition."[7]

---

2. Bernard J. F. Lonergan, *Method in Theology*, Collected Works of Bernard Lonergan vol. 14, ed. Robert M. Doran and John Dadosky. Toronto: University of Toronto Press, 2017.

3. Robert Doran, *Theology and the Dialectics of History*, Toronto: University of Toronto Press, 1990. (Hereafter abbreviated as *TDH*.)

4. See *Psychic Conversion and Theological Foundations*, Milwaukee: Marquette University Press, Second Edition, 2004 and Robert M. Doran, *Subject and Psyche: Ricoeur, Jung, and the Search for Foundations*, Lanham, MD: University of America Press, 1980.

5. Doran, *TDH*, 4.

6. Doran, *TDH*, 12. Doran adds in further explanation of "situation as source of theology" and his difference in understanding of it from Lonergan: "The most obvious of these emphases lies in the assertion that the situation which a theology addresses is as much a course of theology as are the data provided by the Christian tradition" (Doran, *TDH*, 8).

7. Murray writes: "It is classic American doctrine, immortally asserted by Abraham Lincoln, that the new nation which our Fathers brought forth on this continent was dedicated to

Murray entered into formation with the New York Province of the Society of Jesus and was ordained a priest on June 25, 1933.[8] In the course of these years, Murray's superiors had marked him out for his academic prowess. He was sent for further studies at the Pontifical Gregorian University in Rome, which culminated in his doctorate in sacred theology."[9]

After the completion of his doctorate, Murray was assigned to the role of theology professor at his alma mater, Woodstock College[10] and as a writer, and later, editor-in-chief, of *Theological Studies*.[11] He was also invited to form part of the editorial board of the new monthly Catholic news journal, *America*. Murray died in 1967, at the relatively young age of 63, from a heart attack after a visit with his sister in Queens, New York. He had been in poor health, having suffered two previous heart attacks in 1964 and a collapsed lung during the final session of the Second Vatican Council.[12]

---

a 'proposition.' I take it that Lincoln used the word with conceptual propriety. In philosophy a proposition is the statement of a truth to be demonstrated. In mathematics a proposition is at times the statement of an operation to be performed. Our Fathers dedicated the nation to a proposition in both of these senses. The American Proposition is at once doctrinal and practical, a theorem and a problem. It is an affirmation and also an intention. It presents itself as a coherent structure of thought that lays claim to intellectual assent; it also presents itself as an organized political project that aims at historical success. Our Fathers asserted it and most ably argued it; they also undertook to "work it out," and they signally succeeded. Neither as a doctrine nor as a project is the American Proposition a finished thing. Its demonstration is never done once for all; and the Proposition itself requires development on penalty of decadence." John Courtney Murray, *We Hold These Truths: Catholic Reflections on the American Proposition*, Forward by Walter Burghardt and Critical Introduction by Peter Lawler, A Sheed and Ward Classic, Lanham, MD: Rowman & Littlefield Publishers, 1960, 2005, xi (1960c). Note that all articles written by Murray are compiled online by J. Leon Hooper for the Woodstock Theological Library at http://www.library.georgetown.edu/woodstock/Murray. For easier access, articles are listed in the order of publication by year and with an assigned number from Hooper, e.g. (1966e). I will list all references to Murray's works with this designation.

8. Donald E. Pelotte, *John Courtney Murray: Theologian in Conflict*, New York/Ramsey, NJ/Toronto: Paulist Press, 1975–1976, 3.

9. Ibid., 21, footnote 1. Pelotte notes that there was an excerpt of Murray's thesis found in "The Root of Faith: The Doctrine of M. J. Scheeben," *Theological Studies* IX (March 1948), 20–46. (Theological Studies is hereafter abbreviated as *TS*).

10. Dennis P. McCann, "John Courtney Murray (1904–1967)" in *Makers of Christian Theology in America*. 512–517, edited by Mark G. Toulouse and James O. Duke. Nashville: Abingdon Press, 1997 512.

11. Ibid., 513.

12. James Hennesey, "Murray, John Courtney (1904–1967)," in *The Modern Catholic Encyclopedia*, edited by Michael Glazier and Monica Hellwig, Collegeville, MN: Liturgical Press, A Michael Glazer Book, 1992, 591. Note that all future references to *The Modern Catholic Encyclopedia* will be abbreviated as *MCE*.

The Situation of Theology in the United States of America and in Europe at the Start of Murray's Writing

What was the situation of the times in which Murray found himself? To explain this, it is necessary to situate him in the theological and ecclesiastical climate of his time. Pope Leo XIII's 1899 encyclical, *Testem benevolentiae*,[13] was published as a warning against, among other things, "Americanism," which was perceived as being part of the Modernist movement. Americanism was ". . . a theology of history based upon the providential conditions of religious liberty and separation of Church and state which has allowed the Church to flourish in the United States, a Church destined to be the model for Catholicity in the modern world."[14]

With the beginnings of *ressourcement* in Catholic theology from European theologians, Catholic intellectual life began to flourish once again in the United States. Scholarly journals were founded during this time period that promoted the Catholic intellectual life in America. Two such magazines that offered Catholic dialogue with the culture at large were *America*, founded in 1909[15] and, in February 1940, the emergence of the combined academic journal of the Jesuit theological schools of the United States, *Theological Studies*.[16]

Interpreting Murray through Doran

Murray, in the course of his life, underwent a tremendous shift in his perceptions. For this reason, it is important to trace stages of development in his thought.[17] This analysis will employ both the second functional

13. Pope Leo XIII, *Testem Benevolentiae Nostrae*, Concerning New Opinions, Virtue, Nature and Grace, With Regard to Americanism, (January 22, 1899), *Acta Sanctae Sedis* 31: 470–479.

14. Christopher J. Kaufmann, "Americanism," *MCE*, Edited by Michael Glazier and Monika K. Hellwig, Dublin: Gill & Macmillan Ltd., 25–26.

15. Pelotte, 5–6. *America, A Catholic Review of the Week*, was founded in 1909 by the Jesuits of the United States and Canada (See Ciani, John L., "America," *MCE*, 32.)

16. Pelotte, 6.

17. I follow the thinking of Raymond Lafontaine for the spacing of the five periods. However, as I explain below, I explain these periods somewhat differently from Lafontaine, because I use the dialectical method of Doran and not only Lonergan. See Raymond Lafontaine, "Lonergan's Functional Specialties as a Model For Doctrinal Development," *Gregorianum* 89, no. 4 (2007): 780–805 and *The Development of A Moral Doctrine: Religious Liberty and Doctrinal Development in the Works of John Henry Newman and John Courtney Murray*, Excerpta ex Dissertatione ad Doctoratum in Facultate Theologiae Pontificae Universitatis Gregoriane, Romae, (2001).

specialty, interpretation, and the fourth functional specialty, dialectic. Lonergan describes the second functional specialty as offering an "interpretive hermeneutic" of an author. By contrast, he states that the fourth functional specialty performs an "evaluative hermeneutic."[18] An interpretive hermeneutic is used here in offering a chronological narrative of Murray's intellectual journey; however, the fourth functional specialty, dialectic, is already implemented with the fact that Murray's development is characterized in five stages, which implies an evaluation already in progress.

Stage 1 (1940–47) Murray Begins to Treat the Situation as a Source of Theology

This is the period in Murray's life when he identifies the importance of the question of religious freedom as a key question to be addressed in the U.S.A. and elsewhere. This was an impressive exercise in what Doran explains as treating the situation as a source of theology—and identifying a key issue that needed to be addressed theologically. However, at this stage, Murray had arrived recently from his doctoral studies in Rome where he had been formed in a normative notion of culture and a classicist notion of theology. He would make a series of efforts to address the question of religious freedom with the tools at his disposal, before, eventually, recognizing how inadequate they were for his task. Consequently, this stage is one of contrasts in Murray's life: he performs an impressive study of the situation as source of theology; and performs poorly in trying to articulate a systematic theology that would address them.

Much of Murray's opinion about the cultural situation in the USA in the 1940s is captured in an article, "Reversing the Secularist Drift."[19] This article was the fruit of the fact that, from the 1940s onwards, Murray's combination of responsibilities, both academic and journalistic, placed him in an ideal role to recognize what were major characteristics of the culture of the USA and what theological themes were relevant to a study of this situation. During these years Murray's conviction deepened to the point where he would declare: "the most deadly menace to our Christian and American way of living"[20] was not Communism, but secularism.

---

18. Lonergan, *Method in Theology*, 245.

19. Murray, "Reversing the Secularist Drift," *Thought* 24 (March, 1949): 36 (1949g).

20. Administrative Board of the National Catholic Welfare Conference, "The Catholic in Action," in *Catholic Action* XXX (December 1948), 3. See Pelotte, 20.

It is important to note that Murray portrays the U.S.A.'s Founding Fathers as wisdom figures and the secularist drift as representing a betrayal of their ideas. In "Reversing the Secular Drift," Murray suggests that current cultural leaders were doing an injustice to the "American Proposition," as represented by the Founding Fathers of the American Constitution, by not only denying the existence of God but also in rewriting an account of history of Western civilization to suggest that Christianity had not made an important contribution. Murray believes that this "drift" is caused by an atheism associated with the industrial revolution that consciously sets out to be "positive, organic, constructive." He believes that this new thinking succeeds in becoming "a humanism without God, supported by all the resources of science, and invested with messianic pretensions."[21]

In another series of articles, Murray reflects about the possibility of a coalition of religious interests in the U.S.A.—Catholics, Protestants, and Jews etc.—forming an alliance to oppose such secularism. Murray suggests that Catholics could do this without compromising what is particular about the truth-claims that are particular to their denomination of Christianity. He believed that this would be possible by employing natural law arguments. Writing just after the entry of the U.S.A. into World War II, Murray states that for the Catholic Church to refuse such intercredal cooperation would be a major mistake.[22]

At this juncture of his intellectual career, the notion of natural law from which Murray would draw was primarily that articulated by Jacques Maritain (1882–1973). Ultimately, Murray is caught in a theoretical dilemma. He cannot say that a state informed by Catholic values would not be superior to one based only on natural law without deeply offending Protestant sensibilities. Furthermore, he recognizes that in the religiously diverse United States, and given what is stated in the American Constitution, it would be impossible to conceive of the establishment of any one particular religion as the official religion of the state. Within a short time, Murray would recognize that he must abandon his entire method of approaching this question. In the meantime, one recognizes, still in his 1945 argument, a struggle to form conclusions that break free from the abstract universals of a neo-scholastic method of arguing.[23]

---

21. Ibid.

22. Murray, "Current Theology: Christian Co-operation" *TS* 3 (September 1942): 416 (1942b).

23. Murray, "Notes on the Theory of Religious Liberty," 16 (1945e).

Perhaps it was the reluctance of Murray to speak of the superiority of a Catholic social vision that provoked the opposition of some prominent Churchmen to the articles of Murray on religious freedom that were published in 1945. Joseph C. Fenton (1906–1969), editor of *The American Ecclesiastical Review*, offered explicit criticism of Murray and questioned his orthodoxy. Murray, for his part, in addition to feeling the unpleasantness of being caught up in a public controversy, experienced the frustration of sensing that the argument he had been making had been weak in the first place. He recognized that he had been struggling with how to handle the distinction between the individual and social nature of the human person. It began to occur to Murray that social factors are of their nature historical and contingent and that trying to address them with in terms of a scholastic notion of natural law that spoke of *necessary causes* was inevitably going to cause problems. He started reflecting on how to pay more respectful attention to contingent factors in history and to doctrinal development that occurs in the Church over time.[24]

Stage 2 (1948–1955): A Shift to a Historically Conscious Method—the Discovery of the First Phase of Theology

By 1948, Murray would publish an article in which he states: "The discussion of the church's power in the temporal order must proceed from an historical point of view. Nothing is more unhelpful than an abstract starting point."[25] In terms of a dialectical analysis based in the thought of Doran, one can state that it is at this point that Murray recognizes that, in order to adequately treat the situation as a source of theology, he is going to have to change his theological method. From this year until 1955, Murray produces a series of fourteen articles that, while continuing to reflect on the question of religious freedom, adopt an entirely different method.[26]

Murray's study begins with Pope Gelasius I's (d. November 19, 496) dispute with both the emperors Valentinian II and Anastasius I, who wished to exert more control over the Eastern Church. His "Two-sword theory" became the foundational opinion for Church-state relationships for centuries. Gelasius famously wrote in *Duo Sunt* ("On Temporal Power,"

24. Lafontaine, "Lonergan": 788–789.

25. Murray, "Government Repression of Heresy," *Proceedings* of the Third Annual Convention of the Catholic Theological Society of America, 1948: 33 (1948c).

26. Lafontaine, "Lonergan":787.

494). Here he stated: "There are two powers, august Emperor, by which this world is chiefly ruled, namely, the sacred authority of the priests and the royal power."[27] Both orders receive their authority from God. In the Gelasian view, the sacred and the secular must cooperate with each other and are in mutual interdependence with each other, "for it was only in the intermixture of spiritual values and temporal activities that the work of Christ on earth could be accomplished."[28] Murray described the Gelasian thesis as the "Magna Carta" of the Church's freedom and society's spiritual health.[29]

Next, Murray traces how this teaching fell into neglect in the Medieval period, culminating in the "exaggerated claim of the papal court for direct power over the temporal realm, a claim epitomized by Boniface VIII's encyclical *Unam Sanctam*."[30] The document states that the two swords, spiritual and temporal, are under the power of the Church: ". . . the former is to be administered for the Church but the latter by the Church; the former in the hands of the priest; the latter by the hands of kings and soldiers, but at the will and sufferance of the priest."[31] Murray explains this shift of perspective as resulting from the contingent fact that the Church was drawn into engaging with the political order because of the power-vacuum that occurred in the dark ages.

Murray states that, unwittingly, theologians began to make a doctrinal principle out of what was merely a contingent need. He suggested that the time had long since past when there was such immaturity in the political order that it needed such intervention by the Church. Murray argued that the Church of the twentieth century should return to something like the Gelasian understanding of Church-state relations, articulated so long before.

---

27. Gelasius I, "On Spiritual and Temporal Power," translated by J.H. Robinson, Readings in European History, Boston: Ginn, 1905, 72–73. http://legacy.fordham.edu/halsall/source/gelasius1.asp, accessed March 25, 2015.

28. Robert W. McElroy, *The Search for an American Public Theology: The Contribution of John Courtney Murray*, New York/Mahwah, NJ: Paulist Press, 1989, 21, citing Murray, "The Yale University Lectures," I, 12–15. McElroy notes: "Murray's interpretation of this key text relied heavily on the work of Robert and A.J. Carlyle in their *A History of Medieval Political Theory in the West*, Edinburgh: William Blackwood and Sons, 1930 and on R.H. Hull's *Medieval Theories of the Papacy*, London: Burns, Oates, and Westbourne, 1932," (187, footnote 31).

29. Murray stated; "In a true sense, the whole of Catholic theory and practice in the matter of Church-State relationships had taken the form of a speculative interpretation and practical application of this text." "Contemporary Orientations of Catholic Thought on Church and State in the Light of History," *Theological Studies* 10 (June 1949): 196, as quoted in McElroy, 21.

30. McElroy, 24.

31. Boniface VIII, *Unam Sanctam*, November 18, 1302, (The following English translation of 'Unam' is taken from a doctoral dissertation written in the Dept. of Philosophy at the Catholic University of America, and published by CUA Press in 1927, found online at http://legacy.fordham.edu/halsall/source/B8-unam.asp, accessed March 25, 2015.

Stage 3: (1955–62): Deepening Thinking on Social Ethics and Method—Murray's Years of Censure

The Development of Doctrine: Turning to Lonergan

In 1955, Murray's Jesuit superiors, alert to the sensibilities of the Holy Office, imposed an informal censorship on Murray. However, already from 1951 onwards, Murray had begun to receive criticisms for his position.[32] The details of Murray's censure have been much studied by other Church historians and theologians of history. Donald Pelotte places it within the context of an oppressive ecclesial atmosphere in this decade and in the fact that the teachings of Pius XII contained many ambiguities, which neither the Pope nor the Curia were prepared to acknowledge.[33] This censure would prove to be a very painful period in Murray's life. He was a loyal son of the Church, a loyal son of Ignatius, and to have that brought into question in any manner was extremely disconcerting for such a churchman as Murray really was. And yet, his own thoughts were evolving and growing.

For Murray, the terms of his censure in 1955 permitted him to deepen his thinking on a theological issue that might be considered more controversial: that of the development of doctrine. Murray explored these topics in the classroom, teaching Trinitarian theology to Jesuit scholastics.

It is difficult to trace the details of the influence of Lonergan on Murray. It is documented that the two were at least acquainted with each other during the 1930s when they overlapped as students at the Pontifical Gregorian University in Rome. In addition, with his editorship of *Theological Studies*, Murray would have had to approve of the publication of Lonergan's *Verbum* articles in that journal from the years 1946–1949.[34] However, it is most especially in the late 1950s and early 1960s that evidence emerges that Murray was appealing to Bernard Lonergan's epistemology and theological method in his own theology.[35] Further evidence suggests that 1959 was a turning point in Murray's use of Lonergan. In

32. Murray, "For the Freedom and Transcendence of the Church," *The American Ecclesiastical Review* 126 (January 1952): 32 (1952b).

33. Pelotte, 51.

34. Lonergan would eventually collect these articles in *Verbum: Word and Idea in Aquinas*, edited by David B. Burrell, University of Notre Dame Press: Notre Dame, Indiana, 1967.

35. J. Leon Hooper, *The Ethics of Discourse: The Social Philosophy of John Courtney Murray*, Washington, D.C.: Georgetown University Press, 1986, 124.

that year, he organized a meeting of Jesuit theologians at the Catholic Theological Society of America Convention with the specific topic discussed being both Lonergan's theology of the Trinity and Lonergan's recently published work, *Insight*.[36]

During his discussion of the Council of Nicea (325), collected later as *The Way to Nicea*,[37] Lonergan points out that once one accepts that Church councils can represent a process of stating "different expression of the same truth,"[38] the way is open to understand the notion of development of doctrine. Lonergan suggests that those who have undergone intellectual conversion, as proposed in *Insight*, recognize that, in addition to a theoretic differentiation of consciousness, individuals can attain a differentiation of consciousness based on interiority. He states that world-culture is undergoing just such a shift of basic horizon and that Catholic theology needs to be rearticulated in terms of this differentiation of consciousness in order to "raise to the level of its times."[39] Lonergan will come to suggest that the significance of Vatican II lies in just this point and Murray will come to share this opinion.

It seems that Murray engaged in active communication with Lonergan from 1959 onwards. In 1962, Lonergan sent him the draft of an article that would be published later, with the title "The Transition from a Classicist World-View to Historical Mindedness."[40] This title captures Lonergan's point about the need for a shift of horizon from one based on a theoretic differentiation of consciousness (classicism) to one based on an interior differentiation of consciousness (historical consciousness). The phrase will become central to Murray's understanding of the deeper significance of Vatican II.

---

36. Hooper, *Ethics*, (245, footnote 3) details a May 10, 1959 letter addressed to Frederick Crowe which gives the outline for the Jesuit theologian meeting, calling for a discussion of Lonergan's dispenses, "Divinarum processionum conceptionem analogicam evolvit Bernardus Lonergan, S.J. (Rome, 1957)" and "De constitutione Christo ontological et psychological (Rome, 1956)."

37. Lonergan, *The Way to Nicea: The Dialectical Development of Trinitarian Theology*, translated by Conn O'Donovan from the first part of *De Deo Trino*, Philadelphia: The Westminster Press, 1976.

38. Ibid.,10.

39. This phrase is taken from an early draft of a preface to *Insight*, see Frederick Crowe, *Lonergan*, London, Geoffrey Chapman: 1992, 30.

40. Hooper describes this communication between Murray and Lonergan (Hooper, *Ethics*, 125). See also, Lonergan, "The Transition from a Classicist World-View to Historical Mindedness" in *A Second Collection*, Toronto 1974, 5.

Stage 4: (1962–65): Vatican II: A Deepening Conversion to Historical Consciousness

Commentators are united in their opinion that Murray enjoyed remarkable success in influencing Vatican II, especially with regard to the Declaration on Religious Freedom: *Dignitatis Humanae* (hereafter abbreviated as *DH.*) As Robert Doran explains it, Murray began by considering the situation as a source of theology, proceeded to recognize that Catholic teaching was inadequate to address a key aspect of this situation, proposed a new theological doctrine and systematic theology to address this problem, and, eventually succeeded in having his theological doctrine elevated to the position of a church doctrine.[41] Doran's analysis helps to explain the statement by Murray himself: "The Declaration [on Religious Liberty] is a pastoral exercise in the development of doctrine."[42]

In a more general way, he interpreted the events of the Council in terms of Lonergan's epistemology. His work on DH involved many long hours of drafting and committee work. At times he experienced intense opposition from members of the Council minority. At one important moment, he wrote a letter to the bishops of the Council outlining the position of his opponents (the First View) and those who agreed with him (the Second View), he spoke how these two views were not reconcilable with each other and how the bishops would simply have to decide between them.

> This abortive dialogue seems to indicate where the real issue lies. The First and Second View do not confront each other as affirmation confronts negation. Their differences are at a deeper level indeed, at a level so deep that it would be difficult to go deeper. They represent *the contemporary clash between classicism and historical consciousness.*[43]

The bishops decided to vote in favor of the draft of *DH* proposed by Murray. Murray recognized the immense significance of this: "The Declaration [on Religious Liberty] is a pastoral exercise in the development of doctrine.[44]

41. Doran, *WST?*, 59.

42. Murray, "The Declaration on Religious Freedom" in *Concilium 5* (May 1966), 8. Cited in Lafontaine, "Lonergan": 796

43. Murray, "The Problem of Religious Freedom," in *Religious Liberty: Catholic Struggles with Pluralism*, 180. Westminster, MD: Newman Press. 1965 (1965h).

44. Murray, "The Declaration on Religious Freedom" in *Concilium 5* (May 1966), 8. Cited in Lafontaine, 796.

Lafontaine suggests that, at the most explicit level, Murray was involved in both the functional specialties of dialectic and doctrines during the debates at the Council. Regarding the former, Lafontaine praises the civility and clarity with which Murray engaged in debate. He contrasts this with Murray's performance in the early 1950s and states: "Murray's dialectical exercise is no longer an exercise in rhetoric or polemics."[45] Lafontaine notes that the role Murray played in the functional specialty of doctrines was to make it clear to the Council Fathers that it would be up to them to make a decision regarding developing church doctrine or not.[46]

Stage 5 (1966–67): Consolidation and New Departures

In analyzing Murray's short but creative output after the Council, Lafontaine explains that it had two main dimensions: a continuing effort to produce a rigorous systematic explanation of the doctrine of religious freedom and a developing interest in questions other than religious freedom. A Doran-based analysis can accept this analysis as helpful.

Regarding the first point, one notes that the situation that provoked Murray's continuing desire to deepen his systematic explanation of the doctrine on religious freedom was that he felt disappointed with the quality of the final draft of *DH*. In a sense, then, he continued the debates of Vatican II after the closure of the Council in an effort to explain what he thought the Declaration should have stated, but didn't. Regarding Lafontaine's second point, the link to Doran's thought is obvious. Vatican II had so radically changed the position of the Catholic Church on a variety of issues that one was clearly facing a new situation, requiring new theological responses. Such was Murray's alertness to the situation as source of theology that he had the freedom to shift his interest from the question of religious freedom that had occupied him for twenty years.

45. Lafontaine, "Lonergan": 795.

46. Murray was first invited, then, famously, "disinvited," to serve as a *peritus* at the Second Vatican Council; for more information, please see Robert B. Kaiser, *Pope, Council and World*, New York: Macmillan Co., 1963, 65, as cited in Pelotte, 109. In fact, Michael Novak in *The Open Church: Vatican II, Act II*, New York: Macmillan Co., 1964, 257, claims: ". . . the invitation was suddenly and embarrassingly withdrawn); this "snub" caused Murray great personal pain.

After Vatican II: Explaining Dignitatis Humanae

A considerable amount of Murray's writing on the Council continued to be on the topic of religious freedom. In an article entitled "Vers une intelligence du development de la doctrine de l'eglise sur la liberté religieuse," Murray analyzes exactly how *DH* represents a development of doctrine, much as Lonergan had analyzed doctrine developing in *The Way to Nicea*.[47] His point, as always, was that the development at issue was not simply that the doctrine of religious freedom was new, but that proclaiming it constituted a shift of horizon on the part of the Church from one differentiation of consciousness (theoretic) to another (interior). The following quotation, is notable for making explicit mention of Lonergan:

> There is (1), for instance, the generic movement noted in *Humanae Generis*—"toward the elucidation and detailed formulation of matters contained in the deposit of faith only obscurely and in some implicit fashion." This movement is often accomplished by passing from undifferentiated to the differentiated concept—in the technical Scholastic vocabulary, from the "confused" to the "distinct" concept . . . Again (2) development may involve a dialectical process whereby earlier understandings of an affirmation, which were inconsistent with the original sense of affirmation itself are perceived and corrected. Bernard Lonergan has shown this dialectic at work in the series of ante-Nicene writers, in the process that led to the *homoousion* . . . (3) a change of perspective may bring to light a truth which had not been clearly seen or stated before . . . These factors of development are well known. And they may be looked for in the development of the concept of religious liberty.[48]

Point 3 in this quotation mentions "a change of perspective." By this, Murray means the shift, made possible by intellectual conversion, from classicism to historical consciousness.

47. Murray, "Vers une intelligence du developpement de la doctrine de l'eglise sur la liberté religieuse," 114, in *Vatican II: La Liberté Religieuse*, edited by J. Hamer and Y. Congar, Paris: Les Editions du Cerf, 1967, as cited in Hooper, 40.

48. Murray, "Vers une intelligence du developpement de la doctrine de l'eglise sur la liberté religieuse," 114, in *Vatican II : La Liberté Religieuse*, edited by J. Hamer and Y. Congar, Paris: Les Editions du Cerf, 1967, as cited in Hooper, 40. Note: Murray's original English language texts are found in the Murray Archives, file 7–517 (1967m).

After Vatican II: A New Situation Provokes New Theological Reflection

If Murray eventually became "tired of the whole subject"[49] of commenting on *DH*, he by no means became tired of theology in general. In fact, the years before his death witnessed the flourishing of reflections on a wide range of topics not directly related to religious freedom. Here, one might add that the topics he addressed were, in fact, indirectly related to religious freedom.

Vatican II is widely understood to be a Council on the nature of the mission of the Church, both *ad intra* and *ad extra*. It is not surprising that much of Murray's post-conciliar reflection became more ecclesiological than his writings prior to it. Commentators note how Murray, like most other participants in Vatican II, felt enthused and profoundly changed by the Council. In an article published in 1966, he describes the Council as "a splendid event of freedom" adding that it was an event of dialogue which will forever mark and alter the church."[50] In an article written in the same year, "Our Response to the Ecumenical Revolution," Murray indicates that one of the areas of dialogue invigorated by the Council is the search for Christian unity.[51]

One can recall that during the 1940s, Murray had written articles on "intercredal cooperation." At the time, these had been considered progressive, causing Murray to be publicly criticized. However, read in the light of Vatican II, he recognized that his line of argument in those articles was defensive and only reluctantly ecumenical. Now, with his historically conscious understanding of the junctures between both secular culture and Christianity, he recognizes that the Christianity that is in dialogue with the world must be considered to be that Christianity which is only an imperfect model of unity, namely one that includes Catholics, Protestants, and Orthodox believers. Now, Murray states that ecumenism is "a quality inherent in theology, as it is an impulse intrinsic to Christian faith itself."[52] He states that the scandalous fragmentation of the Church implies that the

49. Letter to Paul Webber SJ, 1966, (Cited in Pelotte, 101).

50. Murray, "Freedom, Authority, Community», *America* 115 (December 3, 1966) 734 (1966g).

51. Murray, "Our Response to the Ecumenical Revolution," *Religious Education* 42 (March–April 1967) (1967h); Republished as "Our Response to the Ecumenical Revolution" in *Bridging the Sacred and the Secular*, 330–33.

52. Murray, "Our Response to the Ecumenical Revolution," *Religious Education* 42 (March–April 1967): 91 (1967h).

Church's own salvific mission to the world is now also fragmented. Murray adds that no true theological discussions in the Catholic Church can now take place without being related to ecumenical dialogue with other Christian denominations.[53]

A key article for Murray's systematic-theological reflection on the Church is, "Freedom, Authority, Community," which was published in 1966.[54] Here, Murray devotes considerable time to the first encyclical of Pope Paul VI, *Ecclesiam Suam* (1964),[55] which he describes as "brilliant."[56] He explains it as a striking example of historical consciousness in papal teaching. Murray notes that the Pope describes the Church as a historical process and concludes from this that the Church should be characterized by dialogue, both internal to herself and in its manner of relating to the world. He then turns, primarily, to investigate what dialogue might involve in the internal workings of the Church.

Murray begins his reflection on questions of the communication and dialogue within the Church by accepting the often-quoted principle, "the Church is not a democracy." However, he notes that this principle should not be understood in such a way that expresses classicist presuppositions. He explains that in situations where the Magisterium is negligent in consulting the faithful this tends to produce a *crisis of community* within the Church.[57] This coincides with Lonergan's analysis of community as existing where a group of people accept shared *constitutive meaning*. Murray believes that if lay people do not believe that their insights into their own experience have been attended to, they will feel alienated from judgments and decisions that are subsequently made.[58] To bishops he exhorts the following behaviour: "a willingness to work with others for the sake of cooperative action," an openness to "self-correction," and a willingness not to be a "slave to the flesh."[59]

53. Ibid.

54. Murray, "Freedom, Authority, Community," *America* 115 (December 3, 1966): 734–741 (1966g).

55. Pope Paul VI, *Ecclesiam Suam*, Encyclical on The Church, August 6, 1964, *Acta Apostolica Sedis* 56 (1964): 609–659.

56. Murray, "Freedom, Authority, Community," 740–741.

57. Ibid., 734.

58. Murray, "The Future of Humanistic Education", in Humanistic *Education and Western Civilization*, 231–47, edited by Arthur A. Cohen. New York: Holt, Rinehart, & Winston, 1964 (1964b).

59. Murray, "Freedom, Authority, Community," 739–740.

On the other hand, Murray explains that the final word in matters of doctrinal definition and pastoral decision-making remains with the Magisterium. He states: "there exists among the people no *right* to judge, correct and direct the actions of the teaching of authority."[60] Of course, he presupposes that the judgements that bishops make will have emerged from insights that result from all aspects of a situation having been carefully considered. This is where dialogue with lay people arrives. Murray states that laity can help provide a service within the Christian community of providing a reflection on experience and insights upon which Church authorities will then judge and decide. Writing for an audience that includes Catholic journalists, Murray opines that the Catholic press can help to mediate a process of consultation between magisterium and laity. He recognizes that the point he makes might seem like a small concession to lay people. However, he points out the significance of his argument for promoting change in current Church practice. Murray insists that, because the Church is a human community, lay Catholics have a "public *right* to information that concerns the Church."[61] They are not to remain passive, but are to become active moral agents in the Church as well as in society.

Practical Theology: The Lived Reality of the Situation of the Church

In addition to reflections of a systematic theological nature on the church, Murray offered reflections as a practical theologian. This involved operating in the functional specialty of communications and being ready to comment on the actual situation of the Church and how it is or not living up to the ecclesiological theory to which it aspires.

In an interview given shortly before his untimely death, Murray was blunt about the weaknesses of the Vatican Curia.[62] Murray explains, sympathetically, how bureaucracies take time to accept a shift of constitutive meaning. He distinguishes "religious reform," which occurs in individuals, from "ecclesial reform," which is a matter of bureaucracy. Next, he states

60. Murray, "Information and the Church: The Function of the Catholic Press within the Catholic Church," *Social Survey* 13 (1964): 205 (1964a).

61. Murray, "Information and the Church: The Function of the Catholic Press within the Catholic Church," as cited in Hooper, *Ethics*,181–182.

62. This interview was originally published in the *Toledo Catholic Chronical* 33, no. 29 (May 5, 1967 [1967g]. See Murray, "Toledo Talk," 339 (May 5, 1967) in *Bridging the Sacred and the Secular*, 330–33 (1994).

that the Vatican Curia is experiencing difficulty in shifting from a classicist mentality to a historically conscious one. He suggests that a key indicator of this is a reluctance to recognize that dialogue should characterize Church governance.

In this context, Murray is next asked a question about the Papal Commission on Birth Control. This had been established shortly after the closing of the Council to advise Paul VI on the question of artificial contraception. It is to be noted that Murray died before *Humanae Vitae*[63] was published on July 25, 1968. However, by 1967, this commission on birth control had already produced a *majority opinion* and a *minority opinion*, both of which had been released to the press. Murray (wrongly, it turns out) judges that this had been done with the permission of Pope Paul VI and praises this as representing what he describes as "an internal dialectic process" within the Church. He adds:

> It is up to both people and chancery to do the work of discernment and reconciliation [. . .] on what is going on and try to cooperate to bring as many as possible of the people into the good things and the right things and the true things that are going on. There will always be a fringe on both sides right and left. But try to get as many as possible into the mainstream of the life of the Church today.[64]

Murray does not express an opinion on the merits or otherwise of artificial birth control. However, he does evaluate the method employed by each of the differing groups within the commission. Murray suggests that the question of birth control is one of many issues in the Church that is currently "caught in transition to historical consciousness." He proposes that the arguments of the majority are "intelligently conceived and rationally affirmed"; by contrast, he suggests that those of the minority seem to be characterised by a classicist mentality. Murray notes that the minority report fails to attend to all the data relevant to the question. Above all, he suggests that it neglects to attend to "the total cultural and demographic factors" and, as a result, in the contribution of the minority report, "the church reached for too much certainty too soon and went too far."[65] One

63. Pope Paul VI, *Humanae Vitae*, Encyclical Letter on the Regulation of Birth, *Acta Apostolica Sedis* 60 (1968):481–503.

64. Ibid., "The Toledo Talk," 340 (1967g).

65. Ibid., 381.

is inclined to agree with a commentator who states that *Humanae Vitae* would have been "particularly difficult for Murray to endorse."[66]

A Theological Interpretation of History

There is one final issue upon which Murray wrote which was significant. It involves a theological interpretation of history and so can be attributed to the fifth functional specialty, foundations. Here, Murray accepts that much of his reflection about natural law from preceding years may need to be re-thought. In an article, "The Unbelief of the Christian," he explores questions of the act of faith, taking up the existentialist tone of Vatican II. Murray speaks of how a person who is formally a Catholic may not have made an authentic, subjective, act of self-commitment to Jesus Christ who is seeking to self-communicate to him or her. Conversely, he suggests that God's self-offer in the Holy Spirit occurs outside the boundaries of the Church and that, at times, those who are not Christians may have made a more authentic act of faith than those who are formally Christian.

On this issue, Murray recalls his explanation of how there are two converging processes at work in history: that of secular culture and that of the Church. Now, he suggests "an order of grace is pervasive through all human history, and the action of the Holy Spirit supports history and is also somehow supportive of all human history, including secular history."[67] Murray then returns to the mystery of how Christianity, which has a deeper understanding of the supernatural workings of God in history needs to act in collaboration with all other people of good will. He insists that the Church must recognize its own historicity, as "situated in the interior of history and not above it" and the fact that she is part of culture.[68]

---

66. Hooper, *Ethics*, 180. However, it is worth noting that disagreeing with the method employed in arriving at a conclusion is not the same as disagreeing with the content of the conclusion. One cannot state with any certainty that, had he lived to see the release of *Humanae Vitae*, Murray would have been a vocal dissenter against *Humanae Vitae*. To declare otherwise, one would be engaging in a "What if?" alternate history-type of theology that is neither scholarly or helpful to the pastoral mission of the Church. Some Lonergan scholars suggest that a better argument for *Humanae Vitae* could have been articulated using a critical realist notion of natural law rather than the evidently neo-scholastic one employed in the document. See Andrew Beards, *Insight and Analysis*, (London: Bloomsbury 2010), 169–171.

67. Murray, "The Unbelief of the Christian." In *The Presence and the Absence of God*, 69–83, edited by Christopher Mooney. New York: Fordham University Press, 1969.

68. Ibid.

Catholic AND American: A Staggering Theological Contribution

Even a preliminary outline of Murray's life should make reference to the admiration with which he was held in American public life and how this was expressed clearly after his sudden death in 1967. Murray was regarded by many as a Twentieth-Century model of what it means to be both Catholic and American. By way of a conclusion and an evaluation of Murray through the lens of Doran, it is necessary to note four points:

First, Murray represents an example of someone who employed the situation as source of theology to introduce development to what was held as a doctrine of the Church. It must be noted again that Murray endured censure by the Church for almost ten years for holding this position. It is a remarkable fact that Vatican II accepted the development of doctrine he had been proposing. They not only permitted him to hold this belief as his own theological doctrine, but elevated this opinion to the level of a Church doctrine.

Second, in making his contribution to updating Church doctrine, Murray followed a remarkable path of shifting his thinking about theological method. Consequently, he represents a model of a theologian who shifted from employing a classicist notion of culture as the basis for his theology to one who became historically conscious.

Third, as many as were Murray's strengths, one can also notice some weaknesses. His intellectual conversion, by Lonergan's standards, was incomplete and his psychic conversion was more or less absent, according to the criteria set by Doran. Concerning the former, Frederick Lawrence explains how Murray offered a somewhat naïve and unqualified admiration for the "American proposition."[69] This demonstrates a lack of ability to distinguish progress from decline, which in turn, indicates an incomplete intellectual conversion. Concerning the latter, an absence of psychic conversion is evident in an incomplete exercise of a preferential option for the poor and a near total neglect of the role of symbol both in society and in the religious tradition.

Fourth, Murray has remained a figure of reference in the contextual theology of North America until the present. However, some commentators on Murray exhibit less intellectual and psychic conversion than he did.

69. Lawrence, Frederick G. "John Courtney Murray and Political Theory as Conversational," in *John Courtney Murray and the Growth of Tradition*, edited by J. Leon Hooper and Todd David Whitmore, Kansas City: Sheed & Ward, 1996, 41–59.

This makes it difficult to evaluate the legacy of Murray in the theology of the U.S.A. And, with all that being stated, John Courtney Murray is still the single most important U.S. Roman Catholic theologian of the 20th Century. Walter Burghardt, delivering the funeral homily for John Courtney Murray at the Church of Saint Ignatius Loyola in New York City on August 21, 1967, preached:

> Unborn millions will never know how much their freedom is tied to this man whose pen was a powerful protest, a dramatic march, against injustice and inequality, whose research sparked and terminated in the ringing affirmation of an ecumenical council: "The right to religious freedom has its foundation" not in the Church, not in society or state, not even in objective truth, but "in the very dignity of the human person." Unborn millions will never know how much the civilized dialogue that they take for granted between Christian and Christian, between Christian and Jew, between Christian and unbeliever, was made possible by this man whose life was a civilized conversation. Untold Catholics will never sense that they love so gracefully in this dear land because John Murray showed so persuasively that the American proposition is quite congenial to the Catholic reality.[70]

Doran's views on Murray ring true. By recognizing situation as source of theology, Murray changed the way Catholic theology in the United States was done forever.

---

70. Walter Burghardt, Funeral Homily for John Courtney Murray, (August 21, 1967), quoted in "Memories of "Uncle Jack': A Nephew Remembers John Courtney Murray," in *Finding God in All Things: Celebrating Bernard Longeran, John Courtney Murray, and Karl Rahner*, 98, edited by Mark Bosco and David Stagman, New York: Fordham University Press, 2007.

CHAPTER TWENTY-ONE

ENRICHING LUIGI RULLA'S DIALECTICS OF THE SUBJECT

The Work of Robert Doran

Jake Mudge

Gaudium et Spes' challenge for theologians to use "not only theological principles, but also the findings of the secular sciences, especially of psychology and sociology" was taken up by many scholars after Vatican II as part of the renewed appreciation of the role of the subject in theology.[1] One Jesuit who took up this challenge with vigor was Italian psychiatrist and psychologist, Luigi Maria Rulla S.J. (1922–2002). Although medically trained, his lifelong research focused on the psychology of the Christian vocation and the motivational predispositions that influence inner-freedom and growth in one's calling. Rulla's extensive work in this area, predominantly throughout the 1970s and 1980s, resulted in a three-volume work titled *Anthropology of the Christian Vocation*, which was used as the basis for the coursework and clinical training at the Institute of Psychology at the Gregorian University in Rome.[2]

One of Rulla's key priorities for *Anthropology of the Christian Vocation* (ACV) was that it be interdisciplinary. In particular, he sought to introduce the fields of theology and philosophical anthropology to his existing

1. It states: "Furthermore, theologians, within the requirements and methods proper to theology, are invited to seek continually for more suitable ways of communicating doctrine to the people of their times [. . .] In pastoral care, sufficient use must be made of not only theological principles, but also of the findings of the secular sciences, especially of psychology and sociology, so that the faithful may be brought to a more adequate and mature life of faith." Second Vatican Council, *Gaudium et Spes*, 62.

2. Rulla helped to establish this institute in 1971.

area of expertise (depth psychology), and argued that working together, they could offer a more complete and historically conscious vision of the human person. Rulla acknowledged the challenge of integrating different disciplines—especially philosophical anthropology and theology—and referred briefly to how *Method in Theology* helped with this challenge by explaining dialectical differences in horizons. He also highlighted the contribution of *Insight* and the significance of self-appropriation, especially as it related to the decisions and actions associated with one's vocation. Knowing and deciding, Rulla noted, were the "basis of every vocational choice."[3] Although he made steady reference to Lonergan throughout the ACV series, he admitted that his use of Lonergan remained "very schematic and incomplete."[4]

One aspect of Lonergan's work that Rulla drew upon in some detail, however, was his notion of the basic dialectic of transcendence and limitation found in the subject's thrust towards self-transcendence. The features of this basic dialectic formed the foundation of Rulla's own description of the dialectics of the subject, and, as I hope to argue here, exposed an avenue for reflection on the way that Robert Doran's work enriches Rulla's understanding of the dialectics of the subject even further.

Rulla's Dialectics of the Subject

Aware of the need to consider the concrete, historical experience of the human person, Rulla begins ACV by inviting the subject to reflect on the notion of *value* in the world. If, from experience, one can apprehend and judge that which is of value in the world—that which is objectively good in itself—one can also ask this question in the context of their own vocation: "How might I know and judge the 'real good' as opposed to the 'apparent good' in my Christian vocation?" This Ignatian-Lonerganian starting point, Rulla highlights, forms the basis of the demanding call to self-transcendence.[5]

---

3. Luigi Rulla, *Anthropology of the Christian Vocation Volume 1: Interdisciplinary Bases* (Rome: Gregorian University Press, 1986) 143.

4. Ibid., 51, 140.

5. He notes: "The interdisciplinary approach to the study of the Christian vocation undertaken here addresses the problems noted by Lonergan. [. . .] Basic to this present approach is the assumption that human authenticity cannot simply be taken for granted; and that it is necessary to distinguish constantly between the authentic and the inauthentic in evaluation, decision, and action, and between the real good and the apparent good in Christian vocation." Ibid., 43.

Rulla reminds the theologian that the journey of self-transcendence unfolds in a very human way: there is fundamental tension and struggle involved with the task of intellectual, moral and religious self-transcendence on one hand, and the reality of human need and limitation on the other.[6] Rulla describes this tension as the "basic dialectic of the human person"—a notion he borrows from Lonergan—and argues that it derives from two foundational elements of motivation: appraising something as *important for me* (which relates to intuitive-emotional appraisal and to needs) or appraising something as *important in itself* (which relates to rational-reflective appraisal and to values). He notes:

> As a consequence of theocentric self-transcendence present in the human person, that is, of a transcendence which tends to the Infinite, a basic dialectic arises in the human person, that is, a relation between opposing terms, an opposition of motivational forces, which is inherent in the motivational system of the human person.[7]

Quoting directly from *Method*, Rulla highlights that the dialectic represents the self as *transcending* and the self as *transcended*, and is an ontological feature of the subject.[8] It can also be thought of as an ongoing tension between emotional and rational desire, since an object that one strives for could be either subjectively important (appealing to the subject's needs), or intrinsically important (corresponding to values). From this, Rulla stresses that there can be an ambiguity in our emotional forces: what seems to be a response to a value in our vocation is often (an unconscious) response to a need or gratification.[9] Vocational discernment and accompaniment, he concludes, requires interdisciplinary attention: the careful integration of psychology and the human sciences with a theology and spirituality of the Christian vocation, which strives towards Gospel-centered values.

Rulla describes the basic dialectic of the subject as a tension between the *ideal self* (what one wants to be and do) and the *actual self* (what one

---

6. Here Rulla alludes to an earlier quote from *Gaudium et Spes* (*GS*): "[Humanity] is the meeting point of many conflicting forces. As created beings, people are subject to many limitations, but feel unlimited in their desires and their sense of being destined for a higher life." *GS*, 10.

7. Rulla, *ACV Volume 1*, 150.

8. Ibid., 151. See Bernard Lonergan, *Method in Theology* (Toronto: University of Toronto, 1971) 110.

9. Rulla, *ACV Volume 1*, 136.

actually is and does).[10] By reflecting on this tension, Rulla argues that the subject—and the accompanying spiritual director or psychologist—can arrive at concrete and objective information about unconscious motivations within the subject's psyche; and such information can help one to grow in self-knowledge and inner-freedom in the journey toward both natural and self-transcendent values.

In such a reflection, Rulla notes that we must realize that the basic conscious-unconscious dialectic of the subject tends to "favor the formation of the unconscious by repression."[11] For this reason, the unconscious self—and the action of repression in particular—merit special attention. By reflecting on unconscious repression (the process of restricting data from entering conscious awareness), one can, in turn, judge the role it might play in limiting self-transcendence by maintaining or increasing opposition within the basic dialectic. On the topic of repression, Rulla agrees with Freud's fundamental description that it is a force ultimately capable of distorting perception, memory and judgement. Like many psychologists, however, he criticizes Freud for not placing enough emphasis on the psycho-spiritual implications of repression. To help with this, he employs the work of Wilfried Daim, Viktor Frankl and Viktor von Weizsäcker, who describe the existence of the "data of the spirit" acting in the human psyche.[12] By recognizing the "spirit" in the unconscious self, Rulla notes that discussions about the human psyche can be broadened to accommodate theological notions such as sin or virtue. Further, the data of both the spirit (moral and rational decisions) and the psyche (memories, emotions, images) can be seen to be open to repression, and this may actually be a feature of *normal* human functioning; not necessarily or always a function of sin or pathology.

Taking these foundational distinctions within the basic conscious-unconscious dialectic of the subject, Rulla offers an important (and indeed original) contribution: he suggests that the dialectic of the ideal and actual self—the concrete expression of the basic dialectic of transcendence and limitation—can be expressed via three dimensions or "sub-dialectics."

10. He elaborates: "[The actual self] is the organisation of interdependent motivational forces, *which as a matter of fact* grows towards self-transcendence or resists growth, consciously or unconsciously. This is the self as transcended; it can be called the *actual self*. [. . .] There is also a second structure or motivational organization which aspires to grow *more and more* in its ideals of self-transcendence. This is the self as transcending, and it may be called the *ideal self*." Ibid., 167 (emphasis original).

11. Rulla, *ACV Volume 1*, 151.

12. Ibid., 82–83.

Together, these dimensions help to explain the conscious and unconscious motivations of the subject, and are especially useful for an interdisciplinary study of vocation.[13] He explains:

> It seems that three types of acquired tendencies (of habits, dispositions, states or capacities of action) can be distinguished in the human person. These three types of dispositions may be termed *dimensions*. They are distinct, each from the others, but obviously not separate within the functional dynamic unity of the person.[14]

The notion of three dimensions (dialectics) existing between the structures of the subject (i.e. between the ideal and actual self) is crucial for his wider project, and can be briefly outlined. The first dimension expresses how one might live by predominantly moral or religious ideals, and be disposed to virtue or sin. Rulla says that this dimension derives primarily from the conscious self, since in this dimension the subject is aware of the extent of harmony/agreement present between their ideal self (conscious) and actual self (*predominantly* conscious).[15] From this, the subject can examine the conscious opposition between what one wants to be and do on one hand, and what one actually is and does on the other.[16] The second dimension describes the extent to which the unconscious self and unconscious repression are present in the individual. In this dimension, importantly, the degree of unconscious repression does not imply a tendency to pathology or pathological action.[17] In fact, this dimension helps to express most broadly the dialectic of the apparent versus the real good; since it derives from a combination of both conscious and unconscious motivational elements, and thus represents the human struggle to be aware—and become aware—of

---

13. Tim Healy S.J. suggests that Rulla's account of the three dimensions is one of his "most original contributions." Tim Healy, "The Challenge of Self-transcendence" in ed. Franco Imoda, *A Journey Into Freedom: An Interdisciplinary Approach to the Anthropology of Formation* (Leuven: Peeters, 2000) 77.

14. Rulla, *ACV Volume 1*, 84–85.

15. Ibid., 172.

16. As well as an extensive description of the three dimensions in *ACV Volume 1* (78–89, 162–230), Rulla offers briefer descriptions in other works. See, for example, Luigi M. Rulla, Franco Imoda, and Joyce Ridick, "Anthropology of the Christian Vocation: Conciliar and Postconciliar Aspects" in René Latourelle (ed.) *Vatican II: Assessment and Perspectives Twenty-five Years On* (New York: Paulist, 1989) 402–459.

17. Rulla views this second, intermediate dimension as a new idea since it has the potential to relate the influence of this dialectic on the living of values associated with the spiritual life and to Christian vocation. Rulla, *ACV Volume 1*, 85.

the ambiguity between the ideal and actual self as one negotiates what might be either a subjective or objective good. In essence, it represents the ongoing tension between needs and values. Timothy Costello helps to contextualize this dimension:

> Ambiguity is seen in the mixed motivations out of which many normal people frequently operate: for example, good works undertaken both in order to help another (religious value) and in the expectation of some future reward (natural value); or, prayer that is inspired both by the example of Jesus (religious value) and the feelings of inner peace and relaxation that it engenders (natural value).[18]

Rulla notes that the capacity for this dimension to reflect on the role of both natural and transcendent values means that it is particularly important in the task of psycho-spiritual accompaniment. Rulla highlights that the person's freedom in this dimension can be limited, given that one may only be partly aware of the opposition existing in the tension of this dimension.[19] The third dimension corresponds with our capacity for either normal or pathological functioning and represents, as its particular axiological quality, the predominantly natural values associated with one's capacity for everyday healthy living. The unconscious self, and unconscious repression (with or without biological or physiological changes), are important components of this dimension.[20]

Rulla argues that the framework offered through his dialectics helps the human person to understand their response to self-transcendent values associated with the Christian vocation: to understand what is "good, true,

18. Timothy Costello, *Forming a Priestly Identity: Anthropology of Priestly Formation in the Documents of the VIII Synod of Bishops and the Apostolic Exhortation Pastores Dabo Vobis*. (Rome: Editrice Pontificia Università Gregoriana, 2002) 220.

19. Rulla explains the importance of freedom in one's disposition to self-transcendence: "The notion of an *objective* self-transcendent value implies a relationship of this objective value to the freedom of the subject [. . .] Indeed this value becomes *subjective* only when the subject in fact chooses it freely and this makes it his own. Therefore, in man the subjective self-transcendent value is not a simple reflex of the self-transcendent value of the object. Objective self-transcendent values which are in realities outside the person receive their *ultimate* determination as self-transcendent values from the fact that the freedom of the person finds in them a norm, the 'you ought' of his own theocentric self-transcendence. In other words, the greater the person's inner-freedom, the more the person can pursue self-transcendent values." Rulla *ACV Volume 1*, 189

20. For a cogent explanation of the three dimensions see: Costello, *Forming a Priestly Identity*, 217.

intelligent, and real."[21] He suggests that this framework (which is central to his aim of "objectifying the subject") can be further assisted by understanding the *symbolic* nature of the various dynamic elements within the three dimensions. Highlighting the important contributions of Freud, Paul Ricœur, Wilhelm Dilthey, and Lonergan, he notes the ability of the symbol to "embrace the tensions and the contradictions which logical discourse abhors." Quoting Lonergan, he reflects:

> Granted that a methodological or dialectical approach can embrace the concrete and the dynamic, yet in the history of humanity, the symbol accomplished this before logic or dialectic had been conceived, and continues to do this for the persons who are familiar with neither logic nor dialectic.[22]

Rulla suggests that symbols play a "mediating" role in the three dimensions, and, when understood in the context of the dynamic elements of motivation (such as needs, values, and attitudes—the "product" of needs and values), help to "confer meaning" upon the dialectics of the subject. In addition, Rulla makes special reference to the existence of two vectors (progressive and regressive) operating in every symbol, which he says offer a hermeneutical key to help interpret the subject's journey toward self-transcendent values.[23] Although Rulla notes that linking progression, regression, and the symbolic is a feature of Ricœur's work, he does not make extended reference to Lonergan's work on the symbolic, or on progress and decline. By examining Lonergan's basic dialectic of the subject from the perspective of Doran, we can appreciate how Rulla's dialectics of the subject might be broadened and developed. This is accomplished by reflecting on Doran's treatment of the self-transcending subject, his notion of the derived dialectics of the subject—including psychic conversion—and the role of grace acting in human consciousness.

---

21. He explains: "[The] encounter between objective self-transcendent values on one hand, and [our] conscious intentionality on the other has a profound meaning in [our] life and a great importance for the ultimate sense of human living. [It provides] the basis of the possibility that a vocation can come to [us] from God." Rulla, *ACV Volume 1*, 151, 175–177.

22. Rulla, *ACV Volume 1*, 212–213, paraphrasing Bernard Lonergan, *Method in Theology* (Toronto: University of Toronto, 1971) 64–69.

23. Rulla notes the importance of addressing "the dialectics between the structures [ideal and actual self] which *tend* to symbolize in the progressive manner of the conscious [and] the dialectics which *tend* to symbolize in the regressive manner of the unconscious." Ibid., 221 (emphasis original).

Doran's Dialectics of the Subject

In the opening pages of *Subject and Psyche*, Doran outlines a twofold aim: to show how Lonergan's analysis of human intentionality "allows one to generate categories through which both the human psyche and the science of depth psychology can be profitably understood" and to deepen Lonergan's initial dialogue with depth psychology through the exploration of one's symbolic interiority.[24] Most importantly, these aims are met through a "turn to the subject in every instance—philosophical, psychological [and] theological."[25]

Although obvious for readers of Doran, it is fundamental to recall that his initial description of the subject emerges from a detailed and skilled appreciation of the foundations of the self-transcending Lonerganian subject, from which, he says, "all else derives."[26] In *Theology and the Dialectics of History* (TDH) he dedicates the entire first chapter to Lonergan's notion of the subject, highlighting the importance of the self-affirmation of the knower, knowledge as a function of the desire to know, being and objectivity, and the subject's existential and historical agency. The significance of these initial themes, especially in the context of interdisciplinary study, can be briefly highlighted.

Like Rulla, Doran notes that the first task for the reflective subject is to attend to one's surroundings and context and to "desire to understand [them] correctly."[27] Doran, however, invites the subject to take this basic existential question even further. In reflecting on one's context and surroundings, and beginning the task of self-appropriation, the subject also becomes aware that such operations are taking place within *oneself*: one becomes aware of one's conscious "identity" as a knower, and the existential and intelligible "unity" that this represents within one's conscious operations.[28] Such self-affirmation, Doran highlights, leads to a practical end: not only in the context of one's Christian vocation in general, but in the context of the vocation of the *theologian* endeavouring to offer an interdisciplinary study in the first place. In this way, we see a fundamental

24. Robert Doran, *Subject and Psyche—Second Edition* (Milwaukee WN: Marquette University Press, 1994) 7–8.

25. Ibid., 8.

26. Robert Doran, *Theology and the Dialectics of History* (Toronto: University of Toronto Press, 1990) 19.

27. Doran, *TDH*, 21.

28. Ibid., 21.

application of Doran's attention to the subject for the task of interdisciplinary study: by affirming Lonergan's position on knowing, the theologian is invited to constantly reflect on their own conscious experiences, deliberations, judgements and decisions when completing the task of constructing a collaborative and interdisciplinary study; indeed such as that seen in the ACV series.[29] In this way, Doran alludes to the role that the "transformation of the mentality" of the theologian can play in discerning how various disciplines might cooperate and integrate, and the imperative of such collaboration in the "praxis of theology."[30] The existential and intelligible unity of the knowing subject, in fact, forms the foundation of his vision for interdisciplinary collaboration. Such a framework, he says, will:

> offer a key to the transformation of one science, depth psychology, [and] show that this transformation, joined with Lonergan's work, will ground further interdisciplinary collaboration in the pursuit of integrated science, especially of integrated human science.[31]

With Rulla, Doran holds that the challenge of self-transcendence—and the subsequent apprehension of the "real good" in one's vocation—requires earnest reflection on the basic dialectic of the subject, and attention to the tensions within the dynamics of the conscious and unconscious self. It is this dialectic that Doran sets about grounding firmly in the "dramatic" experiences of the subject's vocation as one strives to live-out the values of the Kingdom authentically and constructively.

---

29. Note, too, Lonergan's reflection in his essay "The Subject." He writes: "So far, our reflections on the subject have been concerned with him as a knower, as one who experiences, understands and judges. We now have to think of him as a doer, as one that deliberates, evaluates, chooses, acts. Such doing, at first sight, affects, modifies, changes the world of objects. *But even more it affects the subject himself.*" Bernard Lonergan, "The Subject" in eds. Frederick Crowe and Robert Doran, *A Second Collection* CWL 13 (Toronto: University of Toronto Press, 1974, reprinted 2016) 63 (emphasis added).

30. He concludes: "That praxis, of course, is itself in part the intellectual, a matter of collaborative interdisciplinary research promoting the reorientation and integration of science and scholarship, of the superstructure of society. And it is also in part education, the formation and transformation of mentality. The praxis of theology, I have concluded, is proximately the transformation of culture, of constitutive meaning, as the condition of the possibility of the transformation of policies, economies, technological structures, and intersubjective communities." Doran, *TDH*, 12.

31. Robert Doran, *Psychic Conversion and Theological Foundations—Second Edition* (Milwaukee WN: Marquette University Press, 2006) 10. Doran's reference to the "Editor's Preface" in *Insight* also provides good background to his point. Here, he reflects on Lonergan's "two reorientations of the modern philosophical differentiation of consciousness." See Doran, *TDH*, 25–26.

Like Rulla, Ricœur, and Jung, Doran places special emphasis on the role of the Freudian censor when reflecting on the dialectics of the subject. He first acknowledges the rich fields of experience that the subject is exposed to each day: the aesthetic, imaginative, biological, intellectual and dramatic.[32] As this vast amount of information enters our "neural manifold"—the biological structures responsible for receiving and processing sensory stimuli—the information competes for the attention of our consciousness. Such an overwhelming (albeit constant) experience leads the intellect to exercise some degree of censorship over what enters our awareness and competes for higher integration by the intellect.[33] Gerard Whelan notes that the role of the censor is particularly significant since it tends to "anticipate" the relevance of certain stimuli associated with acts of insight *prior* to being fully aware of what the importance of a given piece of data might be for the subject.[34] Bias (conscious and unconscious) becomes the obvious by-product of the repressive censor, and it is the experience of conversion, both Rulla and Doran acknowledge, that offers a way to address this.[35]

Interestingly, he notes that Lonergan mainly spoke of the role of the censor in the context of bias.[36] Doran suggests that the censor also exhibits a degree of flexibility according to the type of stimuli received, and can actually function to provide progress and growth for the subject. The censor, he argues, can act *constructively* to assist in the subject's self-awareness and self-knowledge via affective and psychic conversion. A brief outline of Doran's derived dialectics of contraries and contradictories illustrates how this particular experience of conversion unfolds within the dialectics of the subject.

Doran notes that, in addition to the basic dialectic of the conscious-unconscious subject, a secondary dialectic exists within the consciousness.

---

32. Cf. Bernard Lonergan, *Insight: A Study of Human Understanding* CWL 3, eds. Frederick Crowe and Robert Doran, (Toronto: Toronto University Press, 2008) 204.

33. Doran, *TDH*, 70.

34. Gerard Whelan, *Redeeming History: Social Concern in Bernard Lonergan and Robert Doran* (Rome: Gregorian & Biblical Press, 2013) 179.

35. Rulla alludes several times to Lonergan's notions of intellectual, moral, and religious conversion. Rulla, *ACV Volume 1*, 140–144.

36. Lonergan notes: "Again, the censor is neither an agent nor an activity but simply a law or rule of the interrelations between successive levels of integration; the constructive censorship is the admission into consciousness of elements that enter into the higher integration; the repressive censor is the exclusion from consciousness of elements that the higher integration cannot assimilate." Lonergan, *Insight*, 482.

This dialectic is represented by the two types of data received in conscious awareness—spiritual and psychic—and signifies a basic duality in consciousness.[37] This dialectic is important, since both psychic and spiritual data, when working collaboratively, engender a certain harmony between one's intellect and one's affective life—leading to *affective* self-transcendence.[38] At the same time, however, this tension is "ever precarious" since intellectual conversion is still vulnerable to the inflow of psychic data which are received and interpreted uniquely by each person according to their "sensitively experienced movement of life."[39] In essence, the struggle toward affective self-transcendence—the careful negotiation of the world of our emotions and feelings—is not an easy task. As Whelan notes, psychic data tends to *resist* self-transcendence, preferring instead to remain at "a familiar level of sensitive flow rather than accepting its own reorganization at a higher level of intentional consciousness."[40] The subject's progress and growth, argues Doran, is impacted:

> Our psychic energy can be blocked, fixed in inflexible patterns, driven by compulsions, plagued by obsessions, weighed down by general anxiety or specific fears, resistant to insight, true judgement, and responsible action. Then it diverts or derails us from the self-transcendent participation in the humble but exhilarating quest for intelligibility, truth, and the human good through which we discover the direction to be found in the ongoing movement of life.[41]

Doran makes further use of Lonergan's application of dialectic (that which helps to examine "any course of events" including levels of opposition, conflict, breakdown or aberration) and suggests that it can be used to imagine two further dialectics within the conscious self: a dialectic of *contraries* and a dialectic of *contradictories*. The dialectic of contradictories represents a tension of opposites which implies a criteria of exclusion. The dialectic of contraries, however, represents opposites which are "reconcilable at a higher synthesis" and indicates that the dialectic can be fruitful and generative.[42] Since, like Rulla,

37. Doran, *TDH*, 46. See also Bernard Lonergan, *The Triune God: Systematics* CWL 12, eds. Frederick Crowe and Robert Doran, (Toronto: Toronto University Press, 2007) 139.

38. Doran, *TDH*, 51.

39. Ibid., 47.

40. Whelan, *Redeeming History*, 180.

41. Doran, *TDH*, 229.

42. Ibid., 68.

a dialectic helps to express the symbolic dimension of the human psyche, and helps to uncover value and meaning, the affective self (feelings and emotions) provides an ideal conduit for the dialogue between values and symbols.[43] Doran stresses the vital role of discerning value and the human good:

> The key to my thesis is located in the development of Lonergan's thought from cognitional analysis to intentionality analysis. I accord primary importance to the emergence of a notion of a level of human consciousness distinctly concerned with the issue of value, the *notion valoris*, the human good. Values are primordially apprehended in feelings, and feelings are ascertainable, identifiable through symbols.[44]

Doran suggests that the dialectic of contraries, when functioning harmoniously, produces a healthy equilibrium within the subject, and engenders the gifts of affective maturity and progress.[45] The dialectic of contradictories, however, signifies the interference of bias, of position versus counter-position, and the struggle between authenticity and inauthenticity. In this dialectic, harmony and interdependence are replaced by opposition and resistance to self-transcendence. Doran equates such displacement to our hubristic and sinful tendency to defy the call to self-transcendence. In this case, Doran notes, the spirit is held in a type of "captivity."[46]

Certain similarities between both authors can be seen. Both authors, for example, place emphasis on the role of the symbolic in coming to imagine the inner-life of the human psyche and to break open meaning within the various dynamics of the dialectics of the subject. A recurring theme, however, is the way that Doran, using a detailed Lonerganian foundation, develops the notion of intentionality analysis so that the dialectics of the subject might be grounded in the experience of psychic conversion—the transformation of the repressive censor into a constructive role—and be open to progress and growth in the unfolding of their experience as a consequence of this. Part of the reason why Doran's project has the potential to enrich Rulla's framework so much is the way that he carefully links the symbolic, the action of grace, and the healing of the sensitive psyche into his work on dialectics.

---

43. Doran recalls Lonergan's definition of a symbol: "an image of a real or imaginary object that evokes a feeling or is evoked by a feeling." Ibid., 58. See Lonergan, *Method*, 64.

44. Doran, *Subject and Psyche*, 7.

45. Doran, *TDH*, 59, 71.

46. Doran, *TDH*, 55.

Grace, Dialectics, and Healing

Doran suggests that the subject's inner-growth and progress are fostered through what he describes as the "conscious orientation" of the subject to affective conversion, particularly through the unfolding of the dialectic of contraries.[47] This task involves the subject recognizing and accepting aspects of one's personal and affective maturity that need transformation and healing, and—as a consequence of the praxis of self-transcendence—deciding to orient these towards the integration and synthesis that occur at a higher level of consciousness. If aspects of one's personal and affective maturity are left unaddressed through resistance and unwillingness, Doran bluntly suggests that "intellectual inauthenticity" and decline result, since the psyche is left vulnerable to defensive circles which hinder transformation and authenticity.[48]

Like Rulla, Doran notes that the responsible step of promoting the sensitive data of the psyche to higher integration involves the subject negotiating *value* in one's calling; of discerning the "real" rather than the "apparent" good in the vocational journey. Further, it reemphasizes the need for careful recognition of rational and emotional desire within the basic dialectic of the subject and the importance of attending to one's feelings to help with affective maturity and progress. Ignorance of feelings, Doran reiterates, results in bias, decline and "moral impotence."[49]

For Doran, an important feature of the subject coming to realize the value of affective and psychic conversion is the linking of consciousness to the scale of values. The scale, coupled with the willing and responsible activity of affective self-transcendence, enables the subject to ground the basic dialectic, giving it integrity in the process. For Doran, this is ultimately an expression of grace, which "permeates human consciousness" to not only transform and heal, but to expose for the subject the value of being open to the healing effects of conversion in the first place.[50]

---

47. Doran, *Psychic Conversion and Theological Foundations* 144–145.

48. Ibid., 142–143.

49. Ibid., 148. Doran notes the significance of the *dream*; a place whereby "images are released unhindered by the guardianship of waking consciousness under the dominance of the biases." Ibid., 215.

50. Doran, *TDH*, 248. In the seldom-referenced third volume of *ACV*, subtitled "Interpersonal Aspects" (the work only available in Italian), Rulla outlines the role of grace in the Christian vocation. Although he alludes to the presence of grace acting in human consciousness, his reflection takes the form of a general survey rather than an explanation of the action of grace in the dialectics of the subject. Luigi Rulla, *Antropologia della Vocazione Cristiana 3: Aspetti Interpersonali* (Bologna: Edizioni Dehoniane Bologna, 1997) 234.ff.

An important way that Doran envisions the healing activity of grace working in consciousness is seen through a development of the notion of *anagogic* symbols acting within the dialectics of contraries. Anagogic symbols refer to those symbols which pertain distinctly to the individual subject and to their vocational journey—and indeed to their project of dramatic artistry. In Rulla's project, with its specifically therapeutic and accompaniment-based application, Doran's work offers a way to develop the horizon of Rulla's dialectics even further, especially by highlighting the creative *and* healing action of grace working in the dialectics of the subject. To explain this unfolding in the context of anagogic symbols, Doran first recalls the finality of the psyche and notes that, ultimately, our intentions express none other than a natural desire to see and participate in the divine life: a participation of our creative and conscious intentions in the absolute goodness and transcendence of God.[51] Second, when reflecting on the existence of anagogic symbols in vocational accompaniment or psychological therapy, we can note, especially in the context of the dialectic of contraries, that the self-transcending subject, grappling towards the higher integration of discerning the real good in one's vocation, is also participating in the (downward) graced and healing experience of transcendent and divine love.

Doran develops the notion of anagogic symbols further to suggest that—they are "indicative of, indeed productive of, the soteriological differentiation of consciousness that is the human side of the revelation that appears in Israel and Christianity."[52] What Doran is suggesting here is indeed profound: under the therapeutic and healing effects of grace, and by considering symbols such as the anagogic, the subject's psyche can engage fruitfully and cooperatively with "the divinely originated solution to the mystery of evil."[53] As Doran notes, by bringing the creative role of the dialectic of contraries into focus, we see the (Lonerganian) aim of offering a supernatural solution to the problem of evil: "human perfection itself becomes a limit to be transcended, and then, the dialectic is transformed from bipolar to a *tripolar conjunction and opposition*."[54] The goal of psychotherapy, Doran affirms (and of vocational accompaniment, given the nature of Rulla's project), is to confront such tensions, engage in a willingness to self-transcendence, and allow the "dissolving of obstacles to the

51. Ibid., 284–285.

52. Doran, *TDH*, 272–273.

53. Ibid., 273.

54. Ibid., 273–274 (emphasis Doran's).

performance of operations whose normative order constitutes the authentic search for direction in the movement of life."[55]

By attending to the role of anagogic symbols within the dialectics of the subject, Doran provides a way for the subject to negotiate responsibly the tensions and struggles of one's life and to create a fruitful path of development and growth amidst the unfolding of one's vocation, in history. As Doran notes, is it in dialectic that the human person finds "resolution" and realizes oneself as being-in-love: totally grasped, as Lonergan puts it, by *ultimate concern*. In this way, the dialectics of the subject fill a heuristic function for Doran: they offer a way to imagine the subject as both a creative agent in history, yet at the same time totally immersed in the (downward) healing effects of grace—of the love of God—in the unfolding of history itself.

It is hoped that this essay contributes in a small way to bringing the thoughts of Rulla and Doran together. The renewed interest in the work of Luigi Rulla by several contemporary authors, coupled with the highly relevant topic of vocational accompaniment and formation that the work underpins, suggest that further interdisciplinary collaboration in this area could prove fruitful for the mission and task of the Church today. Indeed, it is in the same spirit of collaboration, in the context of the grace-filled unfolding of history, that sees Robert Doran continue to help us make sense of the profound call of the human person to enter into dialogue with the living God, and to help us share that experience with others.

55. Ibid., 276. To complement his work in the ACV series, Rulla established a type of vocational accompaniment known as "Vocational Growth Sessions." The sessions, which take the form of psychotherapy which is spiritually and theological informed, assist with self-knowledge and growth in inner-freedom in living one's vocation. Luigi Rulla, Joyce Ridick and Franco Imoda. *Anthropology of the Christian Vocation Volume 2: Existential Confirmation* (Rome: Gregorian University Press, 1989) 389.

CHAPTER TWENTY-TWO

FOUNDATIONS FOR ECCLESIAL MISSION IN ASIA

The Relevance of General and Special Categories in Robert Doran

Jaime Vidal Zuñiga

In our highly globalized world, we are brought to the awareness of two undeniable realities: first, the scathing and scandalous reality of widespread poverty and suffering in the world; and second, the rich history and inviolable existence of other cultures and other religions with whom we share this world. These realities, though already observable in other continents, are most clearly seen and experienced in the continent of Asia where the economically, culturally, and religious other are immediately outside one's doorstep. Given this peculiar configuration of the Asian situation, by necessity, questions about the mode of existence of the Church in Asia have been increasingly pronounced in recent years. These questions relate both to how ecclesial mission can help promote integral humanization in this vast continent and how Christians are to relate to and collaborate with the greater majority of non-Christians that surround them.

Exploring such questions is a complex task. As a first means of narrowing the focus of this study, after a brief sketch of the social, cultural, and religious profile of Asia, I advert to documents of the Catholic Church on the mission of the Church in Asia, specifically those produced by the Federation of Asian Bishops Conferences (FABC). I note how the Asian bishops speak of the need for a "triple dialogue" with the cultures, religions, and poor of Asia.[1] Next, I identify some tensions that have existed between the

1. FABC Plenary Assemblies I and VII, in *For All the Peoples of Asia: Federation of Asian Bishops' Conferences Documents* (henceforth, *FAPA*) (Manila: Claretian Publications), vol. 1,

Congregation of the Doctrine of the Faith (CDF) and some Asian theologians in the first fifty years of the implementation of Vatican II. While a considerable reduction of these frictions is discernible in the pontificate of Francis, I also suggest that the theological challenges encountered by the FABC in previous decades point to a need for a deepened understanding of the nature and fundamental underpinnings of the triple dialogue. It is in this light that I speak of the value of the foundational reflections provided by Robert Doran. I submit that Doran's work in *Theology and the Dialectics of History* appertains primarily to general theological categories and holds a relevance to two of the FABC's dialogue tripod: with culture and with the poor. I then suggest that Doran's more recent work, *The Trinity in History*, provides special theological categories that have noteworthy implications to the third commitment of the FABC, that is, interreligious dialogue.

The Asian Situation

On the one hand, according to a recent United Nations study: about twenty percent of the Asian population, or approximately 743 million, live in extreme poverty on less than $1.25/day;[2] and about forty percent, or about 1.6 billion, could not afford a decent life living on just $2/day.[3] Knowing that sixty percent or nearly two-thirds of the world's population is found in Asia gives one a better idea of the significance and gravity of this statistic.[4] Problems like malnutrition, unemployment, lack of access to basic education, shelter, and healthcare continue to plague the third world countries of Asia. Wide-scale migration, women and children refugees, and the prevalence of illegal practices like corruption, terrorism, prostitution, drugs, abuse of the environment, and other organized crimes give evidence to the depth and complexity of the problem.[5] All these factors, in turn, contribute to the perpetuation of the systemic cycle of poverty and the ever-widening gap between the rich and the poor.

9.12–16.20 and vol. 3, 2–4 respectively. See also John Paul II, *Ecclesia in Asia*, 23–40. This and all papal documents cited below can be found on the Vatican website, http://www.vatican.va/content/vatican/en.html.

2. UN ESCAP, *Statistical Yearbook for Asia and the Pacific*, Thailand 2013, xi.

3. UN ESCAP, 109.

4. David M. Thompson, "Introduction: Mapping Asian Christianity in the Context of World Christianity," in Sabastian Kim (ed.), *Christian Theology in Asia* (Cambridge: Cambridge University Press, 2008), 11.

5. John Paul II, *Ecclesia in Asia*, 7.

On the other hand, one can also find in Asia a plurality of longstanding cultural traditions and the most ancient world religions, like Judaism, Islam, Hinduism, Buddhism, Confucianism, Taoism, Sikhism, Shintoism, indigenous or folk religions, etc., that pre-existed Christianity in Asia. In most Asian countries, in fact, with the exception of East Timor and the Philippines, Christianity is considered a minority religion, a "little flock,"[6] comprising only about seven percent of the entire Asian population, or about 285 million.[7] The Catholic Christian population would be a smaller fraction thereof. According to Clifford Geertz, religion is at the heart of every culture as its meanings and values shape the worldview and ethos of wider society.[8] One can thus discern a coincidence between pluri-religiosity and multi-culturality. Being comprised of several sub-continents and seven linguistic zones likewise adds to Asia's diversity.[9] Cardinal Stephen Kim Sou-hwan of Korea was thus once able to describe Asia as not only made up of "various nations, but, one might say, many worlds."[10]

Living in a pluralistic context, with all the questions and challenges it offers, is therefore not something new for Asian Christians.[11] Though dialogue on the level of daily life can be said to be happening among naturally friendly and culturally hospitable Asians, it cannot be denied that there have been and continue to be tensions and isolated cases of violence, conflicts, suppression, and discrimination due to religious and cultural differences.[12]

The Federation of Asian Bishops' Conferences (FABC): A Contextual Approach to Mission

Among the concrete fruits of Vatican II, specifically of its teachings on the local church, episcopal collegiality, and the renewed and expanded understanding of ecclesial mission, was the creation of the Federation of Asian

6. John Paul II, *Ecclesia in Asia*, 4.29.50.

7. *Global Christianity: A Report on the Size and Distribution of the World's Christian Population*, in http://www.pewforum.org/2011/12/19/global-christianity-exec/, referenced July 2020.

8. Clifford Geertz, *Interpretation of Cultures* (New York: Basic Books, 1973), 90ff.

9. Peter Phan, "Jesus the Christ with an Asian Face," in *Theological Studies* 57 (1996), 400.

10. Quoted in James H. Kroeger, *Asia-Church in Mission: Exploring* Ad Gentes *Mission Initiatives of the Local Churches in Asia in the Vatican II Era* (Quezon City: Claretian Publications, 1999), 114.

11. M. Thomas Thangaraj, "Religious Pluralism, Dialogue, and Asian Christian Responses," in *Christian Theology in Asia*, 158.

12. Jonathan Y. Tan, *Christian Mission among the Peoples of Asia* (New York: Orbis, 2014), 64–71 and 92–93; and John Paul II, *Ecclesia in Asia*, 6.8.

Bishops' Conferences (FABC). Responding to the need for greater fraternity and cooperation among themselves and to appropriate and pursue the directions laid out by the Council, the bishops of Asia gave birth to the idea of a regional episcopal structure in 1970. In its fifty years of existence, the FABC has not only received and implemented the teachings of Vatican II and the post-conciliar popes. In addition, its members have also brought to the fore specific missiological emphases and trajectories based on their strong pastoral orientation and immersion in and reading of the signs of the times in their region. These they do while, at the same time, being rooted in and aware of the particular worldview, values, and sensibilities of their fellow Asians.[13]

The structure and activities of the FABC are similar to those of the parallel organism in Latin America, the *Consejo Episcopal Latinoamericano* (CELAM), which has been more discussed by European and North-American commentators and theologians. FABC Plenary Assemblies are usually ten-day events of conferences, workshops, liturgies, and fellowships. They are attended by about two hundred participants, half of which are bishop members and the other half are FABC office workers and collaborators.[14] So far, they have held eleven plenary sessions since the FABC's foundation in 1970. The multi-volume work, *For All the Peoples of Asia: Federation of Asian Bishops' Conferences Documents*, published under different times and editorships,[15] compiles the most important documents from these and other gatherings in an orderly fashion.

The FABC documents touch on matters that pertain both to the *ad intra* mission of the Church and its *ad extra* mission. Regarding its *ad intra* mission, one of the main objectives of the FABC is to form a truly local and Asian Church. This comes from the realization that, despite centuries of Christian mission and presence in Asia, the Asian people still consider the Church as foreign and alien due to her origins, links, and practices.[16] This perception is evidently colored by the colonial stigma borne by post-colonial

---

13. Peter C. Phan, "Reception of and Trajectories for Vatican II in Asia," in *Theological Studies* 74/2 (June 2013), 293–312.

14. Edmund Chia, "Thirty Years of FABC: History, Foundation, Context and Theology," in *FABC Papers* No. 106, 9. See http://www.fabc.org/fabc%20papers/fabc_paper_106.pdf, referenced July 2020.

15. FAPA is published in five volumes. Vol. 1 (1997), covers the years 1970–1991, eds. G. Rosales and C. Arevalo; vols. 2–4, editor F.J. Eilers (1997, 2002, 2007), covers the years 1992–2006: and vols. 5–6 (2014, 2017), editor V. Tirimanna, covers the years 2006–2016. For a concise but comprehensive summary of these assemblies, see FABC Plenary Assembly X, in *FAPA*, vol. 5, 51–53.

16. Chia, "Thirty Years of FABC," 21.

Asians who associate the early missionaries and, consequently, the Christian faith with the oppressive memory of their colonizers. Furthermore, such an assessment is also warranted by the present connections and *modus operandi* of the Church in Asia, for example: in recognizing a central Western authority, in depending on and receiving funding from non-Asian churches, in her discipline, architecture, music, arts, etc. As the 1991 FABC Theological Consultation acknowledges: "The Church remains foreign in its lifestyle, in its institutional structure, in its worship, in its western-trained leadership and in its theology."[17] Responding to this assessment, the Asian bishops assert that Christians in the region must become "Asian in their way of thinking, praying, living, communicating their own Christ-experience to others."[18] They further hold that: "The principle of indigenization and inculturation is at the very root of their coming into their own."[19] To impress the critical necessity of this endeavor, they even issue a bleak warning: "If the Asian Churches do not discover their own identity, they will have no future."[20]

The FABC explains that the inculturation of the Church *ad intra* is intrinsically related to the credibility and effectiveness of its mission *ad extra*. The Asian bishops' statements on ecclesial mission are particularly striking as notions deduced from abstract ideas and detached concepts are virtually absent. On the contrary, all their pronouncements are shaped by the consideration of the actual situation to be addressed.[21] Differentiating this approach from the usually metaphysical, theoretical, and disengaged manner of classicist theologizing, Jonathan Tan points out:

> The starting point of the FABC's contextual theological methodology is not the universal precepts of *lex aeterna* and *lex naturalis*, or abstract metaphysical principles pertaining to God, Revelation and the Christian Gospel, or even conciliar, papal or doctrinal pronouncements, but rather the life experiences of the Asian peoples [. . . they are] also the underlying foundation, framework and continuous referent for doing theology in the Asian milieu.[22]

---

17. *FAPA*, vol. 1, 337.

18. *FAPA*, vol. 1, 70.

19. *FAPA*, vol. 1, 72.

20. *FAPA*, vol. 1, 70.

21. A survey of the Asian situation, with both its lights and shadows, from which discernment and reflection part, is a common feature of each of the eleven FABC's documents associated with a plenary assembly.

22. Jonathan Y. Tan, "Theologizing at the Service of Life: The Contextual Theological Methodology of the Federation of Asian Bishops Conferences (FABC)," in *FABC Papers* No. 108, paragraphs 6 and 10. See http://www.fabc.org/fabc%20papers/fabc_paper_108.pdf, referenced July 2020.

The FABC describes the broad lines of its mission *ad extra* by identifying two modes by which it is to be carried out: deeds and dialogue. Regarding deeds, the Asian bishops teach that: "For Christians in Asia, to proclaim Christ means above all to live like him, in the midst of our neighbors of other faiths and persuasions, and to do his deed by the power of his grace."[23] While they maintain that explicit proclamation is not precluded, they stress that living a righteous life is the best, most credible, and at times, the only possible mode of proclamation due to very real external restrictions brought to bear by the Asian context.[24]

Next, the bishops speak a great deal about dialogue. They describe this as the defining characteristic of the new way of being Church that they are proposing for Asia.[25] They explain that dialogue is not a hidden tool to achieve conversions,[26] nor is it something opposed to the explicit proclamation of the Gospel.[27] Neither do they treat it as just one of the aspects or dimensions of the evangelizing mission of the Church. Rather, they consider dialogue to be "intrinsic to the very life of the Church, and the essential mode of all evangelization."[28] According to Luis Antonio Tagle, this is "the basic intuition of the FABC."[29] As early as their first plenary assembly, the Asian bishops have already identified three key areas around which such dialogue should revolve: cultures, religions, and the poor. They detail:

> Indigenization renders the local church truly present within the life and *cultures of our peoples*. Through it all their human reality is assumed into the life of the Body of Christ, so that all of it may be purified and healed, perfected and fulfilled. Through the second task, *the Asian religions* are brought into living dialogue with the Gospel, so that the seeds of the Word in them may come to full flower and fruitfulness within the life of our peoples. Finally, through the "preaching of the good news to *the poor*" (Lk 4:18), Christ's renewing life and the power of His paschal mystery is

23. FABC Plenary Assembly V, in *FAPA*, vol. 1, 282.

24. *FAPA*, vol. 1, 34, 105, 253, 284. See also FAPA vol. 5, 21–22 and 34–35.

25. *FAPA*, vol. 1, 332.

26. *FAPA*, vol. 4, 86.

27. *FAPA*, vol. 1, 120.

28. *FAPA*, vol. 1, 111.

29. Luis Antonio G. Tagle, "The Challenges of Mission in Asia: A View from the Asian Synod," in Peter Phan (ed.), *The Asian Synod: Texts and Commentaries* (New York: Orbs, 2002), 219.

> inserted into our peoples' search for human development, for justice, brotherhood and peace.[30]

The FABC and the Vatican: A Challenge to Clarify Methodological Foundations

These developments in the missiological thinking of the FABC occurred over a fifty-year period while the universal Church was struggling to understand just how to interpret and implement Vatican II. Giuseppe Alberigo describes the key drama of Vatican II as "the comparison and clash between an essentially deductive method and an inductive method." He adds that while the transition to an inductive approach was "imperfect indeed and incomplete," it represented, nevertheless, "a shift of enormous cultural and ecumenical importance, which, over thirty years later, increasingly demonstrates its validity and its fruitfulness."[31] Bernard Lonergan interpreted this shift in terms of an advance from classical mindedness to historical consciousness. Taking a key term of the Council, *aggiornamento*, or updating, he writes:

> The word *aggiornamento* has electrified the world, Catholic and non-Catholic, because it seems to imply a rejection of classicism, a rejection of the view that human nature is always the same [. . .] It opens, or seems to open, the door to historical consciousness, to the awareness that men individually are responsible for their lives and collectively are responsible for the world in which they live them.[32]

Lonergan also anticipated that the full embrace of historical mindedness would take time, adding that, for a period, "[t]here is bound to be formed a solid right that is determined to live in a world that no longer exists." Opposed to this, he predicted the formation of "a scattered left, captivated by now this, now that new development, exploring now this and now that new possibility." In turn, he holds that "what will count is a perhaps not

30. FABC Plenary Assembly I, in *FAPA*, vol. 1, 16.

31. Giuseppe Alberigo, Chapter VIII, "Major Results, Shadows of Uncertainty," in *History of Vatican II: vol. IV, Church As Communion, Third Period and Intersession, September 1964—September 1965* (New York: Orbis, 2004), 624–625.

32. Bernard Lonergan, "*Existenz* and *Aggiornamento*," in Frederick Crowe and Robert Doran (eds.), *Collection, Collected Works of Bernard Lonergan*, vol. 4 (Toronto: University of Toronto Press, 1988), 228–229.

numerous center."[33] He believed that he had provided this center with an adequate program for action when he published *Method in Theology*. During the late 1960s and 70s, Lonergan took various opportunities to comment on the continuing presence of classical mindedness among both theologians and the magisterium. However, he also observed evidence of a scattered left, speaking of "the debacle that followed the pastoral council," remarking that, "an outstanding characteristic of the post-Vatican II horizon is a certain disregard of doctrinal issues."[34]

A study of Church politics in the sixty years since Vatican II provides a further insight: the solid right tended to opt for a Neo-Augustinian approach to theology. Joseph Komonchak describes this paradigm against the backdrop of a more Thomistic approach:

> The typically Augustinian approach works with a sharp and unmediated distinction between sin and grace, natural reason and faith. The natural world appears to have no solidity or substance except as a sign pointing beyond itself to the spiritual and supernatural. The dramatic contest between sin and grace monopolizes attention [. . .] The typically Thomist approach, in contrast, effects a theoretical differentiation of the natural, not in order to deny that the drama of sin and grace is the only real drama of human history but in order to promote a more accurate understanding of it. 'Nature,' if you will, theoretically mediates the practical drama. It has its own solidity or substance, its own laws, its created autonomy.[35]

In 2012, Massimo Faggioli produced a book describing the official conciliar hermeneutic that dominated the first fifty years of the Council's implementation. He entitled it, *Vatican II: A Battle for Meaning*.[36] In the said work, Faggioli suggests that the pontificates of John Paul II and Benedict XVI were characterized by a predominantly Neo-Augustinian perspective, as manifest in several magisterial interventions on theological questions, with

33. Lonergan, "Dimensions of Meaning," in *Collection*, 245.

34. Lonergan, "Horizons and Transpositions," in Robert C. Croken and Robert M. Doran (eds.), *Philosophical and Theological Papers: 1965–1980, Collected Works of Bernard Lonergan*, vol. 17 (Toronto: University of Toronto Press, 2004), 427 and 410.

35. Joseph A. Komonchak, "A Postmodern Augustinian Thomism?," in Lieven Boeve—Mathijs Lamberigts—Maarten Wisse (eds.), *Augustine and Postmodern Thought, A New Alliance Against Modernity?* (Leuven: Peeters, 2009), 123.

36. Massimo Faggioli, *Vatican II: A Battle for Meaning* (Mahwah: Paulist Press, 2012).

consequences on missiological directions that were usually cautious with regards to Church-world relations. Faggioli pays particular attention to the intervention of the CDF in Latin America, not least with a document published in 1984, "Instruction on Certain Aspects of Liberation Theology."[37] This document expresses concern about a tendency to employ Marxist categories in talking about a preferential option for the poor, as well as other signs of academic immaturity in that emerging theological school.

A study of the interaction between the central magisterium and the FABC shows that the same dynamics were at work between Rome and the Church in Asia. In terms of the triple dialogue, one perceives that the concern for the first dialogue, that with the poor, bears a resemblance to the themes treated in Latin American liberation theology. The concerns of the CDF, therefore, were relevant to the liberation theologians of Asia as well. Regarding the dialogue with culture, one can trace that the call for an "inculturation" of the Christian faith had first emerged from the Church in Africa. However, in that case, Rome had continued to adopt a Neo-Augustinian approach and to advise caution against cultural relativism, syncretism, and isolationism. In contrast, concern for inculturation outside the West tended to be spontaneously more Thomist than Augustinian. Komonchak offers a reason for this: "St. Thomas could embrace the new world opened to Christian culture by Aristotle's philosophy and by Arabian science without believing, as many Augustinians did at the time, that this was a profanation of the sacred."[38]

It is in the sphere of interreligious dialogue where the Church in Asia was most innovative and distinctive. It is also the field in which Asia received the most severe Roman interventions. Edmund Chia recognizes that the encyclical *Dominus Iesus* had a particular intention of warning against wrongful approaches to interreligious dialogue in Asia. Similarly, he calls to mind the treatment of the eminent Jesuit theologian Jacques Dupuis, the excommunication and eventual reinstatement of Sri Lankan OMI Tissa Balasuriya, and the notification on and condemnation of the works of Indian Jesuit Anthony de Mello.[39] In addition, he narrates how the Vatican closely monitored some bishops and theologians:

---

37. CDF, "Instruction on Certain Aspects of Liberation Theology" (1984), in http://w2.vatican.va/roman_curia/congregations/cfaith/documents/rc_con_cfaith_doc_19840806_theology-liberation_en.html, referenced July 2020.

38. Komonchak, "A Postmodern Augustinian Thomism?," 123.

39. Edmund Chia, "Wanted: Interreligious Dialogue in Asia," in *Studies in Interreligious Dialogue* 12/1 (2002), 103–105.

> In the mid-1990s a group of Indian bishops were summoned by the CDF for a seminar or "dialogue session" during which the works of their theologians were discussed. In the past year, the editors of a reputable theological journal in India were also privileged with a "dialogue session" on the theological positions taken by some of the journal's contributors.[40]

It would be a mistake to neglect the valuable role that such CDF interventions played. It must be admitted that the Church in Asia likewise witnessed excessive and reductive interpretations of some conciliar precepts that led to unorthodox positions like cultural relativism, radical pluralism, and a regnocentrism without Christ. These properly merited the correction and clarification of the post-conciliar magisterium. During the volatile period after the Council, when a lot of items still needed to be defined and specified, the universal magisterium, in many respects, ably and validly performed its incumbent duty to authentically interpret the faith and address prevalent misunderstandings in order to protect the deposit of faith and preserve the Church in truth. In retrospect, these criticisms also providentially served as catalysts for the greater precision and development of Asian theology. Be that as it may, one may qualify this point by suggesting that magisterial positions had the characteristic of the solid right making accurate criticisms of the scattered left. Moving forward, what is needed is a theological support for the triple dialogue that is historically conscious and yet fully orthodox. As Lonergan points out, providing such foundations is a question of epistemology and theological method.

The theological climate in Rome changed with the election of Pope Francis in 2013. Walter Kasper observes that this pontificate represents a swing to a Thomist approach to pastoral reflection from a largely Neo-Augustinian one that characterized Benedict XVI.[41] He specifies that Francis represents a form of Thomism in dialogue with modern thought, pointing out that the key difference between Francis and his predecessors "concerns theological method and its concomitant emphases."[42] He also explains that this form of Thomism passed through the perspective of the Latin American Church and the "Theology of the People," which was an expression of liberation theology found in Argentina.[43] Doran expresses

40. Edmund Chia, "*Dominus Iesus* and Asian Theologies," in *Horizons* 29/2 (2002), 288.

41. Walter Kasper, *Pope Francis' Revolution of Tenderness and Love* (Mahwah: Paulist Press, 2015), 7 and 12.

42. Kasper, *Pope Francis' Revolution of Tenderness and Love*, 7 and 12.

43. See Kasper, Chapter 3, "A Historical-Theological Classification—Argentine and European Roots," in *Pope Francis' Revolution of Tenderness and Love*, 16–17.

opinions similar to Kasper, stating that: "Pope Francis is probably the first non-classicist pope, the first who does not take a particular set of cultural meanings and values, however noble they may have been in their origins, as normative for genuine humanity."[44] The apostolic exhortation *Evangelii Gaudium* [EG] serves as a kind of manifesto of the thinking of Francis and, six years into his papacy, it is clear that he has been systematically attempting to implement its vision.

One telling feature of the Francis papacy is the opposition it has provoked, especially among senior churchmen. It is reasonable to suspect that resistance to Francis has a lot to do with an abiding classicism in some members of the Roman Curia who refuse to yield to historical mindedness. I concur with what *La Civiltà Cattolica* writes: "Francis is a pope of the Second Vatican Council, not because he affirms it and defends it constantly, but because he gathers the intimate value of rereading the Gospel in the light of contemporary experience [. . .] The resistances to Francis are resistances to the Council."[45] How then to support the initiatives undertaken by the current pope? One option is to bring explanatory depth and apologetic value to his teachings by employing a critical realist theological method that bring to the surface and clarify foundational issues. Incidentally, this venture coincides with what we have proposed above for the FABC. The links between EG and the FABC's triple dialogue are, after all, not hard to find.[46] In what follows, I explore how the thought of Doran can ground the teachings of the FABC, aware that such reflection is supportive of the missiological options of Pope Francis.

The FABC and Doran of *Theology and the Dialectics of History*

Doran's intellectual career can be divided into two major periods. The first begins with his doctoral studies until it culminates with the publication of *Theology and the Dialectics of History* in 1990. The second has involved the project of producing a multi-volume work, *The Trinity in History*, of which

44. Robert M. Doran, "Foreword," in Gerard Whelan SJ, *A Discerning Church: Pope Francis, Lonergan, and a Theological Method for the Future* (Mahwah: Paulist Press, 2018).

45. "Cinque anni di Papa Francesco," editorial, *La Civiltà Cattolica*, March 17, 2018, 1, Translation is mine.

46. Pope Francis speaks of dialogue with the poor in EG 48.186–216.233; of dialogue with culture in EG 61–75.90.115–118.122–126.132–134.143; and of dialogue with other religions in EG 22.247–258.

he is currently completing the third installment. At the risk of oversimplification, I suggest that the first period of Doran's career was primarily concerned with developing what Lonergan calls general theological categories, whereas the second involves the exploration of special theological categories. Relating these to the FABC's triple dialogue, I posit that the first period is especially relevant to the first two of the dialogues mentioned by the FABC: with the poor and with culture. By contrast, Doran's reflections on special theological categories are uniquely well-suited to ground interreligious dialogue.

Before exploring what *Theology and the Dialectics of History* has to say about the poor and about culture, two fundamental notions have to be discussed. Firstly, it is important to draw attention to Doran's understanding of dialogue in general. Here he develops the little that Lonergan has to say about how theological method is open to the situation not only at the beginning of the mediating phase, Research, but also at the end of the mediated phase, Communications. Reflecting further on the eighth functional specialty, Doran states that "the situation which a theology addresses is as much a source of theology as are the data provided by the Christian tradition."[47] The situation is thus a *locus theologicus* at both ends of the method, activating a recurrent cycle of constantly considering and re-considering the input offered by history.[48] He adds that this "provides a new source for theology, one that perhaps will demand a profound rethinking and reorientation of much of the tradition itself."[49] In this way, Doran anchors in functional specialization the process that is more loosely called dialogical or inductive, which takes seriously what *Gaudium et Spes* describes as "the signs of the times."

Secondly, one needs to recognize the broad foundations for ecclesiology outlined by Doran. He explores how religious conversion can differentiate itself into soteriological conversion, that is, a conversion possible only for Jews and Christians who explicitly believe that the divine solution to the problem of evil has already occurred. He describes how those who enjoy soteriological conversion are particularly well-suited to promote the integral dialectics of culture. While he acknowledges that Judaism is a soteriological religion, he underscores the value of Christianity in its particular focus on questions of salvation. He emphasizes how it is in Jesus Christ that the outer word of historical revelation brings to fulfillment the expectations raised by the inner

47. Robert M. Doran, *Theology and the Dialectics of History* (Toronto: University of Toronto Press, 1990), 8.

48. Doran, *Theology and the Dialectics of History*, 12–13.

49. Doran, *Theology and the Dialectics of History*, 8.

word of interior revelation that occurs in religious conversion. This is why he states, "Christianity has some genuine *universal* significance."[50]

In relation to this, Doran explains that the Church, as a continuation of the saving presence of Jesus Christ in history, seeks to respond to our current global situation that is marked by different forms of decline. He proposes a notion of the church as a "catalytic agent of an alternative situation in the world, through its fidelity to the just and mysterious law of the cross."[51] He further describes that "the resistant community to be evoked by theology is first the church, and only then, through the ministry of the church, a world-cultural humanity."[52] It is important to note, however, that though the Church is the sacrament of Christ, her members are not automatically soteriologically converted by virtue of their religious affiliation alone. It is therefore imperative to promote Jesus Christ and the law of his cross more clearly, deeply, and extensively even within ecclesial boundaries.

Within this broad notion of the soteriological mission of the church, we can now relate Doran's ideas to the teaching of the FABC. Regarding the dialogue with culture, Doran appropriates Lonergan's understanding of theology as mediating between religion and culture and as infusing the meanings and values of Christ to dominant culture. He stresses the intellectual service and responsibility theology affords to the cultural superstructure as a praxis of meaning and as a cosmopolitan activity. As he affirms: "Within ecclesial ministry, as we will see, there lies a cosmopolitan intellectual collaboration whose responsibility is the integrity of culture."[53] In line with this, he is convinced that: "A methodical theology has a transformative objective."[54] Through the praxis of meaning on the level of cultural superstructure, with the help of integrally converted cosmopolitan theologians, the whole socio-cultural landscape may be influenced and improved. It is in this sense that theology is discussed as a crucial attribute of Doran's understanding of the Church and her mission. He writes:

> By its participation in evoking through the ministry of the church these globally shared cultural values on the ground of the self-appropriation of the crosscultural constituents of human integrity,

50. Doran, *Theology and the Dialectics of History*, 108.

51. Doran, *Theology and the Dialectics of History*, 126. See also *Ibid.*, 109 and 110.

52. Doran, *Theology and the Dialectics of History*, 418.

53. Doran, *Theology and the Dialectics of History*, 107.

54. Robert M. Doran, *Psychic Conversion and Theological Foundations* (Toronto: University of Toronto Press, 1981), 46.

> theology will have an effect on the political, economic, and technological constituents of the dialectic of community, and on the dramatic intersubjectivity that is the dialectical counterpart of these elements. By evoking a new set of cultural values, theology promotes the establishment of the dialectic of community as an integral and concrete unfolding of linked but opposed principles of change facilitating the creation of the human world, of personal relations, and of subjects as genuine works of art.[55]

Doran explains that a soteriologically converted church recognizes that she is not alone in the project of redeeming history. Her suffering servanthood in pursuit of the human good prompts her to participate in the life of the wider community. This opens the doors for intercultural and interreligious dialogue and collaboration with other religiously converted individuals and communities where the inner word is at work.

Next, Doran suggests that his account of how soteriological conversion works on both the self-transcending spirit and the psyche presents a "transcendental grounding" for the notion of preferential option for the poor. He argues:

> Our position on the scale of values constitutes in effect a defense from the standpoint of a transcendental anthropology of the insights of theologians of liberation regarding, first, the hermeneutically privileged position for theology of the most grievously victimized peoples of our globe and, second, the preferential option for the poor that must govern the church's exercise of all its ministry.[56]

In explaining this point, Doran indicates how psychic and affective conversion enables one not only to feel and accord with the normative scale of values, but also to perceive its aberrations in personal or social actuality. Through these conversions, one can discern the gap between the ideal and the real and decide to choose what is the truly good versus the only apparently good. Moreover, "psychic conversion, when critically appropriated, speaks to the issue of the universal victimhood of humanity"[57] as it highlights the effect of a sinful history and an oppressive society to the human

55. Doran, *Theology and the Dialectics of History*, 423.

56. Doran, *Theology and the Dialectics of History*, 421.

57. Rohan M. Curnow, *The Preferential Option*: A Short History and a Reading Based on the Thought of Bernard Lonergan (Wisconsin: Marquette University Press, 2014), 150.

subjects' psyche.[58] Seeing and sensing the injustice in the world, persons imbued with religious and soteriological values could decide and act for the re-shaping of culture and society. One commentator explains:

> Doran suggests that living in fidelity to the law of the cross expands naturally to an "option for the poor" [. . .] Witnessing this exclusion of some from the material well-being that is normal for others, can scandalize religiously converted individuals as it seems to deprive these marginalized people from the chance to feel loved.[59]

Such reflections, brief as they are, indicate how Doran's *Theology and the Dialectics of History* helps provide methodological foundations for the triple dialogue proposed by the FABC, especially as regards dialogue with culture and with the poor. The said work indicates the role of the Church in the dialectics of history, with a special emphasis on human intellectual and existential agency and the Church's ministry to culture, towards an alternative situation that more closely resembles the reign of God and benefits the poor. A discussion of soteriological conversion and comments on the "genuine *universal* significance"[60] of Christianity have obvious significance for interreligious dialogue. However, it is in the next phase of his intellectual career that Doran will his make his most valuable contributions to a foundational understanding of interreligious relations.

The Trinity in History: *Foundations for Interreligious Dialogue*

For some years now, Doran has been working on a multi-volume project of producing a comprehensive systematic theology anchored in a single notion, that is, how an individual, Christian or non-Christian, participates, by grace, in the inner relations of the Trinity. As with so much of Doran's thought, he develops a theme mentioned briefly by his mentor Lonergan. In Lonergan's writings on Trinitarian theology, he spoke of a "four-point hypothesis" which, for Doran, could provide a conceptual nucleus for all of systematic theology:

---

58. Curnow, *The Preferential Option*, 152.

59. Gerard Whelan, *Redeeming History: Social Concern in Bernard Lonergan and Robert Doran* (Rome: G&B Press, 2013), 197–198.

60. Doran, *Theology and the Dialectics of History*, 108.

> First, there are four real divine relations, really identical with the divine substance, and therefore there are four very special modes that ground the external imitation of the divine substance. Next, there are four absolutely supernatural realities, which are never found uninformed, namely, the secondary act of existence of the incarnation, sanctifying grace, the habit of charity, and the light of glory. It would not be inappropriate, therefore, to say that the secondary act of existence of the incarnation is a created participation of paternity, and so has a special relation to the Son; that sanctifying grace is a participation of active spiration, and so has a special relation to the Holy Spirit; that the habit of charity is a participation of passive spiration, and so has a special relation to the Father and the Son; and that the light of glory is a participation of sonship, and so in a most perfect way brings the children of adoption back to the Father.[61]

Doran expands this insight into a work that will soon comprise three volumes, intending this as merely the beginning of a systematic theology that will be appropriately sophisticated for use in the twenty-first century. I do not pretend to outline all the developments included in the first two volumes of this series which have so far been published. Rather, I indicate some broad lines of how Doran's thought grounds and supports the notion of interreligious dialogue, as called for by the FABC. Above all, I stress that Doran's discussion of the four-point hypothesis sheds light on: (1) the dynamism of universalist faith to pursue the human good through acts of charity as a free response to the universal offer of sanctifying grace; and (2) the Christian faith to work for the closer approximation of the reign of God through witnessing according to the law of the cross as a response to the knowledge and love of Jesus Christ.[62]

Firstly, through this synthetic theological construct that relates the processions, missions, and relations in the Trinity to created contingent external terms, sanctifying grace and the habit of charity are introduced as participations in or imitations of the eternal relations of active and passive spiration, respectively. Sanctifying grace evoking the habit of charity in a person imitates the Father and Son spirating the Spirit in active spiration;

---

61. Bernard Lonergan, *The Triune God: Systematics, Collected Works of Bernard Lonergan*, vol. 12, eds. Robert M. Doran and Daniel M. Monsour (Toronto: University of Toronto Press, 2009), 471 and 473.

62. Robert M. Doran, *Trinity in History a Theology of the Divine Missions: Missions and Processions*, vol. 1 (Toronto: University of Toronto Press, 2012), 86–98.

and the habit of charity as a response to the prompting of sanctifying grace participates in the Spirit loving back the Father and the Son in passive spiration. Thus, those who are so graced with God's love and who respond to such love with a charitable life are especially related to the Father, Son, and Spirit. They can be said to participate in the Trinitarian life, implicated in the spiral of receiving love and loving in return.

Given the dogmatic certainty that grace is offered to all and since the loving response to God and neighbor can be observed even outside the confines of the Church, then even non-Christians, whose lives are marked with faith, hope, and charity, can be said to participate in the life of God. As Doran explains:

> For those who do not know the revelation of this trinitarian gift, charity takes the form of a love of wisdom and a purified transcendence that in fact if not in name is a love of God with all one's heart and all one's mind and all one's strength and a love of one's neighbor as oneself.[63]

For Doran, therefore, both universalist and Christian faith are fruits of sanctifying grace from which usher a life characterized by the habit of charity that is willing to return good for evil. When this dynamic of the life of grace is existentially self-appropriated through interiorly and religiously differentiated consciousness, a theological-anthropological ground for interreligious dialogue and collaboration comes to the fore. We decide to work for peaceful and harmonious relations with followers of other religions not only because it is what the Church teaches, but because, with the eyes of love, we experience, understand, and judge that God is indeed actively at work in their lives as well.

Secondly, through the gift of sanctifying grace that catalyzes conversion towards a more authentic human existence, a person, Christian or not, can be a source of meanings and an agent of values that can influence and shape his socio-cultural milieu. Human participation in and imitation of divine life and love can facilitate the implementation of the divine solution to the problem of evil through "supernatural" charitable acts that promote progress and reverse decline. The healing grace of God, coursed through free human subjects, in and beyond the Church, can therefore tilt the dialectics of history

63. Robert M. Doran, "'As the Father Has Sent Me': The Mission of the Church in a Multi-Religious World," talk delivered at the Lonergan Colloquium at Marquette University (02–03 Nov 2011), 6 in http://www.lonerganresource.com/conference.php?8, referenced July 2020.

towards integration and a closer approximation of the reign of God. Thus, should there be a critical mass of religiously converted subjects who think and act authentically and collectively in history, dominant culture may be reformed, which may redound to societal infrastructural changes that would pursue and serve the common good. The imperative of preferential option for the poor thus no longer only comes from external moral commands, but also from a stronger internal imperative and commitment of a life endeavoring to return God's love through love of neighbor.

Therefore, through the use of the four-point hypothesis, with a focus on the created participations in active and passive spiration and their impact on history, interreligious dialogue and collaboration for the redemption of history are given sure Trinitarian foundations with a more solid pneumatological emphasis. It helps to further describe the peculiarities of both universalist and Christian faith in order to understand the possibility of their healthy dialogue and collaboration.

According to Doran, the other religions that have been gifted with the inner word, the invisible missions of the Spirit and the Son, together with their externalizations of such inner word, are thus to be respected and acknowledged as vital and important for the establishment of the reign of God on earth and the recapitulation of all things in Christ. As their externalizations of the inner word come from the same foundation of religious experience, the same invisible missions of the Spirit and the Son, they can manifest points of intersection, creating a platform on the level of explicit meanings and values, where mutual understanding and common pursuit of the real, true, and good are made possible across traditions.[64] Doran posits:

> Articulating those common judgments of value represents, I believe, the locus of interreligious dialogue today, which, as it engages in such articulation, will in fact be making explicit the invisible mission of the divine Word [. . .] The articulation of those common judgments of value will raise our community with the people of the world's religions from the potential community constituted by a shared experience to the formal and actual state generated by shared understanding and affirmation, and because the judgments in question are judgments of value, also to the status of a community that can act in solidarity in the collaborative constitution of the human world.[65]

64. Doran, *The Trinity in History*, vol. 1, 80.

65. Doran, *The Trinity in History*, vol. 1, 80–81.

For Doran, the mission of the Son is therefore not limited to the Christian realm. It is "carried on, participated in, both in and beyond the church, partly through the gifts and vocations of theologians, philosophers, scientists both natural and human, and scholars, all speaking intelligible words of truth, justice, and reconciliation to a broken world."[66] Through his invisible mission, his meanings and values penetrate other religions and cultures, articulated in words of truth that spirate love due to a memory of being loved, making them pursue the common good and the integrity of the scale of values. As Doran writes:

> The global implications of Lonergan's scale of values provide an extraordinary litmus test regarding the major authenticity of the various religious traditions in our world, where 'major authenticity' refers not to the authenticity of individuals vis-à-vis their traditions but to the authenticity of the traditions themselves as currently appropriated and implemented or exercised.[67]

With such a positive evaluation of other religions, it remains for Doran to make explicit just what is the "universal significance" of Christianity. Here, he explains that Christian faith is a specific differentiation of universalist faith. It is the believer's response or judgment of value to the revelation and love of God in Jesus Christ, the outer word and the visible mission of the Son. It is received in the context of the Church that is imbued with both the visible and invisible missions of the Spirit, where it can be deepened to the point that Christ lives in each Christian. Doran explains that, with the coming of Jesus Christ, the implicit has become explicit, the conscious has become known, and the movement from the world of immediacy to the world of meanings contributes a particular intelligibility both to one's personal operations and to one's history and culture-forming activities.

Doran, however, qualifies that there is something more contained in the revelation of Jesus Christ vis-à-vis the ineffable knowledge of universalist faith and its externalizations. He locates this difference in the explicit relationship that Christians have to the story of Jesus Christ, and especially the paschal mystery of his death and resurrection. He explains that the particular form of sanctifying grace enjoyed by the Church is intimately related to the symbol of the Cross and will thus emanate into a habit of charity that is patterned on the unconditional and salvific charity of God,

66. Doran, *The Trinity in History*, vol. 1, 100.

67. Robert M. Doran, "Social Grace," in *Method: Journal of Lonergan Studies* 2/2 (2011), 133.

exhibited in Christ, which is in accordance with the just and mysterious law of the cross. Doran explains:

> The unique contributions that Christianity offers to this world-cultural matrix are three: the incarnation of the eternal Word of God in Jesus of Nazareth, the Trinitarian nature of God, and the resurrection of Jesus from the dead. Closely tied to these are the implications of the passion, death, and resurrection of Jesus for a non-violent response to the scandal of evil in the world.[68]

Doran is aware that Christians may feel a pang of conscience reading such words and ask if the actual practice of the Church is in accordance with this high ideal. However, he insists: "Remove any one of these, and Christianity has been eviscerated of the very marrow of its bones, however much hierarchical structures may continue to function."[69]

In the light of such systematic insights, Doran proposes that evangelization has two dimensions:

> First, it proceeds from the conviction that the incarnation of the eternal Word marks the definitive revelation of the gift that God is always pouring forth by flooding human hearts with God's love by the Holy Spirit given them. But if that gift, now revealed, is offered universally, then evangelization entails speaking a word that assists others to recognize God's gift of love in their own lives, including in their own cultures and religious traditions. Second, as rooted in the revelation that occurs precisely in Jesus and so in the paschal mystery, evangelization addresses specifically the problem of evil, and it does so from the standpoint of the Law of the Cross as the revelation of the divinely ordained response to evil.[70]

In sum, Christian faith is the fruit of both the invisible and visible missions of the Spirit and the Son. Given her unique externalization and distinctive message, the Church has the non-transferrable duty to share the soteriological meanings and values of Christ and the law of his cross to greater society. She performs this mission in respect, dialogue, and collaboration with other authentic religious traditions with whom she shares not only the invisible missions of the Sprit and the Son, but also the project of

68. Doran, *The Trinity in History*, vol. 1, 66.

69. Doran, *The Trinity in History*, vol. 1, 66.

70. Doran, "'As the Father Has Sent Me,'" 8–9.

participating in the divine solution to the problem of evil. The implications for interreligious dialogue are immense.

Conclusion

In this chapter, we have located both the thought of Doran and the FABC within the drama of the past fifty-five years of conciliar interpretation and implementation. We have suggested that the pontificate of Francis makes it an opportune time to provide adequate methodological foundations for understanding the mission of the Church in Asia, as in the other regions of the world. We then explored how Doran's general and special categories can serve as foundation for ecclesial mission in a multicultural and interreligious context towards the redemption of history. It proves to be a transcultural and credible proposal, open to dialogue and collaboration, while remaining rooted in an orthodox Trinitarian theology and promotive of Vatican II's teachings and pastoral and dialogical spirit.

In sum, integrating Doran's special and general categories, I trace how, as the privileged bearer of the meanings and values of Jesus Christ (soteriological and religious values), the Church, through her words and deeds (personal values), has the task and responsibility of shaping the meanings and values constitutive of dominant culture through her witnessing and theology (cultural values) in order to evoke an alternative situation (social and vital values) that approximates more closely the reign of God. I gather that it is in this sense that the Church continues the missions of the Spirit and the Son, helping mediate the healing and redemption of history, with other cultures and religions.

LIST OF CONTRIBUTORS

Brian Bajzek is Visiting Assistant Professor of Theology at Marquette University. He holds a Ph.D. in Theological Studies from Regis College and University of Toronto (2018). His current work explores the roles of intersubjectivity and otherness in God's healing, elevation, and redemption of human relationality. He has published in *The Heythrop Journal, International Philosophical Quarterly, Theological Studies*, and several edited volumes. He is also the director of the Philosophy component of the International Institute for Method in Theology.

Jeremy W. Blackwood is Assistant Professor of Systematic Theology and Director of Admissions at Sacred Heart Seminary and School of Theology in Hales Corners, Wisconsin. He is the author of *'And Hope Does Not Disappoint': Love, Grace, and Subjectivity in the Work of Bernard J. F. Lonergan, S.J.*, as well as articles in *Theological Studies*, *Irish Theological Quarterly*, and *Method: Journal of Lonergan Studies*. His research interests focus on Bernard Lonergan's theology and philosophy, Trinitarian theology, and racial justice.

Lucas Briola is Assistant Professor of Theology at Saint Vincent College (Latrobe, PA). With Joseph Ogbonnaya, he coedited a collection of essays entitled *Everything Is Interconnected: Towards a Globalization with a Human Face and an Integral Ecology* (Marquette University Press, 2019). His articles have appeared in *Theological Studies*, *New Blackfriars*, *The Lonergan Review*, *Journal of Moral Theology*, and *Downside Review*, and he coordinates the ecological culture section of the International Institute for Method in Theology. He is currently completing a manuscript tentatively entitled "Worship and Care in Our Common Home: Perspectives from Bernard Lonergan."

Anne M. Carpenter is an Associate Professor in the Department of Theology and Religious Studies at Saint Mary's College of California. She received her doctorate in theology from Marquette University. She has published on Christian monasticism, theological aesthetics, Bernard Lonergan, Maurice Blondel, and Hans Urs von Balthasar. Her book *Theo-Poetics: Hans Urs von Balthasar and the Risk of Art and Being* was published with the University of Notre Dame Press.

Rev. John P. Cush is a priest of the Diocese of Brooklyn, New York (USA). He serves as the academic dean and as a formation advisor at the Pontifical North American College in Rome, Italy. Fr. Cush holds the Doctorate in Sacred Theology (STD) from the Pontifical Gregorian University in Rome where he also serves as an adjunct professor of Theology. He also is an adjunct professor of Contemporary Church History at the Pontifical University of the Holy Cross in Rome, Italy. Fr. Cush is the author of *The How to Book of Catholic Theology* (Our Sunday Visitor Press, 2020) as well as a forthcoming book on priestly spirituality and priestly formation.

John D. Dadosky, Ph.D., S.T.D. is professor of theology and philosophy at Regis College/University of Toronto since July 2001. He is author of The Structure of Religious Knowing (SUNY Press, 2004), The Eclipse and Recovery of Beauty (University of Toronto Press, 2014), co-editor of four volumes of the Collected Works of Bernard Lonergan, including Method in Theology (2017) and the final archival volume (2019). In 2018, he published Image to Insight: The Art of William Hart McNichols, which won the 2019 Arizona-New Mexico Book Award in Art. He has published numerous articles on Lonergan bringing his thought into engagement with ecclesiology, Vatican II, and dialogue with Buddhism. He is currently the director of the Monsignor John-Mary Fraser Centre for Practical Theology at Regis College (Toronto).

Darren J. Dias is a professor in the Faculty of Theology of the University of St Michael's College. His research focuses on the intersection of Trinitarian doctrine and the life and practice of the church today. His publications on religious diversity include: "Peace and Religions in a Changing World: From Consensus to Difference," "A Circuitous Route: Implementing *Nostra Aetate* in Canada," "Fifty Years and Learning: Developments in the Roman Catholic Church's Encounter with Religions," and "Why Dialogue?" He is also an appointee of the Canadian Conference of Catholic Bishops to the Hindu-Roman Catholic Dialogue.

Gregory P. Floyd, Ph.D., teaches in the Department of the Core at Seton Hall University. His areas of teaching and scholarship include the history of philosophy, philosophy and literature, and the thought of Bernard Lonergan.

Joseph K. Gordon is Associate Professor of Theology at Johnson University (Knoxville, TN). The author of *Divine Scripture in Human Understanding: A Systematic Theology of the Christian Bible* (University of Notre Dame Press, 2019), he has also published journal articles in *Theological Studies*, *Nova et Vetera*, *Method: A Journal of Lonergan Studies*, *The Lonergan Review*, and the *Stone-Campbell Journal*, and his essays appear in collections published by the University of Notre Dame Press, Marquette University Press, and Pickwick. He is the coordinator of the Critical-Realist Hermeneutics group of the International Institute for Method in Theology and was a postdoctoral fellow in the Lonergan Institute at Boston College (2018–2019). He is currently completing the Cascade Companion to Bernard Lonergan and is editing a collection of essays on critical realism and scriptural interpretation.

Jonathan Heaps specializes in twentieth-century Roman Catholic philosophy and systematic theology, particularly the thought of Bernard Lonergan. He has published articles with *The Heythrop Journal*, *American Catholic Philosophical Quarterly*, and *Theological Studies* on such topics as the embodiment of cognition, the problem of forgiveness in philosophical hermeneutics, and the metaphysics of gender and sexuality. His most recent work explores how contemplative spiritual practices can help address the problem of verification in the humanities. He currently lives and teaches in Austin, TX.

Ryan Hemmer is an acquisitions editor at Fortress Press in Minneapolis, Minnesota. He earned his Ph.D. in religious studies from Marquette University, where he wrote a dissertation on Lonergan and speculative theology under the direction of Robert Doran.

Christopher Krall, S.J., is a priest of the Society of Jesus and doctoral candidate in the interdisciplinary research of systematic theology and neuroscience at Marquette University. He is currently writing his dissertation under the direction of Fr. Doran. The title of his dissertation is "The Human Person Fully Alive: The Transformation of the Body, Brain, Mind, and Soul of Humanity in the Encounter with the Divinity." He also has previous degrees from Boston College (BA, BS, MDiv, ThM, STL), University of Toronto (MA), and Oxford University (MSt).

Cecille Medina-Maldonado is a doctoral student in systematic theology at Marquette University. Her research interests include Trinitarian theology, especially the contributions of Bernard Lonergan and Robert Doran, and the connection between the Trinity, deification, and grace. She is also interested in Catholic bioethics, particularly reproductive ethics. She has received degrees from the University of Illinois at Urbana-Champaign and Loyola University Chicago.

Joseph C. Mudd is Associate Professor of Religious Studies at Gonzaga University where he also directs the Catholic Studies program. His research focuses on sacramental theology and the thought of Bernard Lonergan. He is the author of *Eucharist as Meaning: Critical Metaphysics and Contemporary Eucharistic Theology* (Liturgical Press, 2014). A volume on the sacraments in general informed by Lonergan and Robert M. Doran's treatise *The Trinity in History* is forthcoming.

Jacob M. Mudge is a Lecturer in Pastoral Studies and Systematic Theology at Catholic Theological College, University of Divinity in Melbourne, Australia, and a priest of the Diocese of Sandhurst. He serves as the Director of Pastoral Work at Corpus Christi College, the Regional Seminary for Victoria and Tasmania. His research interests include Christian formation, interdisciplinary studies, and the role of history in theology. He completed his doctorate in Fundamental Theology at the Gregorian University under the guidance of Professor Gerard Whelan SJ.

Joseph Ogbonnaya, Ph.D., is Associate Professor of Theology, Marquette University in Milwaukee, Wisconsin. In addition to articles in peer-reviewed journals, he has previously published these books: *African Perspectives on Culture and World Christianity* (2017), *Lonergan, Social Transformation and Sustainable Human Development* (2013), *African Catholicism and Hermeneutics of Culture* (2014). He coedited *Everything is Interconnected: Towards a Globalization with a Human Face and Integral Ecology* (2019), *Christianity and Culture Collision* (2016) and *The Church as Salt and Light* (2011).

Dr. Cyril Orji is Professor of Systematic Theology and Core Integrated Study at the University of Dayton, Ohio, USA. He specializes in fundamental and constructive theology, with particular emphasis on the theology and philosophy of Bernard Lonergan, which he brings into conversation with the works of the American pragmatist and semiotician, Charles Sanders Peirce, and the German Lutheran theologian, Wolfhart Pannenberg. He has published numerous journal articles. He has also published several books, including, *A Semiotic Christology* (Pickwick, 2020), *An Introduction to Religious and Theological Studies* 2nd edition (Cascade, 2020), *A Science-Theology Rapprochement: Pannenberg, Peirce, and Lonergan in Conversation* (Cambridge Scholars, 2018), *A Semiotic Approach to the Theology of Inculturation* (Pickwick, 2015), *The Catholic University and the Search for Truth* (Anslem Academic, 2013), and *Ethnic and Religious Conflicts in Africa: An Analysis of Bias and Conversion Based on the Work of Bernard Lonergan* (Marquette University Press, 2008). He has a forthcoming book, *Unmasking the African Ghost: How to Overcome the Nightmare of a Failed State* (Fortress Press, 2022).

Gordon Rixon, S.J., completed undergraduate studies in philosophy and mathematics at Gonzaga University in Spokane, Washington, a Master of Divinity and Licentiate in Theology at Regis College, Toronto, and doctoral studies in theology at Boston College. After working at the Jesuit Center for Social Faith and Justice in Toronto, Gordon joined the faculty of Regis College at the University of Toronto, where he teaches and publishes in the area of systematic theology, Ignatian spirituality and contemporary social theory. He is a Research Scholar at the Lonergan Research Institute and a member of the Board of Directors of St Paul University in Ottawa, Ontario. Gordon has been a Senior Resident at Massey College at the University of Toronto, a Scholar in Residence at the Institute for Ecumenical and Cultural Research at St. John's University, Collegeville, Minnesota and a guest lecturer at the Jesuit College of Spirituality in Melbourne, Australia. He represented the Canadian Conference of Catholic Bishops on the Churches' Council on Theological Education and served as Dean of Regis College from 2005–2014. Gordon participates in a collaborative project with Crivella West Inc, a knowledge firm based in Pittsburgh that explores the application of advance algorithms to the analysis of digitized texts in the humanities. He contributed to the design of the 2016–2017 exhibit "Mystical Landscapes: Masterpieces from Monet, van Goph and More," which was presented at the Art Gallery of Ontario in Toronto and the Musée d'Orsay in Paris. He has also contributed to the interpretive programing of Tafelmusik baroque orchestra and chamber choir in Toronto and the "Réseau International d'Innovation et de Prospective," a multidisciplinary initiative base in Montreal that promotes innovative economic, social, and cultural leadership. Gordon complements his academic and consulting work by preaching regularly in local parishes and offering educational seminars in the community.

Josephat John Rugaiganisa is a priest of the Franciscan Friers Minor (OFM). He obtained a Ph.D in Sacred Theology, specialized in *Fundamental Theology*, from Gregorian University in Rome, Italy. He is currently working in the Archdiocese of Mwanza-Tanzania. Among the duties, he is the Superior (Guardian) of the Franciscan Formation House Ilemela. He runs the programs of Initial & On-going formation for different groups and is assists in the parish of Butimba.

Eugene R. Schlesinger, Ph.D. (Marquette University), is Lecturer in the Department of Religious Studies at Santa Clara University. He specializes in systematic theology, working especially at the intersection of ecclesiology, sacramental theology, and mission, and has a distinct interest in the theology of sacrifice. He is a member of the ecology section of the International Institute for Method in Theology. He is the author of *Missa Est! A Missional Liturgical Ecclesiology* (Fortress Press, 2017) and *Sacrificing the Church: Mass, Mission, and Ecumenism* (Lexington Books/Fortress Academic, 2019).

Andrew T. Vink is a doctoral candidate at Boston College in Systematic Theology with a minor in Theological Ethics. His research interests concern Latin American Liberation Theology, Political Theology, Catholic Social Teaching, and the thought of Bernard Lonergan. Andrew has had articles accepted by *The Heythrop Journal* and *Irish Theological Quarterly*, and has presented both nationally and internationally. Andrew's latest two articles include "In the Midst of Our Sorrows: An Existential-Phenomenological Analysis of Evil," in *The Heythrop Journal* Volume 56, Issue 1, January 2015 and "History from the View of the Cross: An Exploration of Lonergan and Latin American Theologies of Liberation" in *Irish Theological Quarterly* Volume 82, Issue 3, August 2017.

Gerard Whelan, S.J., is an Irish Jesuit and Professor of Fundamental Theology at the Pontifical Gregorian University. He lived in Kenya for twelve years and is author of *Redeeming History: Social Concern in the Thought of Bernard Lonergan and Robert Doran* (2013) and *A Discerning Church: Pope Francis, Bernard Lonergan and Theological Method in Changing Times* (Paulist Press, 2019).

Jaime Vidal Zuñiga was ordained a priest of the Archdiocese of Manila in 2009. He works as an adjunct professor in the seminary of Manila and is completing a doctorate in the Gregorian University, Rome, entitled, "Foundations for Ecclesial Mission in Asia: A Dialogue Between Robert Doran and Recent Magisterial Teachings."

INDEX